Angel Diary

vol. 7

Kara · Lee YunHee

Yen
Press

• A WORD FROM THE CREATORS •

THIS IS THE SEVENTH VOLUME OF *ANGEL DIARY*. IT'S BEEN THREE YEARS SINCE WE FIRST STARTED WORKING ON THE BOOK. WE HOPE THAT WE'LL BE ABLE TO SEE THE STORY ALL THE WAY THROUGH TO THE END.

WE ALSO HOPE THAT OUR CATS STAY HEALTHY SO WE CAN FOCUS ON OUR JOBS WITHOUT WORRYING ABOUT THEM. (SINCE HEALTH INSURANCE DOESN'T APPLY TO PETS, MEDICAL BILLS CAN REALLY ADD UP.)

BY KARA

THIS IS LUCKY NO. 7! ^^ SEVEN IS ONE OF MY FAVORITE NUMBERS. THIS VOLUME WILL SURPRISE YOU WITH LOTS OF REVEALED SECRETS ABOUT THE CHARACTERS.

I CREATED A WEBSITE FOR NEW STORIES PUT TOGETHER WITH OTHER PEOPLE I KNOW. I'M GLAD FOR THE CHANCE TO TELL YOU ABOUT IT IN *ANGEL DIARY*. ^^; VISIT US AT HTTP://JISANG.NET (IT'S IN KOREAN!). IF YOU'RE INTERESTED IN FANTASY NOVELS, YOU'RE GOING TO LOVE IT. YOU CAN CHAT WITH ME IF YOU VISIT THE BULLETIN BOARD. (PARDON? YOU DON'T WANT TO? I'M GONNA CRY! ¡_¡)

BY YUNHEE LEE

CONTENTS

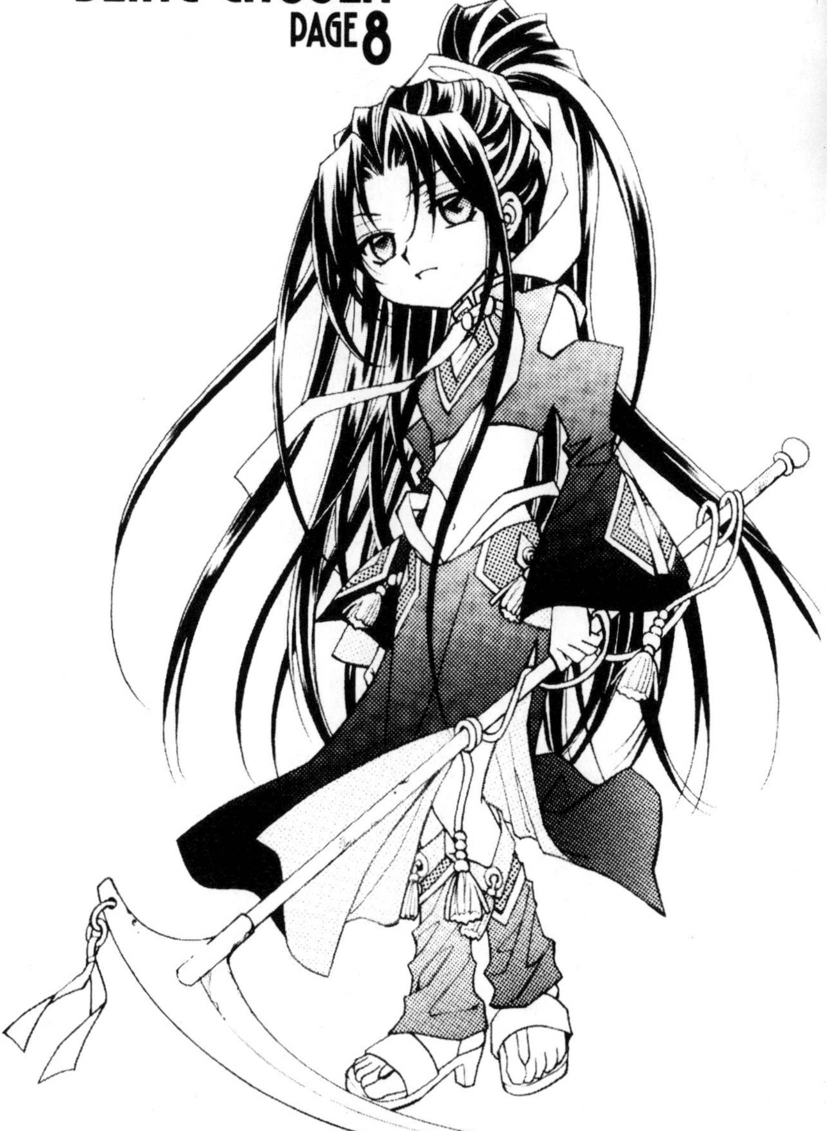

VII CHOOSING AND BEING CHOSEN

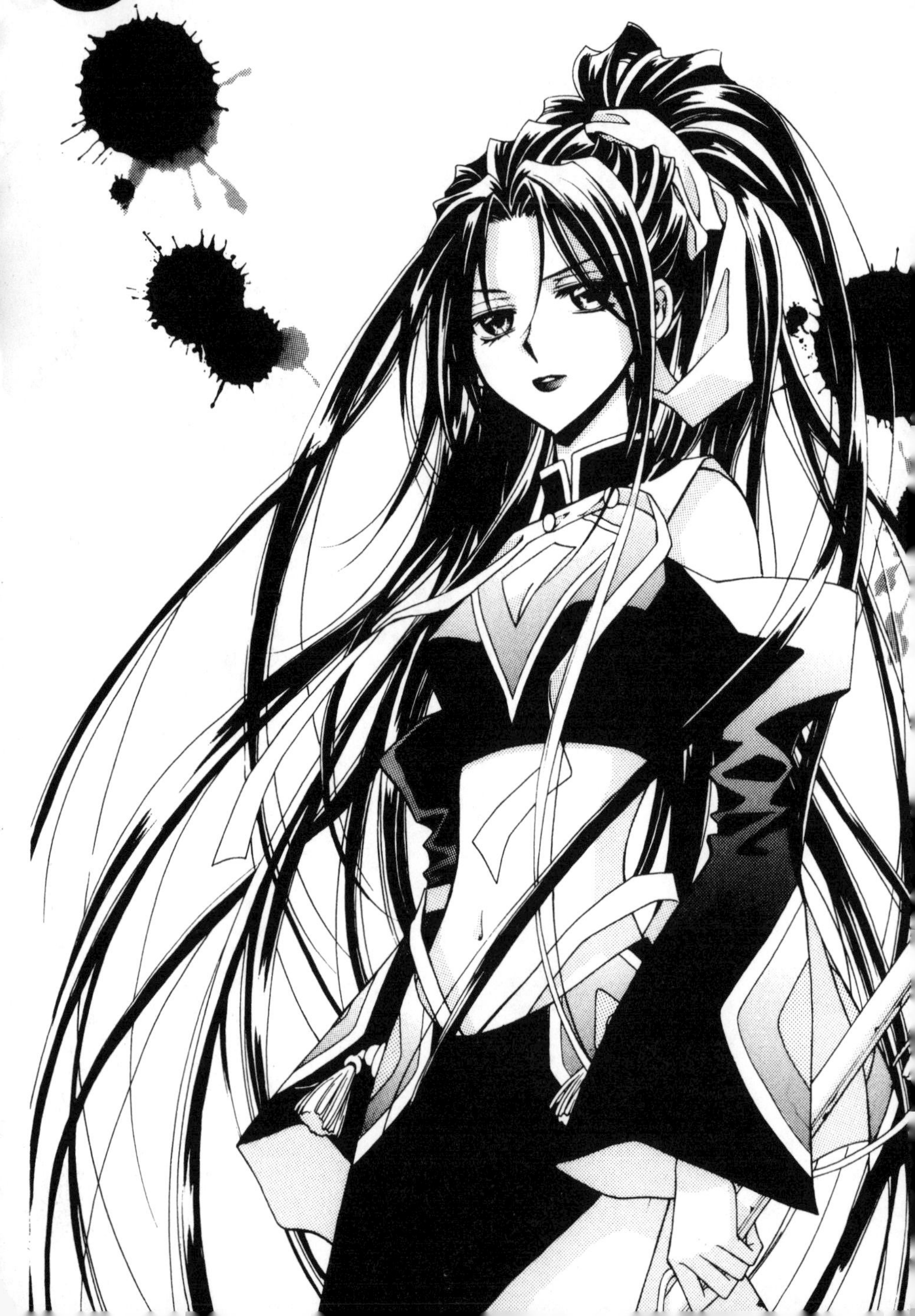

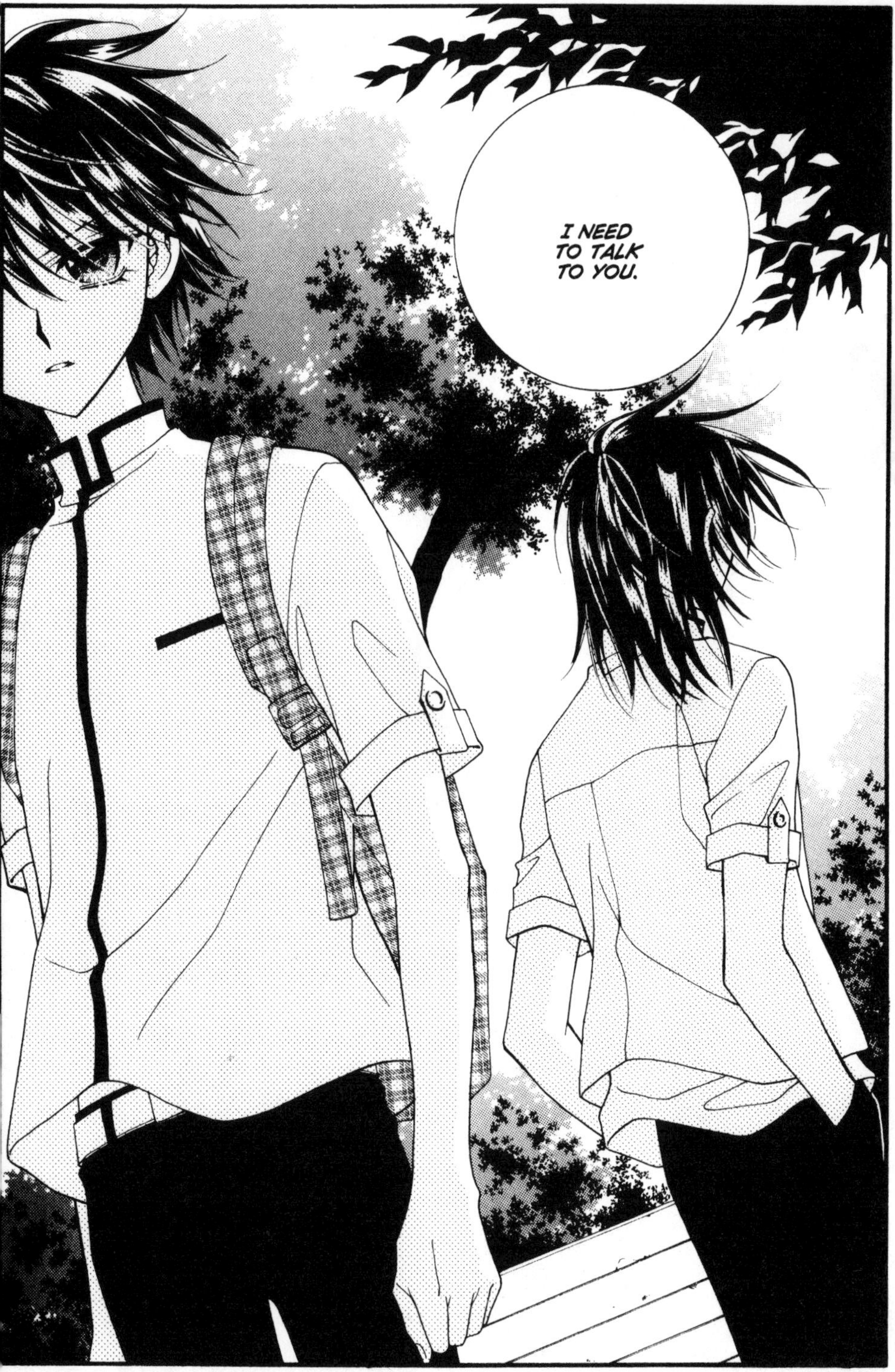
I NEED TO TALK TO YOU.

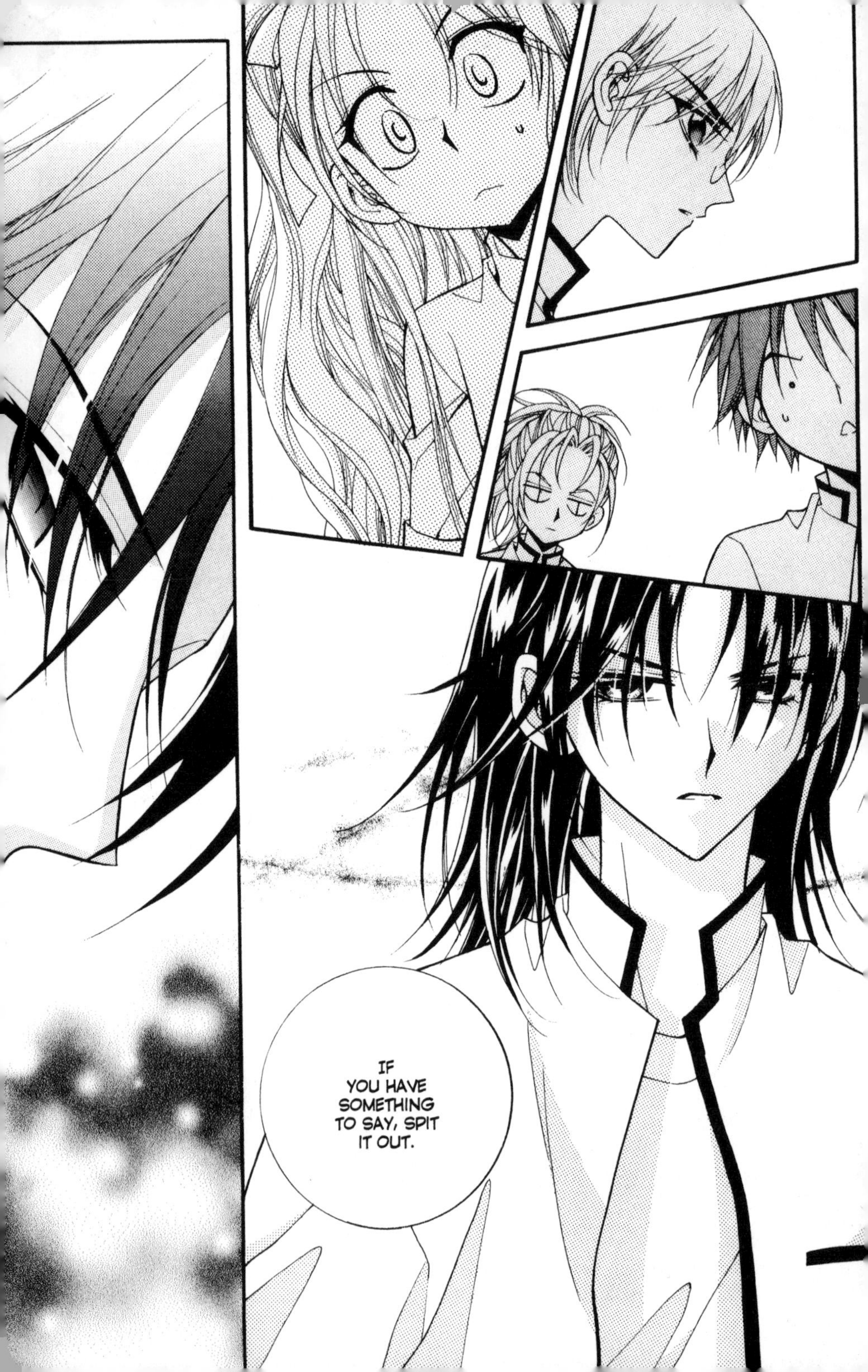
IF YOU HAVE SOMETHING TO SAY, SPIT IT OUT.

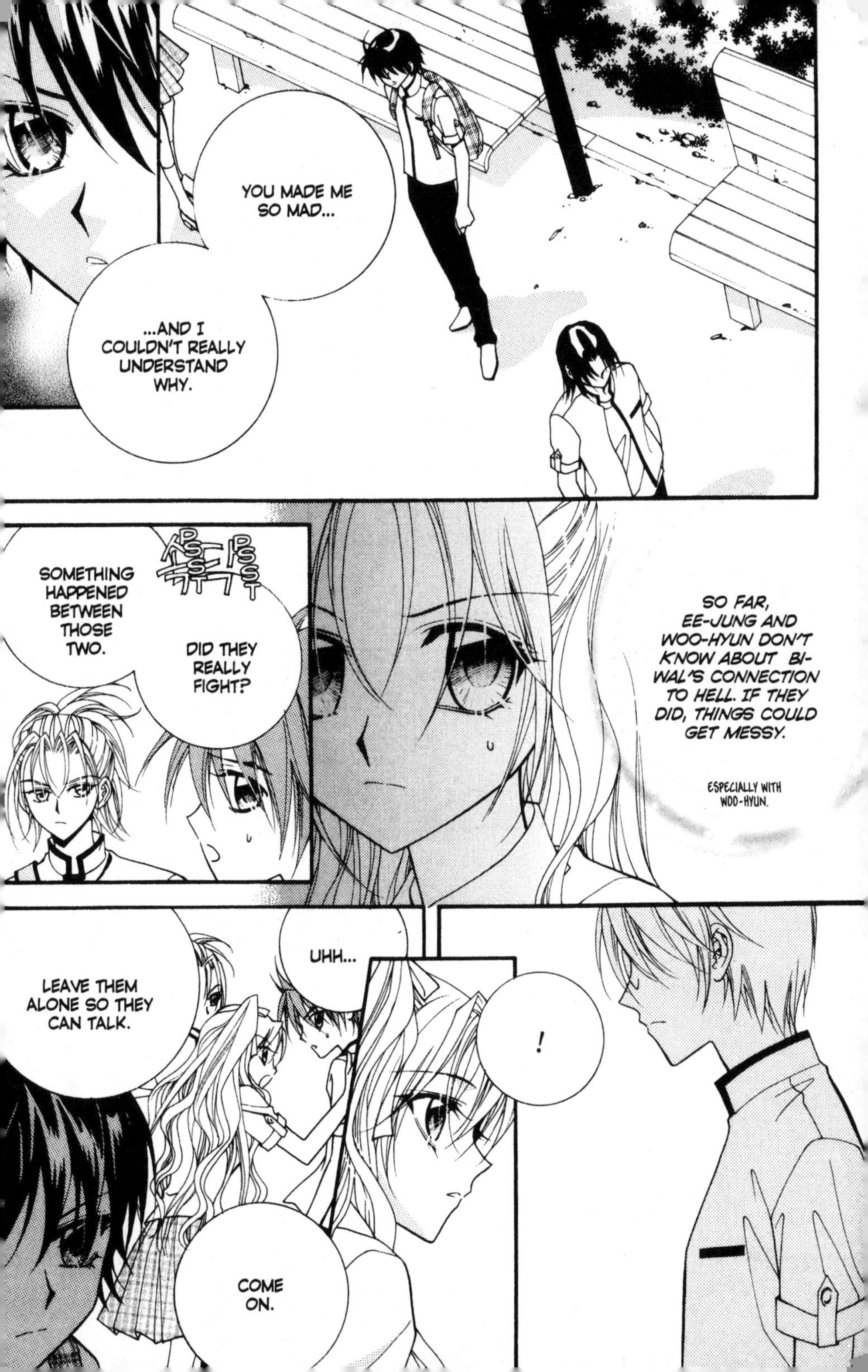
YOU MADE ME SO MAD...
...AND I COULDN'T REALLY UNDERSTAND WHY.
SOMETHING HAPPENED BETWEEN THOSE TWO.
PSST PSST
DID THEY REALLY FIGHT?
SO FAR, EE-JUNG AND WOO-HYUN DON'T KNOW ABOUT BI-WAL'S CONNECTION TO HELL. IF THEY DID, THINGS COULD GET MESSY.
ESPECIALLY WITH WOO-HYUN.
LEAVE THEM ALONE SO THEY CAN TALK.
UHH...
COME ON.
!

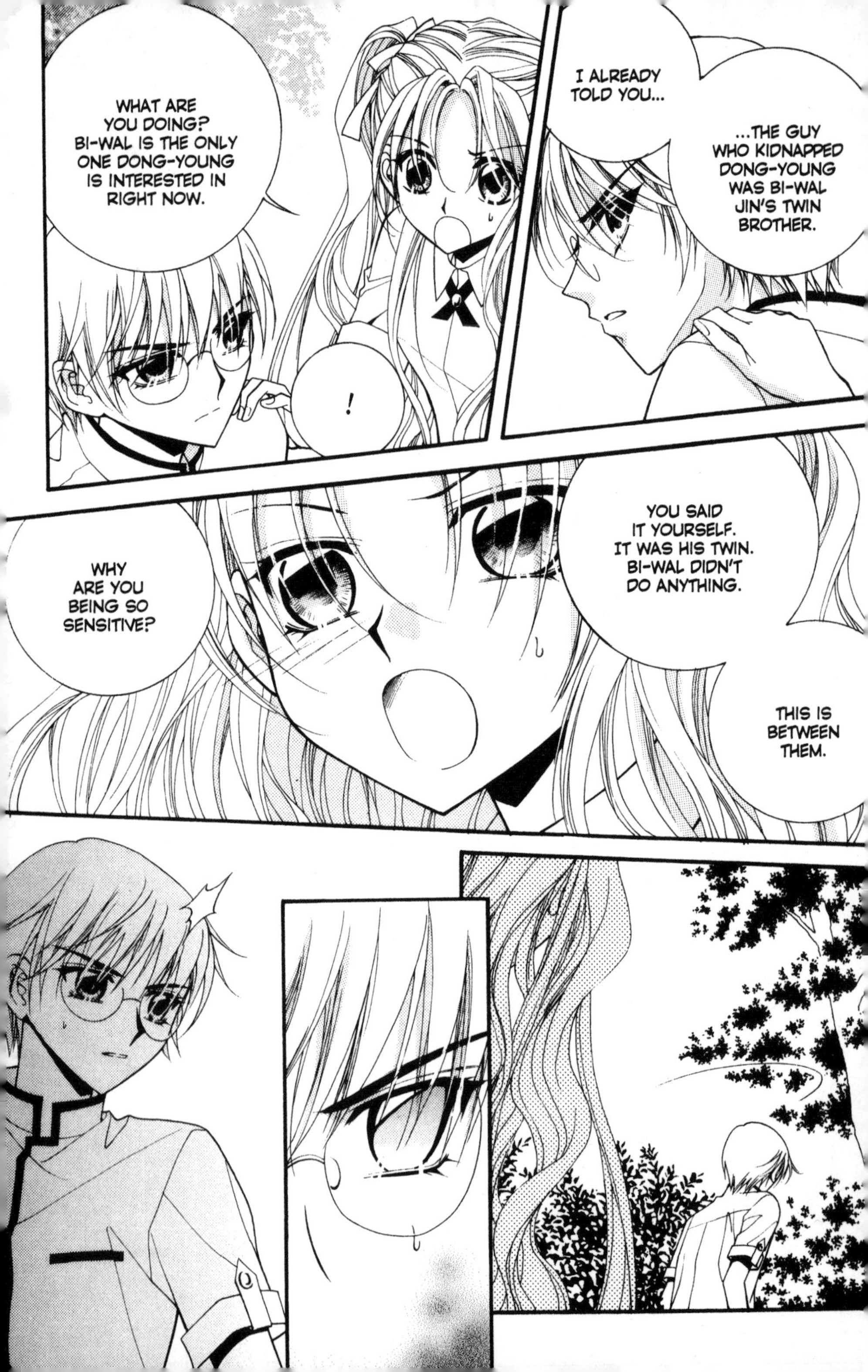
WHAT ARE YOU DOING? BI-WAL IS THE ONLY ONE DONG-YOUNG IS INTERESTED IN RIGHT NOW.
!
I ALREADY TOLD YOU...
...THE GUY WHO KIDNAPPED DONG-YOUNG WAS BI-WAL JIN'S TWIN BROTHER.
WHY ARE YOU BEING SO SENSITIVE?
YOU SAID IT YOURSELF. IT WAS HIS TWIN. BI-WAL DIDN'T DO ANYTHING.
THIS IS BETWEEN THEM.

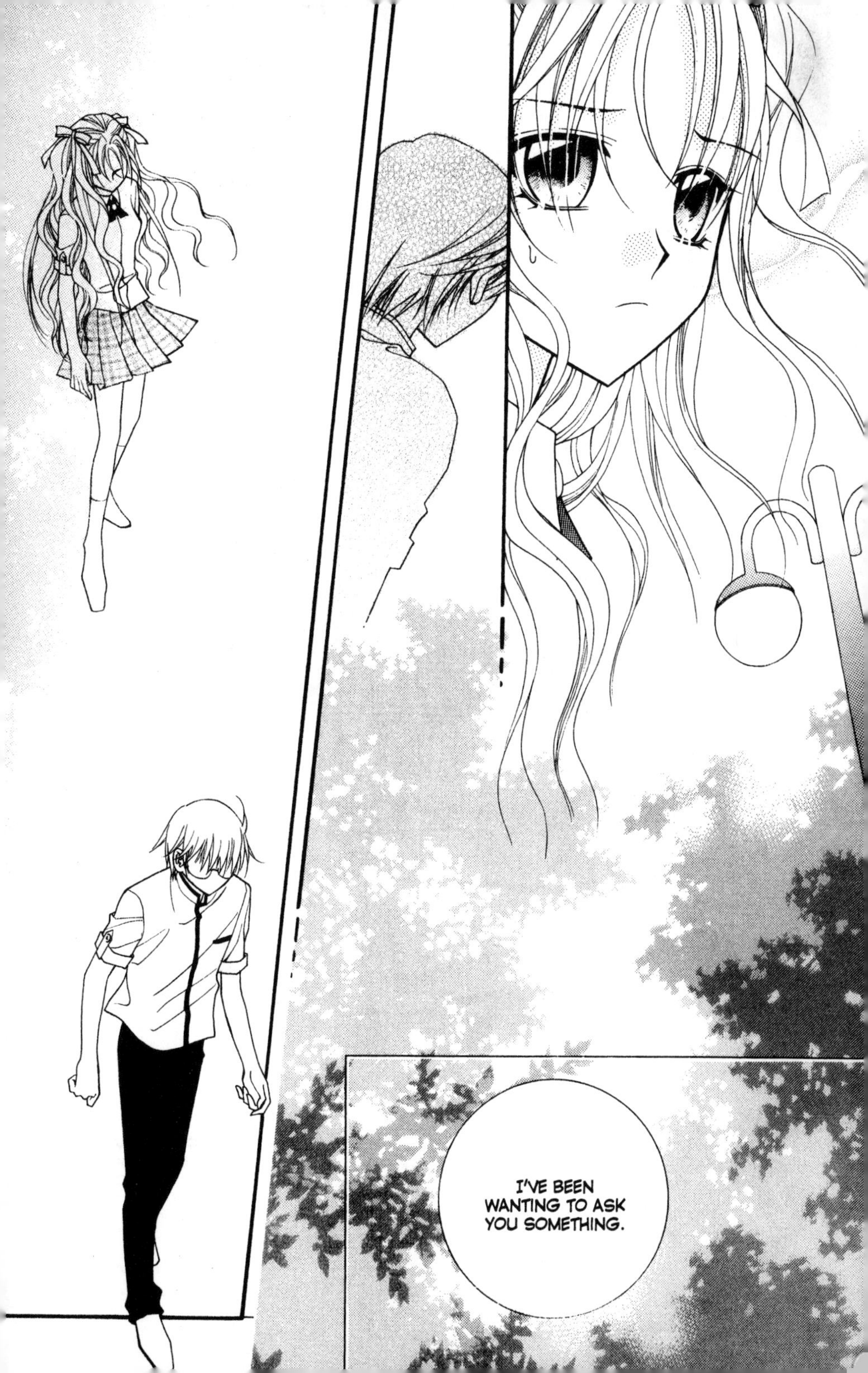
I'VE BEEN WANTING TO ASK YOU SOMETHING.

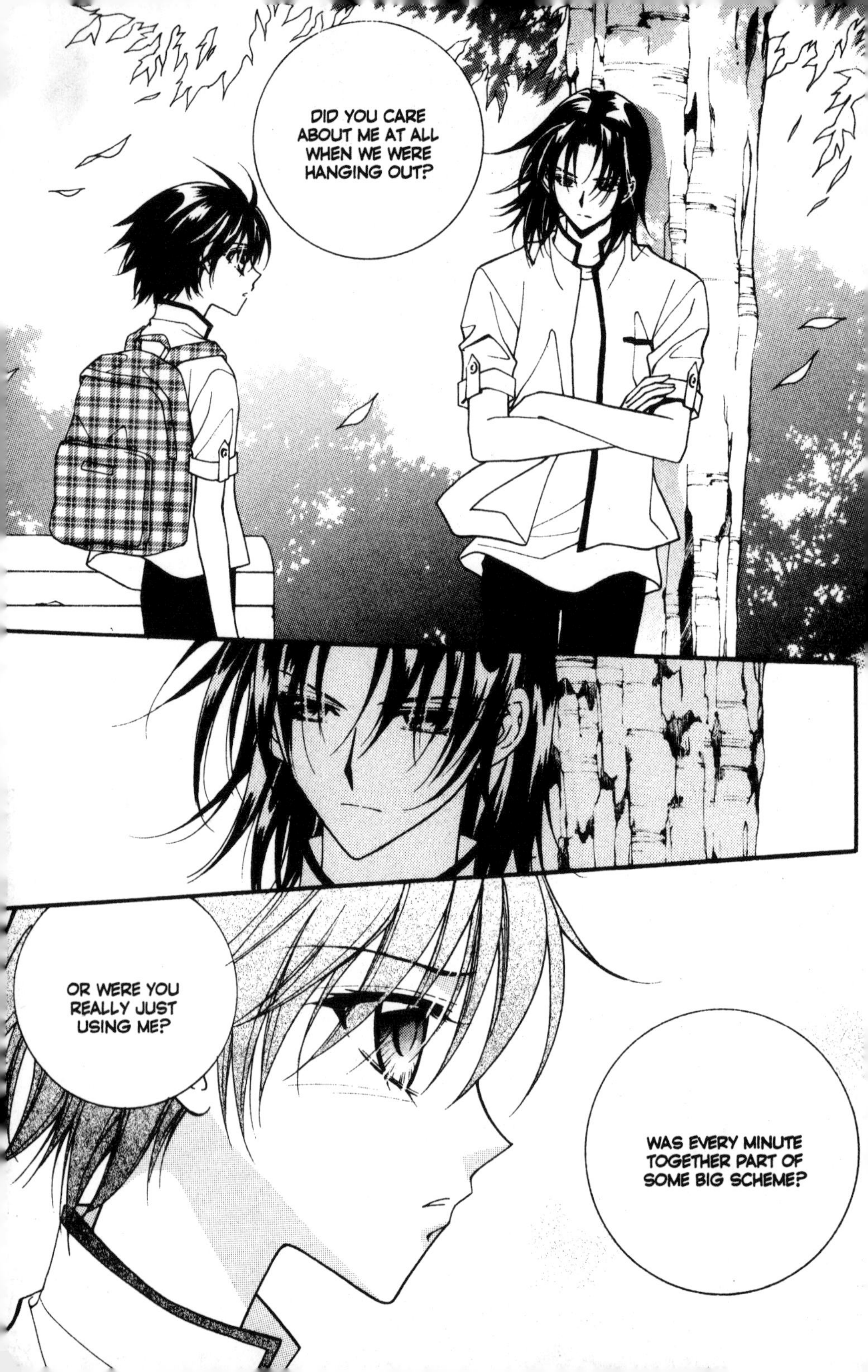
DID YOU CARE ABOUT ME AT ALL WHEN WE WERE HANGING OUT?
OR WERE YOU REALLY JUST USING ME?
WAS EVERY MINUTE TOGETHER PART OF SOME BIG SCHEME?

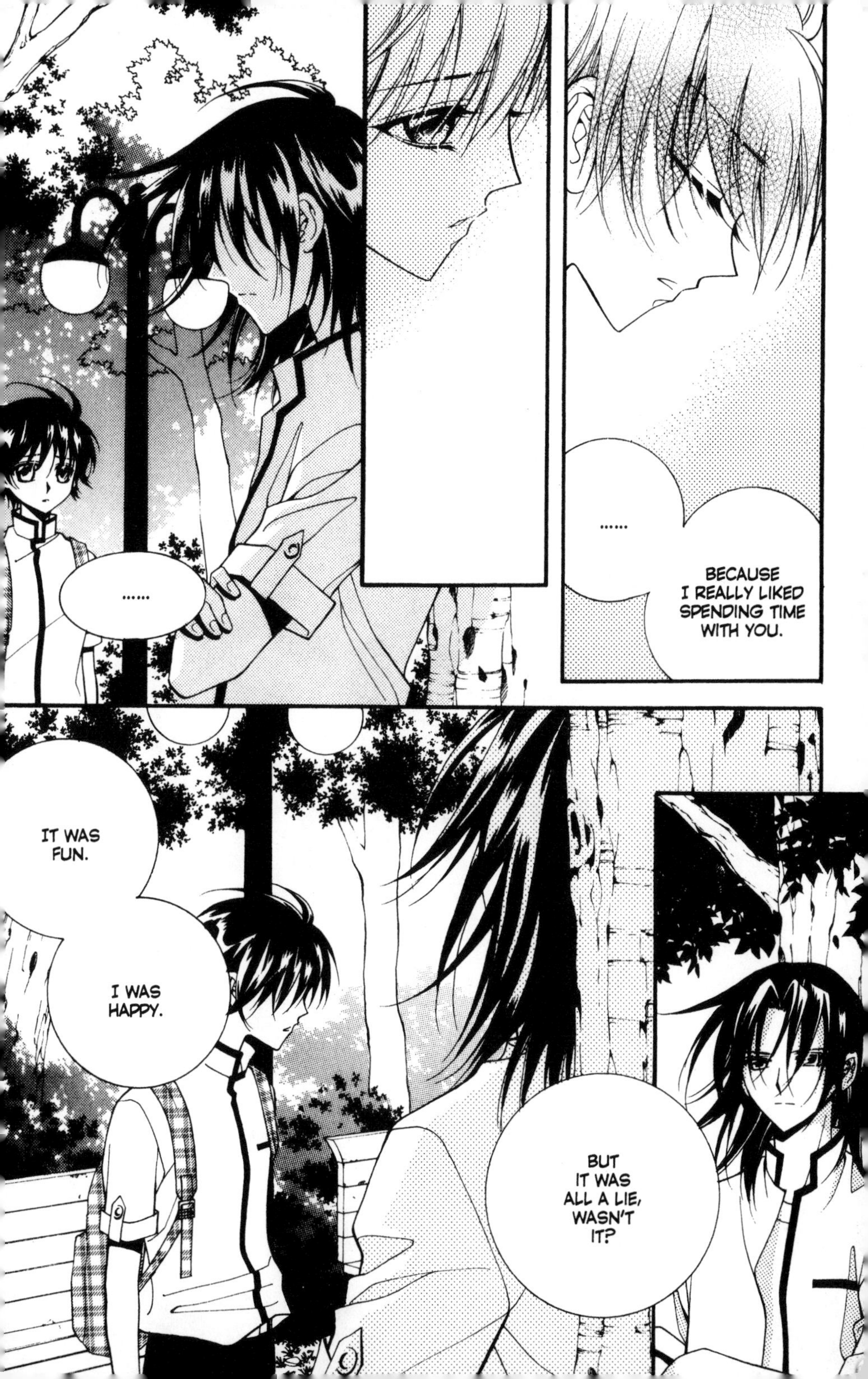
......
......
BECAUSE I REALLY LIKED SPENDING TIME WITH YOU.
IT WAS FUN.
I WAS HAPPY.
BUT IT WAS ALL A LIE, WASN'T IT?

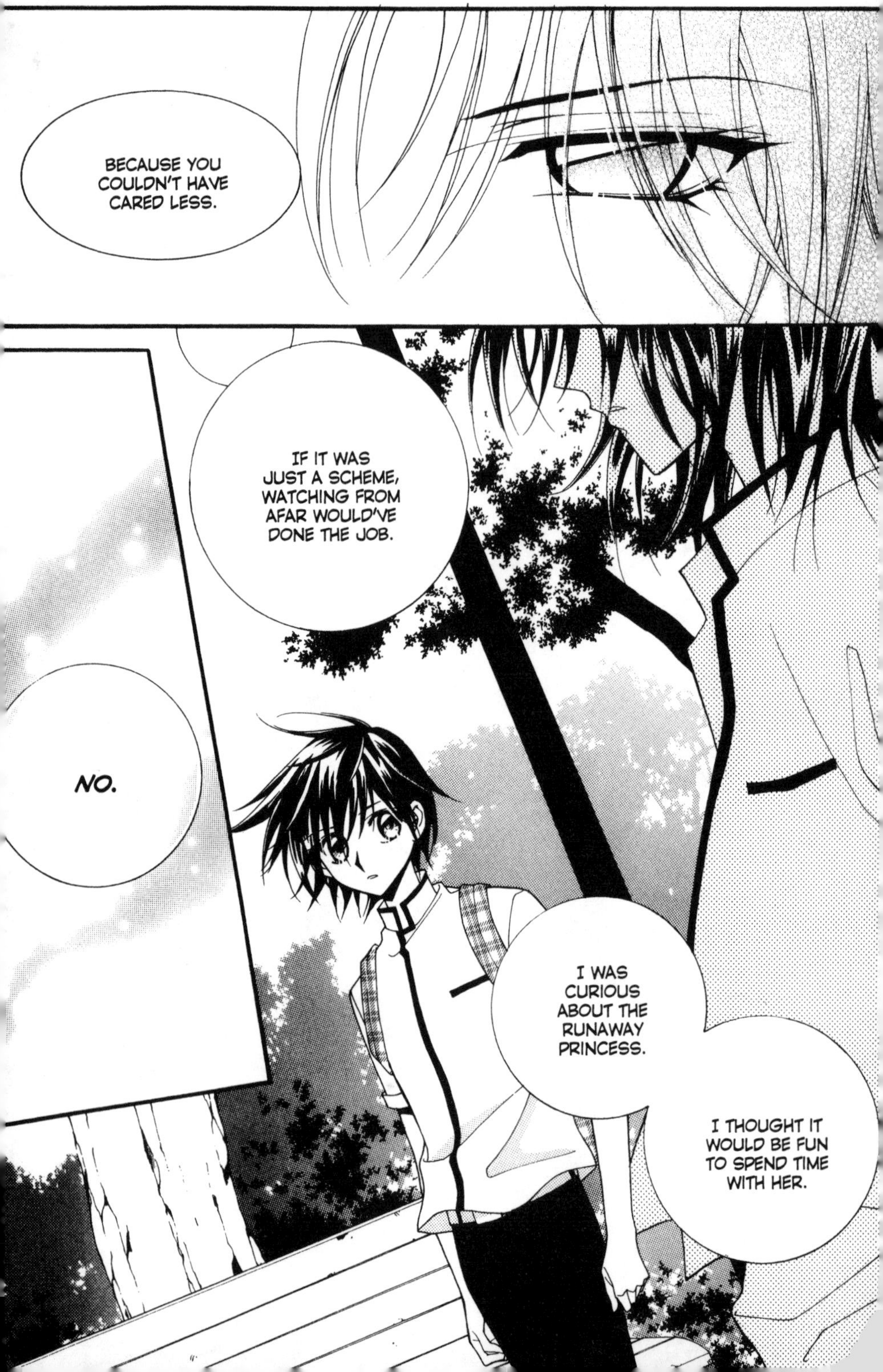
BECAUSE YOU COULDN'T HAVE CARED LESS.
IF IT WAS JUST A SCHEME, WATCHING FROM AFAR WOULD'VE DONE THE JOB.
NO.
I WAS CURIOUS ABOUT THE RUNAWAY PRINCESS.
I THOUGHT IT WOULD BE FUN TO SPEND TIME WITH HER.

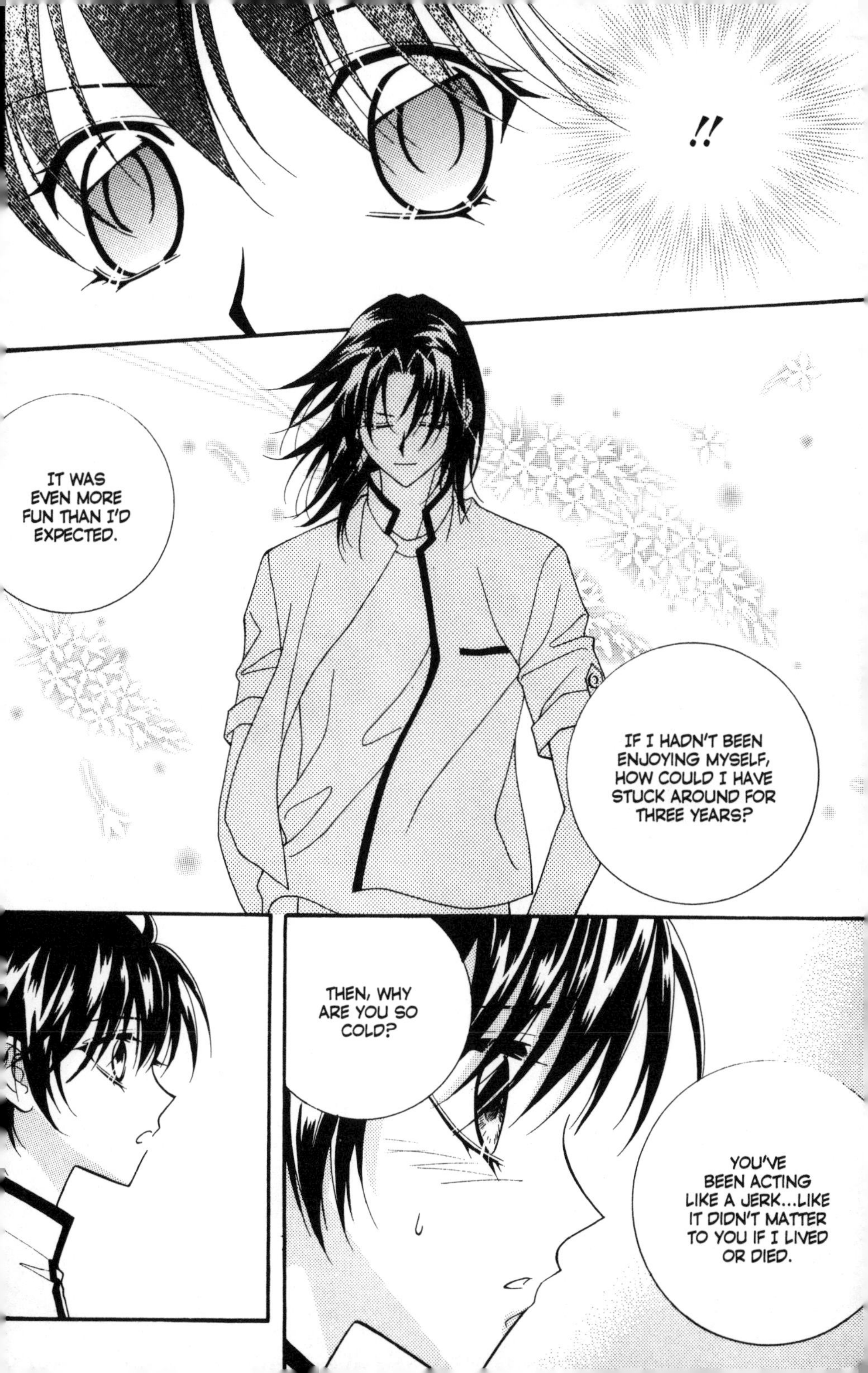
!!
IT WAS EVEN MORE FUN THAN I'D EXPECTED.
IF I HADN'T BEEN ENJOYING MYSELF, HOW COULD I HAVE STUCK AROUND FOR THREE YEARS?
THEN, WHY ARE YOU SO COLD?
YOU'VE BEEN ACTING LIKE A JERK...LIKE IT DIDN'T MATTER TO YOU IF I LIVED OR DIED.

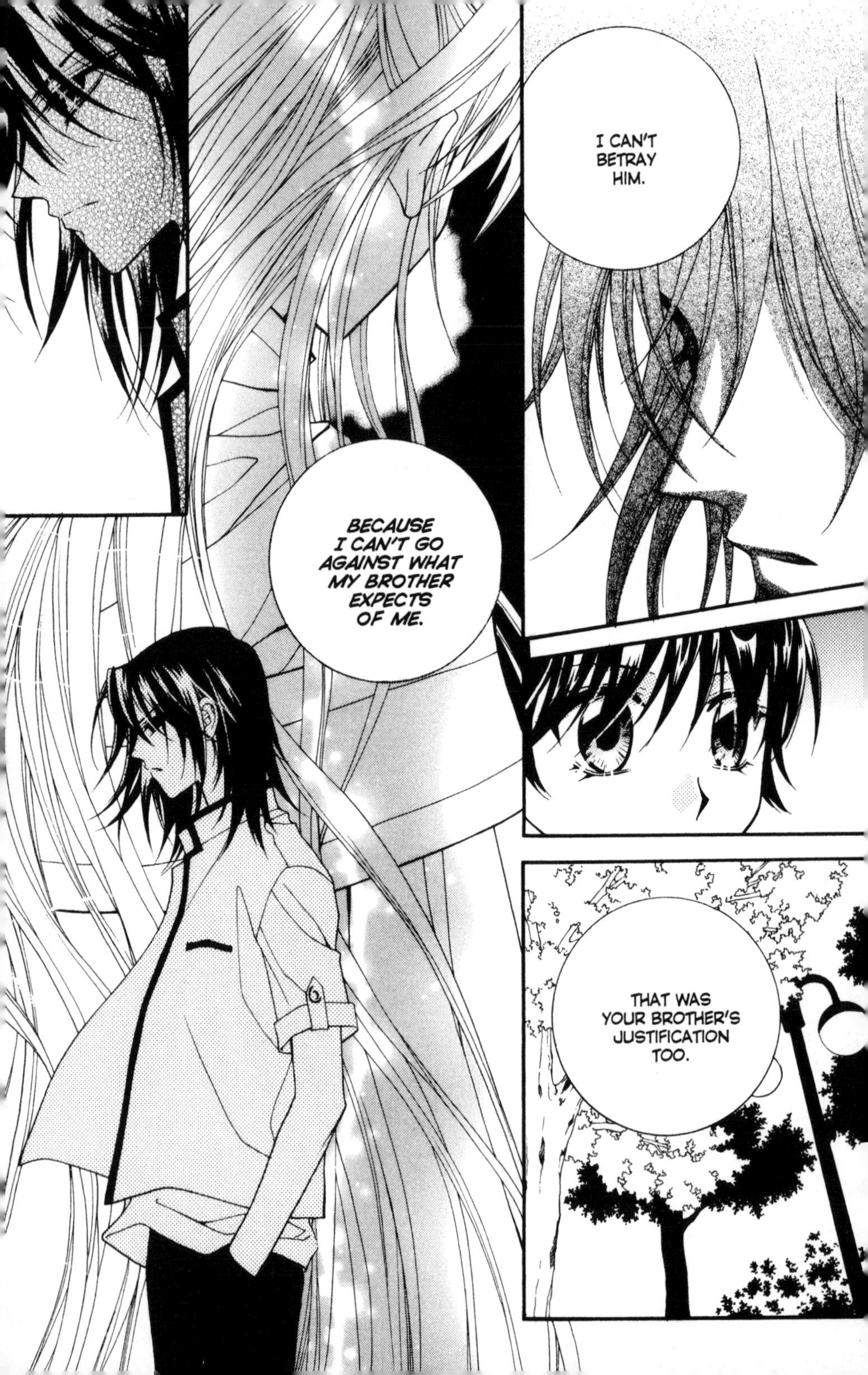
BECAUSE I CAN'T GO AGAINST WHAT MY BROTHER EXPECTS OF ME.
I CAN'T BETRAY HIM.
THAT WAS YOUR BROTHER'S JUSTIFICATION TOO.

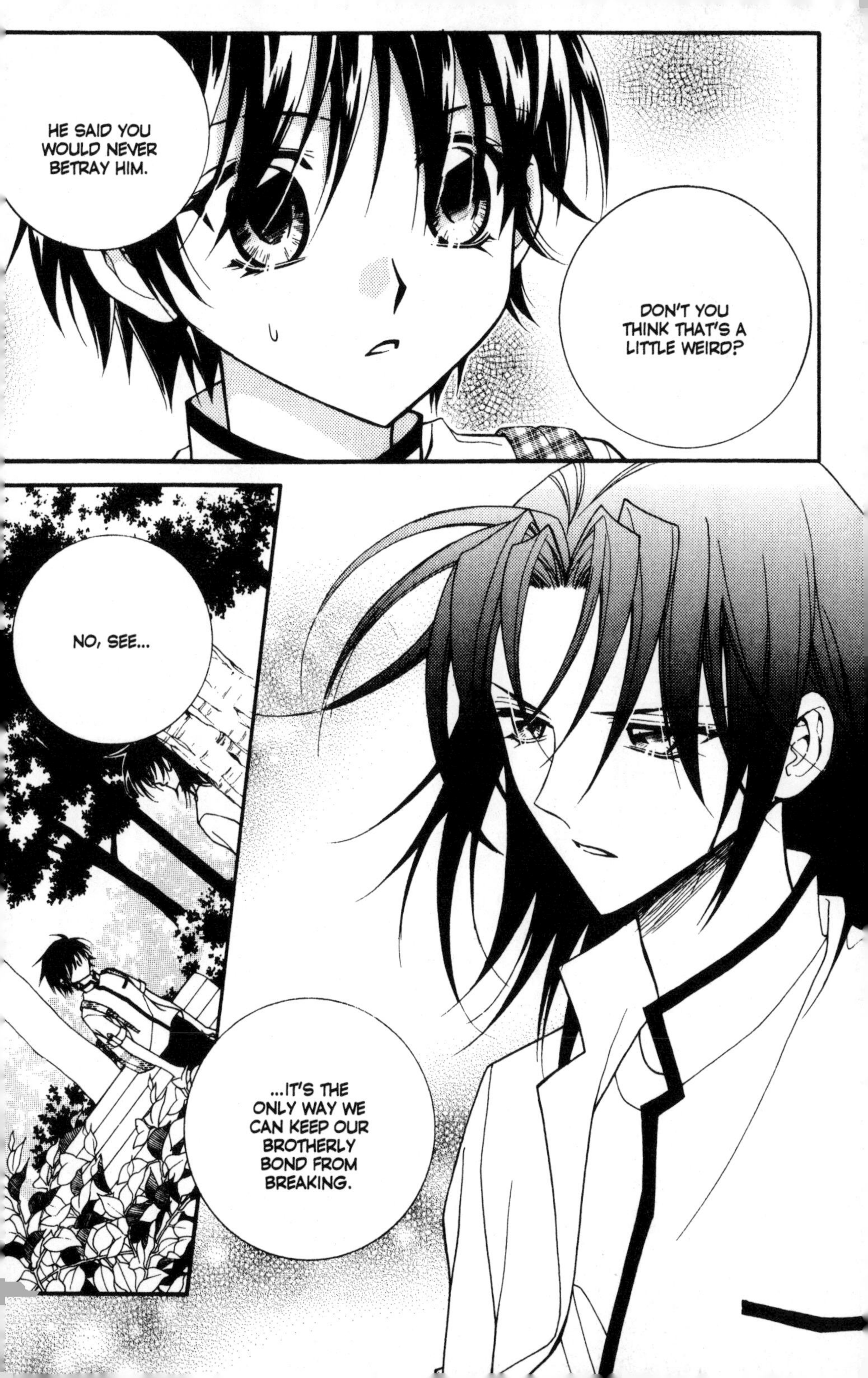
HE SAID YOU WOULD NEVER BETRAY HIM.
DON'T YOU THINK THAT'S A LITTLE WEIRD?
NO, SEE...
...IT'S THE ONLY WAY WE CAN KEEP OUR BROTHERLY BOND FROM BREAKING.

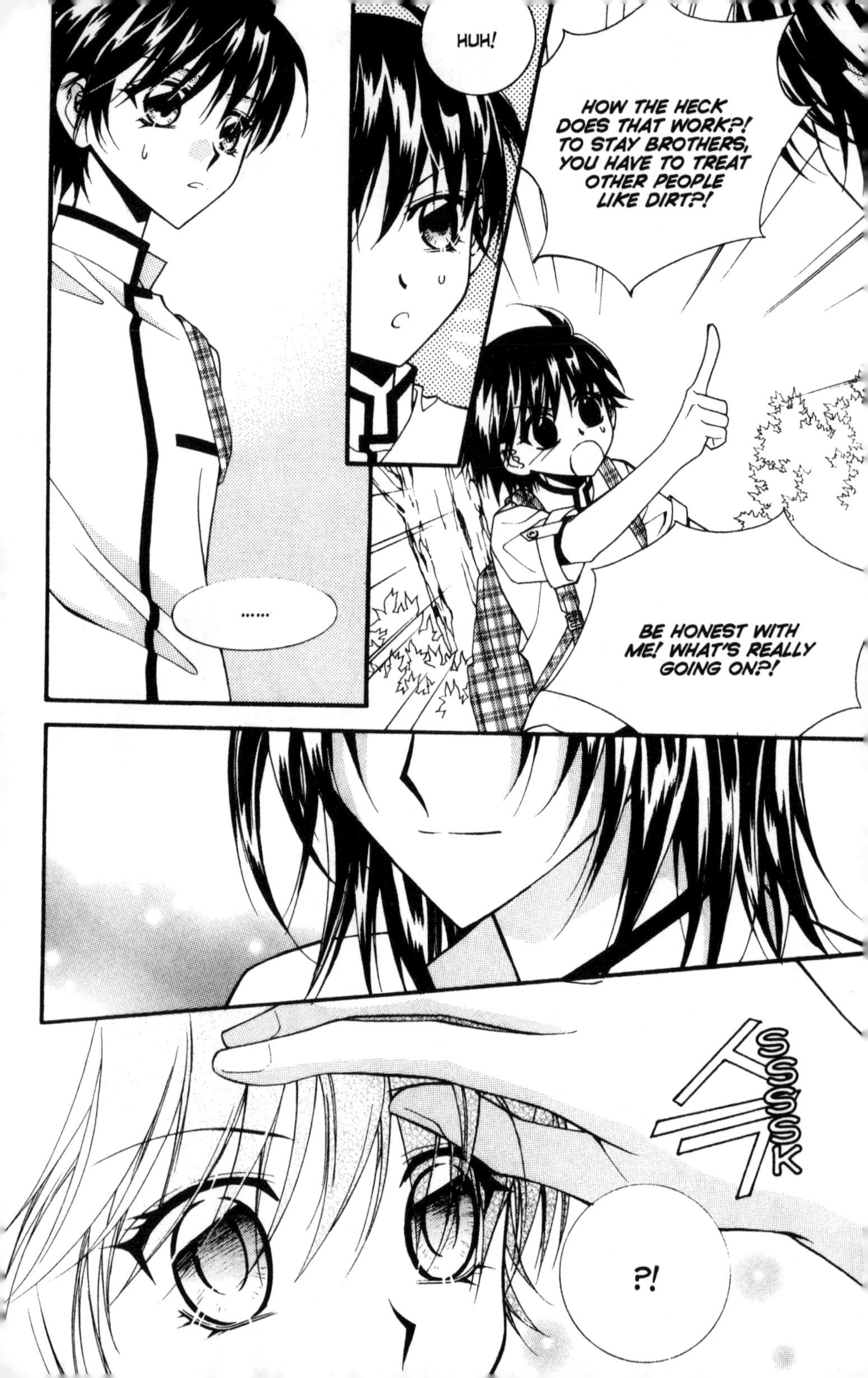
......
HUH!
HOW THE HECK DOES THAT WORK?! TO STAY BROTHERS, YOU HAVE TO TREAT OTHER PEOPLE LIKE DIRT?!
BE HONEST WITH ME! WHAT'S REALLY GOING ON?!
SSSSK
?!

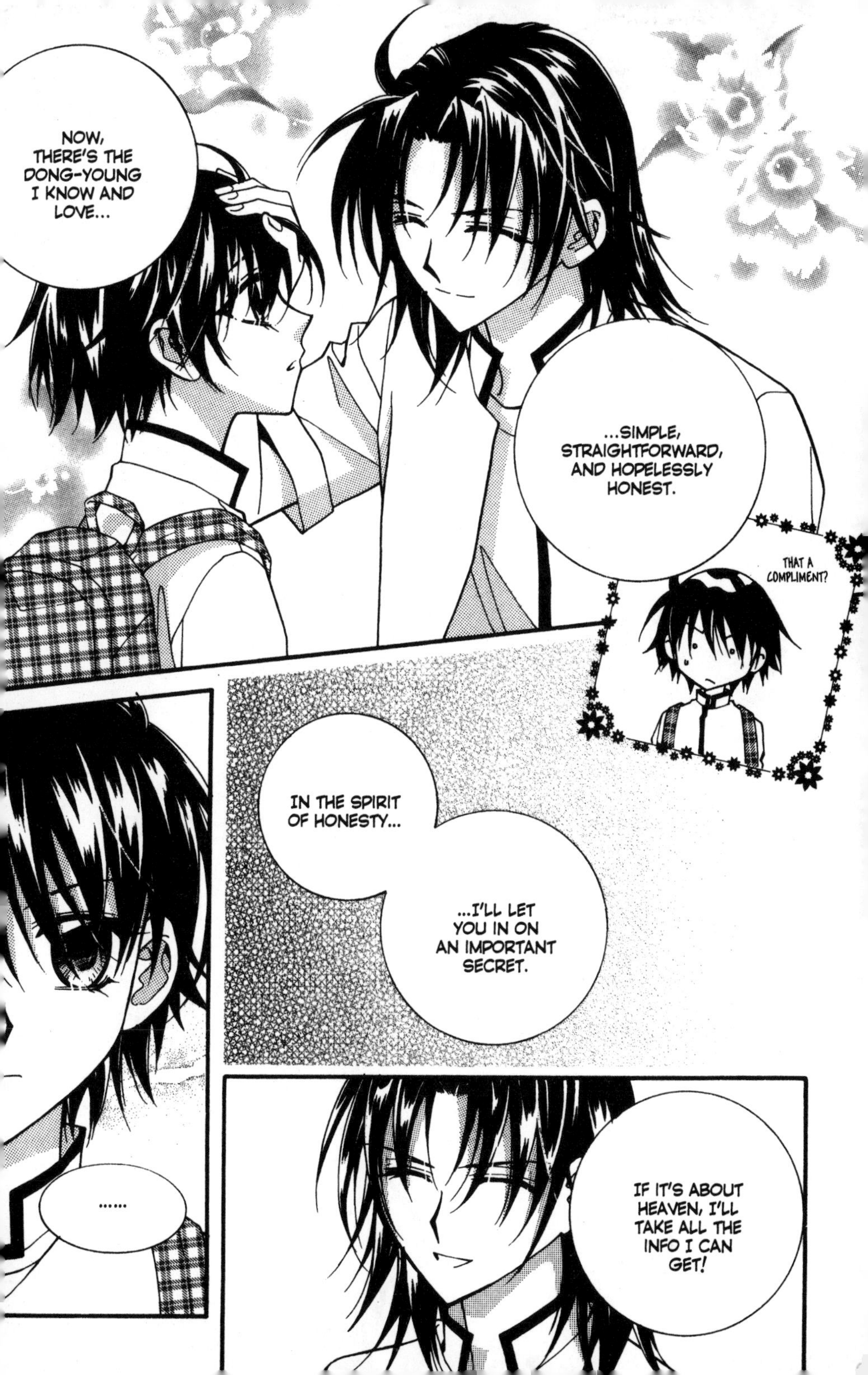
NOW, THERE'S THE DONG-YOUNG I KNOW AND LOVE...
...SIMPLE, STRAIGHTFORWARD, AND HOPELESSLY HONEST.
THAT A COMPLIMENT?
......
IN THE SPIRIT OF HONESTY...
...I'LL LET YOU IN ON AN IMPORTANT SECRET.
IF IT'S ABOUT HEAVEN, I'LL TAKE ALL THE INFO I CAN GET!

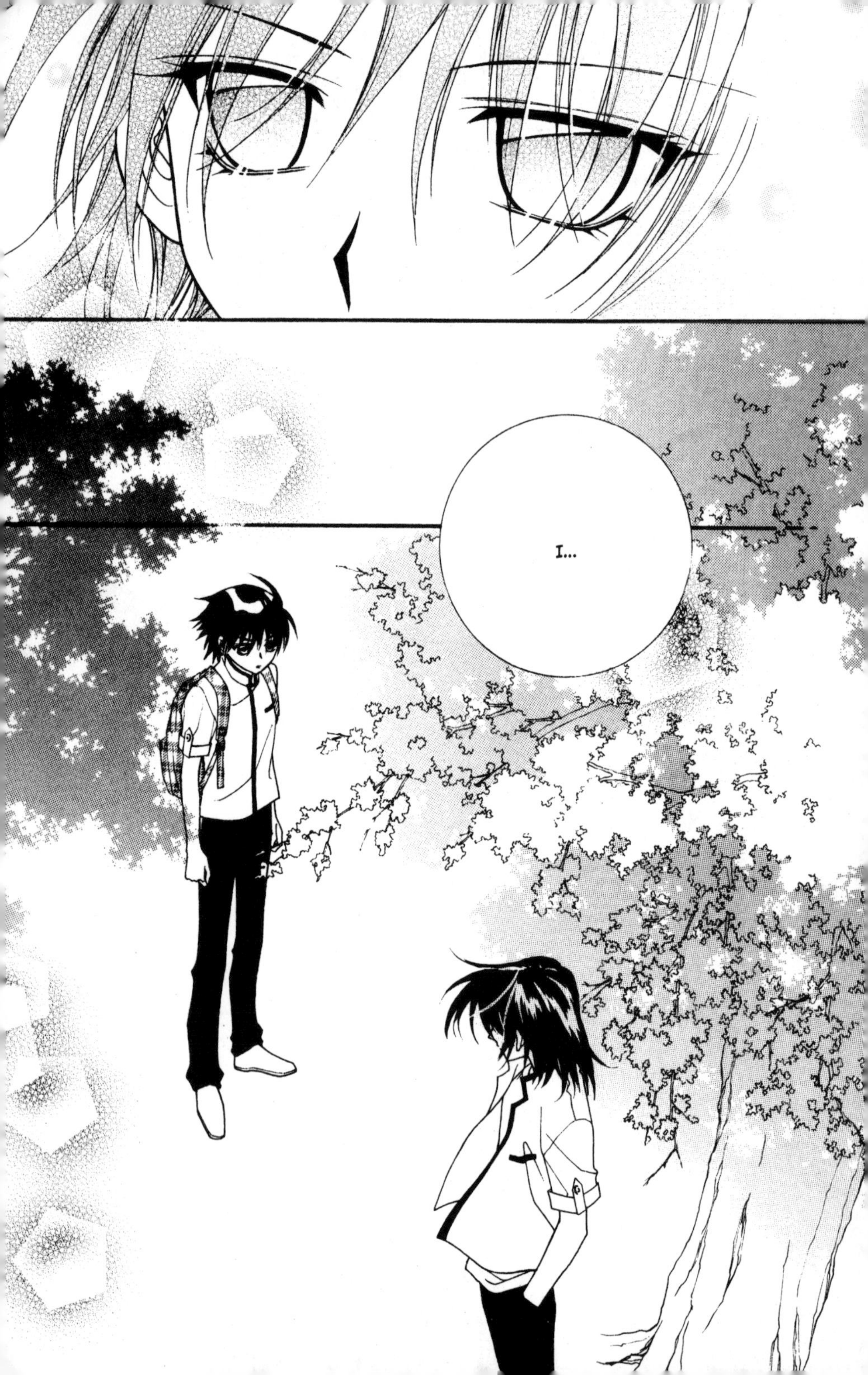
I...

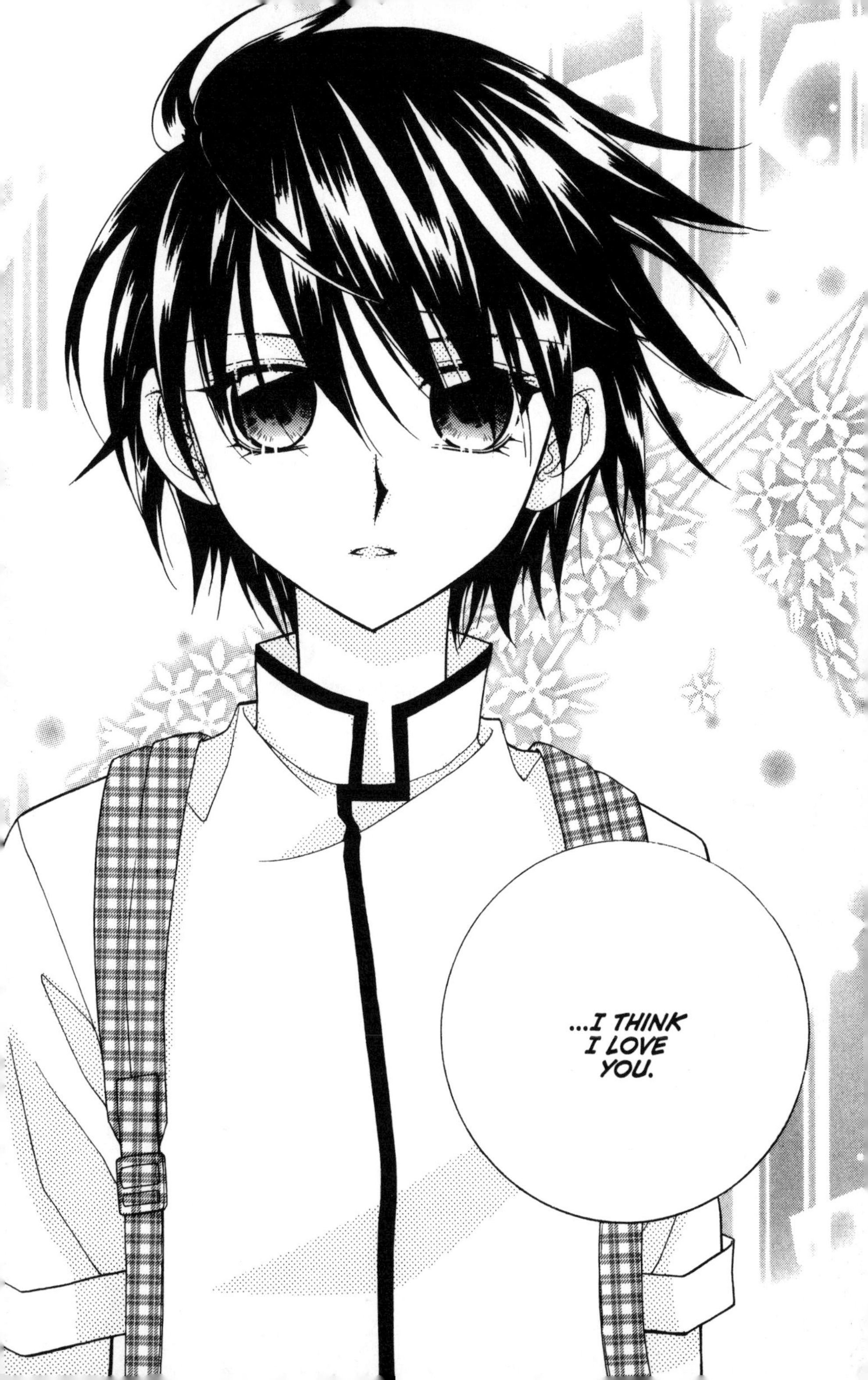
...I THINK I LOVE YOU.

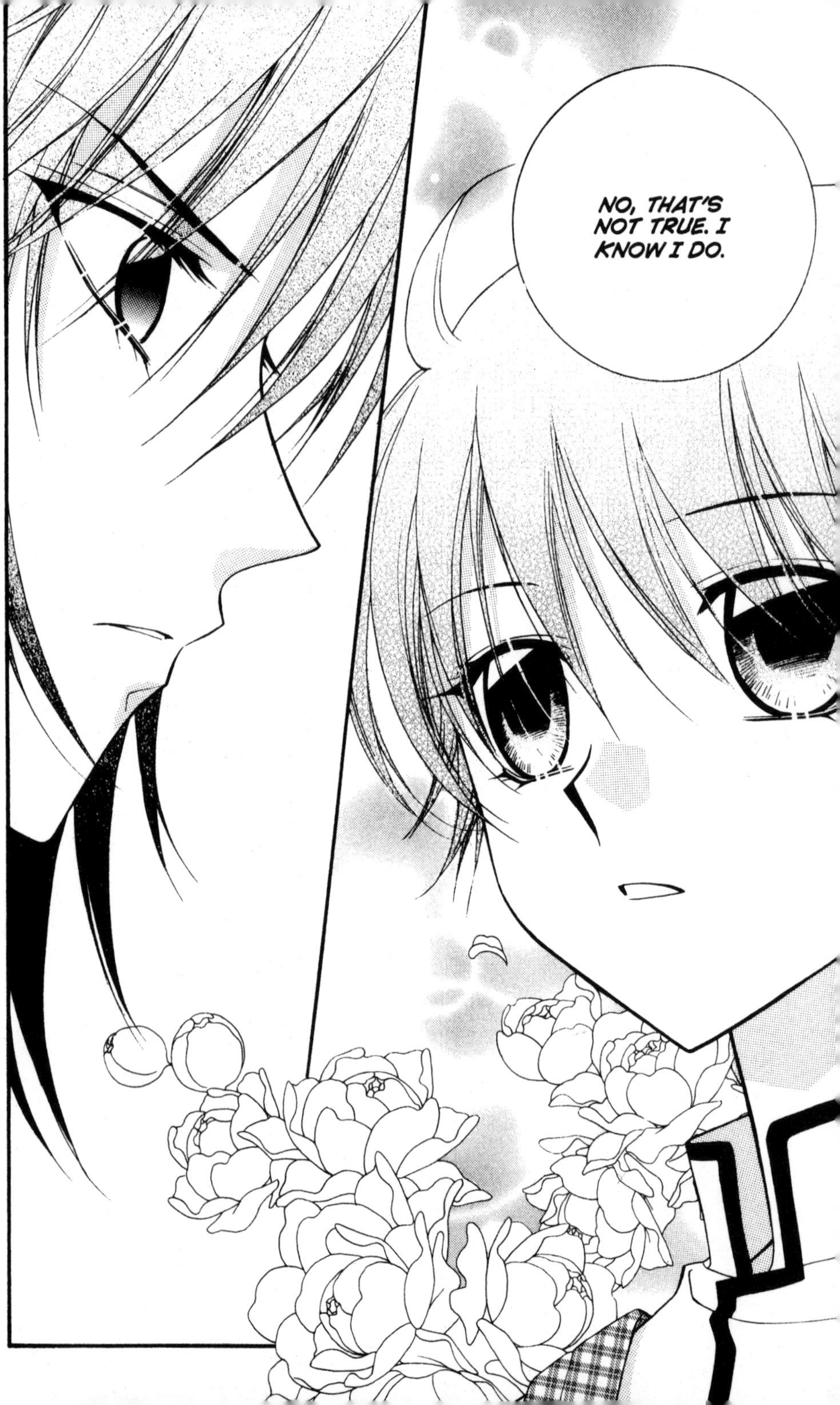
NO, THAT'S NOT TRUE. I KNOW I DO.

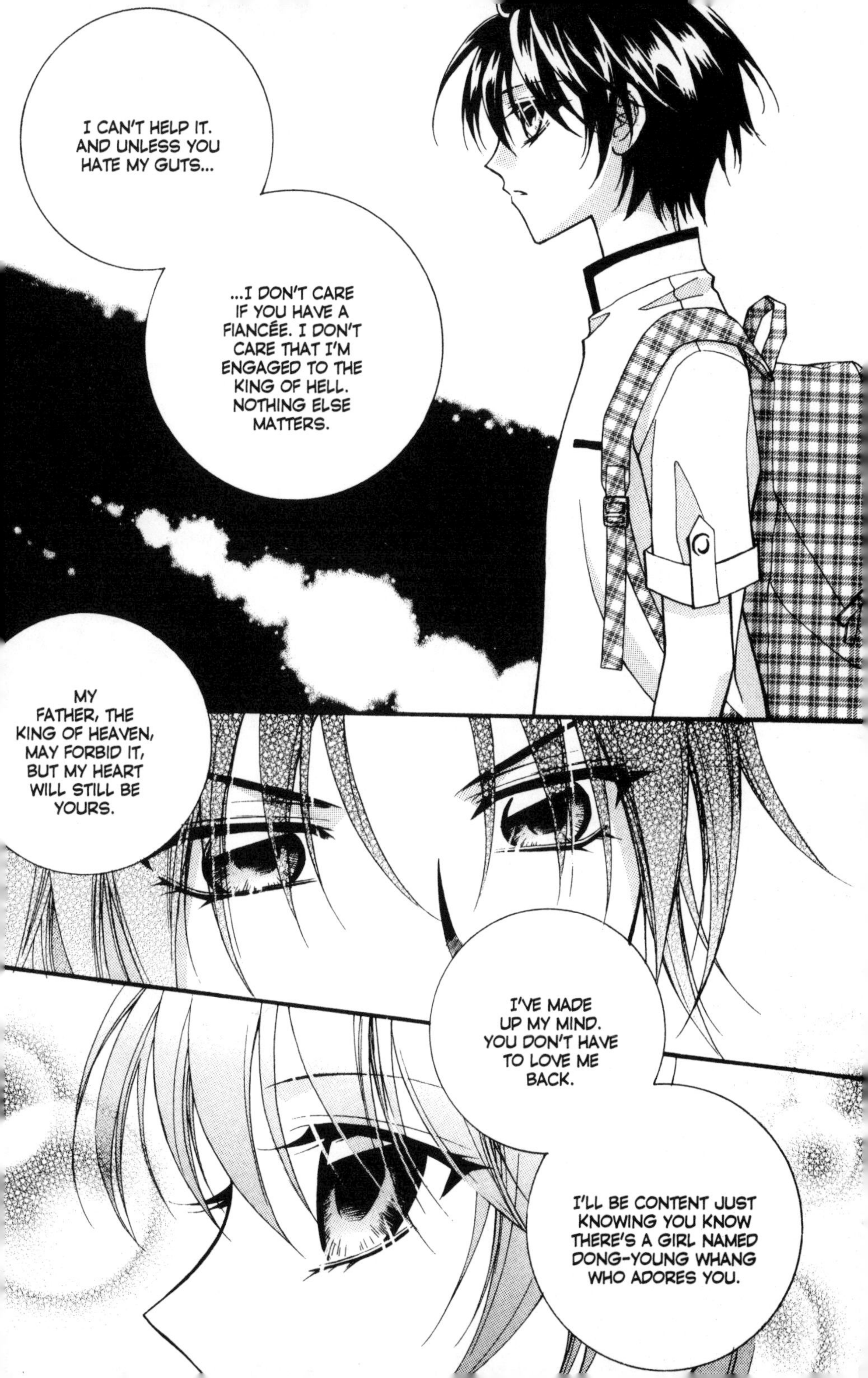
I CAN'T HELP IT. AND UNLESS YOU HATE MY GUTS...
...I DON'T CARE IF YOU HAVE A FIANCÉE. I DON'T CARE THAT I'M ENGAGED TO THE KING OF HELL. NOTHING ELSE MATTERS.
MY FATHER, THE KING OF HEAVEN, MAY FORBID IT, BUT MY HEART WILL STILL BE YOURS.
I'VE MADE UP MY MIND. YOU DON'T HAVE TO LOVE ME BACK.
I'LL BE CONTENT JUST KNOWING YOU KNOW THERE'S A GIRL NAMED DONG-YOUNG WHANG WHO ADORES YOU.

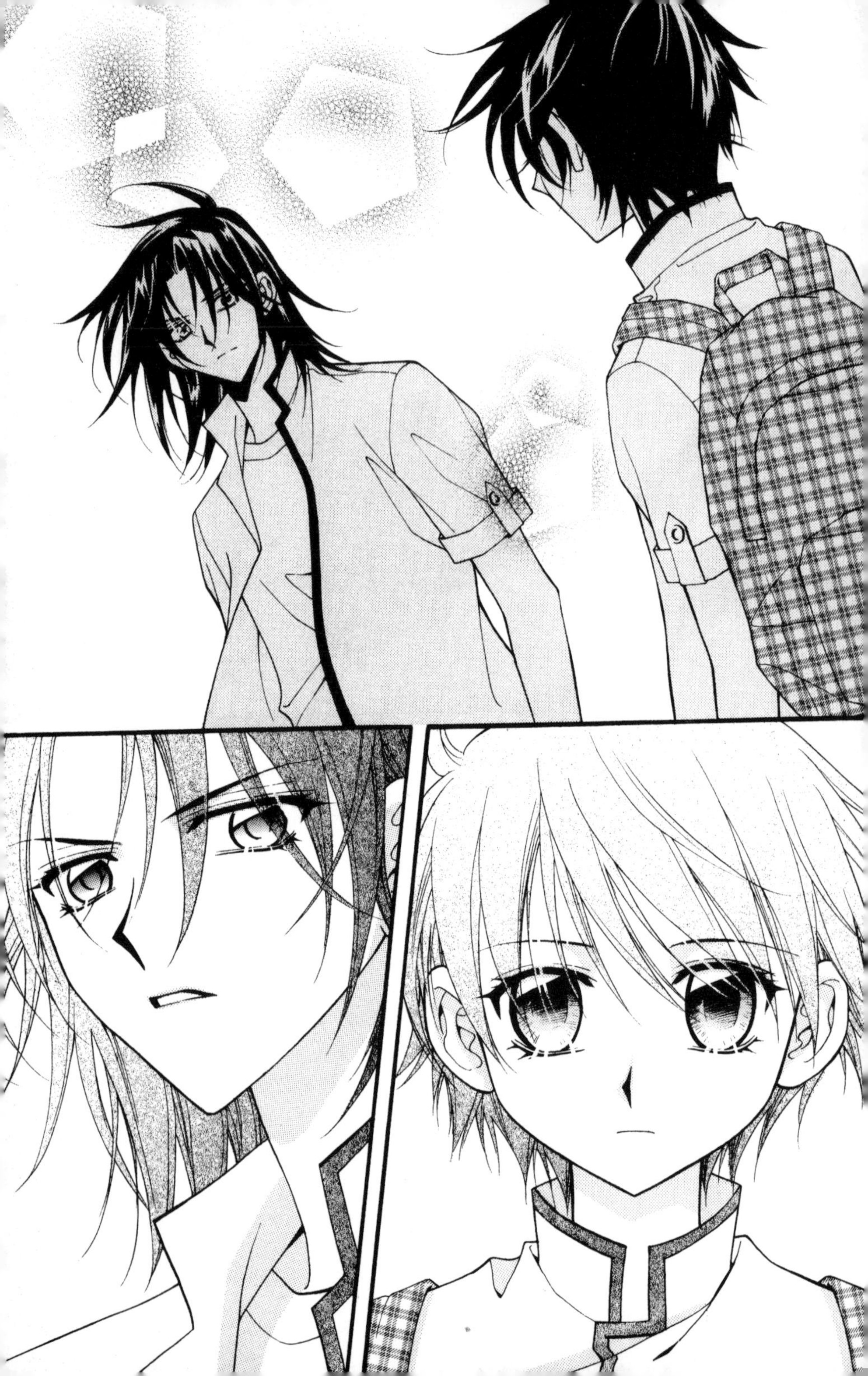

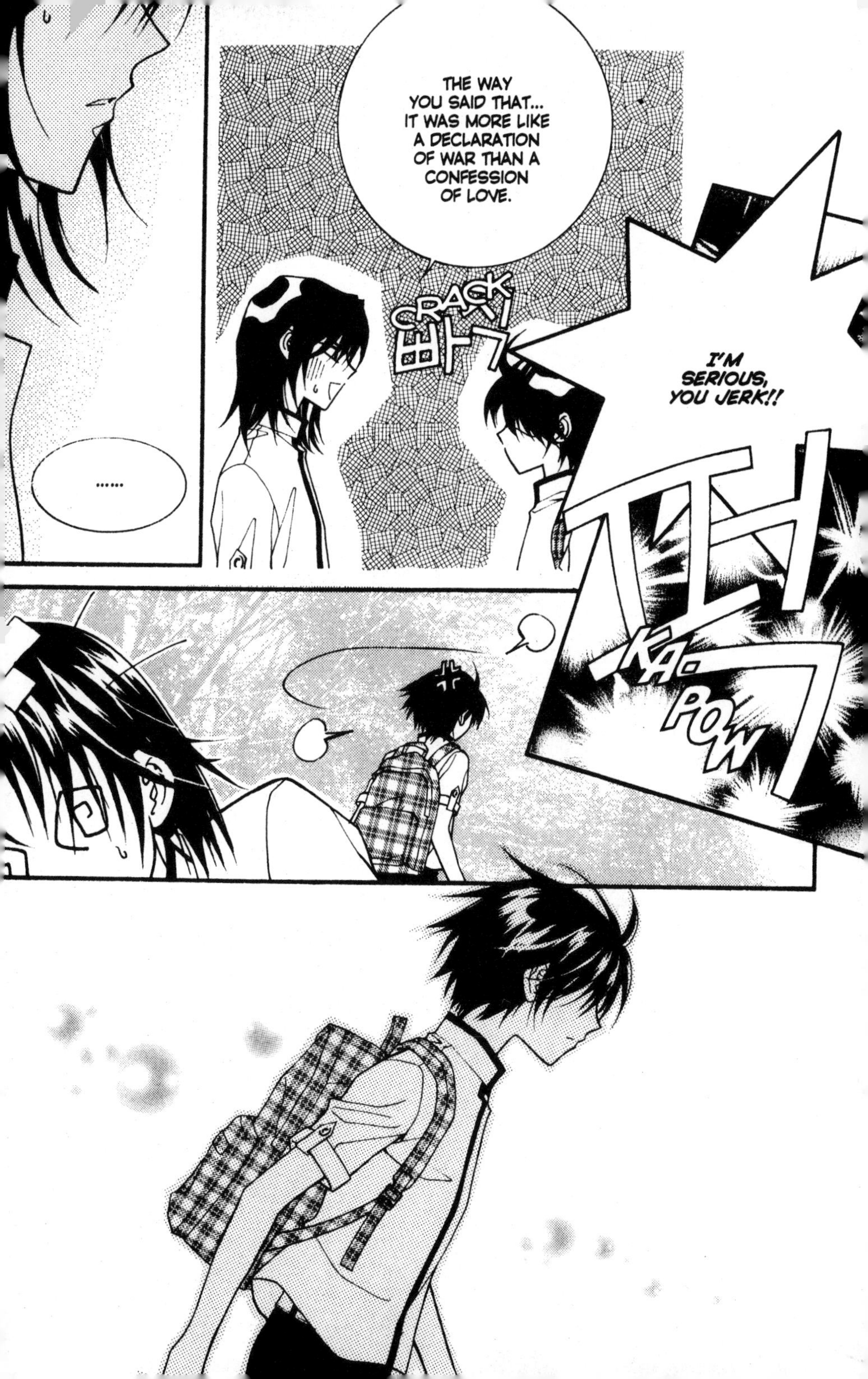

......
THE WAY YOU SAID THAT... IT WAS MORE LIKE A DECLARATION OF WAR THAN A CONFESSION OF LOVE.
CRACK!
빠각
I'M SERIOUS, YOU JERK!!
퍽
KA-POW

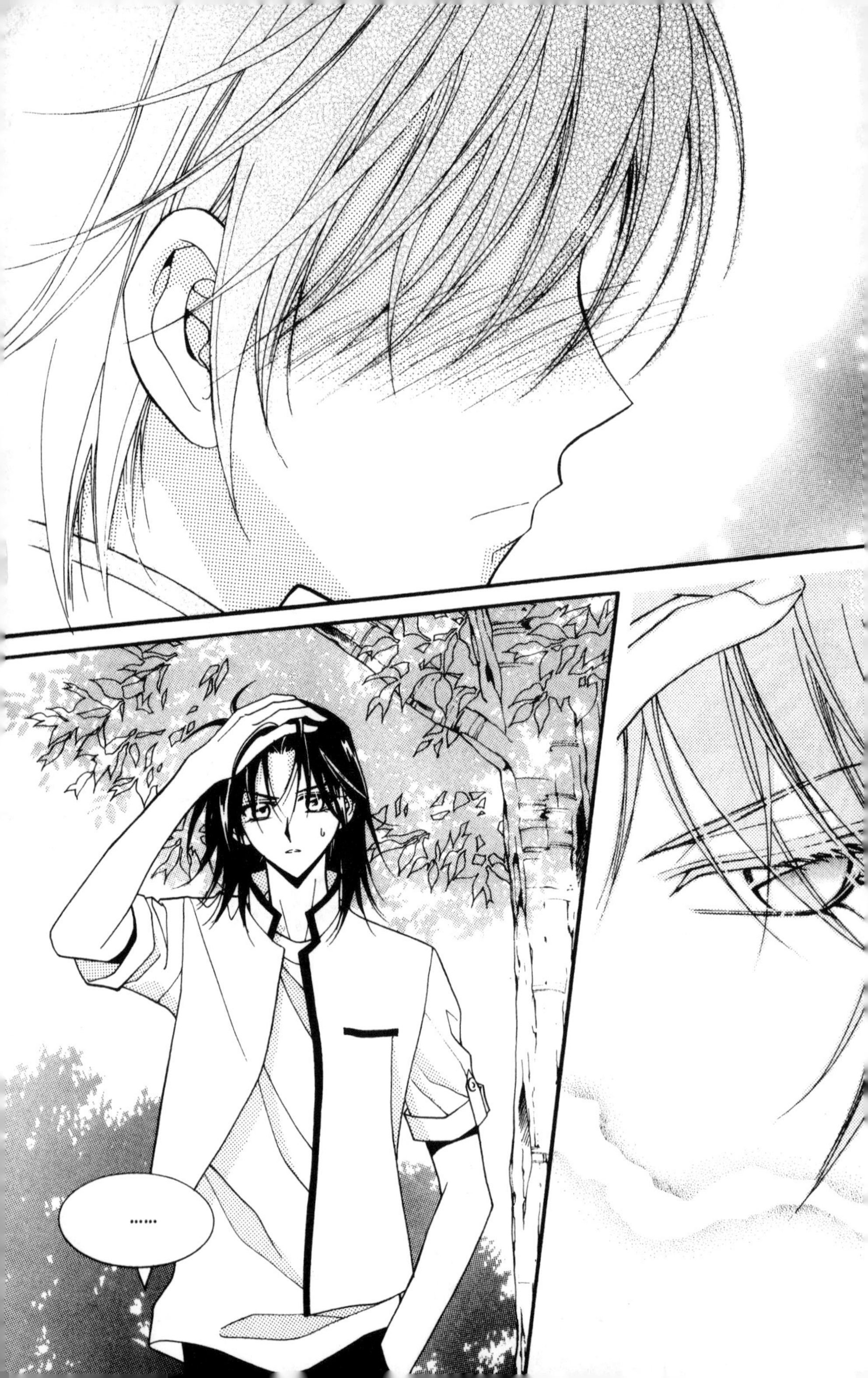
……

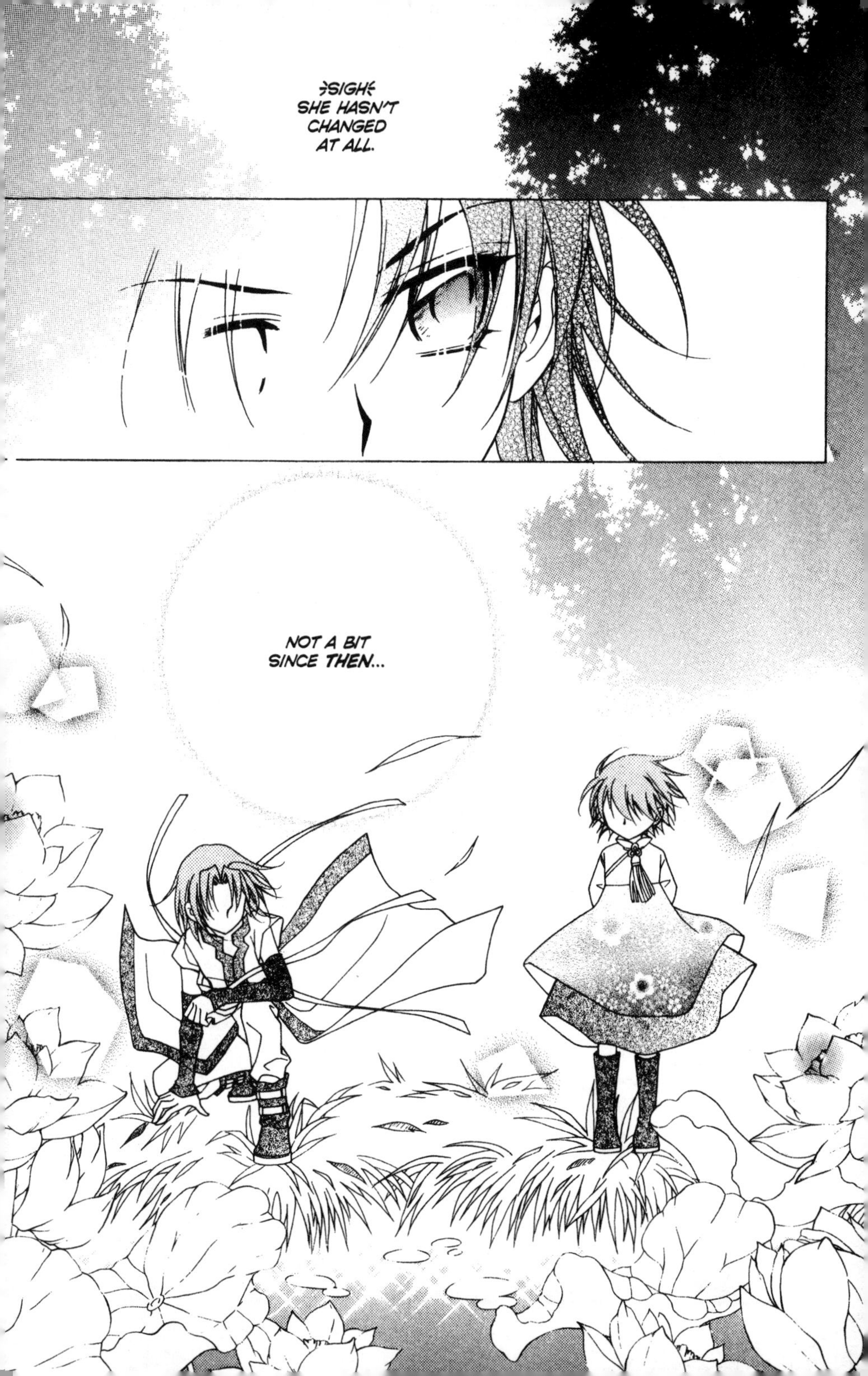

SIGH
SHE HASN'T CHANGED AT ALL.
NOT A BIT SINCE THEN...

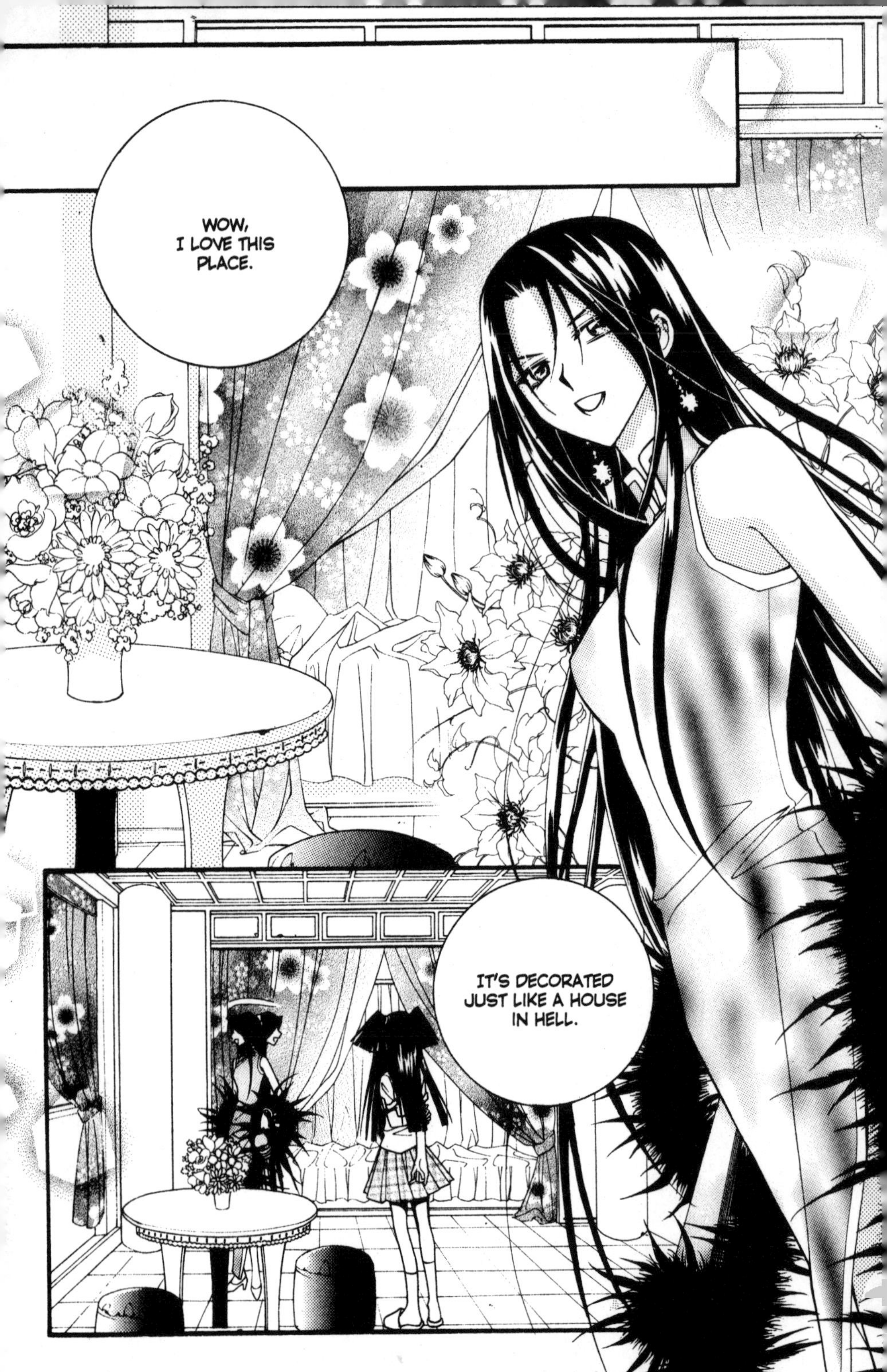
WOW, I LOVE THIS PLACE.
IT'S DECORATED JUST LIKE A HOUSE IN HELL.

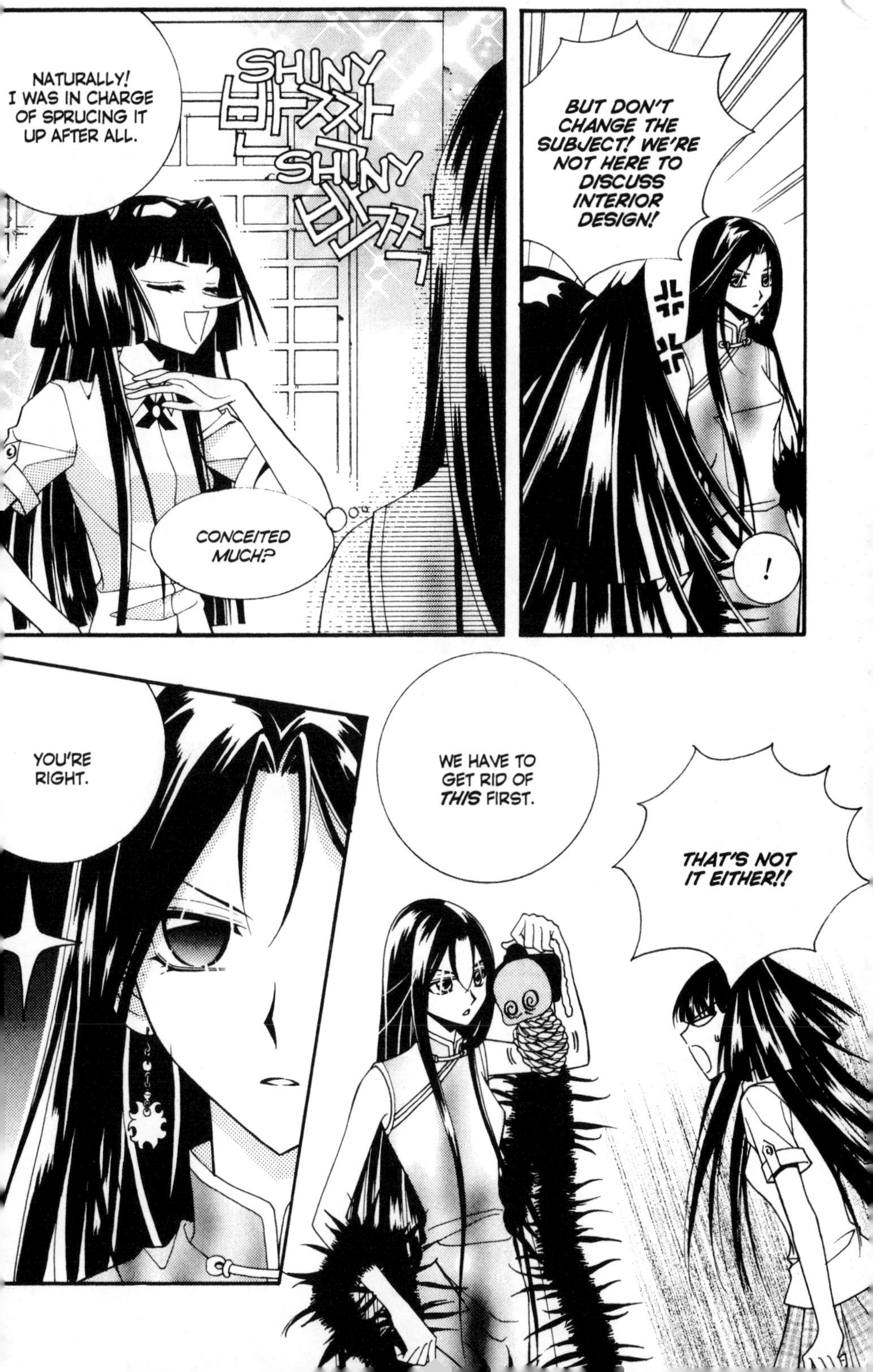
NATURALLY! I WAS IN CHARGE OF SPRUCING IT UP AFTER ALL.
SHINY 반짝 SHINY 반짝
CONCEITED MUCH?
BUT DON'T CHANGE THE SUBJECT! WE'RE NOT HERE TO DISCUSS INTERIOR DESIGN!
!
YOU'RE RIGHT.
WE HAVE TO GET RID OF *THIS* FIRST.
THAT'S NOT IT EITHER!!

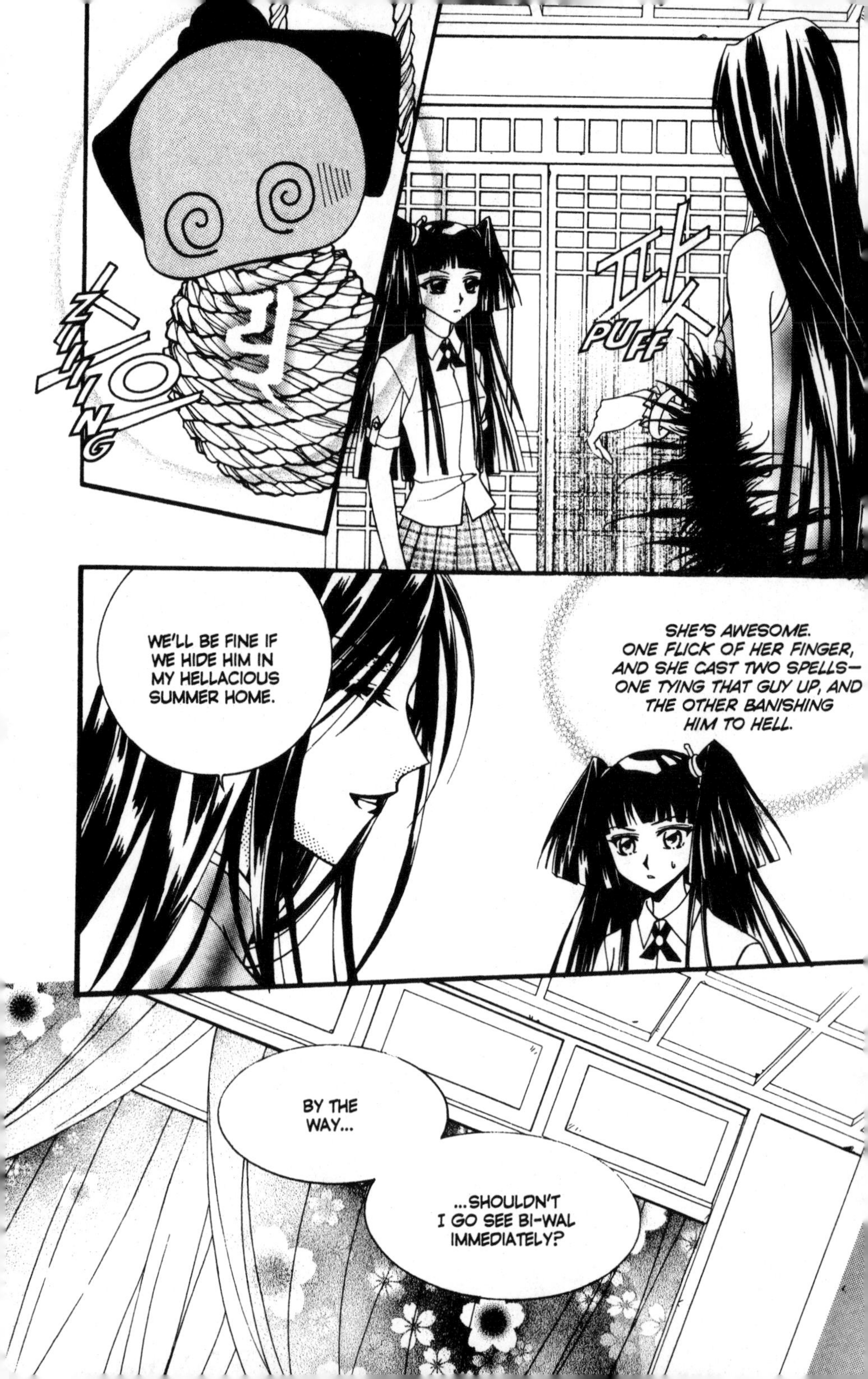
ZIIING
PUFF
WE'LL BE FINE IF WE HIDE HIM IN MY HELLACIOUS SUMMER HOME.
SHE'S AWESOME. ONE FLICK OF HER FINGER, AND SHE CAST TWO SPELLS—ONE TYING THAT GUY UP, AND THE OTHER BANISHING HIM TO HELL.
BY THE WAY...
...SHOULDN'T I GO SEE BI-WAL IMMEDIATELY?

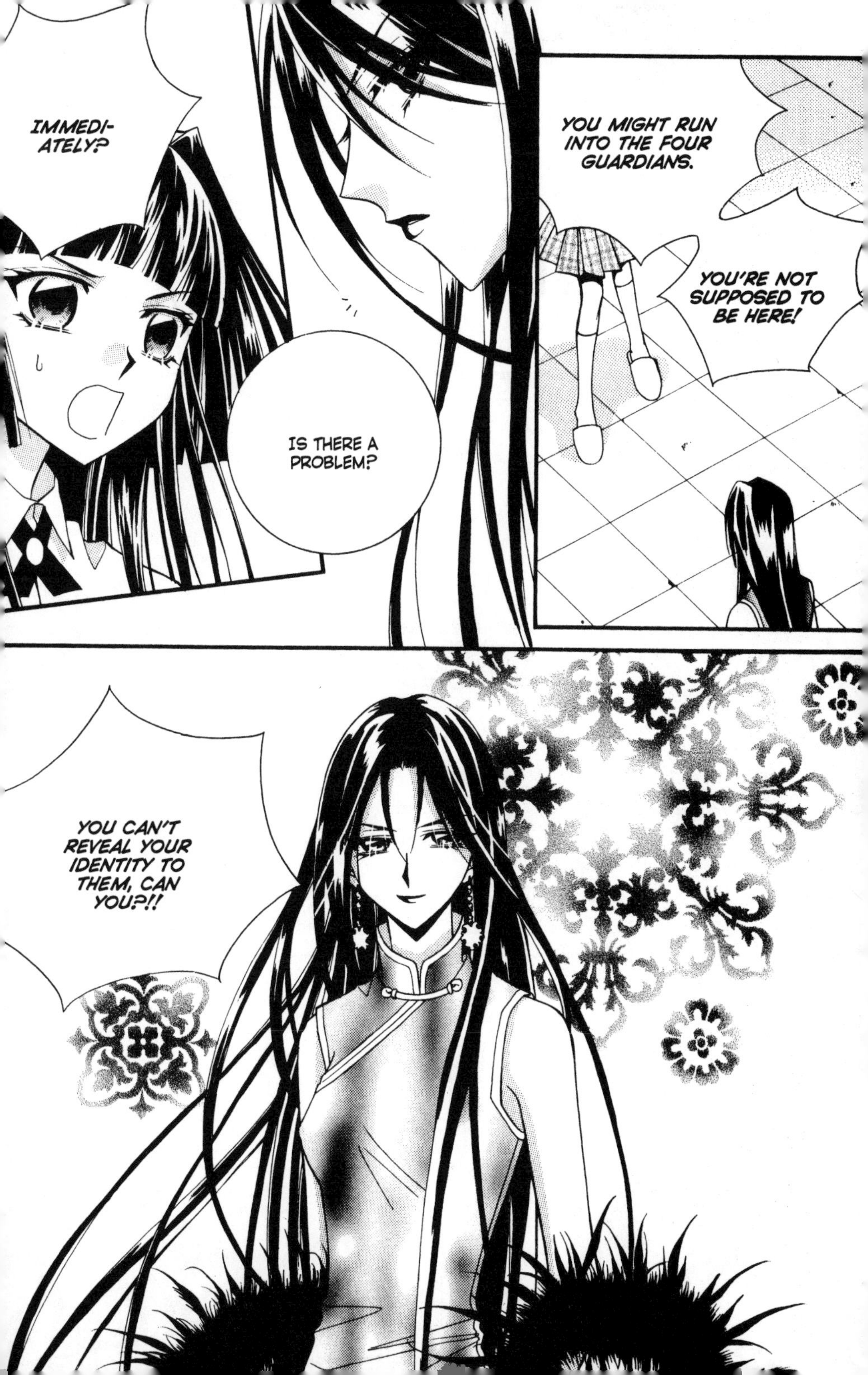
IMMEDI-ATELY?
IS THERE A PROBLEM?
YOU MIGHT RUN INTO THE FOUR GUARDIANS.
YOU'RE NOT SUPPOSED TO BE HERE!
YOU CAN'T REVEAL YOUR IDENTITY TO THEM, CAN YOU?!!

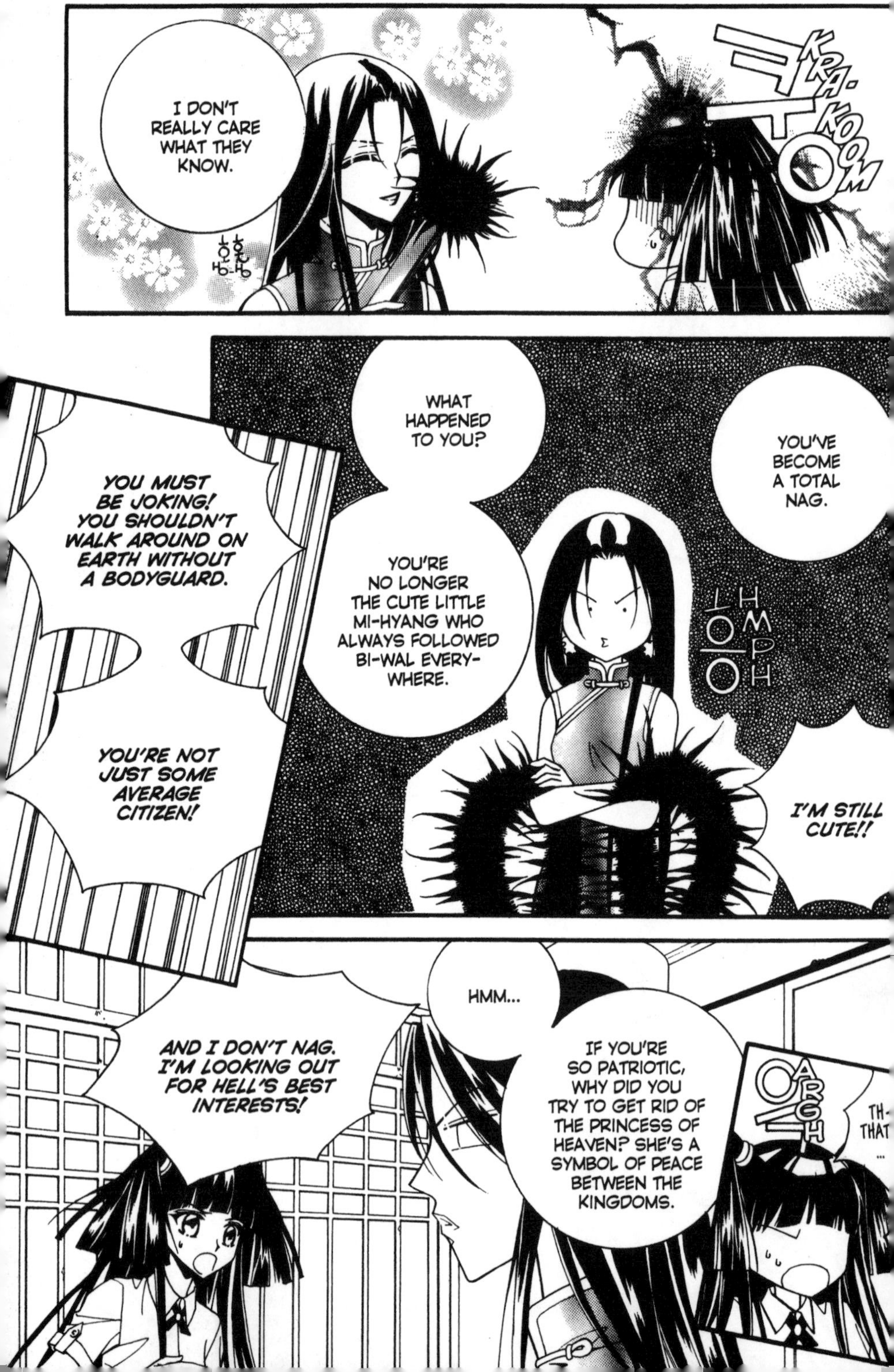
I DON'T REALLY CARE WHAT THEY KNOW.
KRA-KOOM
YOU MUST BE JOKING! YOU SHOULDN'T WALK AROUND ON EARTH WITHOUT A BODYGUARD.
YOU'RE NOT JUST SOME AVERAGE CITIZEN!
WHAT HAPPENED TO YOU?
YOU'RE NO LONGER THE CUTE LITTLE MI-HYANG WHO ALWAYS FOLLOWED BI-WAL EVERY-WHERE.
YOU'VE BECOME A TOTAL NAG.
HMPH
I'M STILL CUTE!!
AND I DON'T NAG. I'M LOOKING OUT FOR HELL'S BEST INTERESTS!
HMM...
IF YOU'RE SO PATRIOTIC, WHY DID YOU TRY TO GET RID OF THE PRINCESS OF HEAVEN? SHE'S A SYMBOL OF PEACE BETWEEN THE KINGDOMS.
ARGH
TH-THAT...

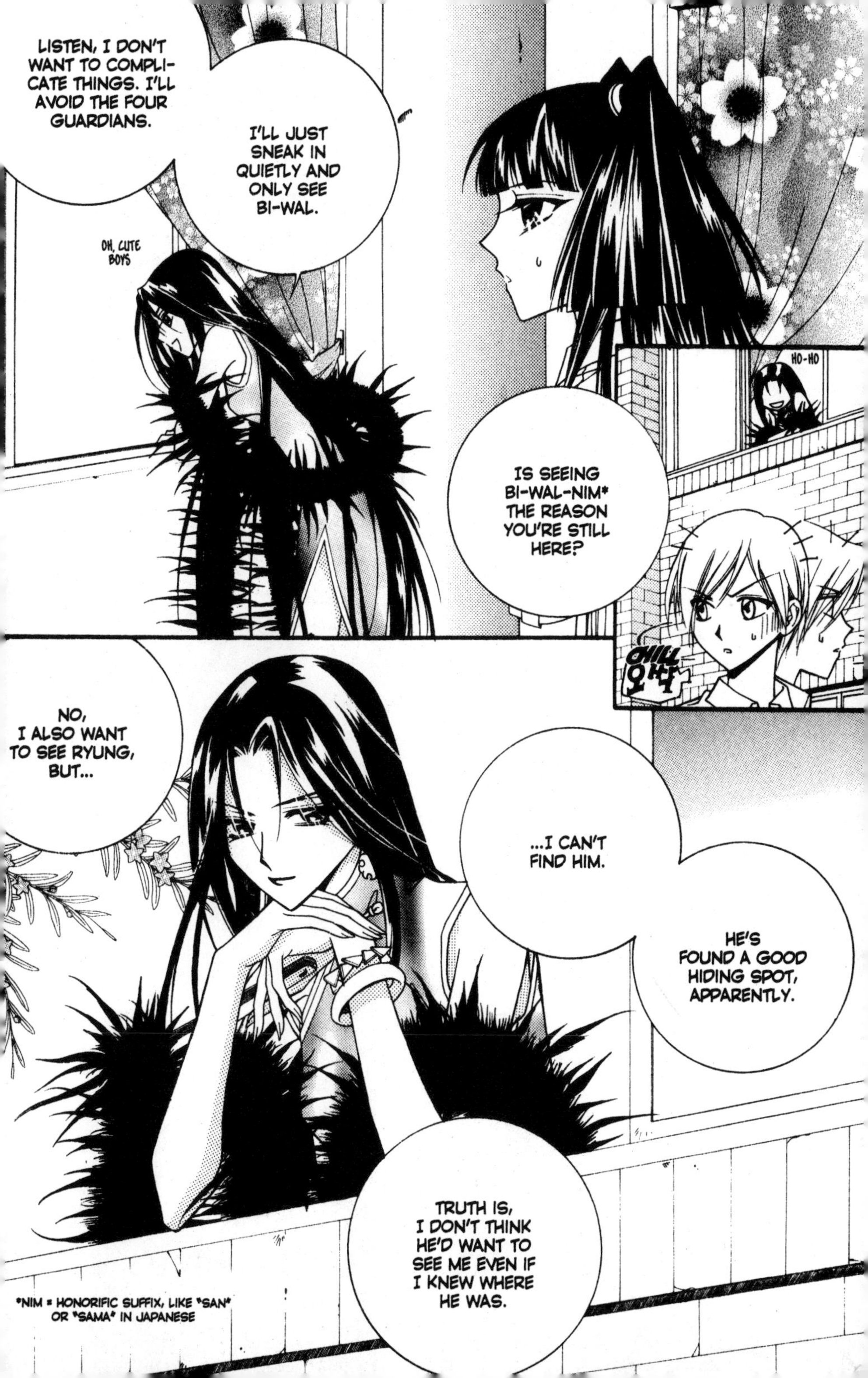
LISTEN, I DON'T WANT TO COMPLI-CATE THINGS. I'LL AVOID THE FOUR GUARDIANS.
I'LL JUST SNEAK IN QUIETLY AND ONLY SEE BI-WAL.
OH, CUTE BOYS
IS SEEING BI-WAL-NIM* THE REASON YOU'RE STILL HERE?
HO-HO
CHILL
오싹
NO, I ALSO WANT TO SEE RYUNG, BUT...
...I CAN'T FIND HIM.
HE'S FOUND A GOOD HIDING SPOT, APPARENTLY.
TRUTH IS, I DON'T THINK HE'D WANT TO SEE ME EVEN IF I KNEW WHERE HE WAS.

*NIM = HONORIFIC SUFFIX, LIKE "SAN" OR "SAMA" IN JAPANESE

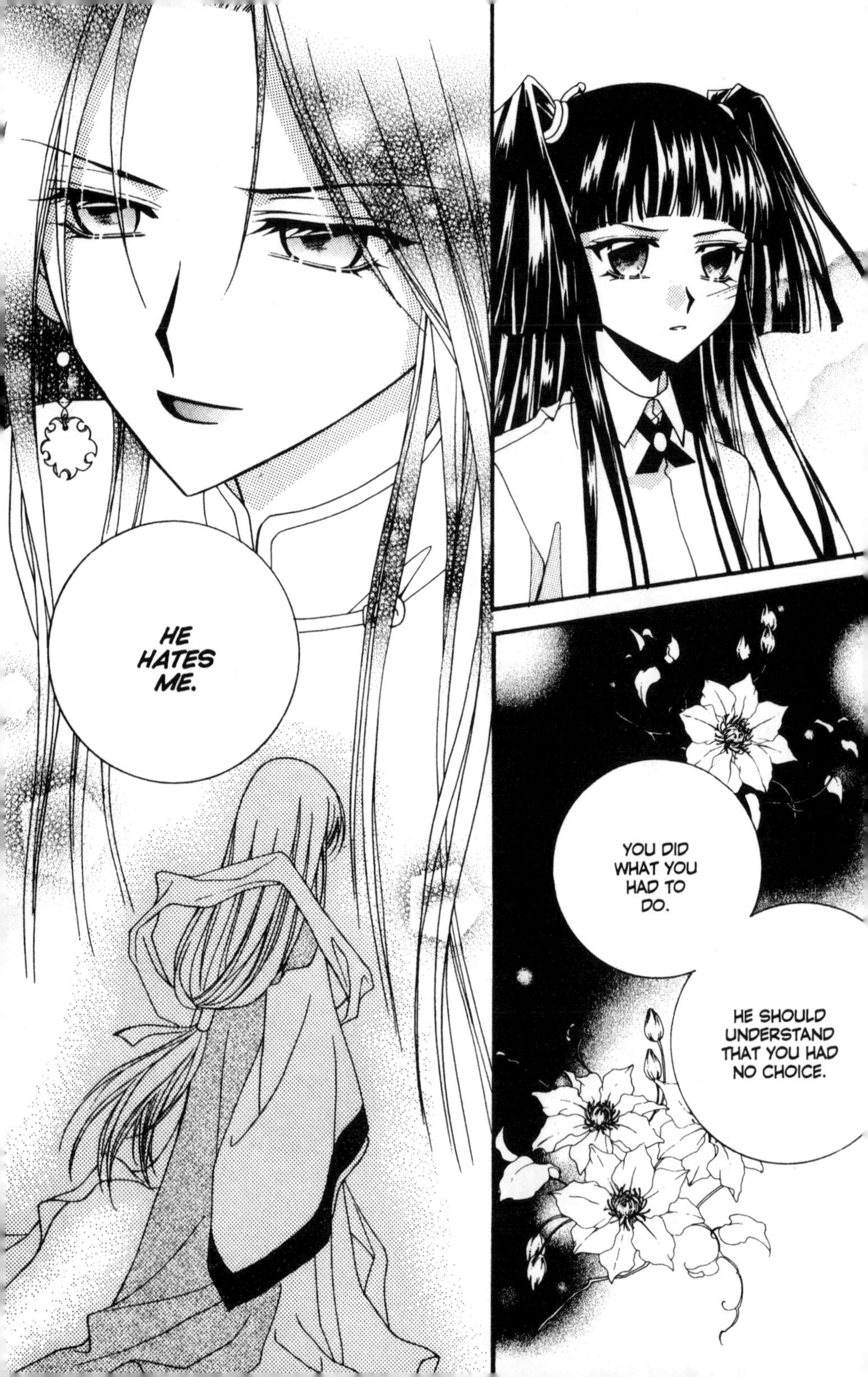
HE HATES ME.
YOU DID WHAT YOU HAD TO DO.
HE SHOULD UNDERSTAND THAT YOU HAD NO CHOICE.

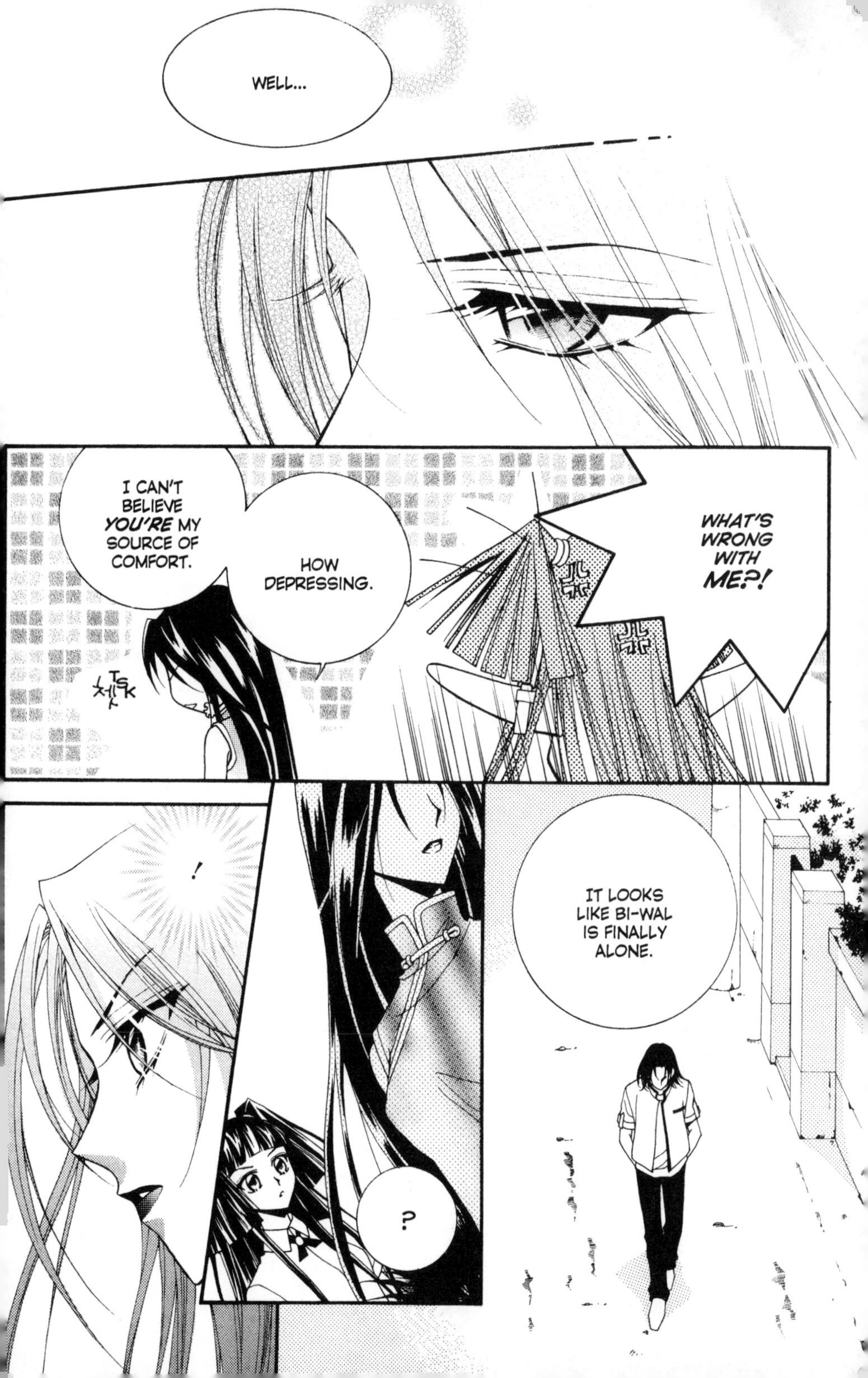
WELL...
I CAN'T BELIEVE *YOU'RE* MY SOURCE OF COMFORT.
HOW DEPRESSING.
TSK
*WHAT'S WRONG WITH **ME?!***
!
?
IT LOOKS LIKE BI-WAL IS FINALLY ALONE.

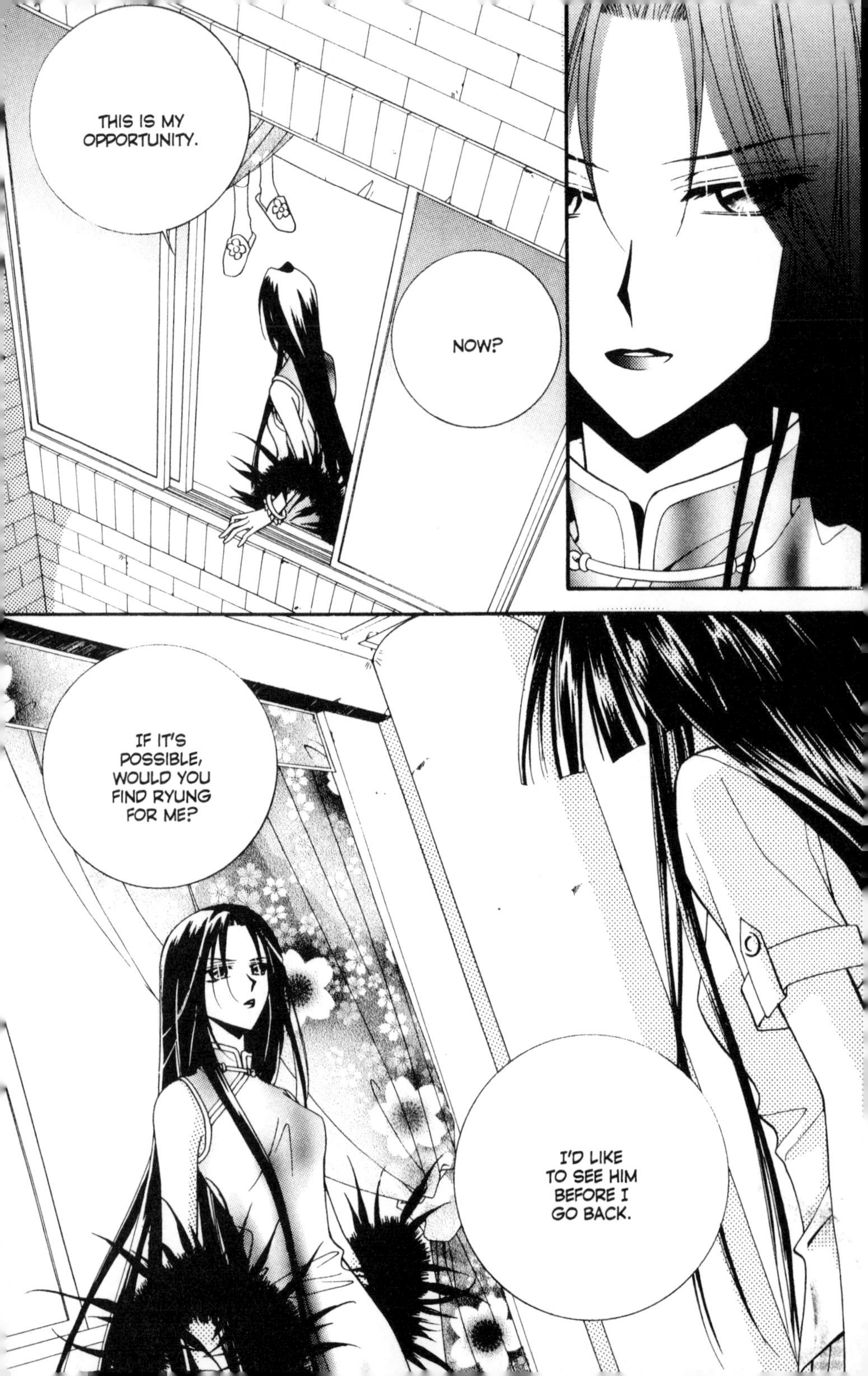
THIS IS MY OPPORTUNITY.
NOW?
IF IT'S POSSIBLE, WOULD YOU FIND RYUNG FOR ME?
I'D LIKE TO SEE HIM BEFORE I GO BACK.

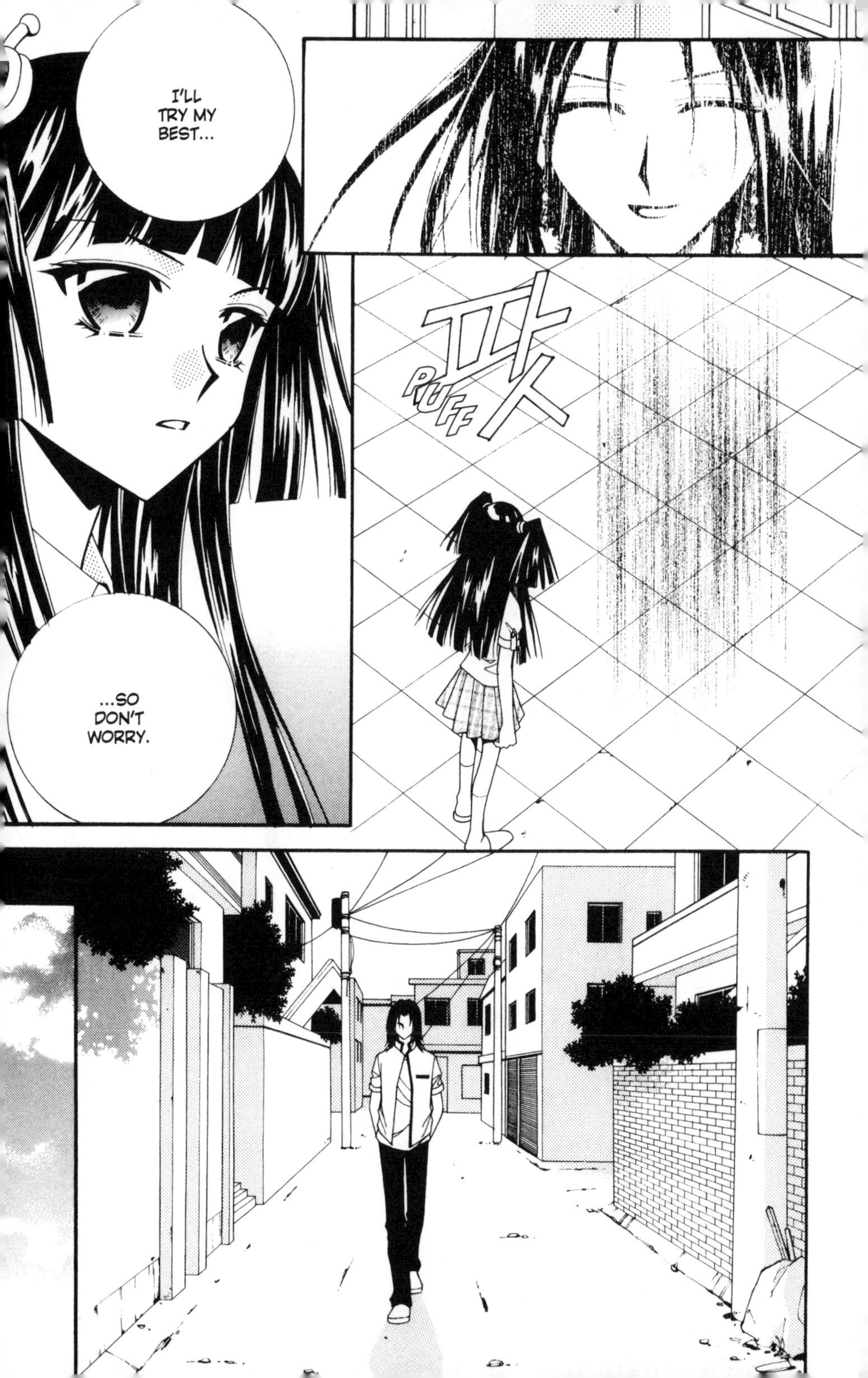
I'LL TRY MY BEST...
...SO DON'T WORRY.
PUFF

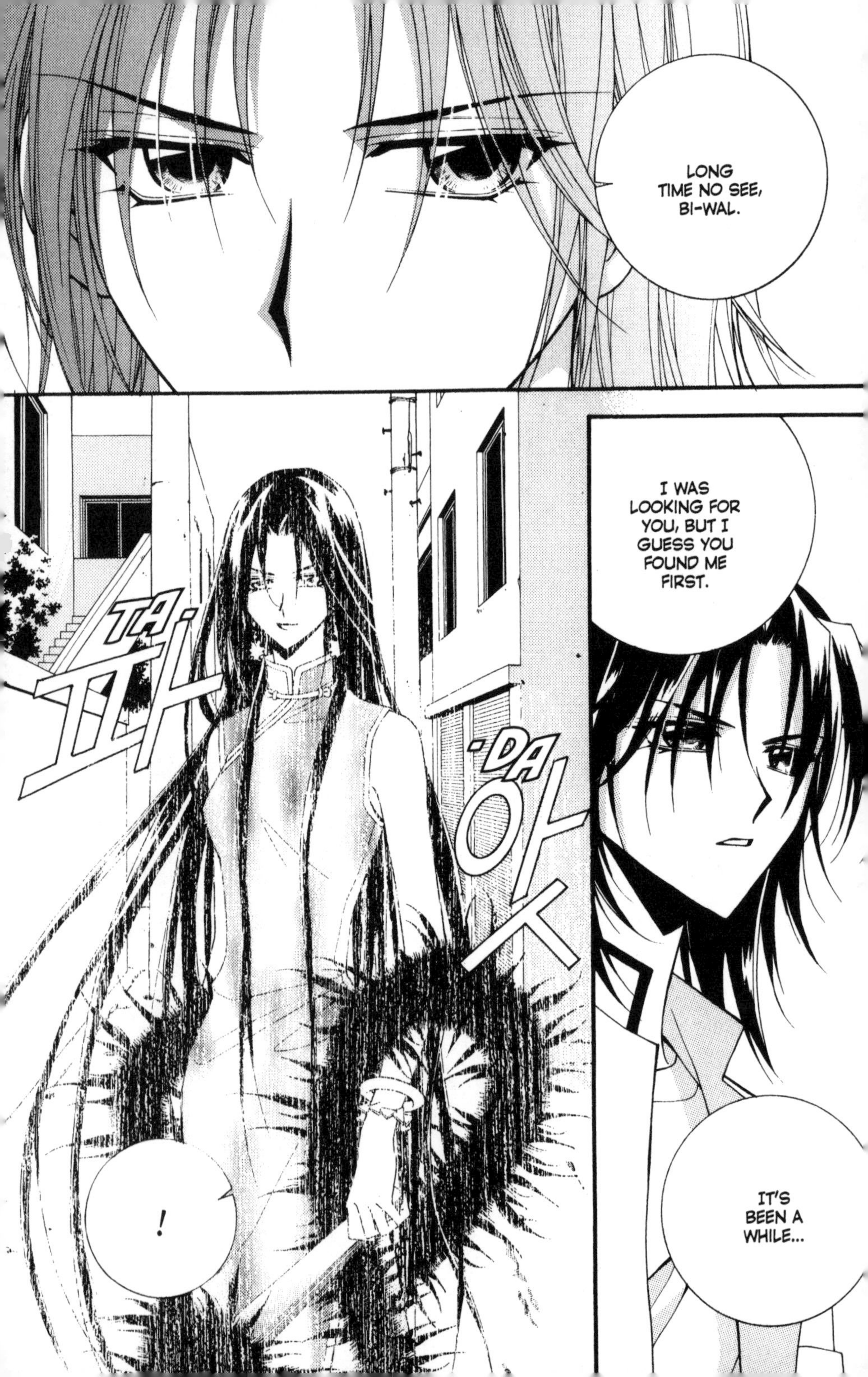
LONG TIME NO SEE, BI-WAL.
TA-
-DA
!
I WAS LOOKING FOR YOU, BUT I GUESS YOU FOUND ME FIRST.
IT'S BEEN A WHILE...

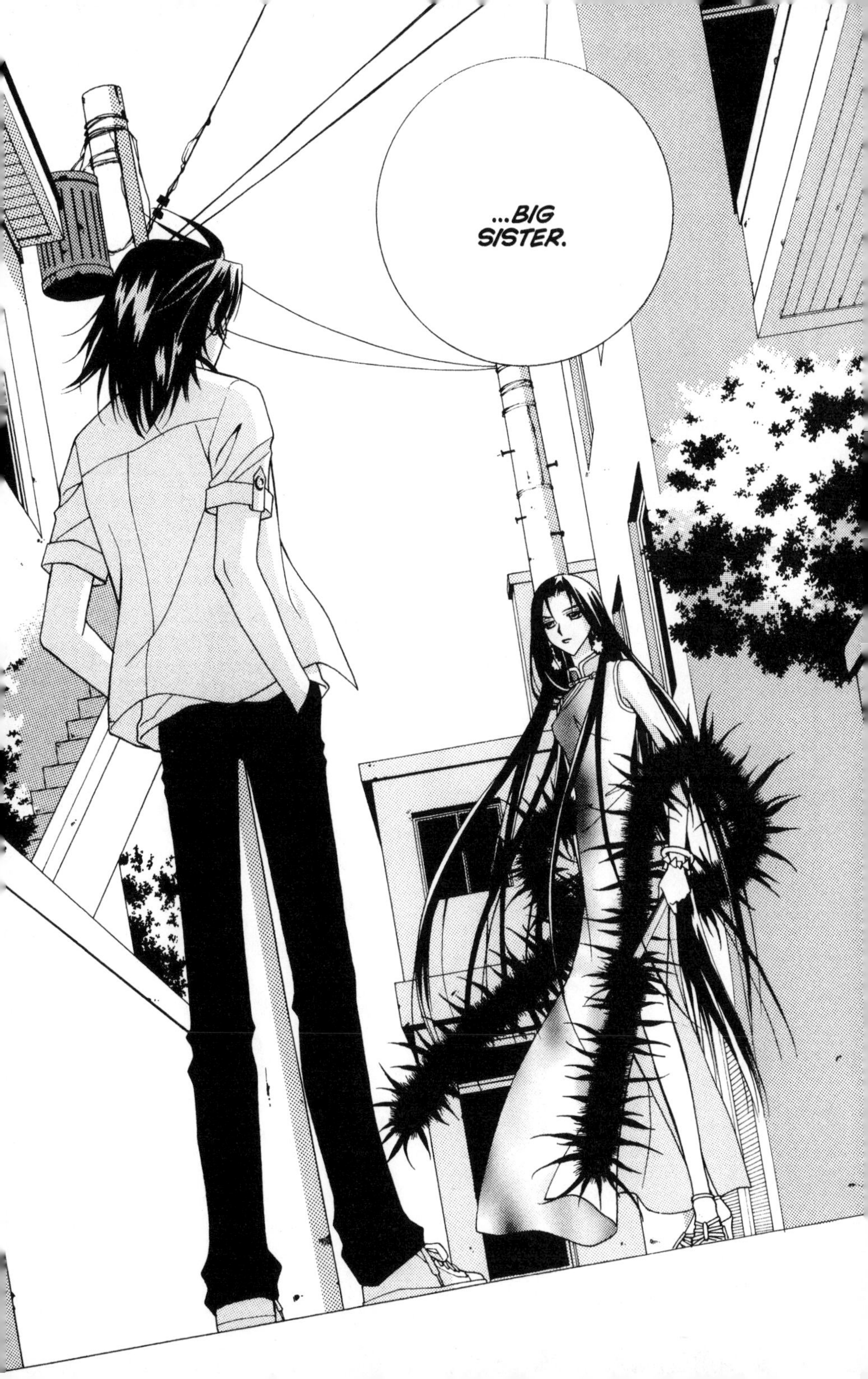
...BIG SISTER.

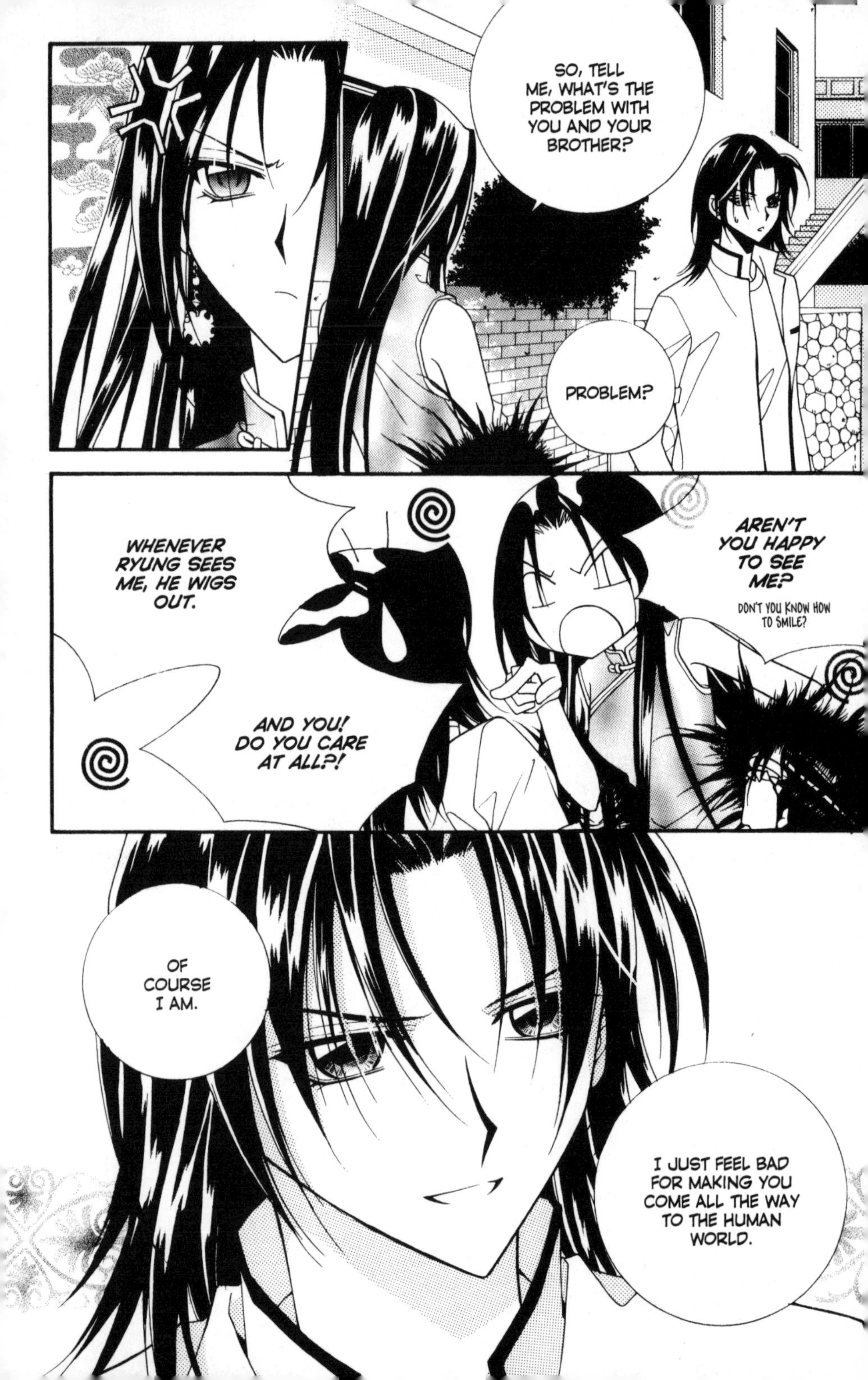
SO, TELL ME, WHAT'S THE PROBLEM WITH YOU AND YOUR BROTHER?
PROBLEM?
WHENEVER RYUNG SEES ME, HE WIGS OUT.
AREN'T YOU HAPPY TO SEE ME?
DON'T YOU KNOW HOW TO SMILE?
AND YOU! DO YOU CARE AT ALL?!
OF COURSE I AM.
I JUST FEEL BAD FOR MAKING YOU COME ALL THE WAY TO THE HUMAN WORLD.

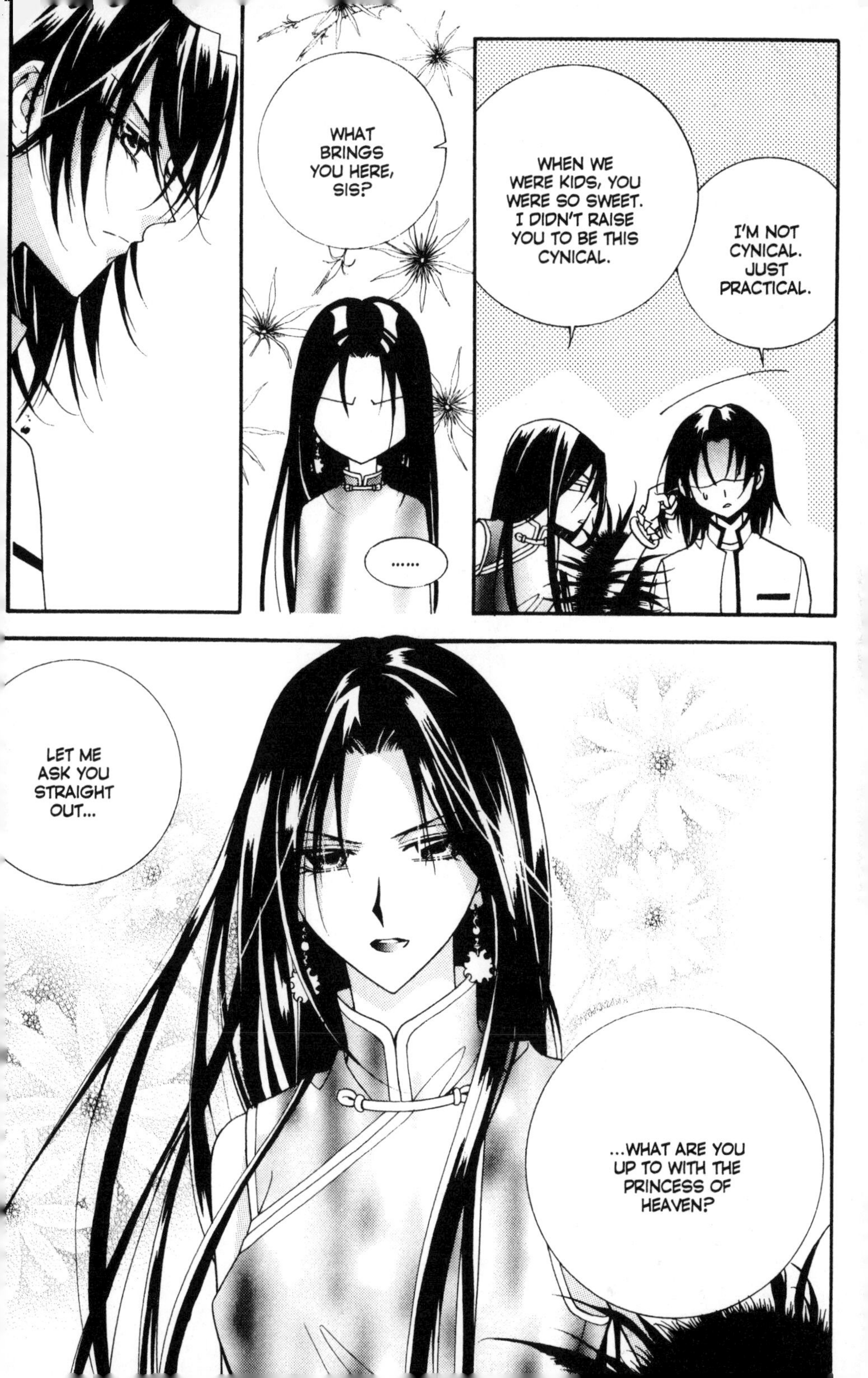
WHAT BRINGS YOU HERE, SIS?
......
WHEN WE WERE KIDS, YOU WERE SO SWEET. I DIDN'T RAISE YOU TO BE THIS CYNICAL.
I'M NOT CYNICAL. JUST PRACTICAL.
LET ME ASK YOU STRAIGHT OUT...
...WHAT ARE YOU UP TO WITH THE PRINCESS OF HEAVEN?

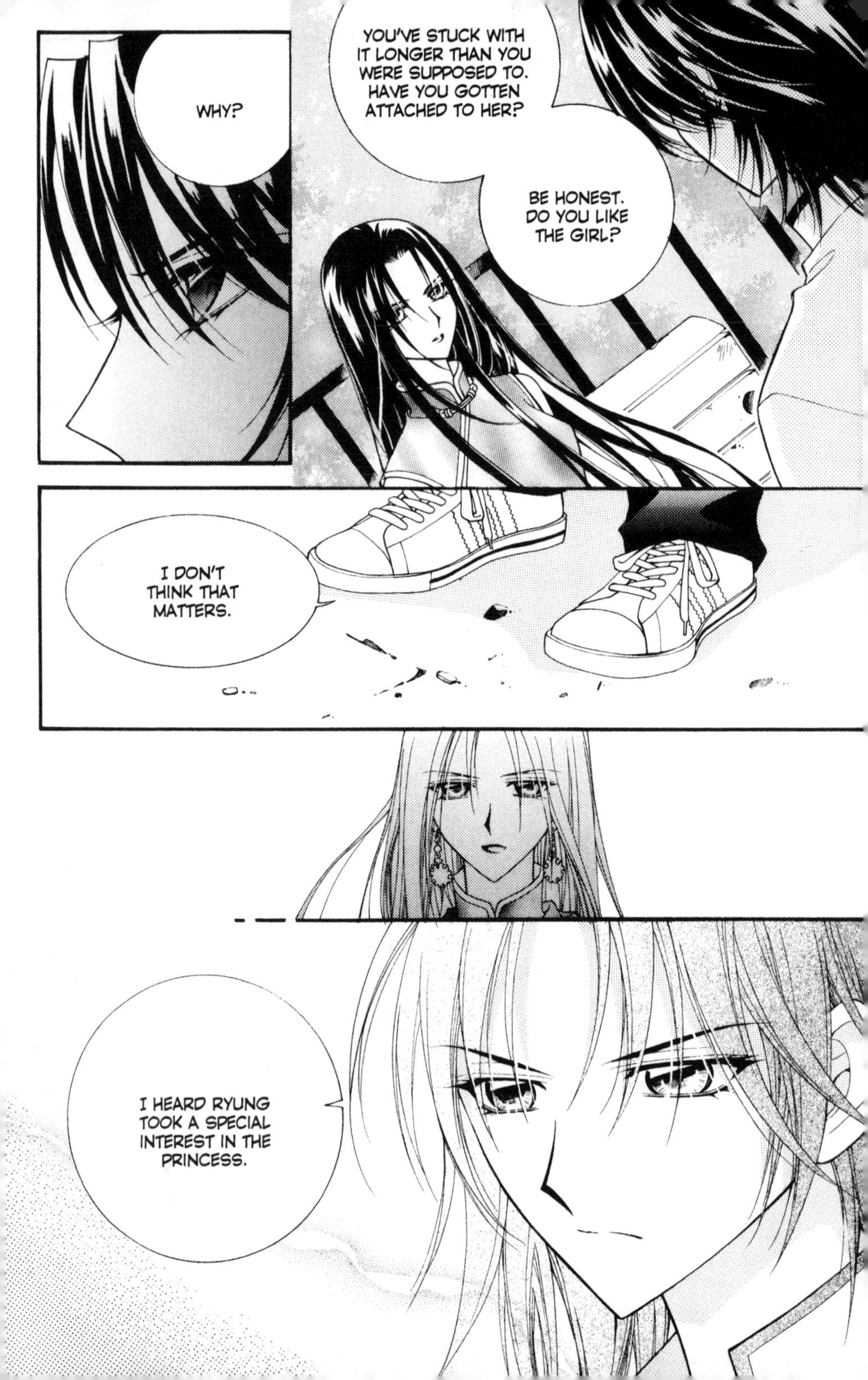
WHY?
YOU'VE STUCK WITH IT LONGER THAN YOU WERE SUPPOSED TO. HAVE YOU GOTTEN ATTACHED TO HER?
BE HONEST. DO YOU LIKE THE GIRL?
I DON'T THINK THAT MATTERS.
I HEARD RYUNG TOOK A SPECIAL INTEREST IN THE PRINCESS.

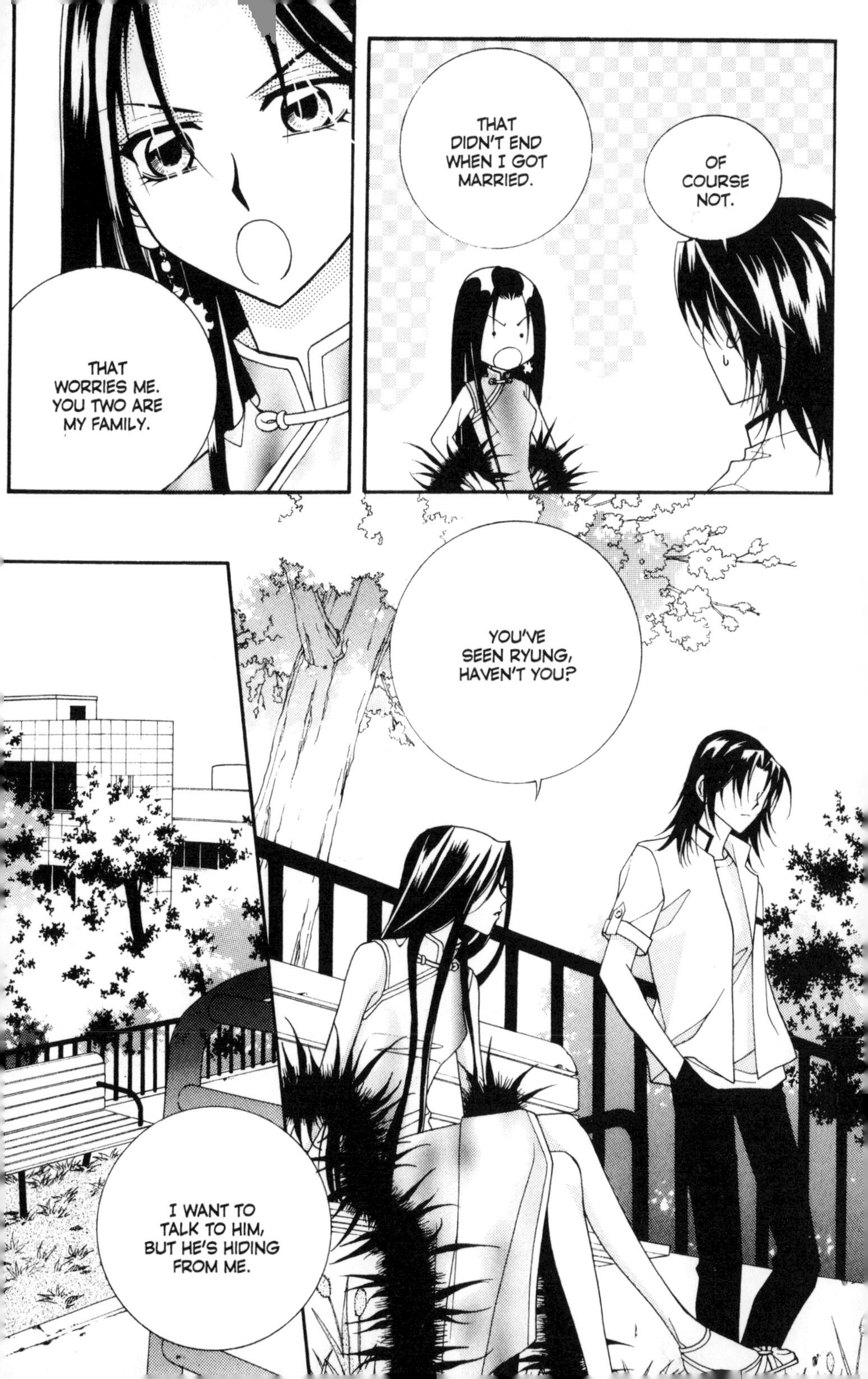
THAT WORRIES ME. YOU TWO ARE MY FAMILY.
THAT DIDN'T END WHEN I GOT MARRIED.
OF COURSE NOT.
YOU'VE SEEN RYUNG, HAVEN'T YOU?
I WANT TO TALK TO HIM, BUT HE'S HIDING FROM ME.

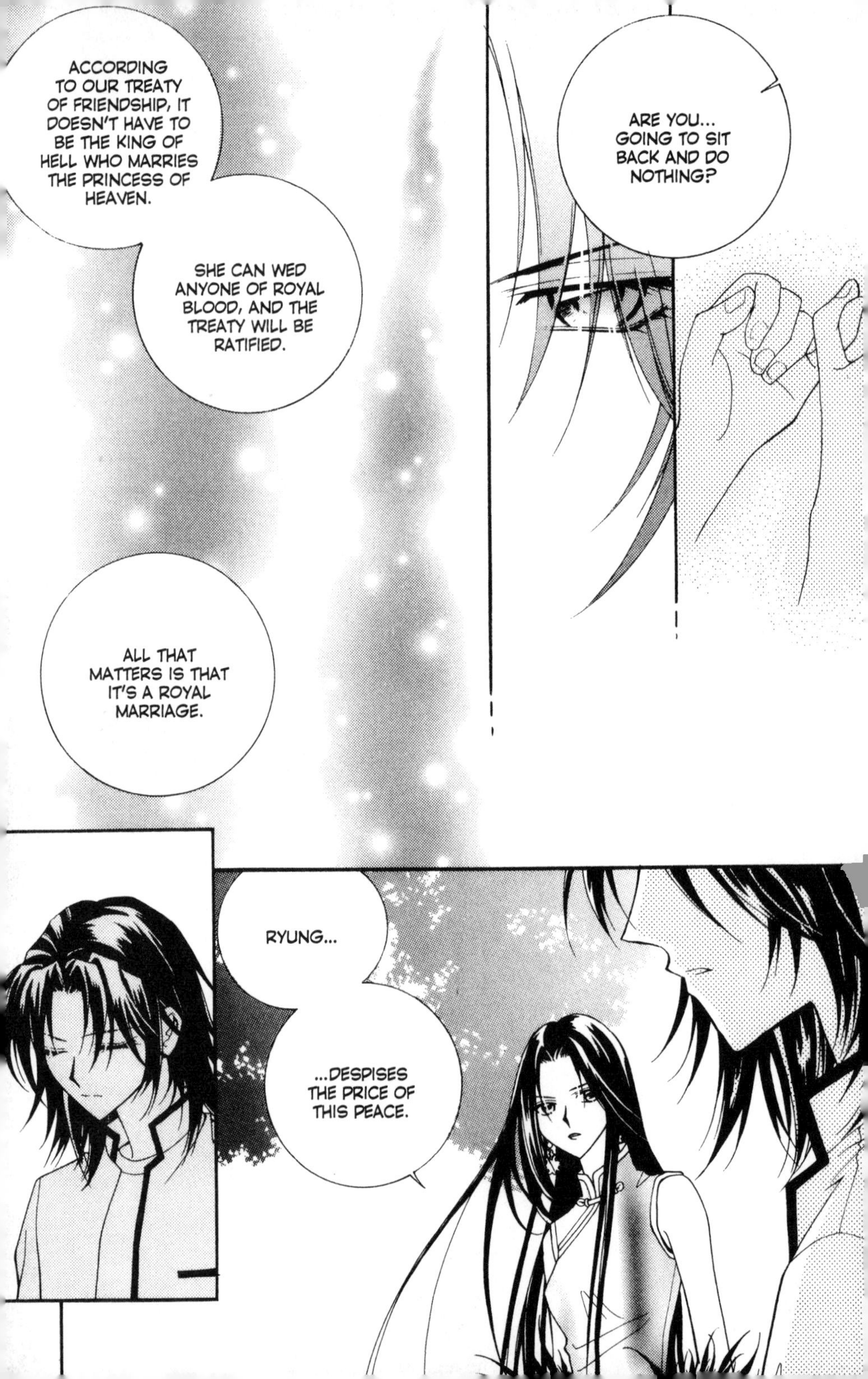
ACCORDING TO OUR TREATY OF FRIENDSHIP, IT DOESN'T HAVE TO BE THE KING OF HELL WHO MARRIES THE PRINCESS OF HEAVEN.
SHE CAN WED ANYONE OF ROYAL BLOOD, AND THE TREATY WILL BE RATIFIED.
ALL THAT MATTERS IS THAT IT'S A ROYAL MARRIAGE.
ARE YOU... GOING TO SIT BACK AND DO NOTHING?
RYUNG...
...DESPISES THE PRICE OF THIS PEACE.

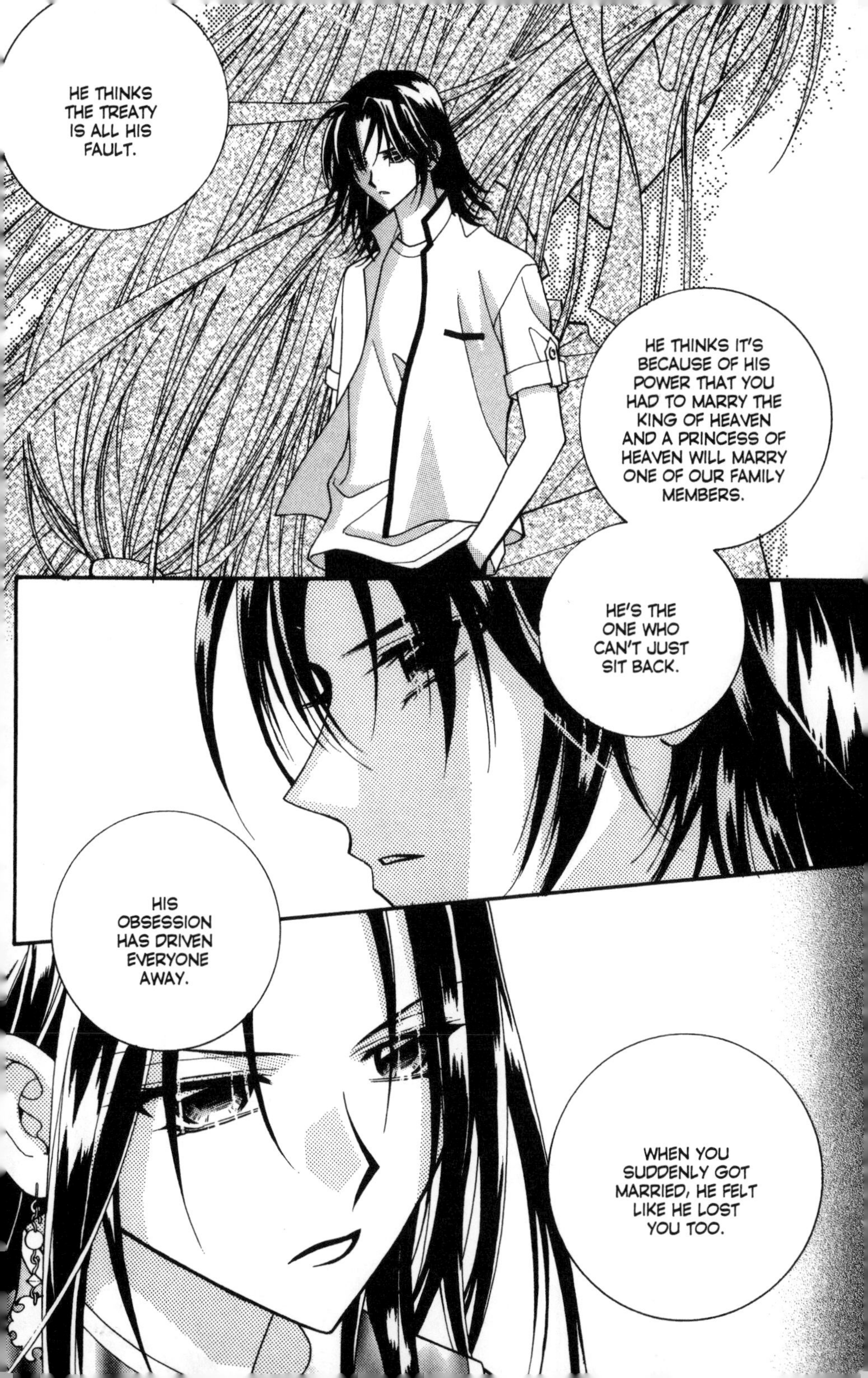
HE THINKS THE TREATY IS ALL HIS FAULT.
HE THINKS IT'S BECAUSE OF HIS POWER THAT YOU HAD TO MARRY THE KING OF HEAVEN AND A PRINCESS OF HEAVEN WILL MARRY ONE OF OUR FAMILY MEMBERS.
HE'S THE ONE WHO CAN'T JUST SIT BACK.
HIS OBSESSION HAS DRIVEN EVERYONE AWAY.
WHEN YOU SUDDENLY GOT MARRIED, HE FELT LIKE HE LOST YOU TOO.

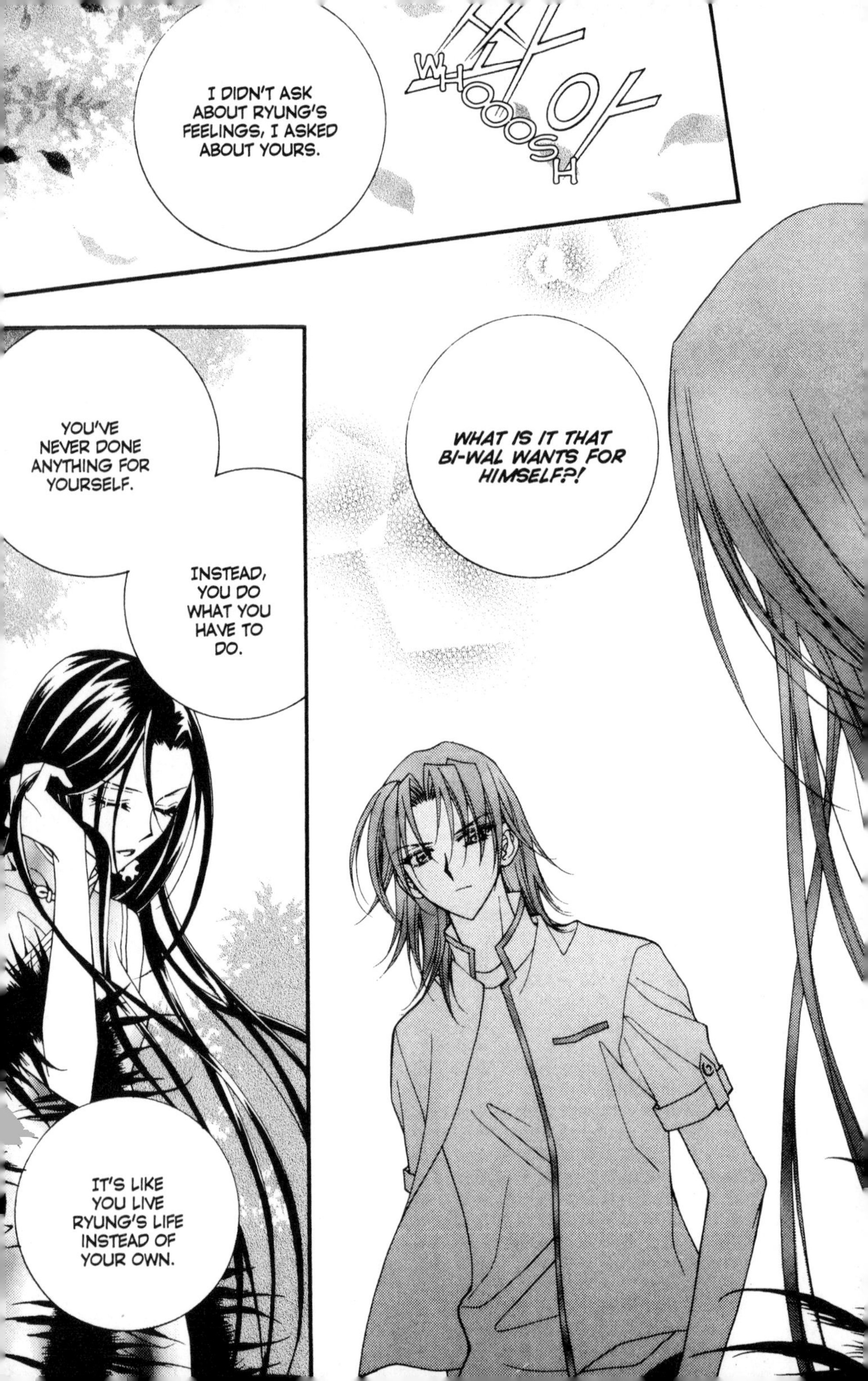
I DIDN'T ASK ABOUT RYUNG'S FEELINGS, I ASKED ABOUT YOURS.
HEY OY
WHOOOSH
YOU'VE NEVER DONE ANYTHING FOR YOURSELF.
INSTEAD, YOU DO WHAT YOU HAVE TO DO.
IT'S LIKE YOU LIVE RYUNG'S LIFE INSTEAD OF YOUR OWN.
WHAT IS IT THAT BI-WAL WANTS FOR HIMSELF?!

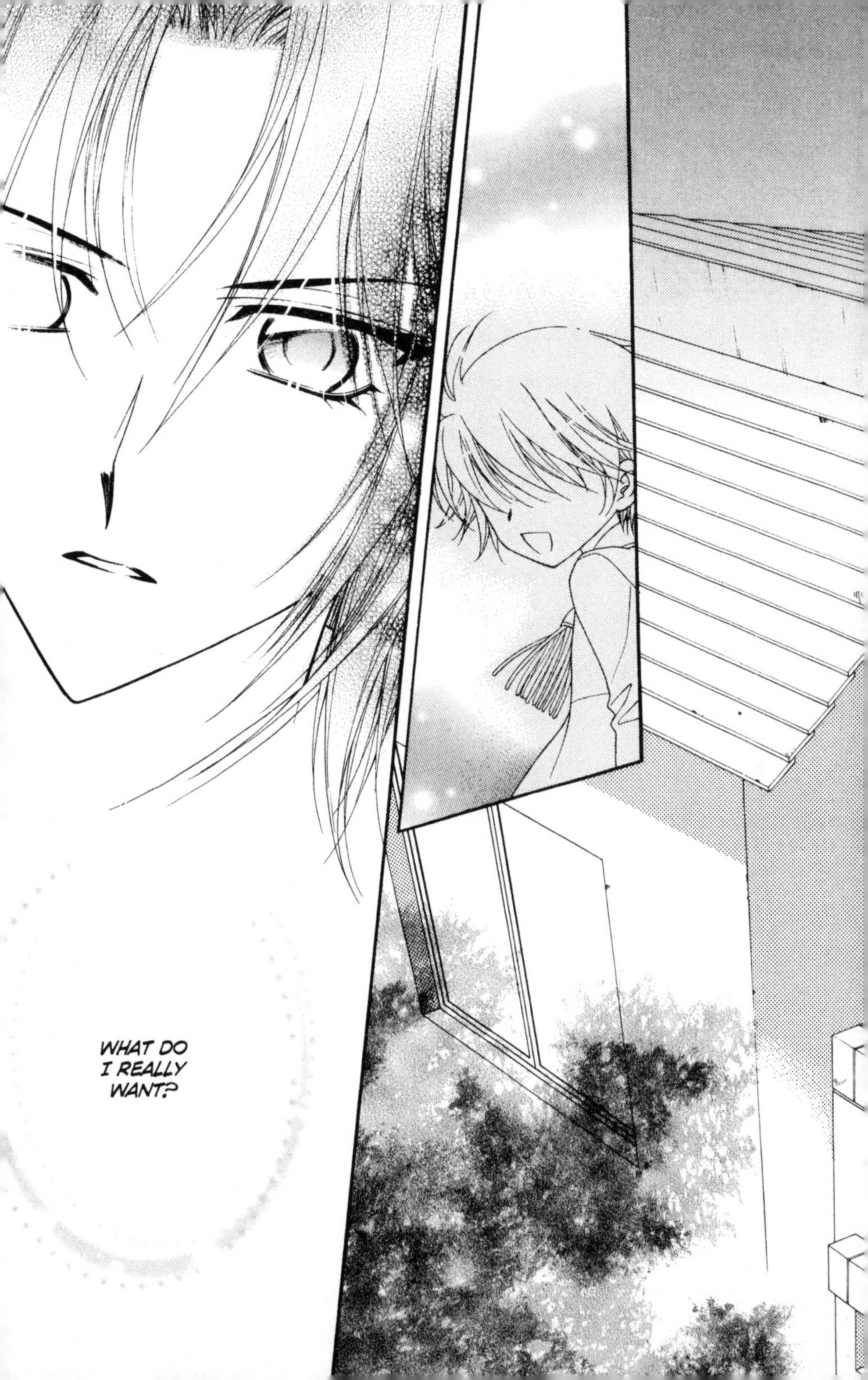
WHAT DO I REALLY WANT?

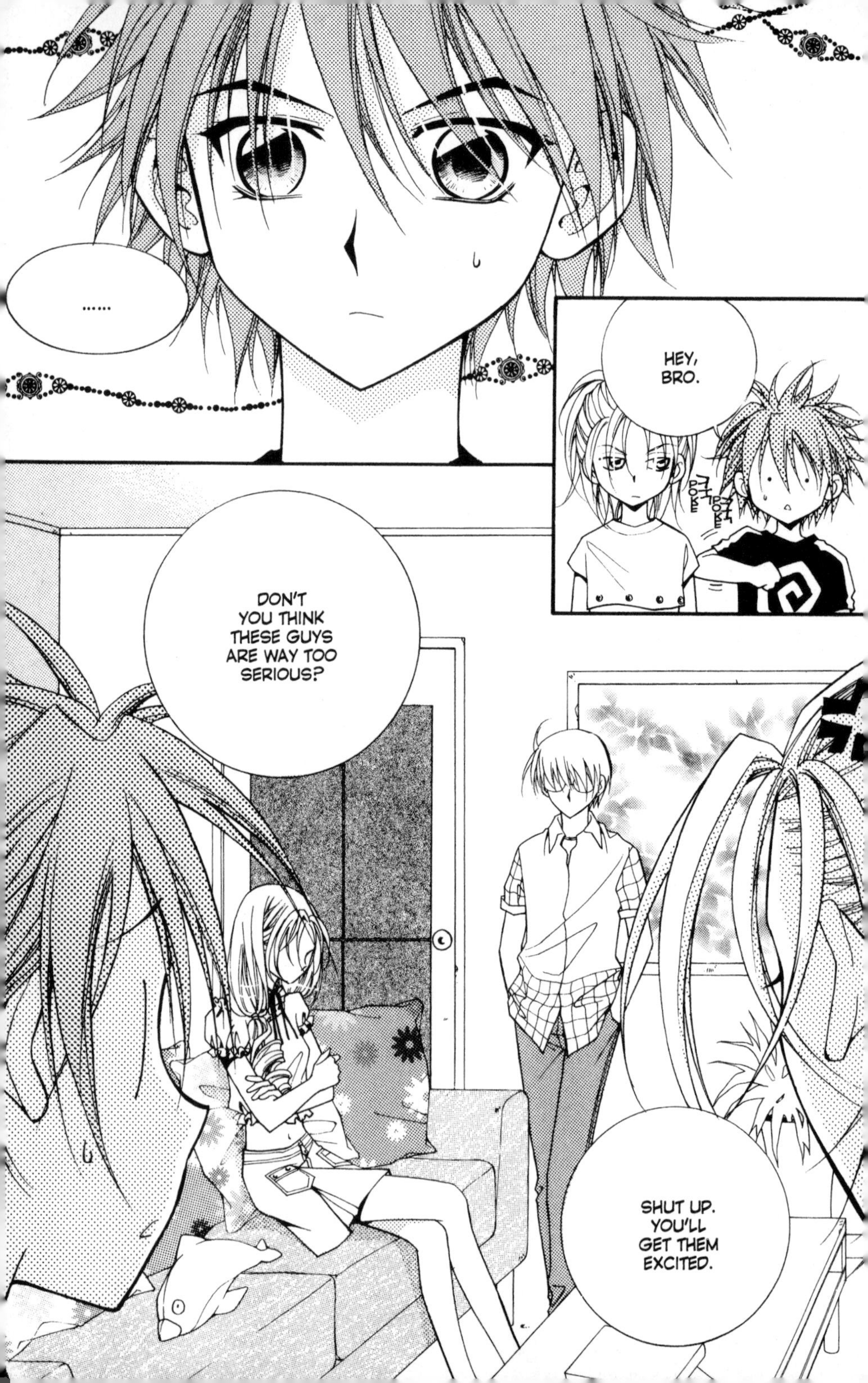
......
HEY, BRO.
POKE POKE
DON'T YOU THINK THESE GUYS ARE WAY TOO SERIOUS?
SHUT UP. YOU'LL GET THEM EXCITED.

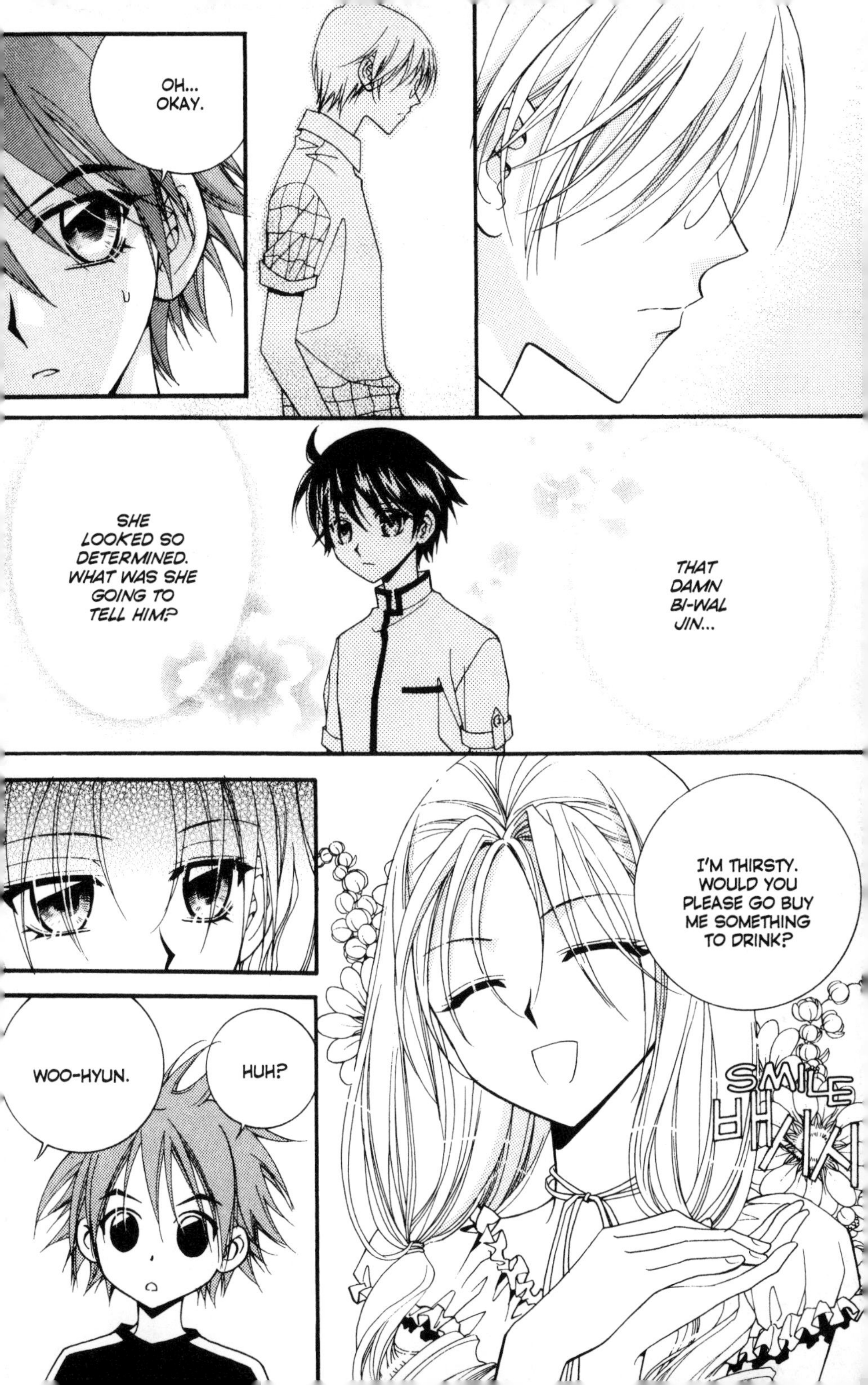
OH... OKAY.
SHE LOOKED SO DETERMINED. WHAT WAS SHE GOING TO TELL HIM?
THAT DAMN BI-WAL JIN...
I'M THIRSTY. WOULD YOU PLEASE GO BUY ME SOMETHING TO DRINK?
WOO-HYUN.
HUH?
SMILE

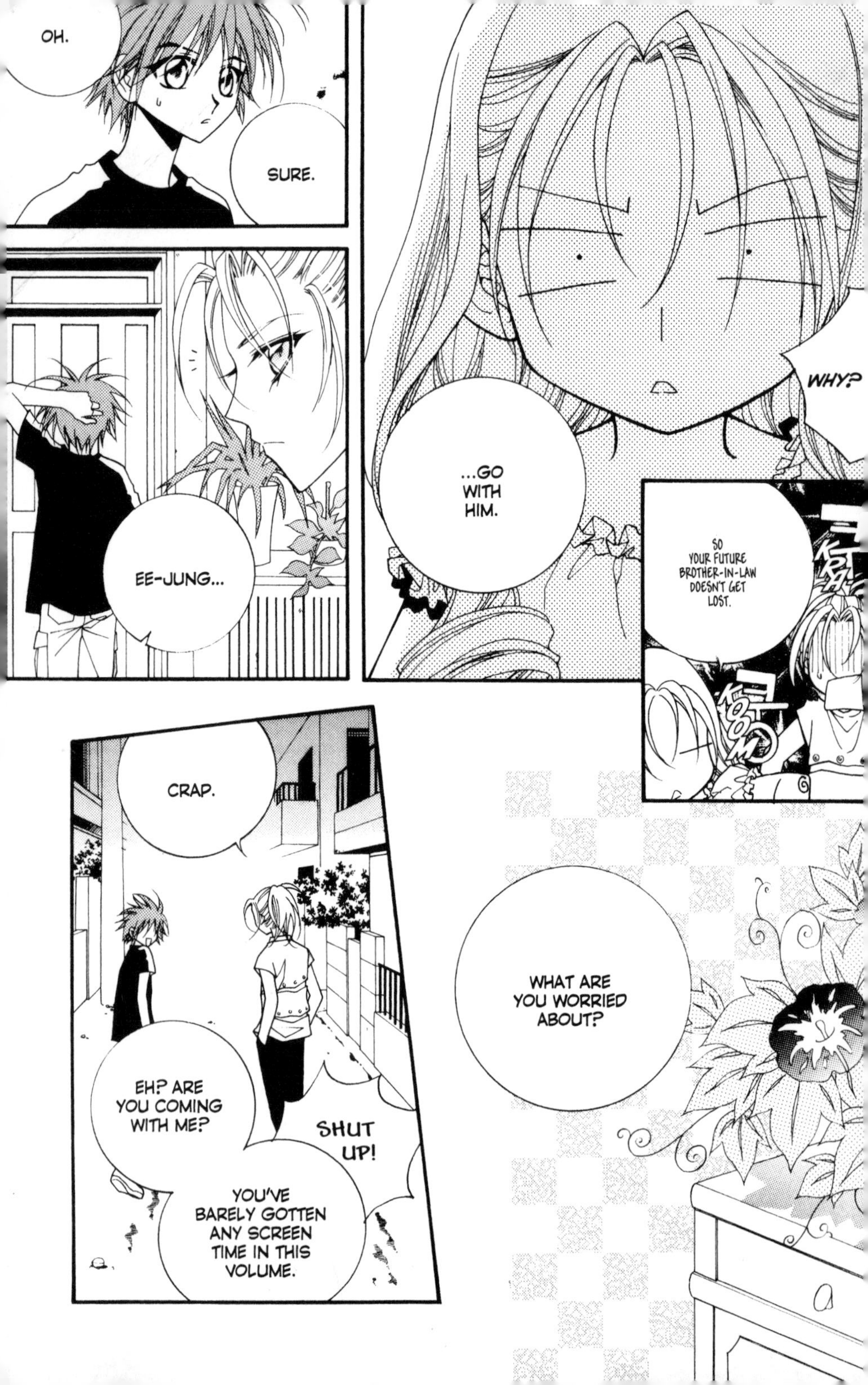
OH.
SURE.
EE-JUNG...
WHY?
...GO WITH HIM.
SO YOUR FUTURE BROTHER-IN-LAW DOESN'T GET LOST.
CRAP.
EH? ARE YOU COMING WITH ME?
SHUT UP!
YOU'VE BARELY GOTTEN ANY SCREEN TIME IN THIS VOLUME.
WHAT ARE YOU WORRIED ABOUT?

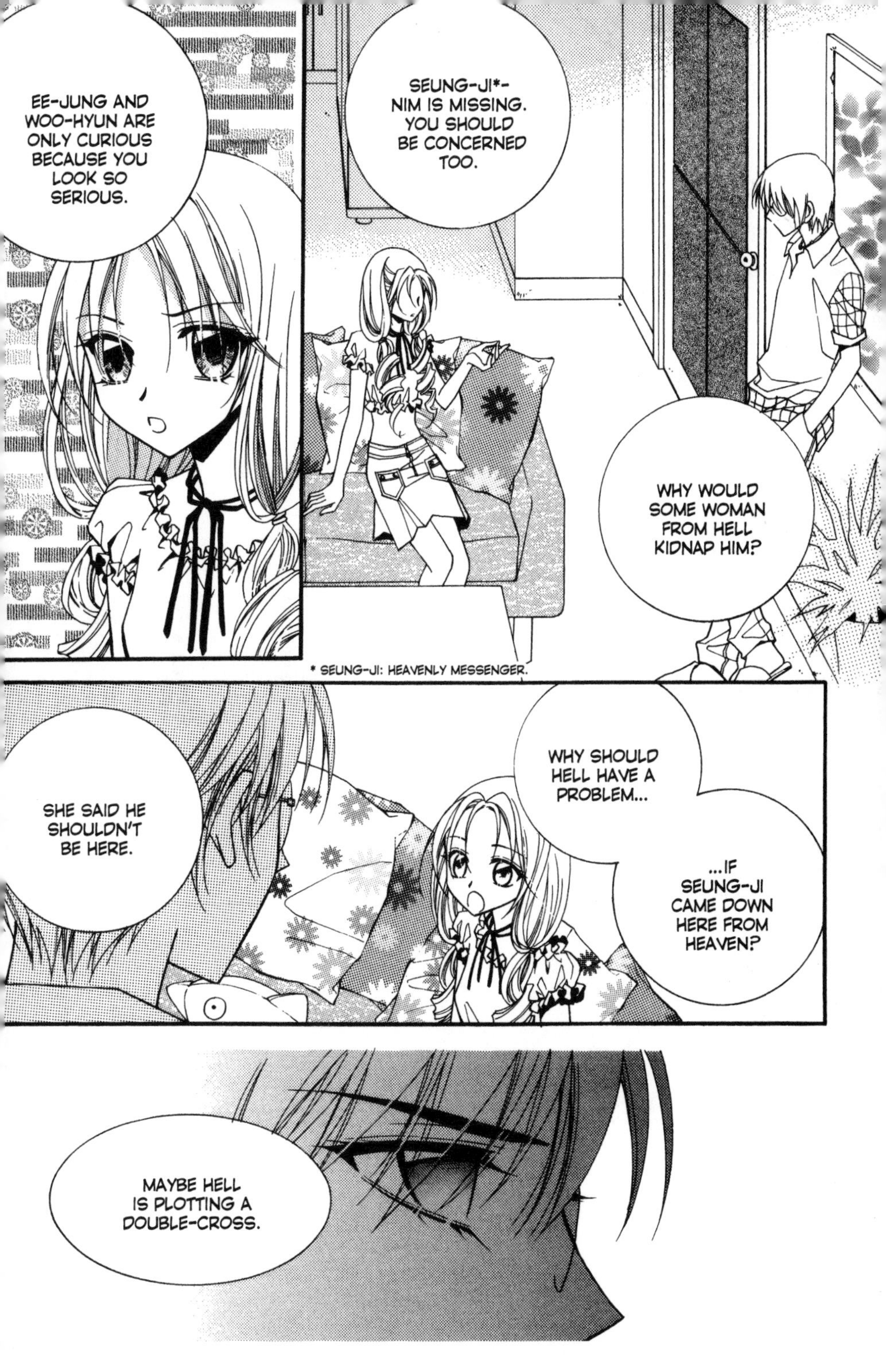
EE-JUNG AND WOO-HYUN ARE ONLY CURIOUS BECAUSE YOU LOOK SO SERIOUS.
SEUNG-JI*-NIM IS MISSING. YOU SHOULD BE CONCERNED TOO.
WHY WOULD SOME WOMAN FROM HELL KIDNAP HIM?
SHE SAID HE SHOULDN'T BE HERE.
WHY SHOULD HELL HAVE A PROBLEM...
...IF SEUNG-JI CAME DOWN HERE FROM HEAVEN?
MAYBE HELL IS PLOTTING A DOUBLE-CROSS.

* SEUNG-JI: HEAVENLY MESSENGER.

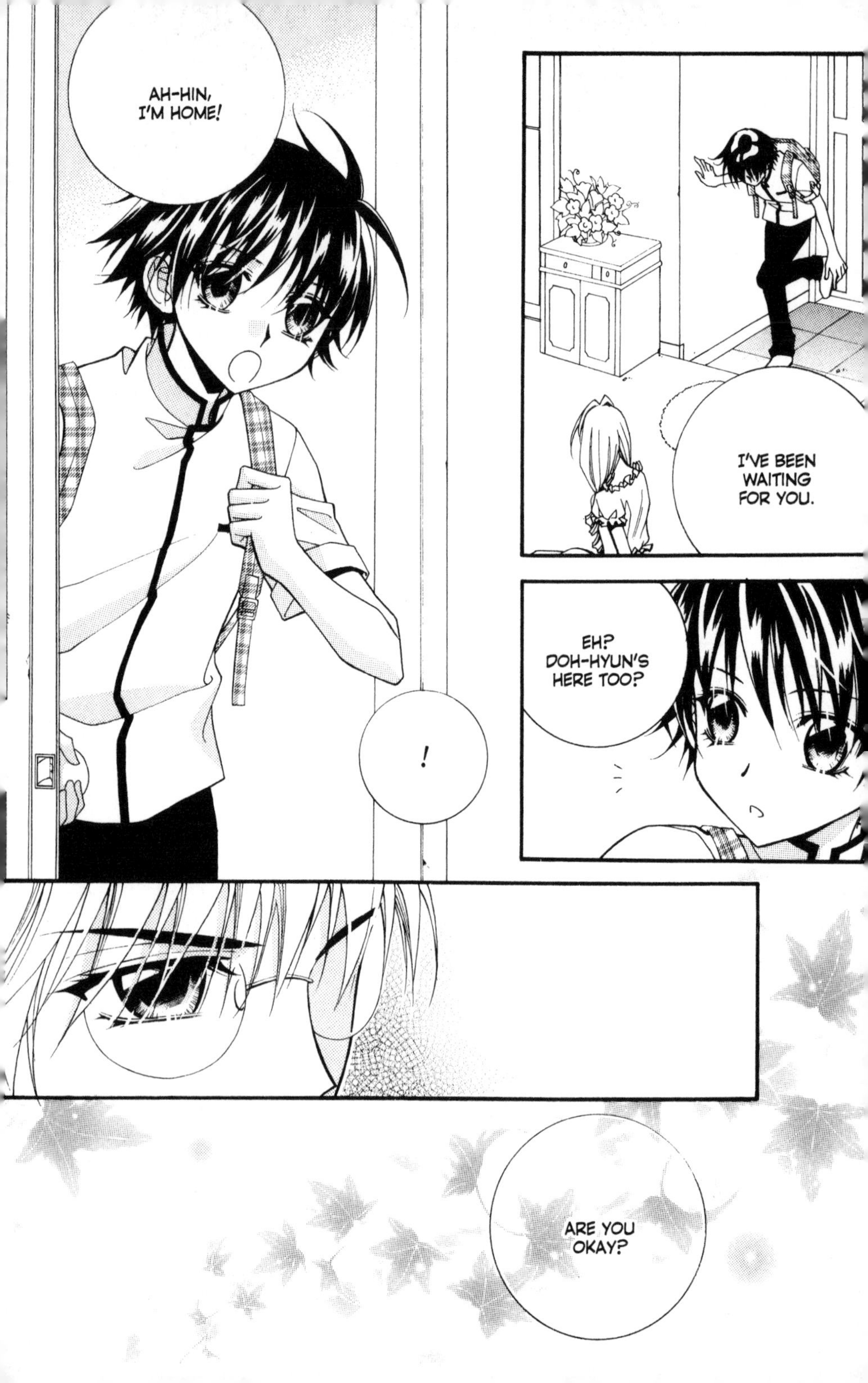
AH-HIN, I'M HOME!
!
I'VE BEEN WAITING FOR YOU.
EH? DOH-HYUN'S HERE TOO?
ARE YOU OKAY?

EH...? WHY?!

WHAT HAPPENED?

WHY ARE YOU BLUSHING?

...I THINK... I CONFESSED TO BI-WAL...

SO... UH...

CONFESSED?

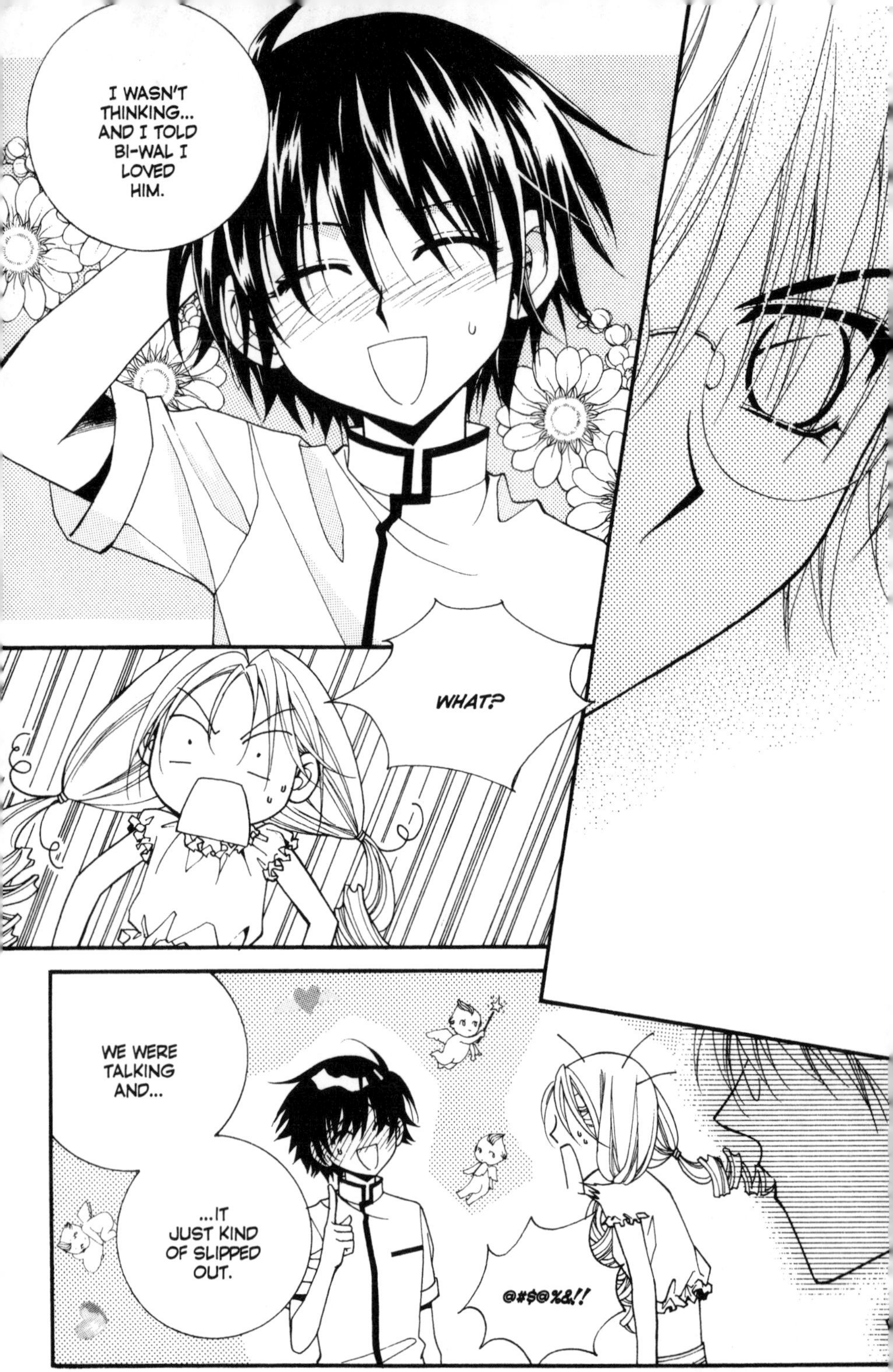
I WASN'T THINKING... AND I TOLD BI-WAL I LOVED HIM.
WHAT?
WE WERE TALKING AND...
...IT JUST KIND OF SLIPPED OUT.
@#$@%&!!

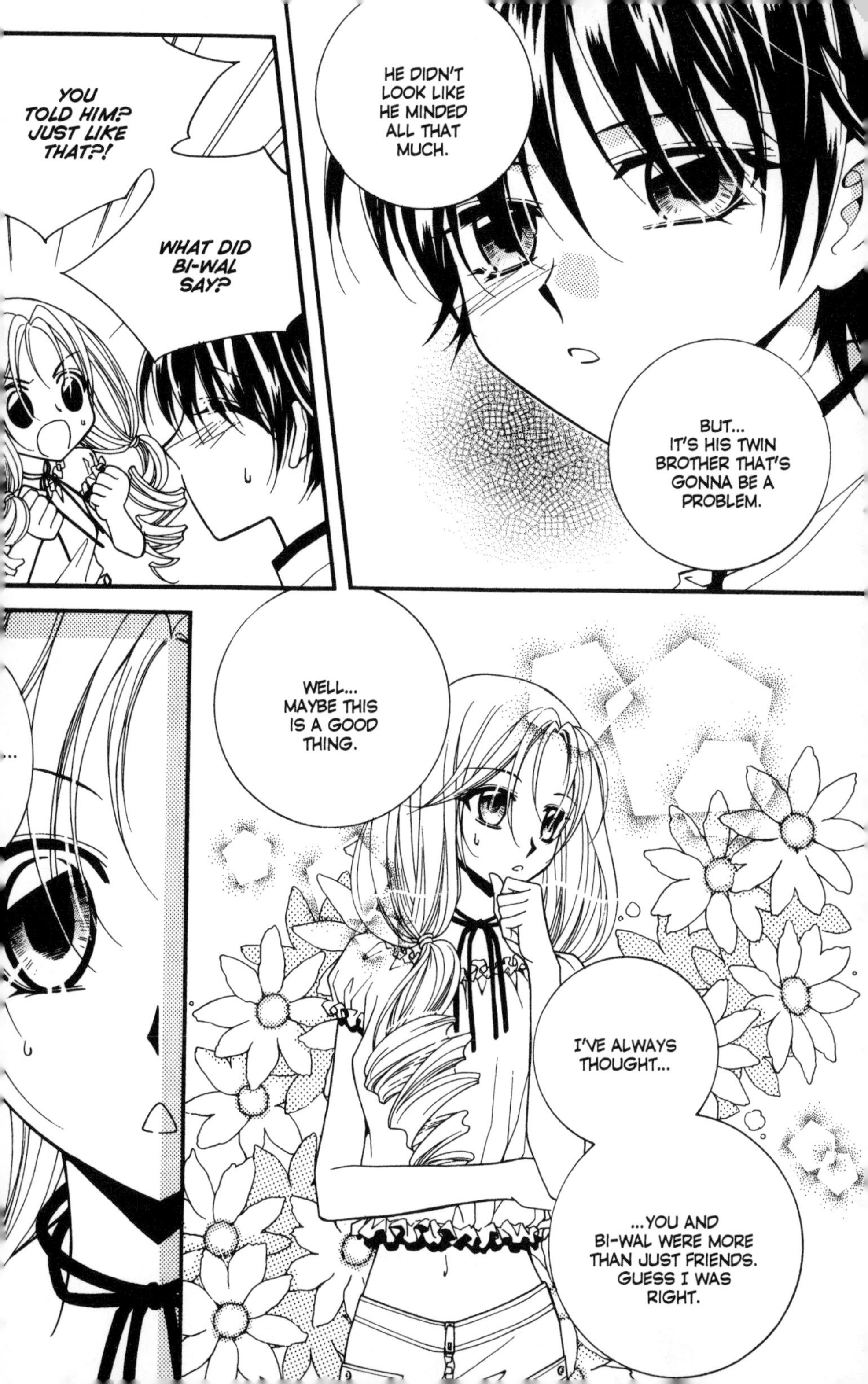
YOU TOLD HIM? JUST LIKE THAT?!
WHAT DID BI-WAL SAY?
HE DIDN'T LOOK LIKE HE MINDED ALL THAT MUCH.
BUT... IT'S HIS TWIN BROTHER THAT'S GONNA BE A PROBLEM.
...
WELL... MAYBE THIS IS A GOOD THING.
I'VE ALWAYS THOUGHT...
...YOU AND BI-WAL WERE MORE THAN JUST FRIENDS. GUESS I WAS RIGHT.

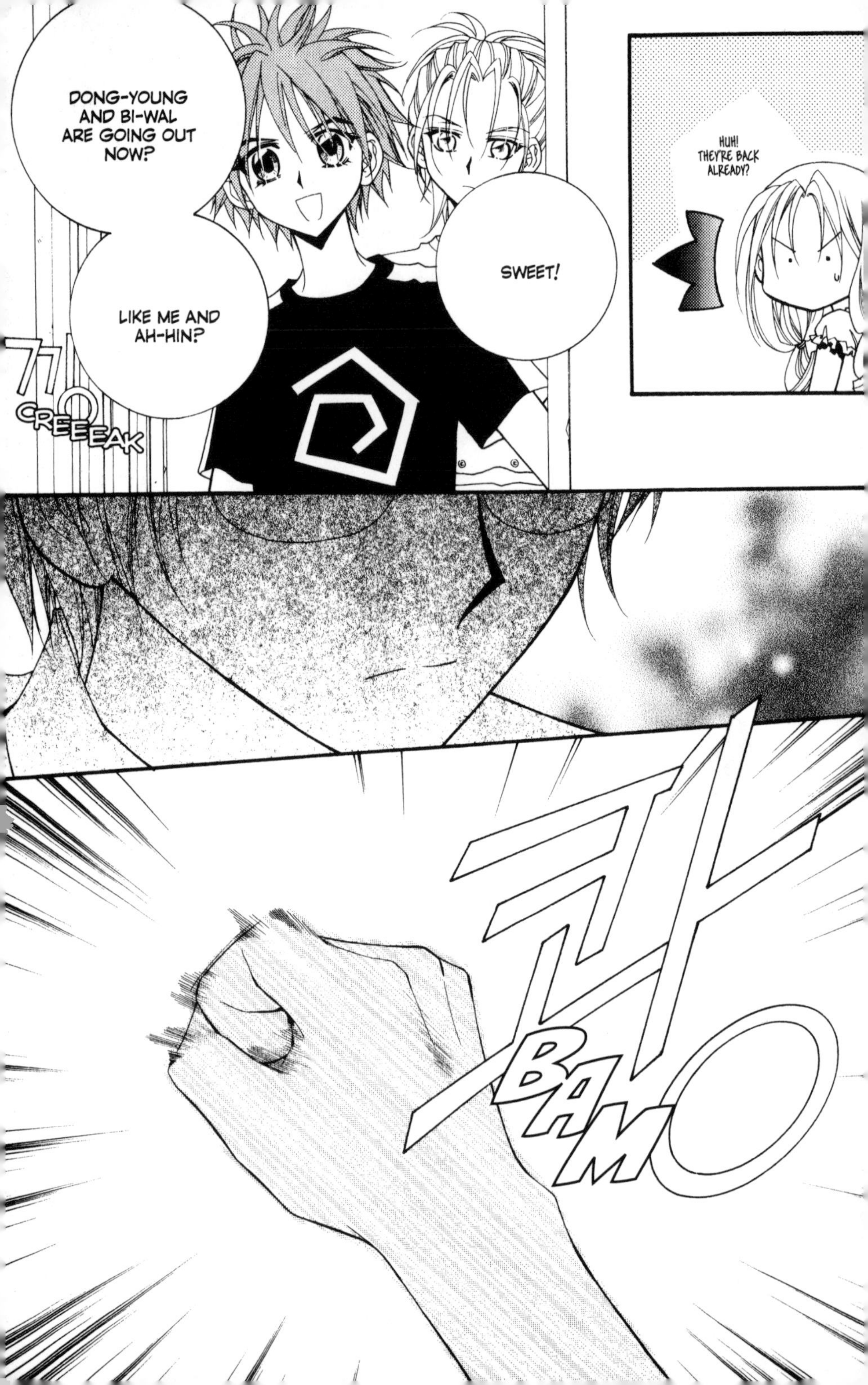
DONG-YOUNG AND BI-WAL ARE GOING OUT NOW?
LIKE ME AND AH-HIN?
CREEEEAK
SWEET!
HUH! THEY'RE BACK ALREADY?
BAM

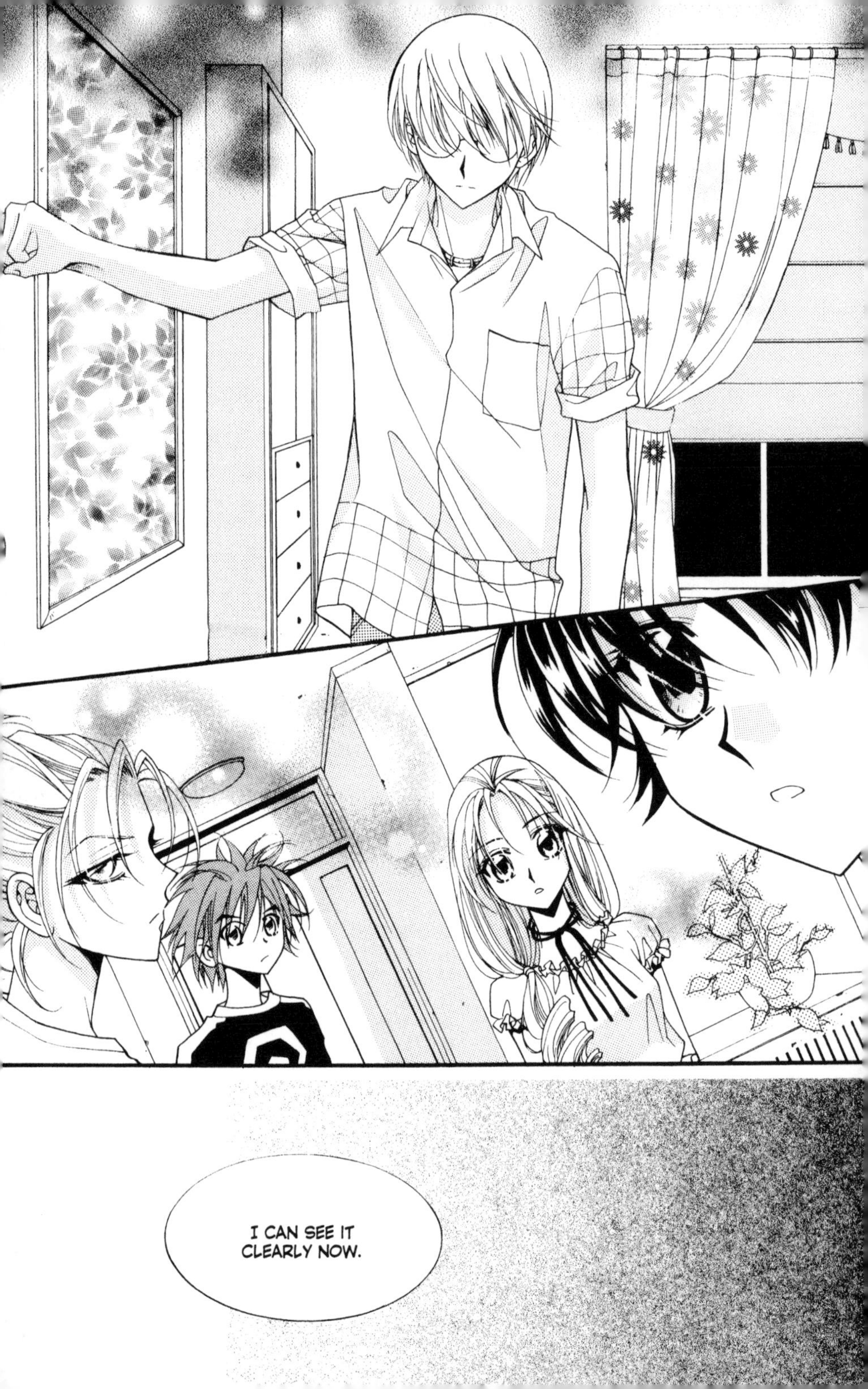
I CAN SEE IT CLEARLY NOW.

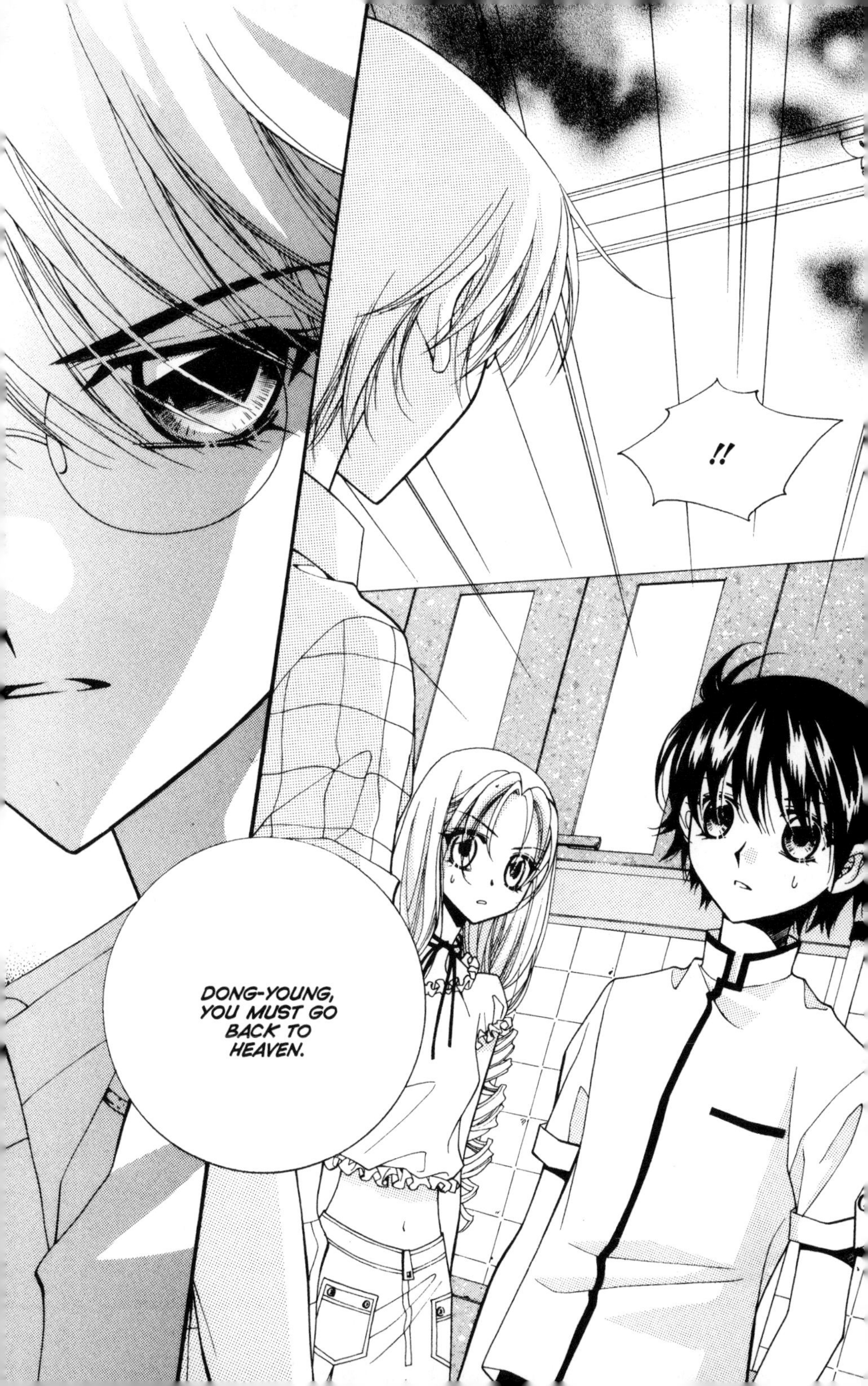
!!
DONG-YOUNG, YOU MUST GO BACK TO HEAVEN.

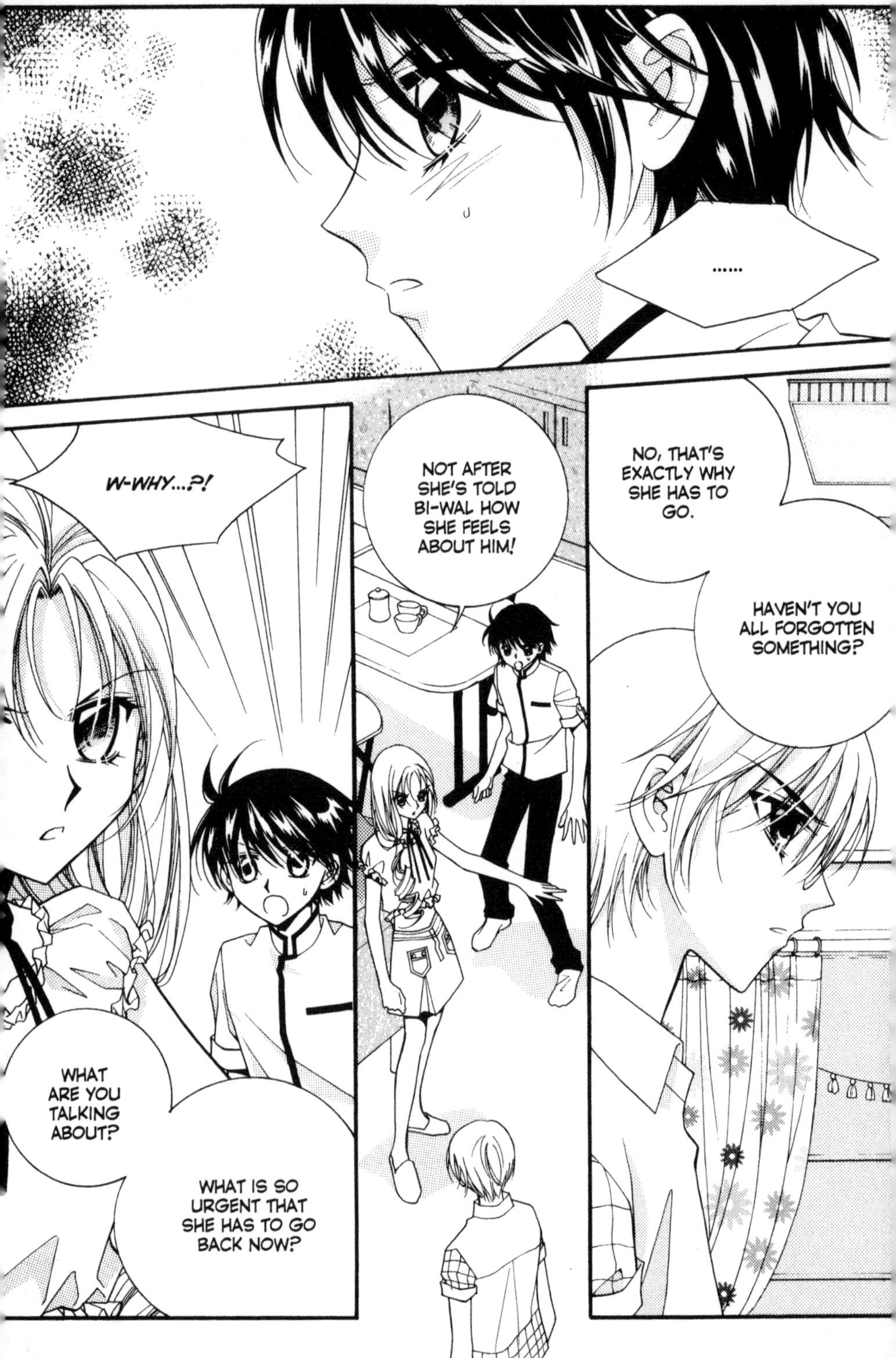
......
W-WHY...?!
WHAT ARE YOU TALKING ABOUT?
WHAT IS SO URGENT THAT SHE HAS TO GO BACK NOW?
NOT AFTER SHE'S TOLD BI-WAL HOW SHE FEELS ABOUT HIM!
NO, THAT'S EXACTLY WHY SHE HAS TO GO.
HAVEN'T YOU ALL FORGOTTEN SOMETHING?

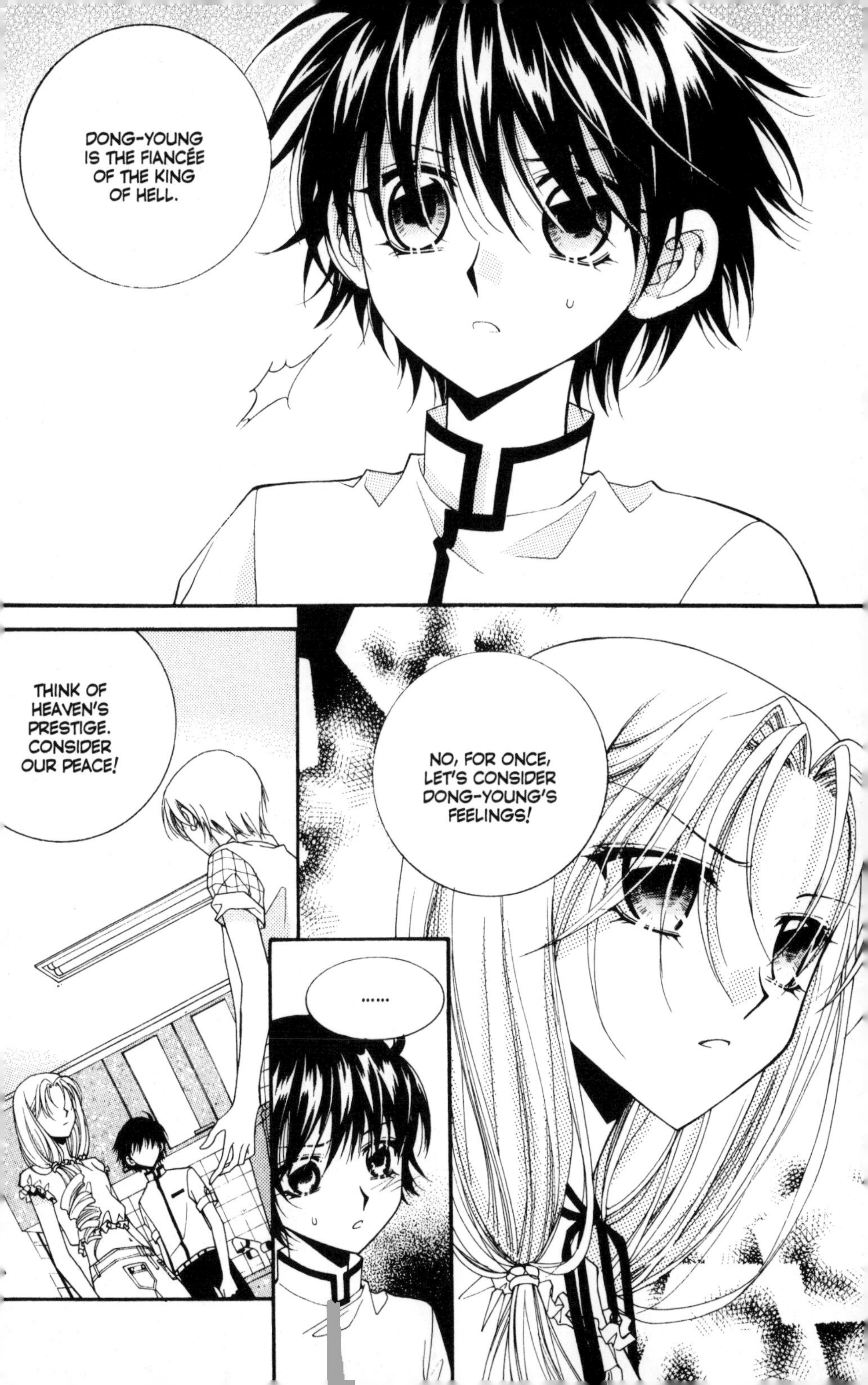
DONG-YOUNG IS THE FIANCÉE OF THE KING OF HELL.
THINK OF HEAVEN'S PRESTIGE. CONSIDER OUR PEACE!
NO, FOR ONCE, LET'S CONSIDER DONG-YOUNG'S FEELINGS!
......

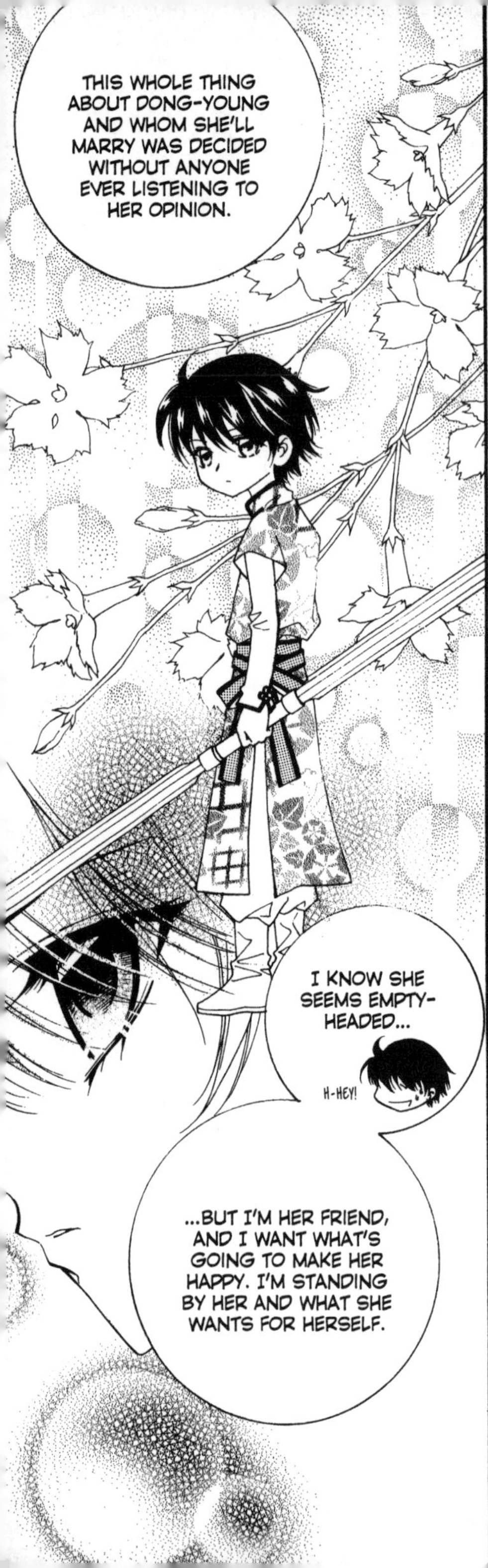
THIS WHOLE THING ABOUT DONG-YOUNG AND WHOM SHE'LL MARRY WAS DECIDED WITHOUT ANYONE EVER LISTENING TO HER OPINION.
I KNOW SHE SEEMS EMPTY-HEADED...
H-HEY!
...BUT I'M HER FRIEND, AND I WANT WHAT'S GOING TO MAKE HER HAPPY. I'M STANDING BY HER AND WHAT SHE WANTS FOR HERSELF.
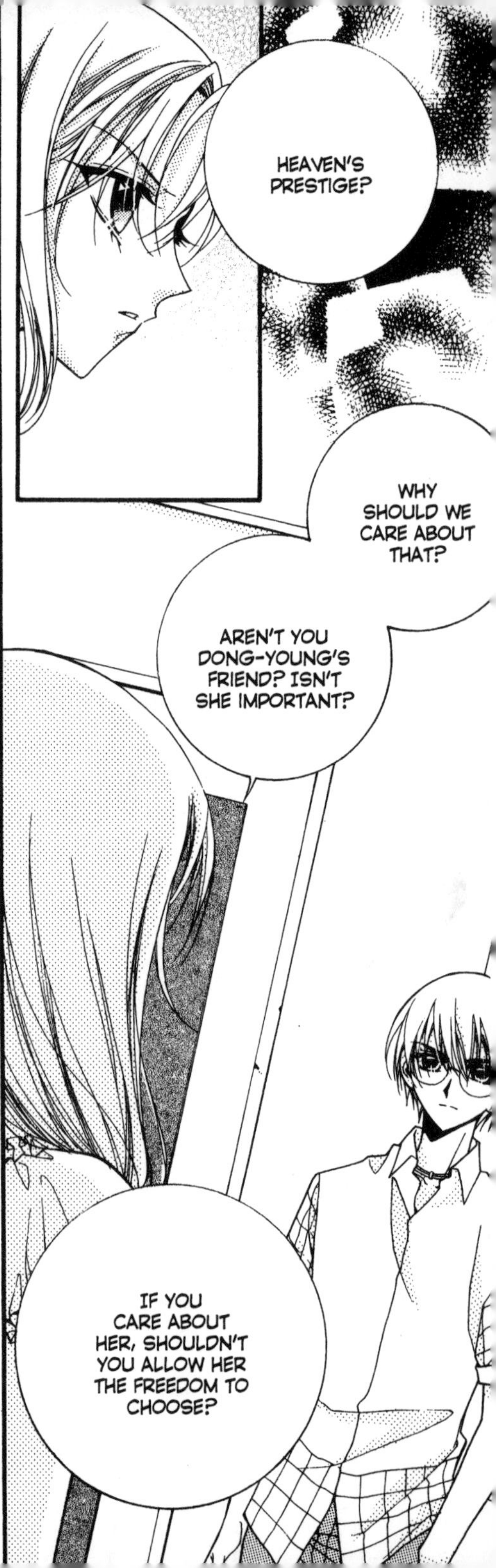
HEAVEN'S PRESTIGE?
WHY SHOULD WE CARE ABOUT THAT?
AREN'T YOU DONG-YOUNG'S FRIEND? ISN'T SHE IMPORTANT?
IF YOU CARE ABOUT HER, SHOULDN'T YOU ALLOW HER THE FREEDOM TO CHOOSE?

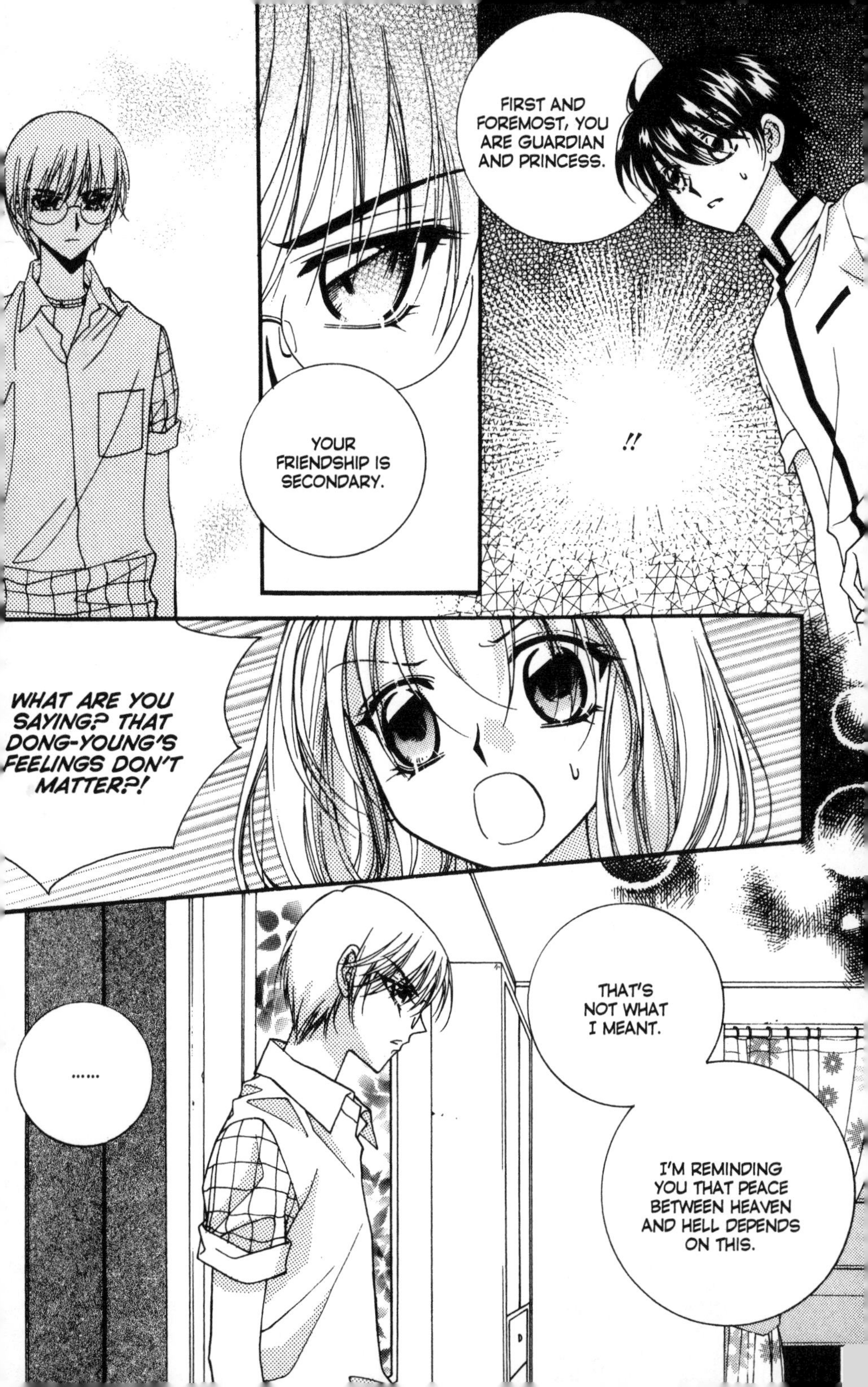
YOUR FRIENDSHIP IS SECONDARY.
FIRST AND FOREMOST, YOU ARE GUARDIAN AND PRINCESS.
!!
WHAT ARE YOU SAYING? THAT DONG-YOUNG'S FEELINGS DON'T MATTER?!
......
THAT'S NOT WHAT I MEANT.
I'M REMINDING YOU THAT PEACE BETWEEN HEAVEN AND HELL DEPENDS ON THIS.

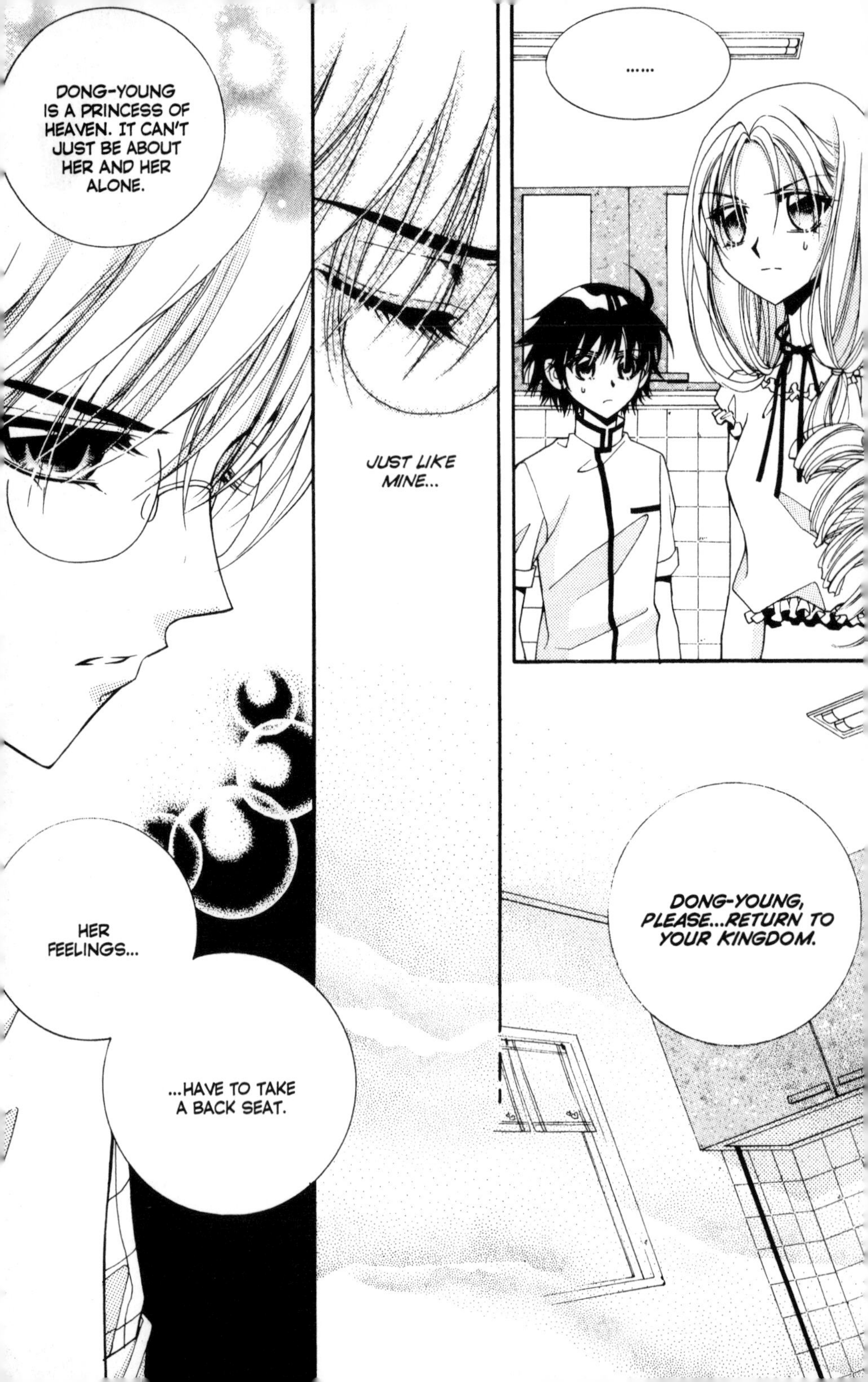
DONG-YOUNG IS A PRINCESS OF HEAVEN. IT CAN'T JUST BE ABOUT HER AND HER ALONE.
HER FEELINGS...
...HAVE TO TAKE A BACK SEAT.
JUST LIKE MINE...
......
DONG-YOUNG, PLEASE...RETURN TO YOUR KINGDOM.

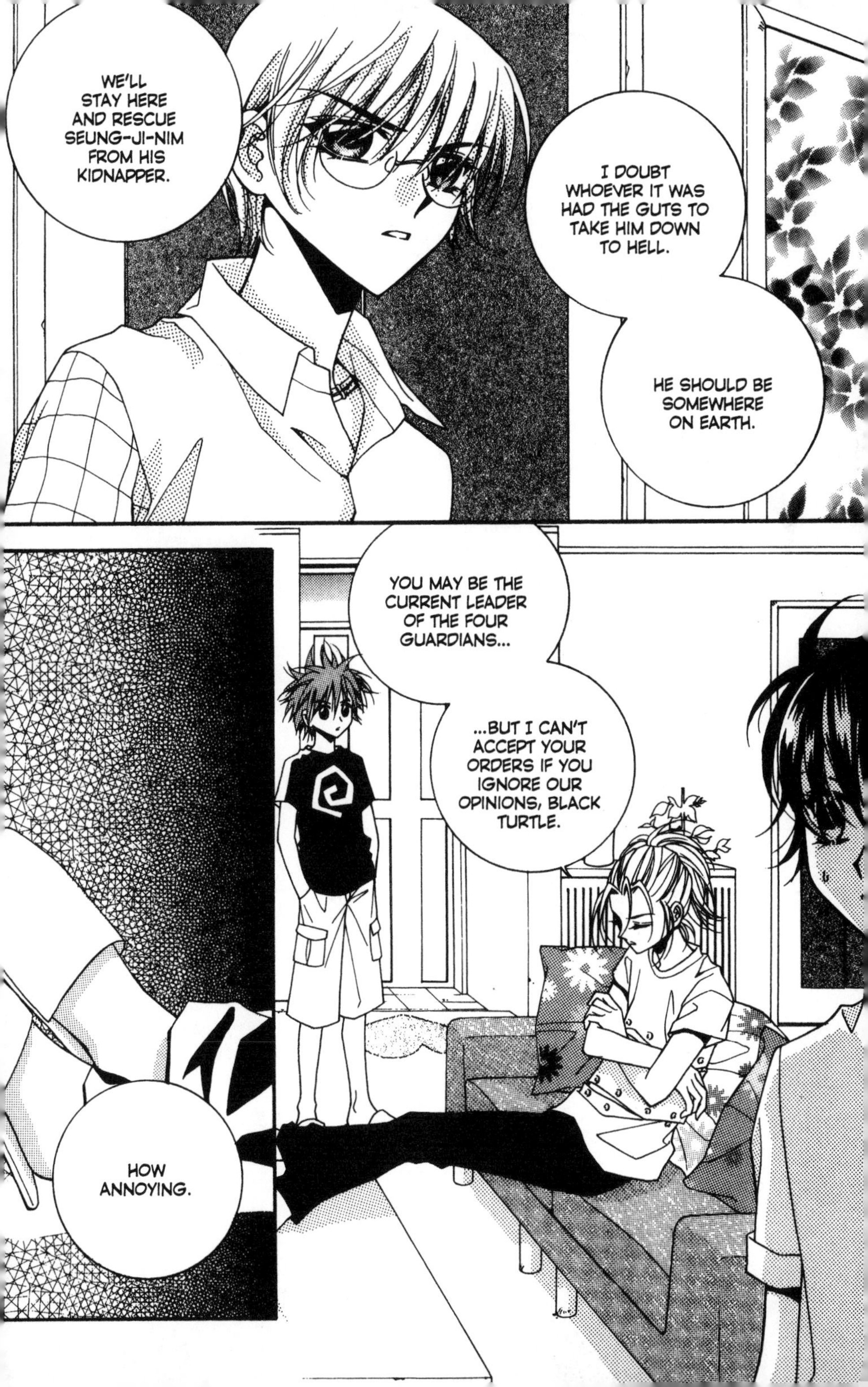
WE'LL STAY HERE AND RESCUE SEUNG-JI-NIM FROM HIS KIDNAPPER.
I DOUBT WHOEVER IT WAS HAD THE GUTS TO TAKE HIM DOWN TO HELL.
HE SHOULD BE SOMEWHERE ON EARTH.
YOU MAY BE THE CURRENT LEADER OF THE FOUR GUARDIANS...
...BUT I CAN'T ACCEPT YOUR ORDERS IF YOU IGNORE OUR OPINIONS, BLACK TURTLE.
HOW ANNOYING.

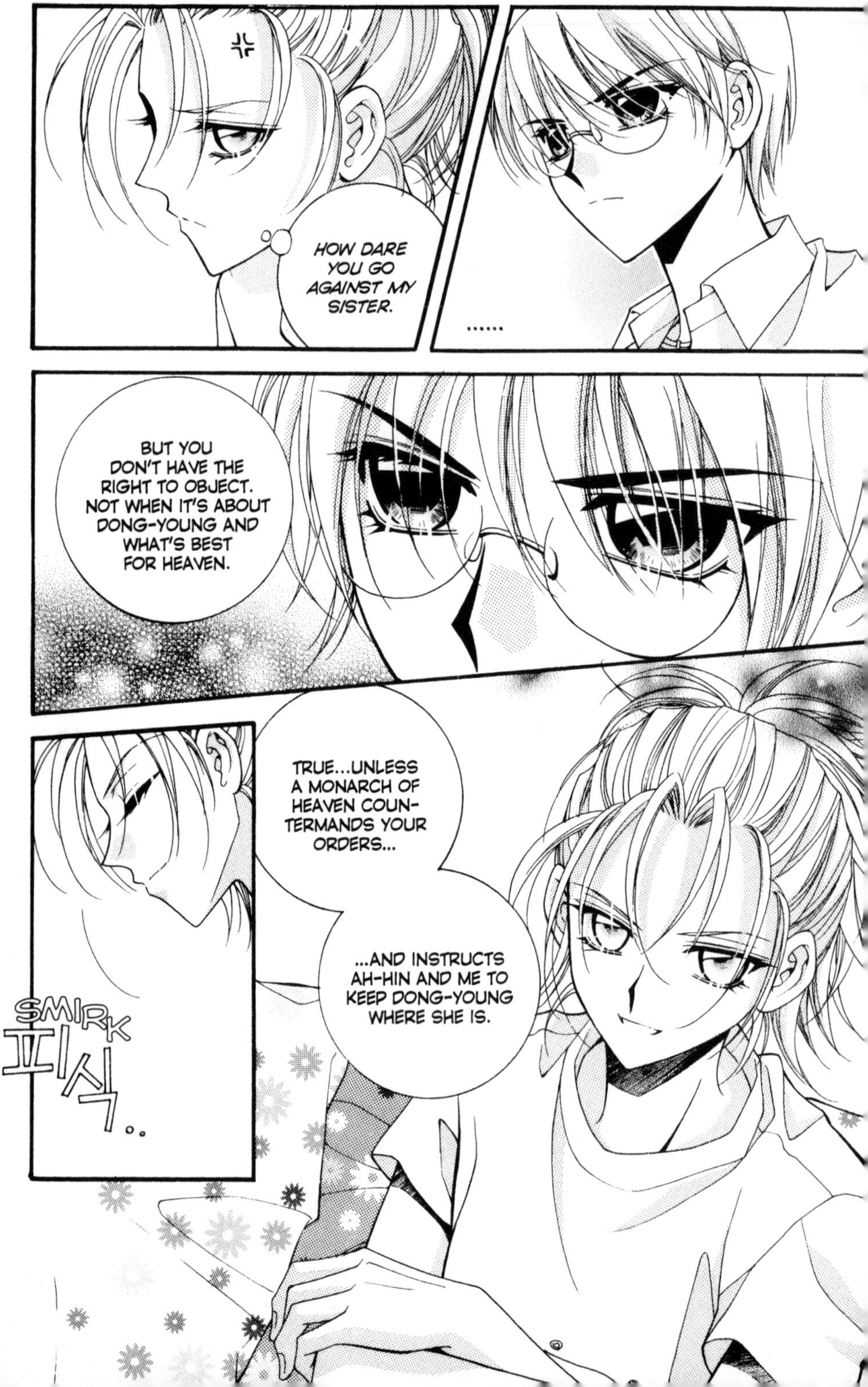
HOW DARE YOU GO AGAINST MY SISTER.
......
BUT YOU DON'T HAVE THE RIGHT TO OBJECT. NOT WHEN IT'S ABOUT DONG-YOUNG AND WHAT'S BEST FOR HEAVEN.
SMIRK
피식..
TRUE...UNLESS A MONARCH OF HEAVEN COUN-TERMANDS YOUR ORDERS...
...AND INSTRUCTS AH-HIN AND ME TO KEEP DONG-YOUNG WHERE SHE IS.

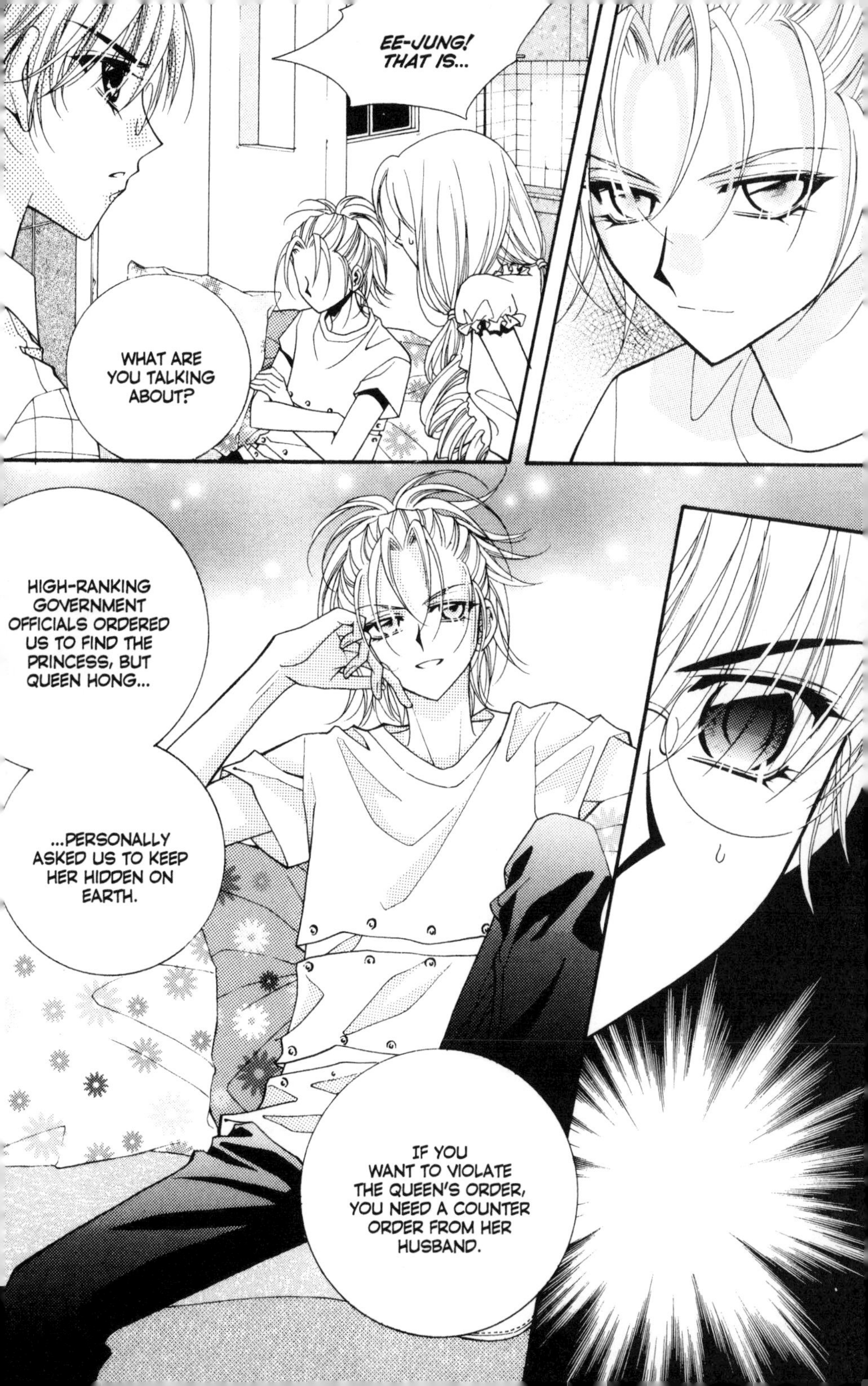
EE-JUNG! THAT IS...
WHAT ARE YOU TALKING ABOUT?
HIGH-RANKING GOVERNMENT OFFICIALS ORDERED US TO FIND THE PRINCESS, BUT QUEEN HONG...
...PERSONALLY ASKED US TO KEEP HER HIDDEN ON EARTH.
IF YOU WANT TO VIOLATE THE QUEEN'S ORDER, YOU NEED A COUNTER ORDER FROM HER HUSBAND.

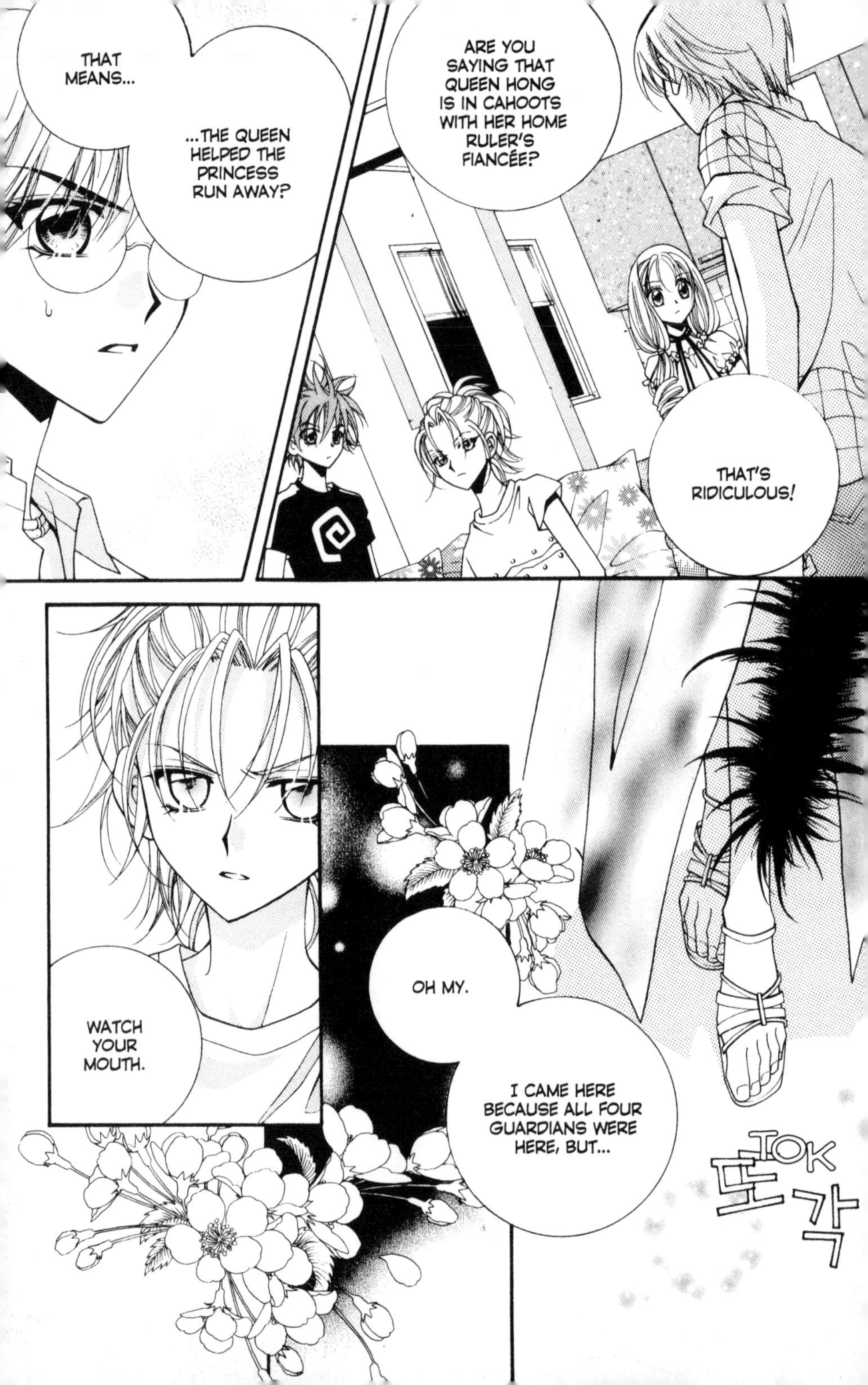
THAT MEANS...
...THE QUEEN HELPED THE PRINCESS RUN AWAY?
ARE YOU SAYING THAT QUEEN HONG IS IN CAHOOTS WITH HER HOME RULER'S FIANCÉE?
THAT'S RIDICULOUS!
WATCH YOUR MOUTH.
OH MY.
I CAME HERE BECAUSE ALL FOUR GUARDIANS WERE HERE, BUT...
TOK
또각

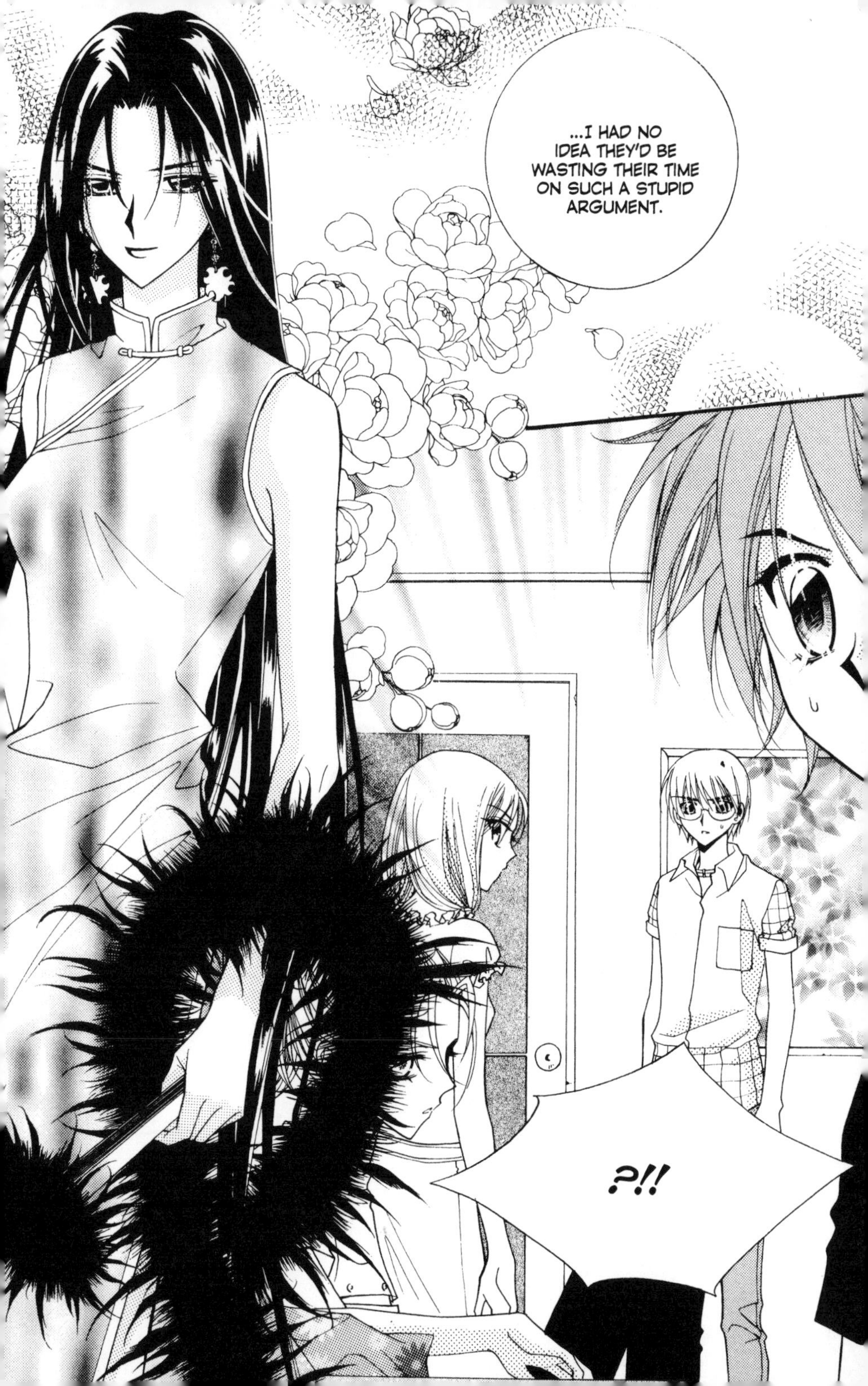
...I HAD NO IDEA THEY'D BE WASTING THEIR TIME ON SUCH A STUPID ARGUMENT.
?!!

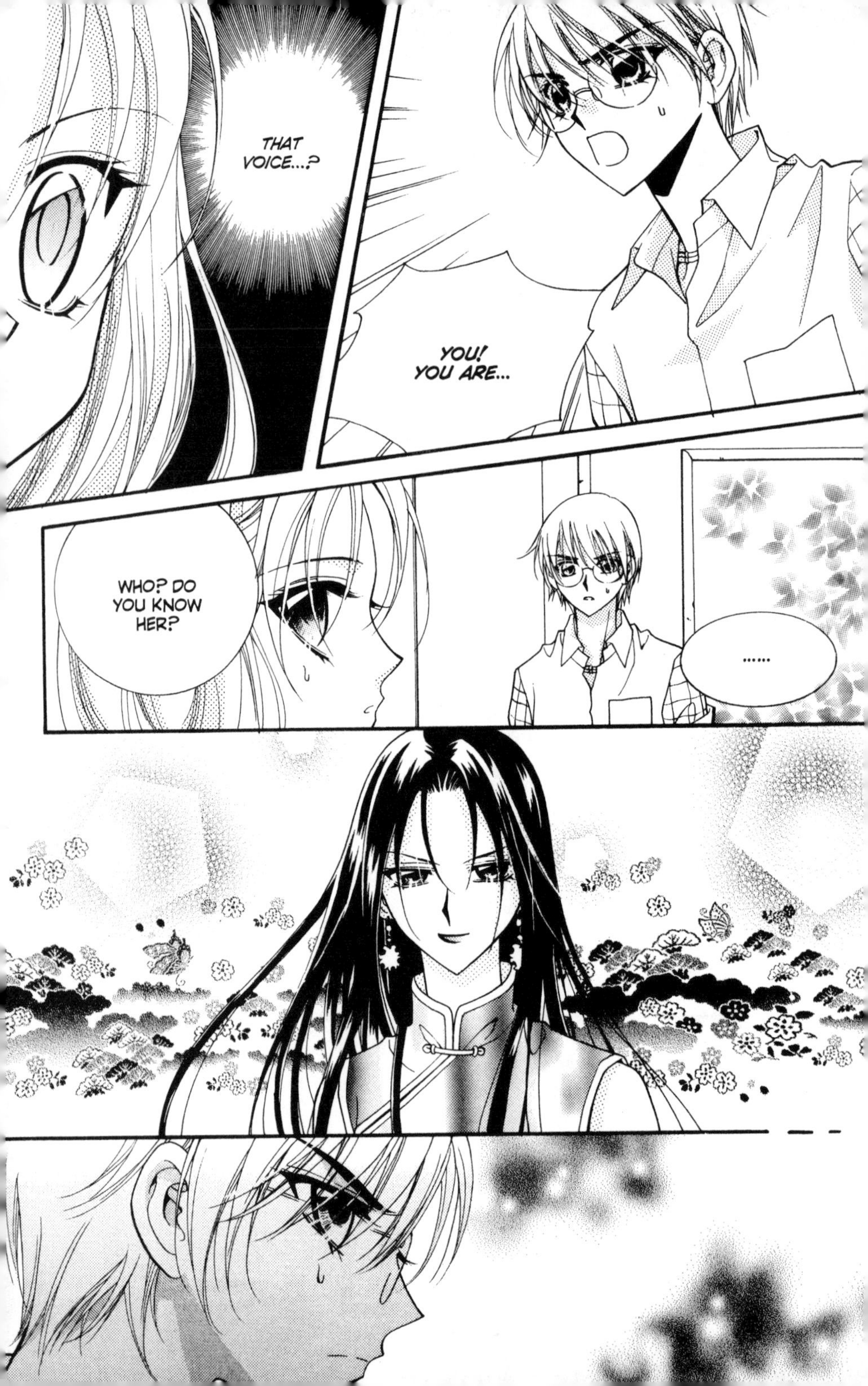
THAT VOICE...?
YOU! YOU ARE...
WHO? DO YOU KNOW HER?
......

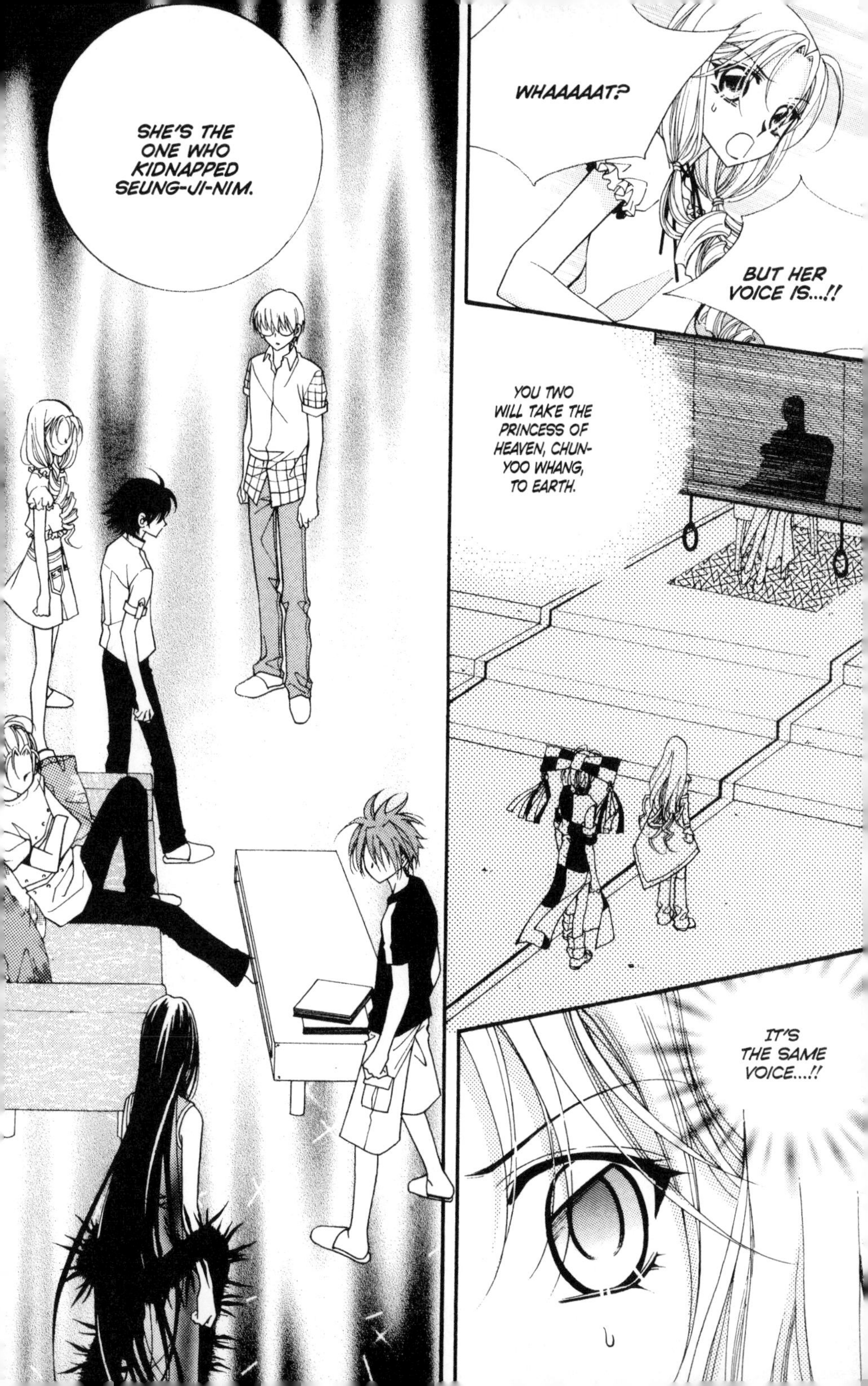
SHE'S THE ONE WHO KIDNAPPED SEUNG-JI-NIM.
WHAAAAAT?
BUT HER VOICE IS...!!
YOU TWO WILL TAKE THE PRINCESS OF HEAVEN, CHUN-YOO WHANG, TO EARTH.
IT'S THE SAME VOICE...!!

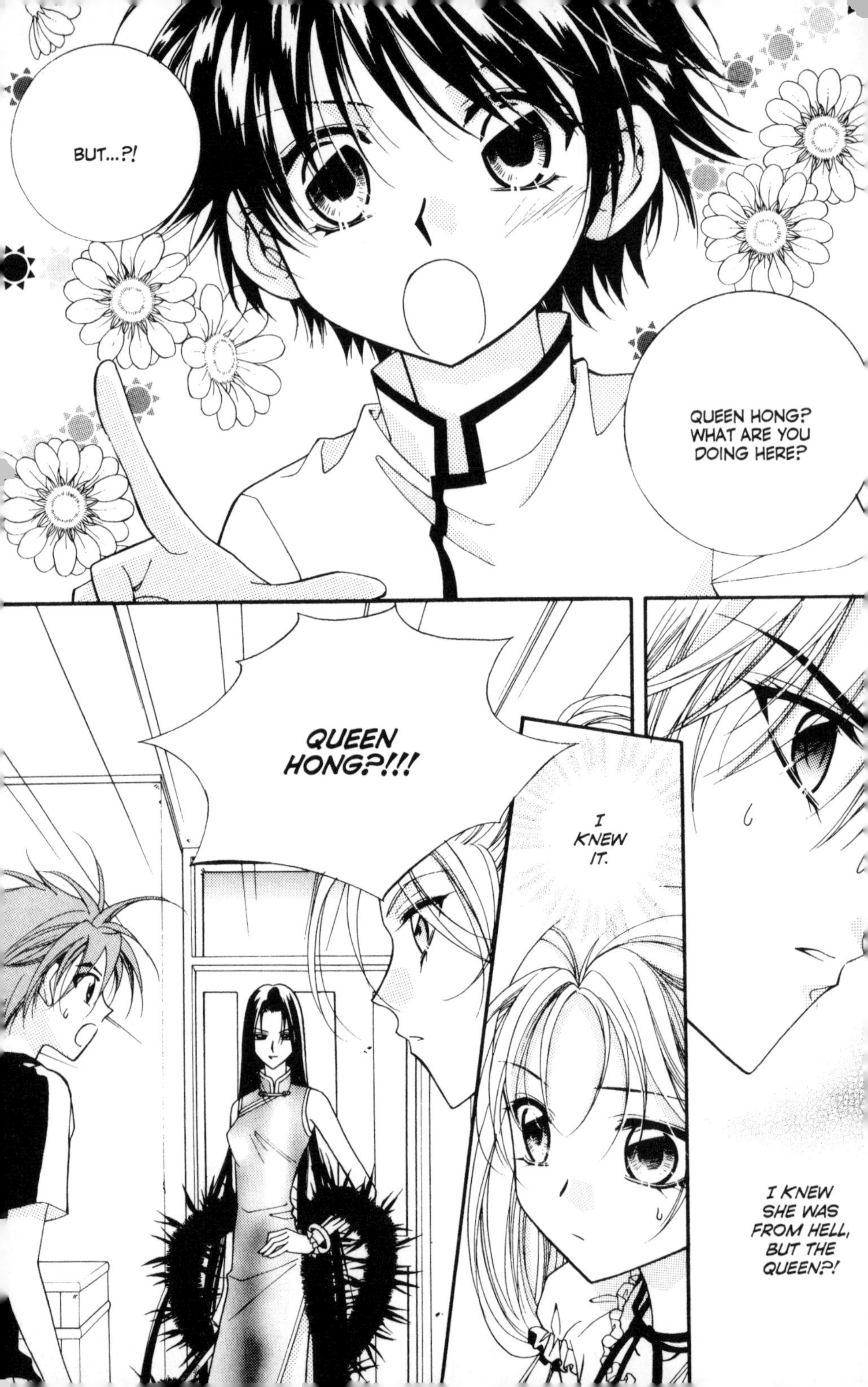
BUT...?!
QUEEN HONG? WHAT ARE YOU DOING HERE?
QUEEN HONG?!!!
I KNEW IT.
I KNEW SHE WAS FROM HELL, BUT THE QUEEN?!

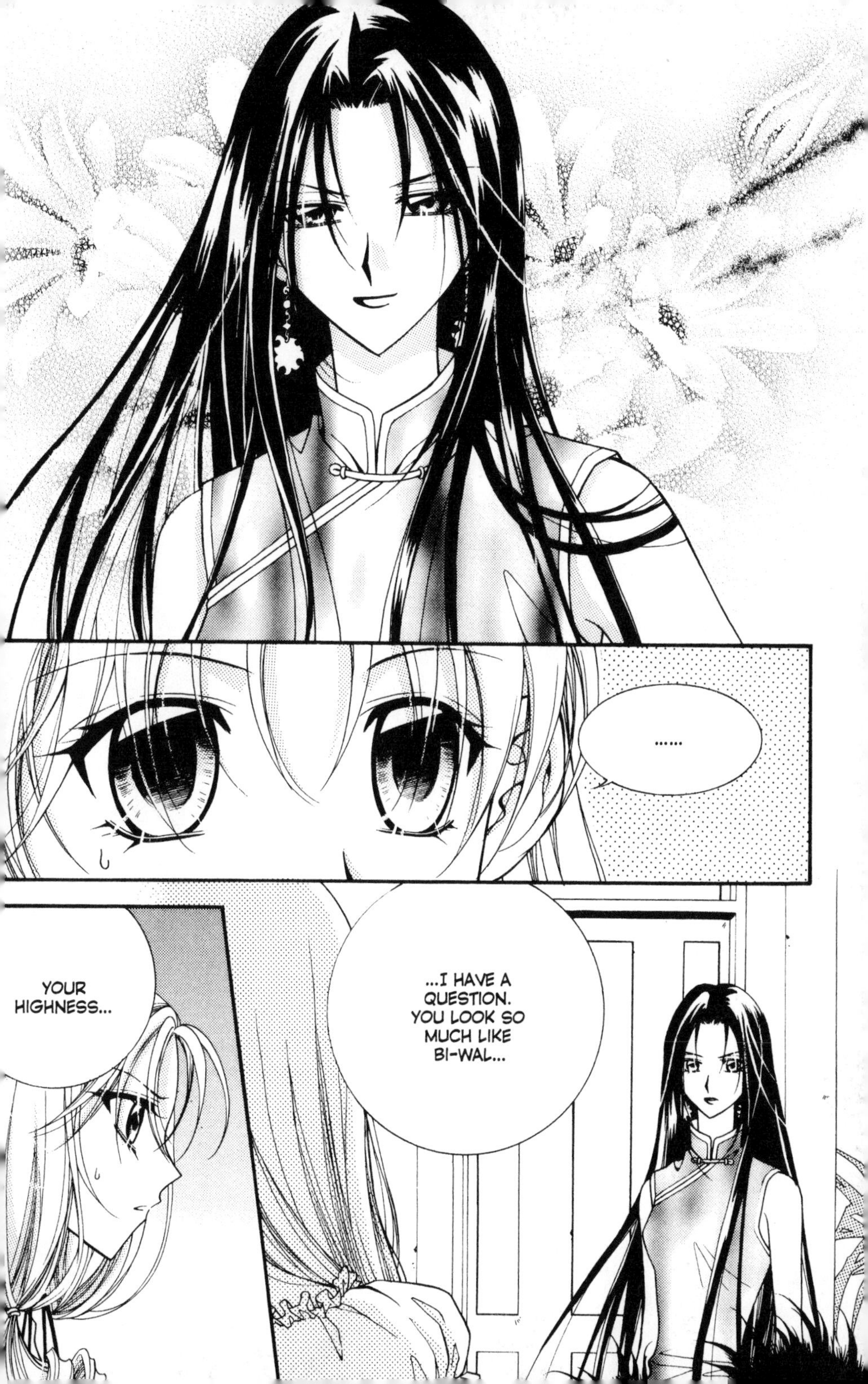
......
YOUR HIGHNESS...
...I HAVE A QUESTION. YOU LOOK SO MUCH LIKE BI-WAL...

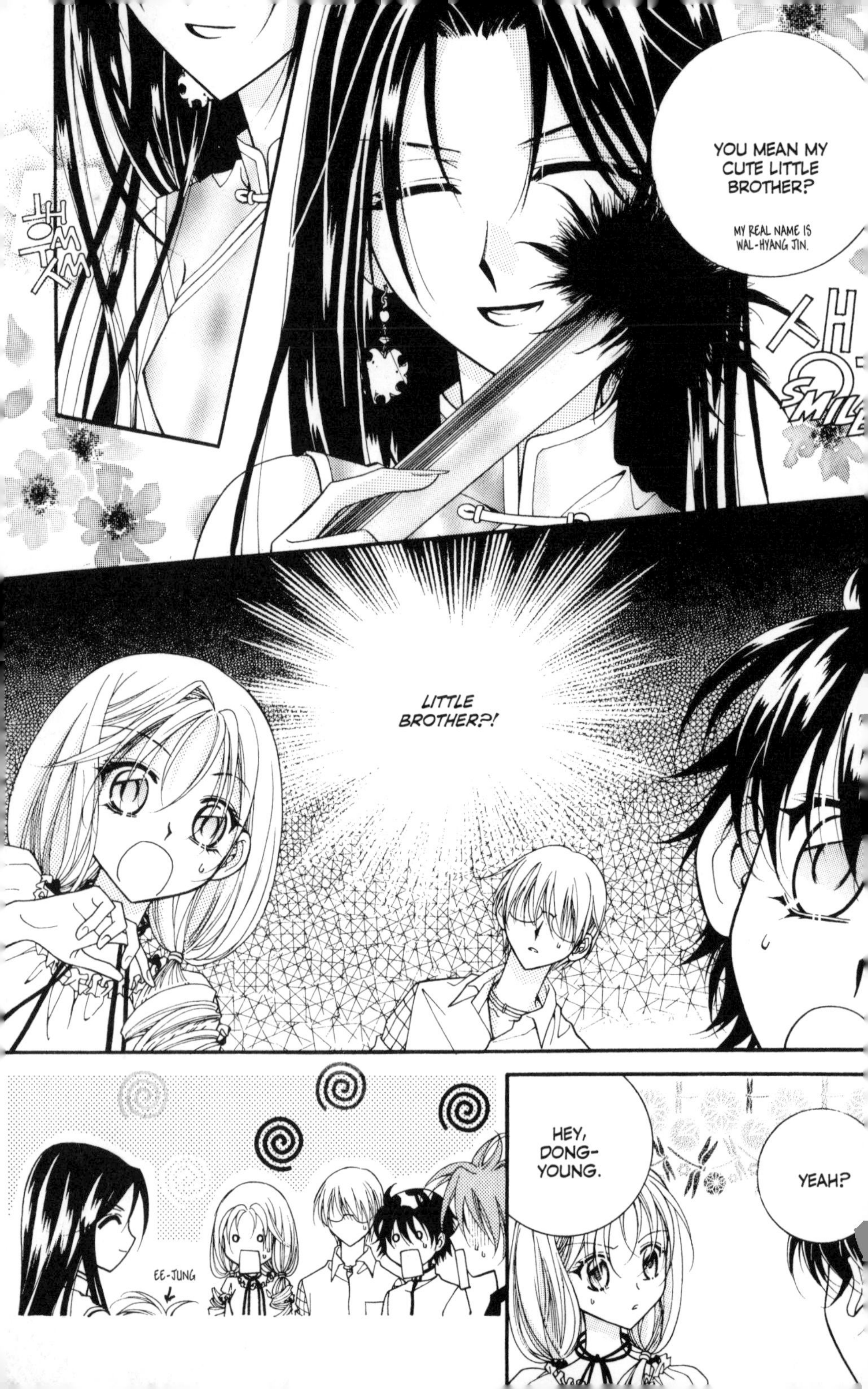

YOU MEAN MY CUTE LITTLE BROTHER?
MY REAL NAME IS WAL-HYANG JIN.
SMILE
LITTLE BROTHER?!
EE-JUNG
HEY, DONG-YOUNG.
YEAH?

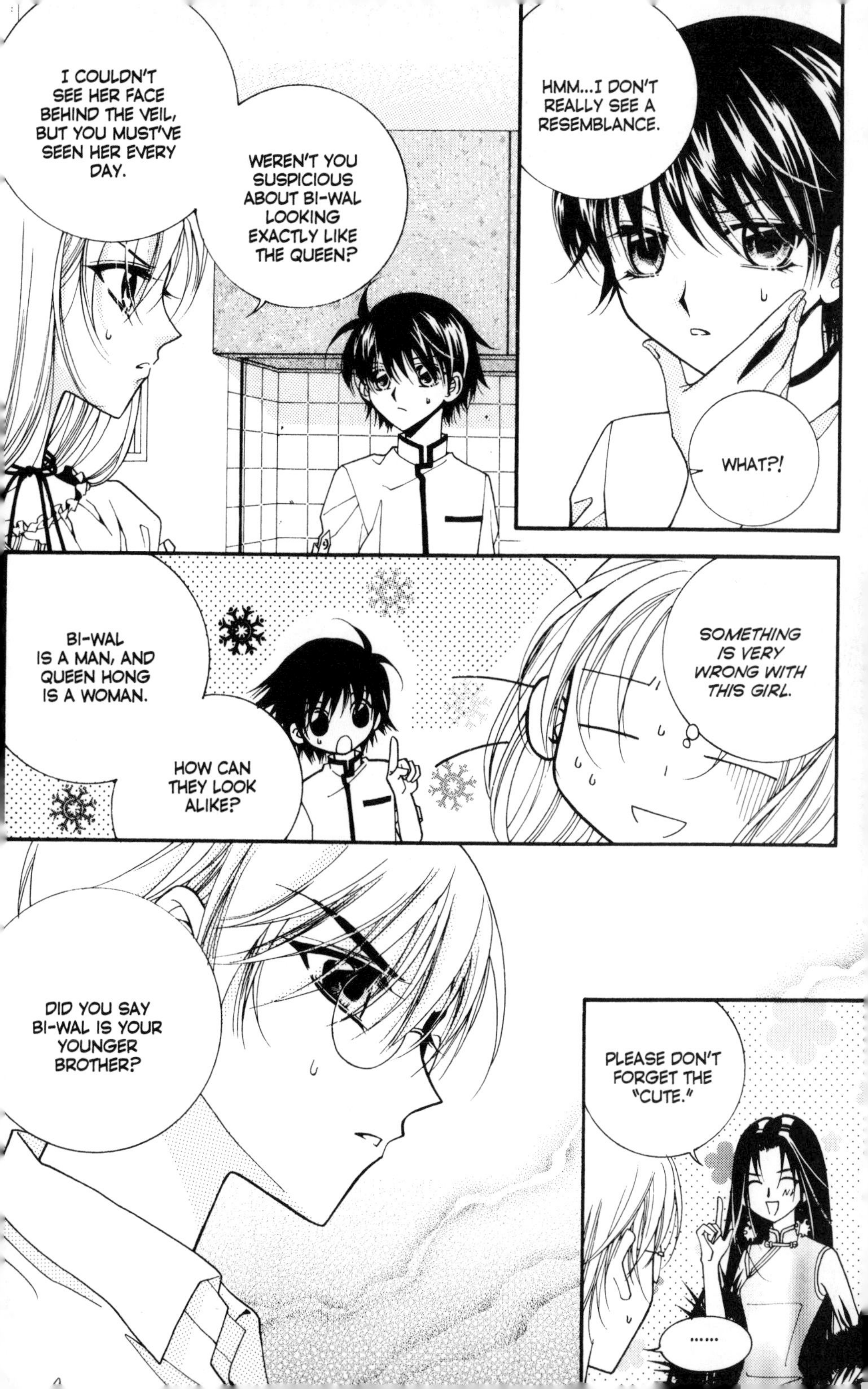
I COULDN'T SEE HER FACE BEHIND THE VEIL, BUT YOU MUST'VE SEEN HER EVERY DAY.
WEREN'T YOU SUSPICIOUS ABOUT BI-WAL LOOKING EXACTLY LIKE THE QUEEN?
HMM...I DON'T REALLY SEE A RESEMBLANCE.
WHAT?!
BI-WAL IS A MAN, AND QUEEN HONG IS A WOMAN.
HOW CAN THEY LOOK ALIKE?
SOMETHING IS VERY WRONG WITH THIS GIRL.
DID YOU SAY BI-WAL IS YOUR YOUNGER BROTHER?
PLEASE DON'T FORGET THE "CUTE."
......

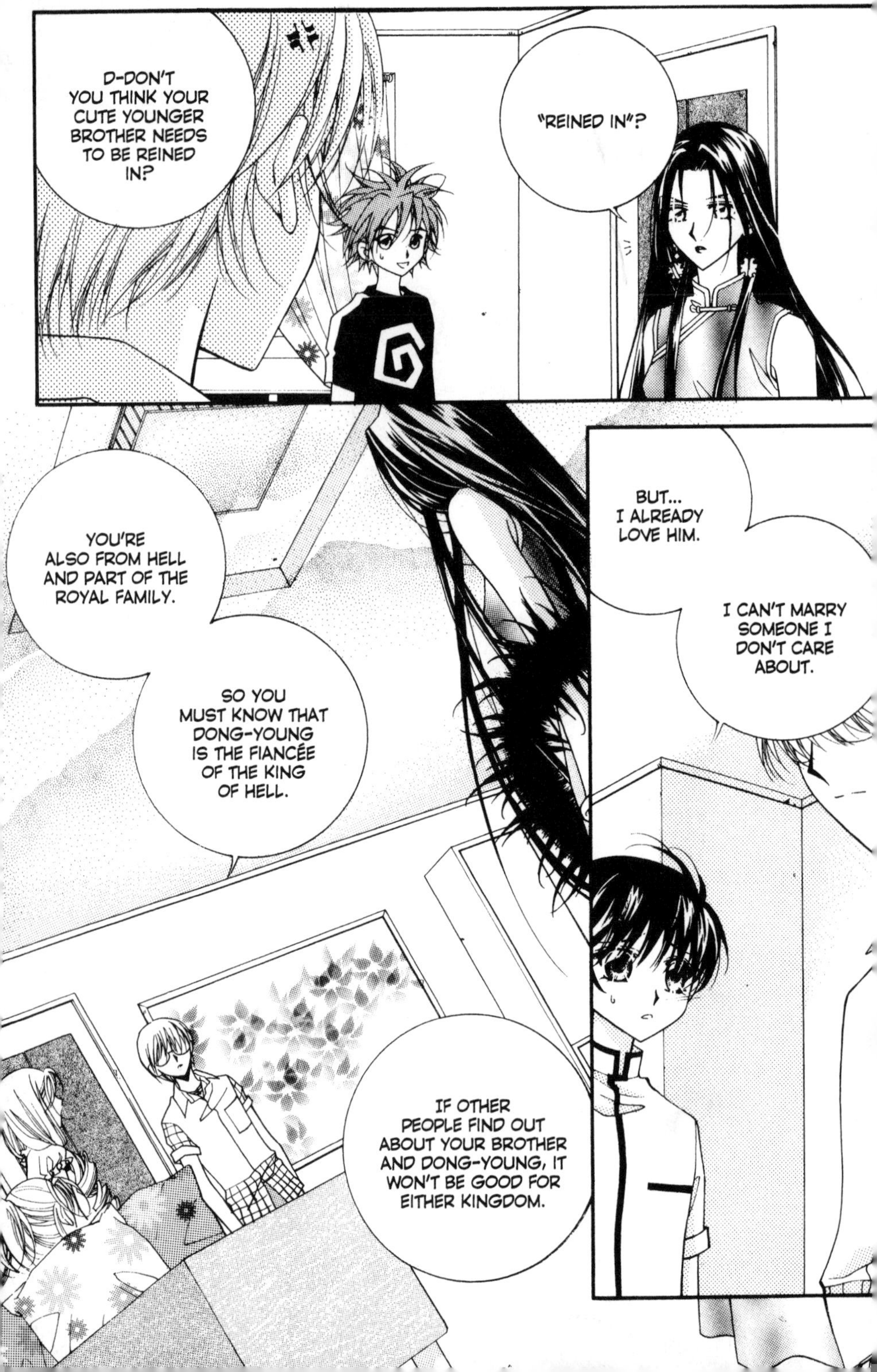
D-DON'T YOU THINK YOUR CUTE YOUNGER BROTHER NEEDS TO BE REINED IN?
"REINED IN"?
YOU'RE ALSO FROM HELL AND PART OF THE ROYAL FAMILY.
SO YOU MUST KNOW THAT DONG-YOUNG IS THE FIANCÉE OF THE KING OF HELL.
IF OTHER PEOPLE FIND OUT ABOUT YOUR BROTHER AND DONG-YOUNG, IT WON'T BE GOOD FOR EITHER KINGDOM.
BUT... I ALREADY LOVE HIM.
I CAN'T MARRY SOMEONE I DON'T CARE ABOUT.

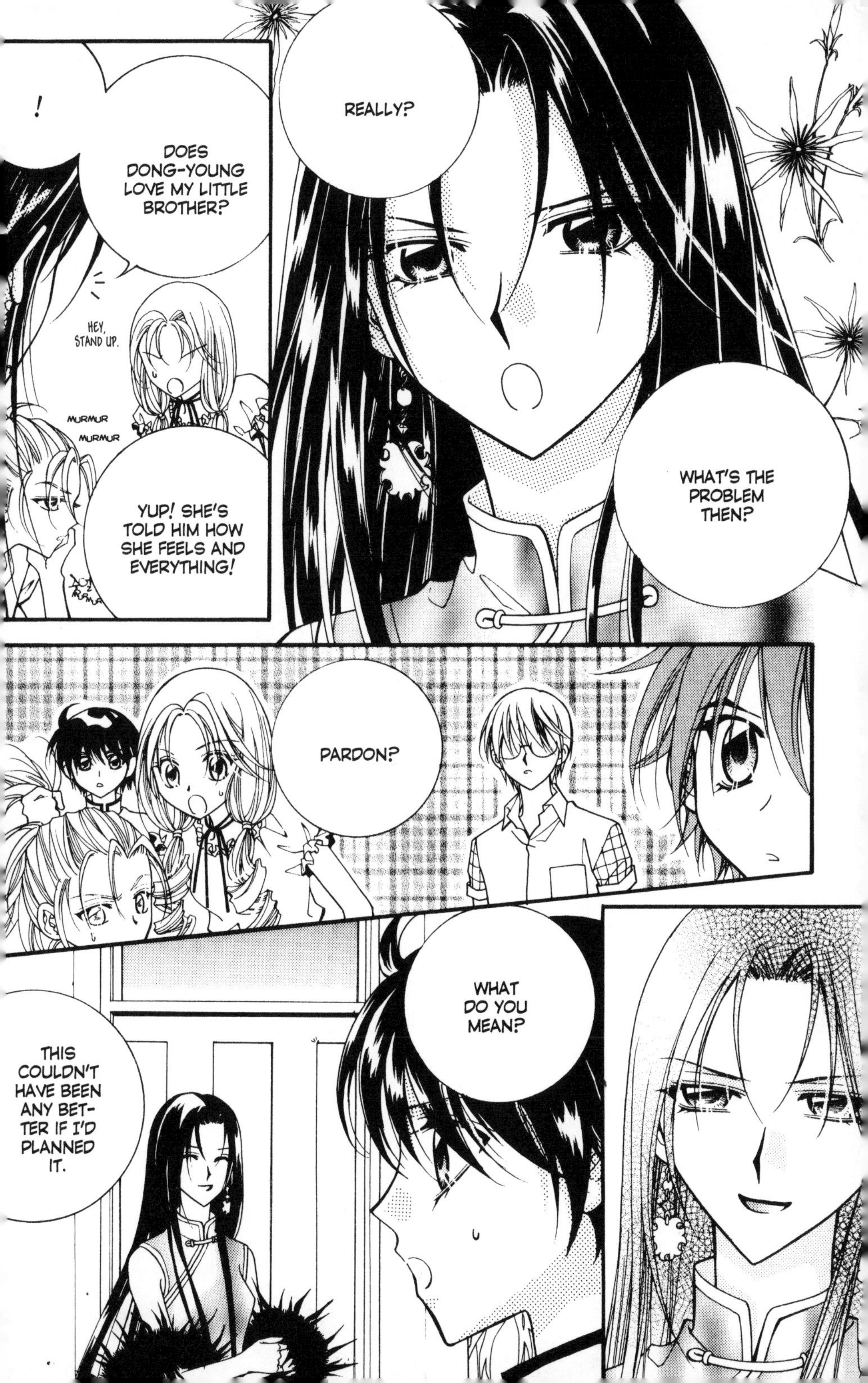
!
DOES DONG-YOUNG LOVE MY LITTLE BROTHER?
HEY, STAND UP.
MURMUR
MURMUR
YUP! SHE'S TOLD HIM HOW SHE FEELS AND EVERYTHING!
REALLY?
WHAT'S THE PROBLEM THEN?
PARDON?
THIS COULDN'T HAVE BEEN ANY BET-TER IF I'D PLANNED IT.
WHAT DO YOU MEAN?

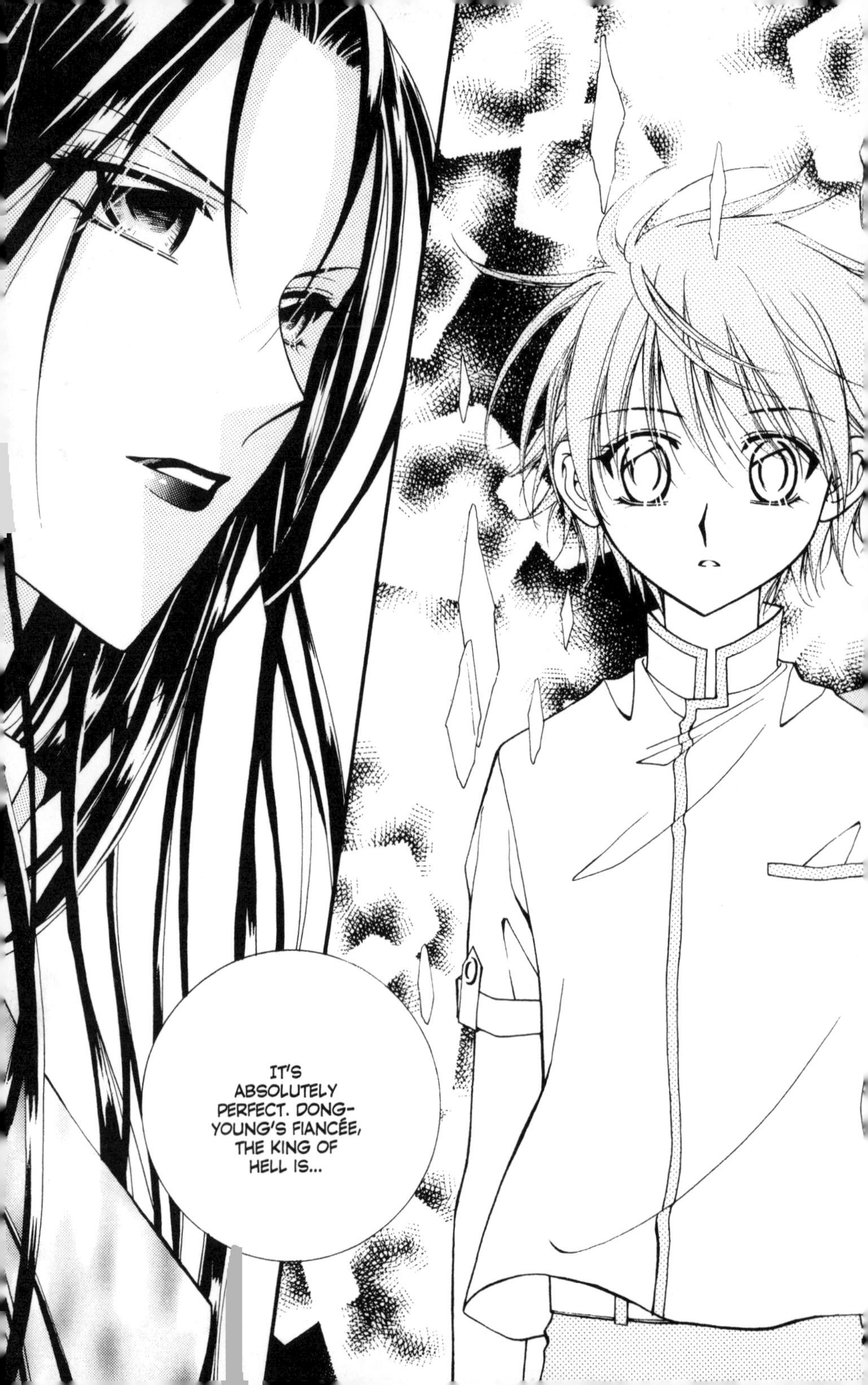
IT'S ABSOLUTELY PERFECT. DONG-YOUNG'S FIANCÉE, THE KING OF HELL IS...

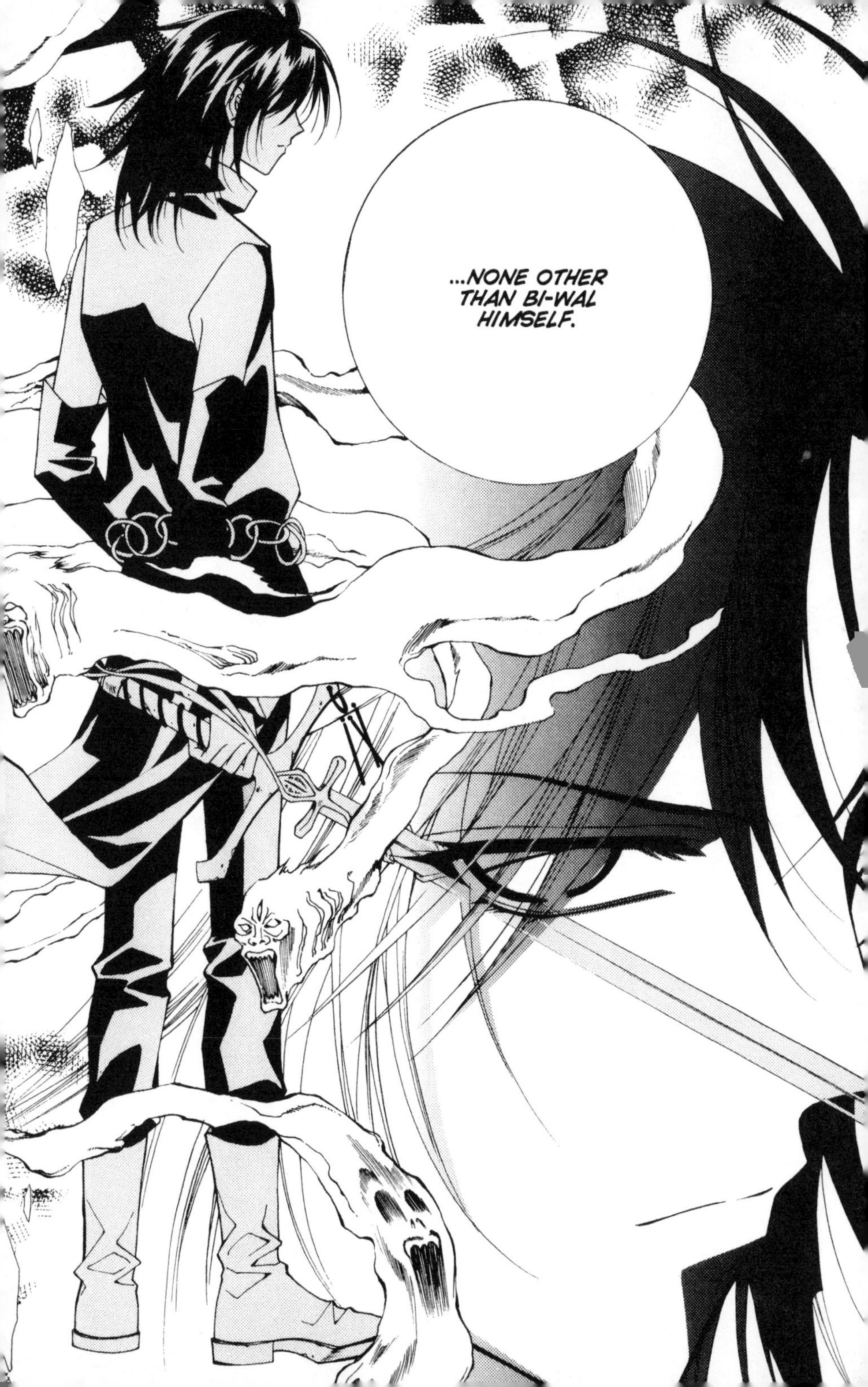
...NONE OTHER THAN BI-WAL HIMSELF.

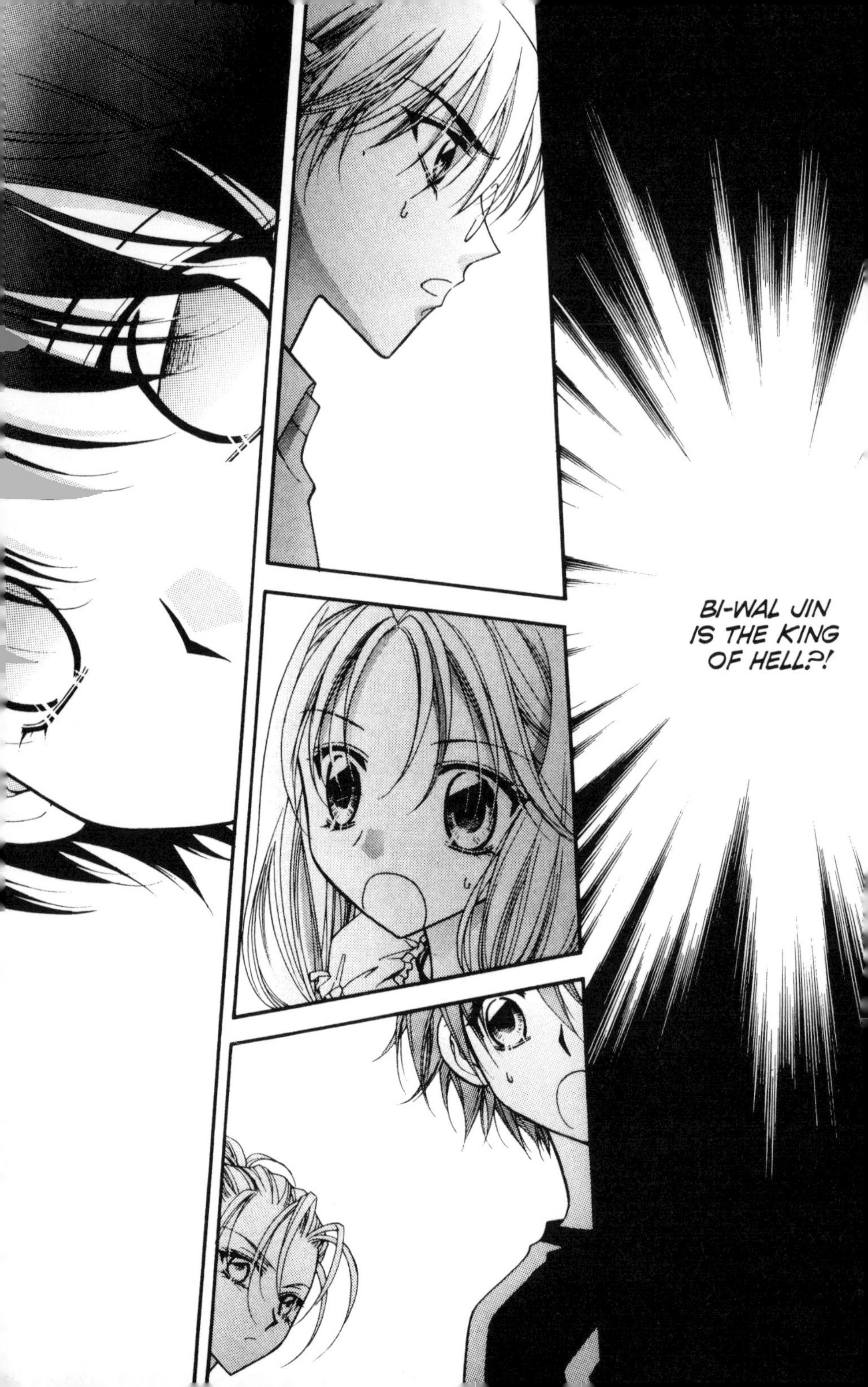
BI-WAL JIN
IS THE KING
OF HELL?!

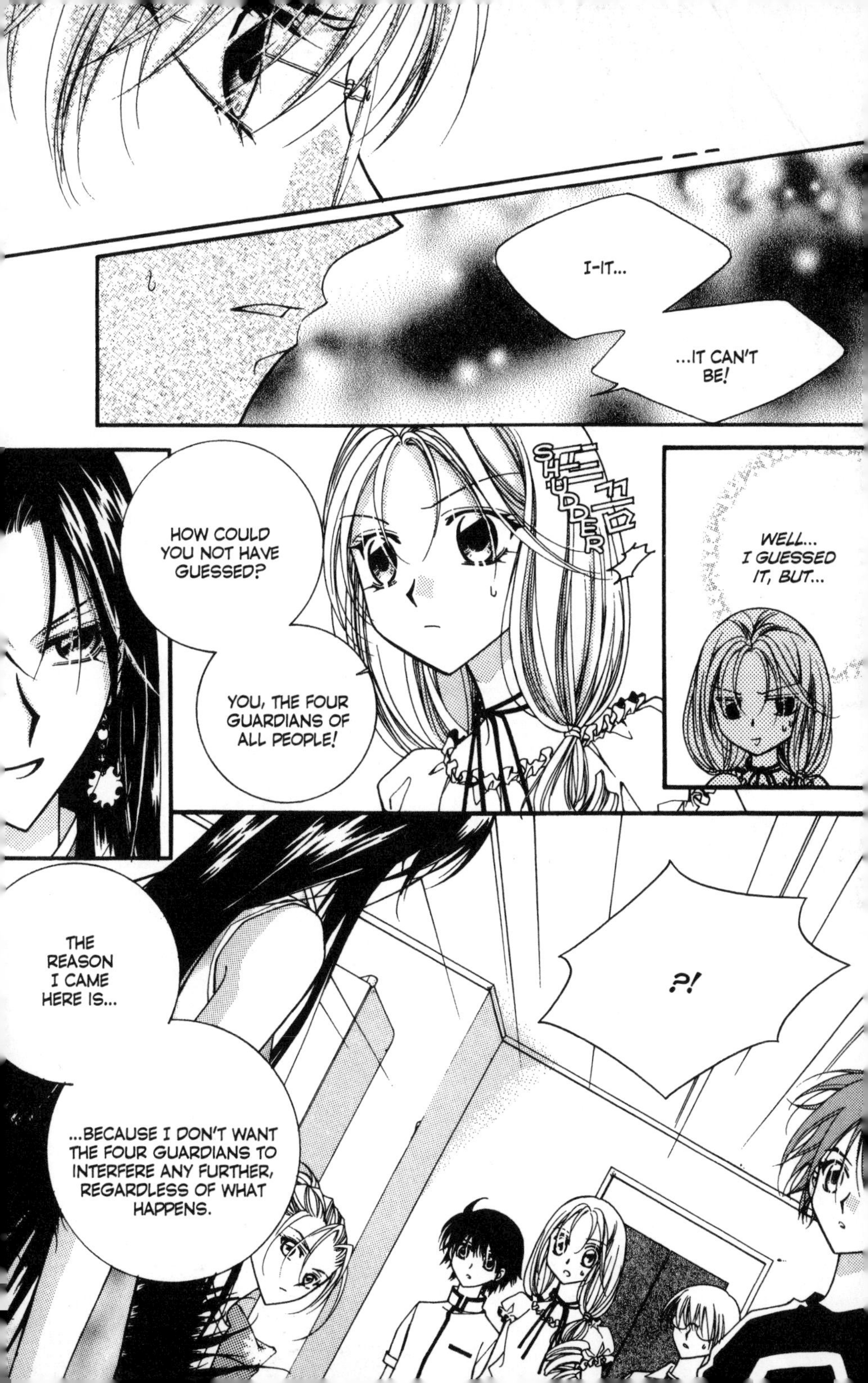
I-IT...
...IT CAN'T BE!
HOW COULD YOU NOT HAVE GUESSED?
YOU, THE FOUR GUARDIANS OF ALL PEOPLE!
SHUDDER
WELL... I GUESSED IT, BUT...
THE REASON I CAME HERE IS...
...BECAUSE I DON'T WANT THE FOUR GUARDIANS TO INTERFERE ANY FURTHER, REGARDLESS OF WHAT HAPPENS.
?!

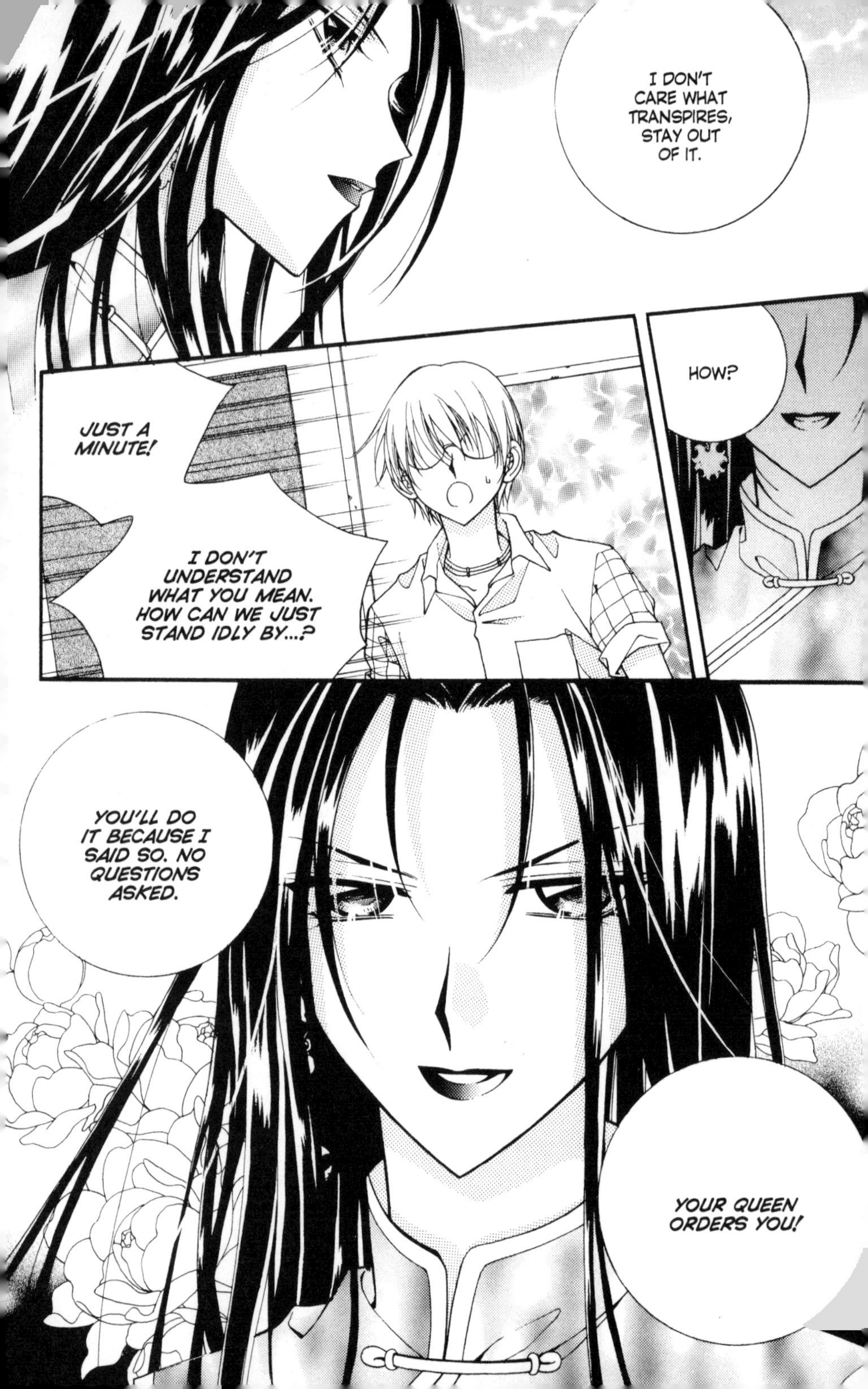
I DON'T CARE WHAT TRANSPIRES, STAY OUT OF IT.
JUST A MINUTE!
I DON'T UNDERSTAND WHAT YOU MEAN. HOW CAN WE JUST STAND IDLY BY...?
HOW?
YOU'LL DO IT BECAUSE I SAID SO. NO QUESTIONS ASKED.
YOUR QUEEN ORDERS YOU!

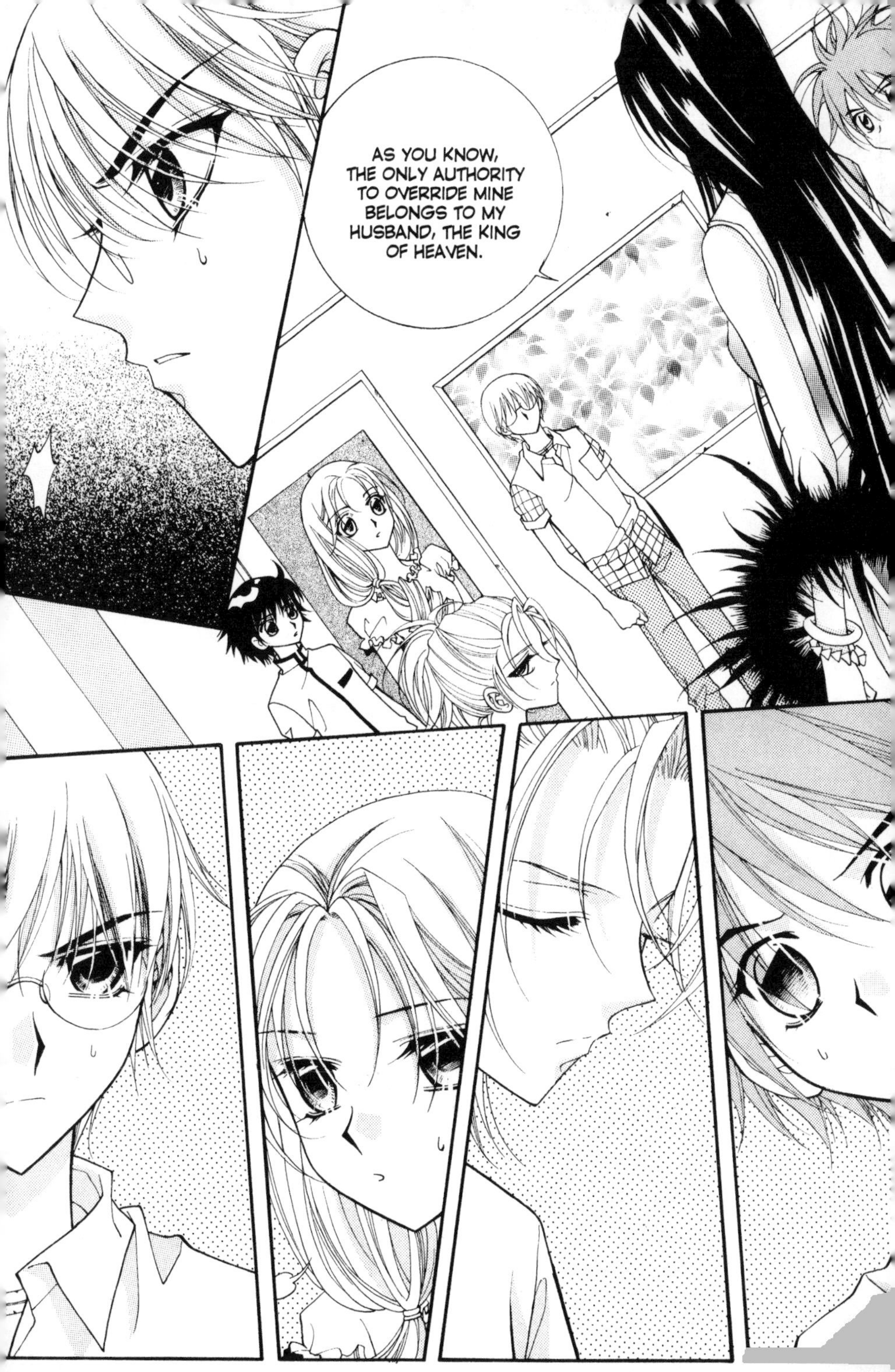
AS YOU KNOW, THE ONLY AUTHORITY TO OVERRIDE MINE BELONGS TO MY HUSBAND, THE KING OF HEAVEN.

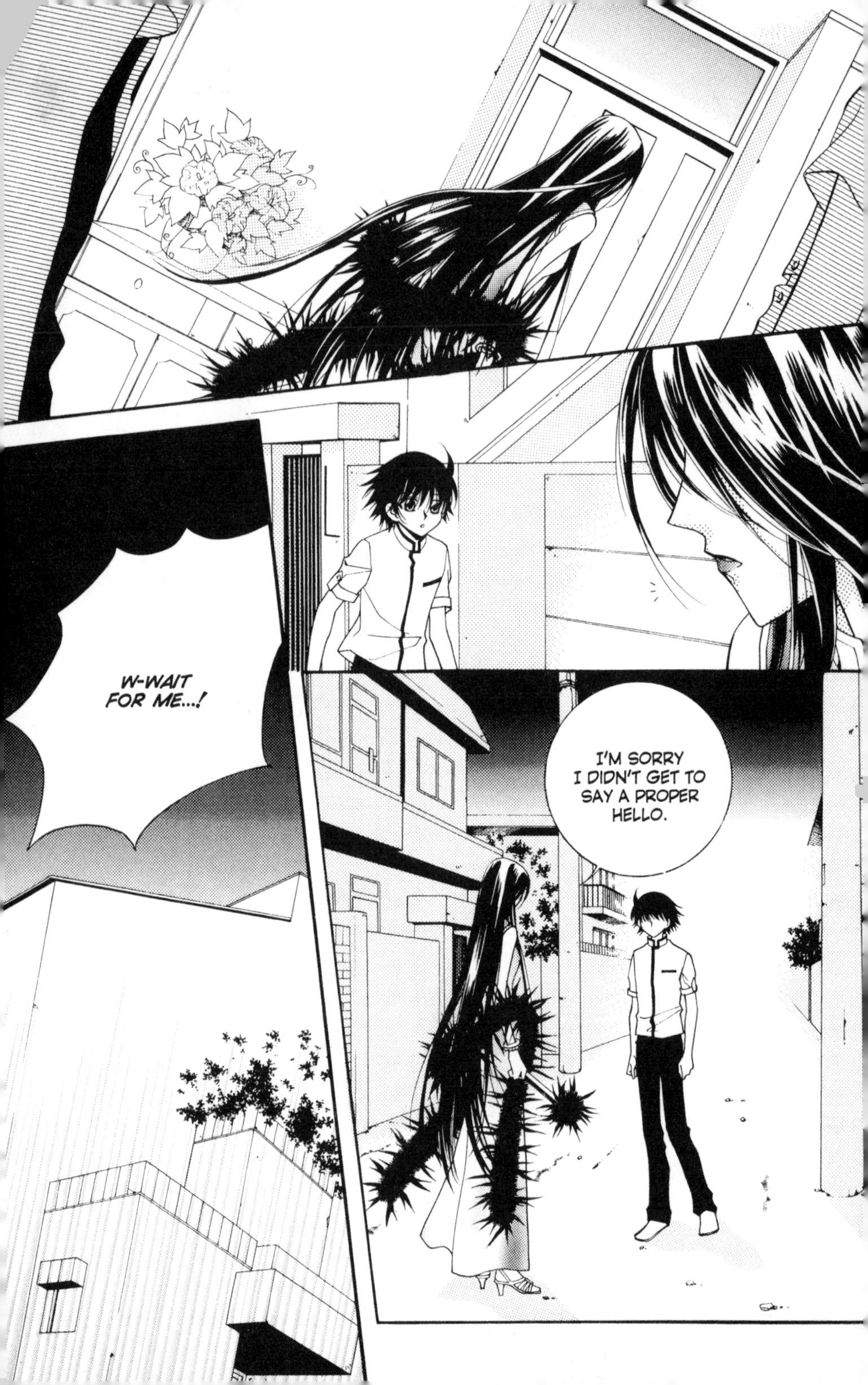
W-WAIT FOR ME...!
I'M SORRY I DIDN'T GET TO SAY A PROPER HELLO.

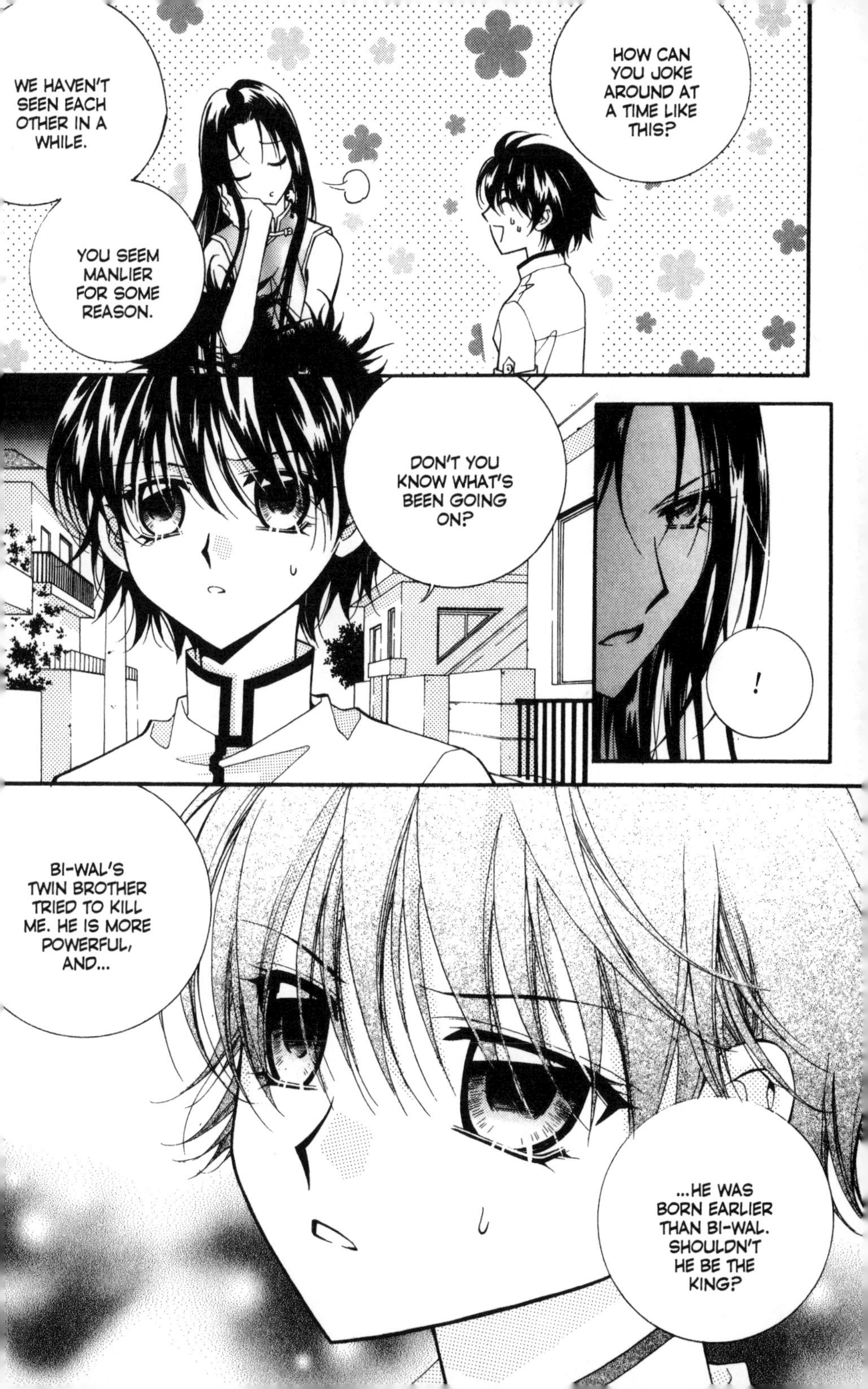
WE HAVEN'T SEEN EACH OTHER IN A WHILE.
YOU SEEM MANLIER FOR SOME REASON.
HOW CAN YOU JOKE AROUND AT A TIME LIKE THIS?
DON'T YOU KNOW WHAT'S BEEN GOING ON?
!
BI-WAL'S TWIN BROTHER TRIED TO KILL ME. HE IS MORE POWERFUL, AND...
...HE WAS BORN EARLIER THAN BI-WAL. SHOULDN'T HE BE THE KING?

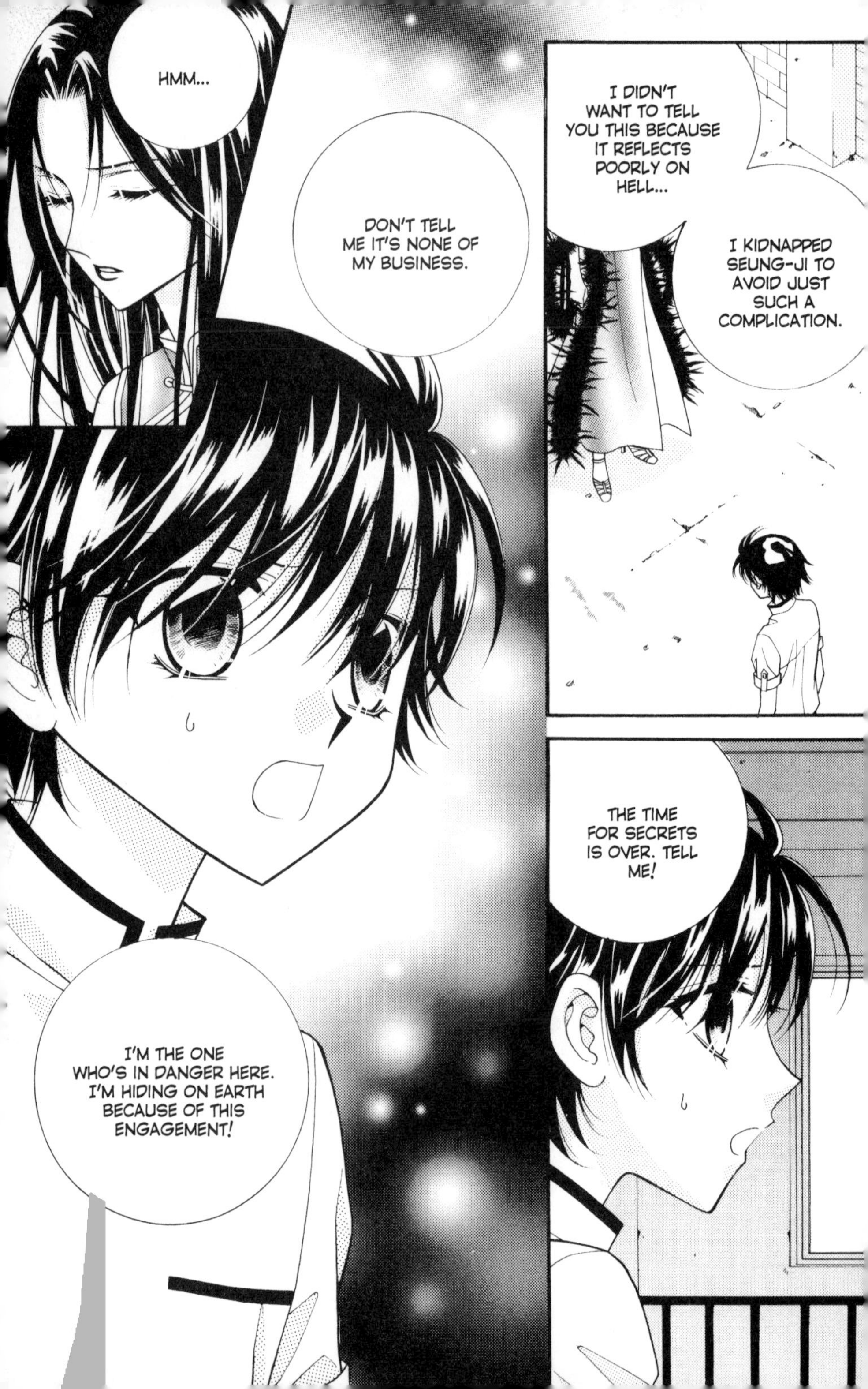
HMM...
DON'T TELL ME IT'S NONE OF MY BUSINESS.
I'M THE ONE WHO'S IN DANGER HERE. I'M HIDING ON EARTH BECAUSE OF THIS ENGAGEMENT!
I DIDN'T WANT TO TELL YOU THIS BECAUSE IT REFLECTS POORLY ON HELL...
I KIDNAPPED SEUNG-JI TO AVOID JUST SUCH A COMPLICATION.
THE TIME FOR SECRETS IS OVER. TELL ME!

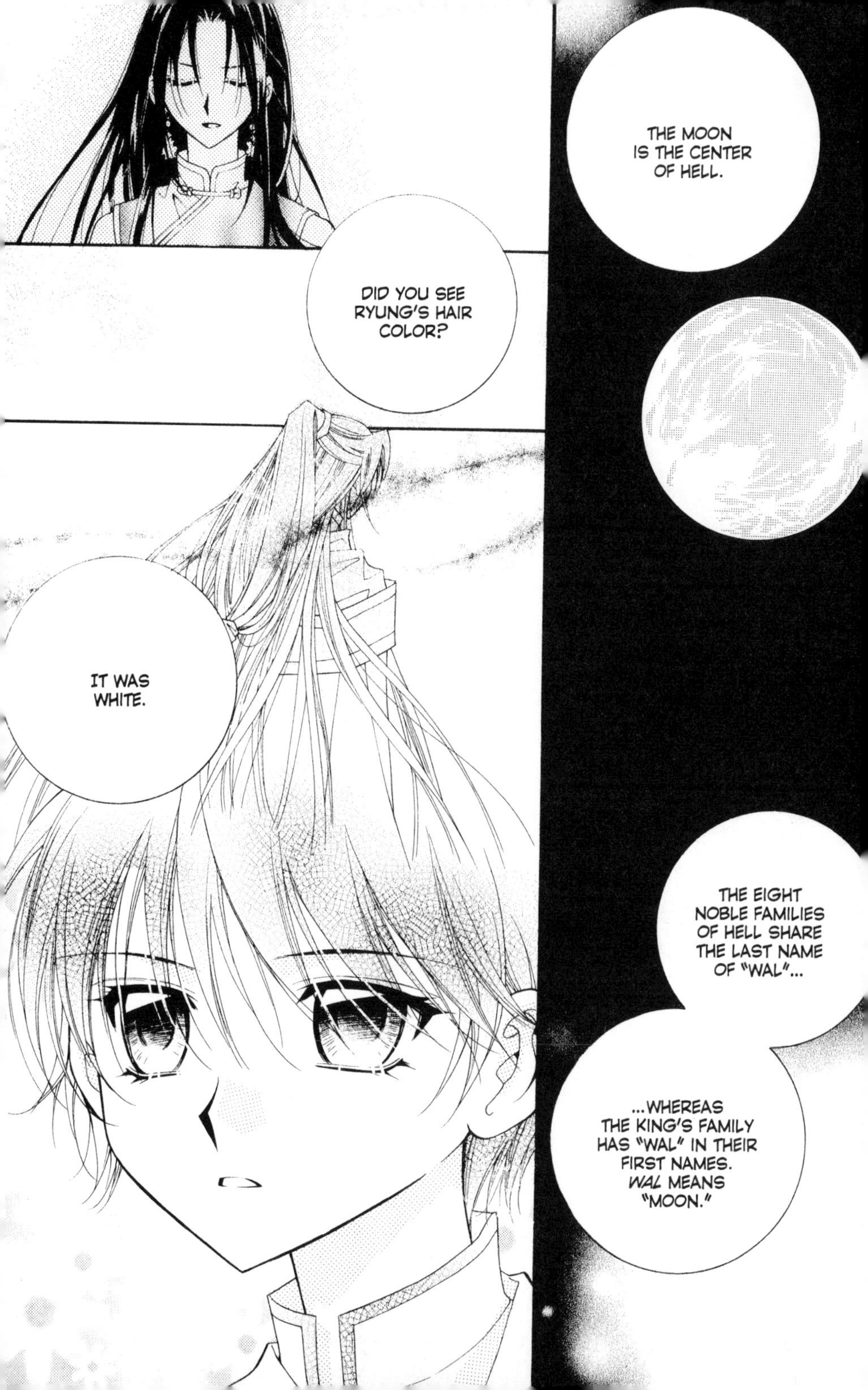
DID YOU SEE RYUNG'S HAIR COLOR?
IT WAS WHITE.
THE MOON IS THE CENTER OF HELL.
THE EIGHT NOBLE FAMILIES OF HELL SHARE THE LAST NAME OF "WAL"...
...WHEREAS THE KING'S FAMILY HAS "WAL" IN THEIR FIRST NAMES. *WAL* MEANS "MOON."

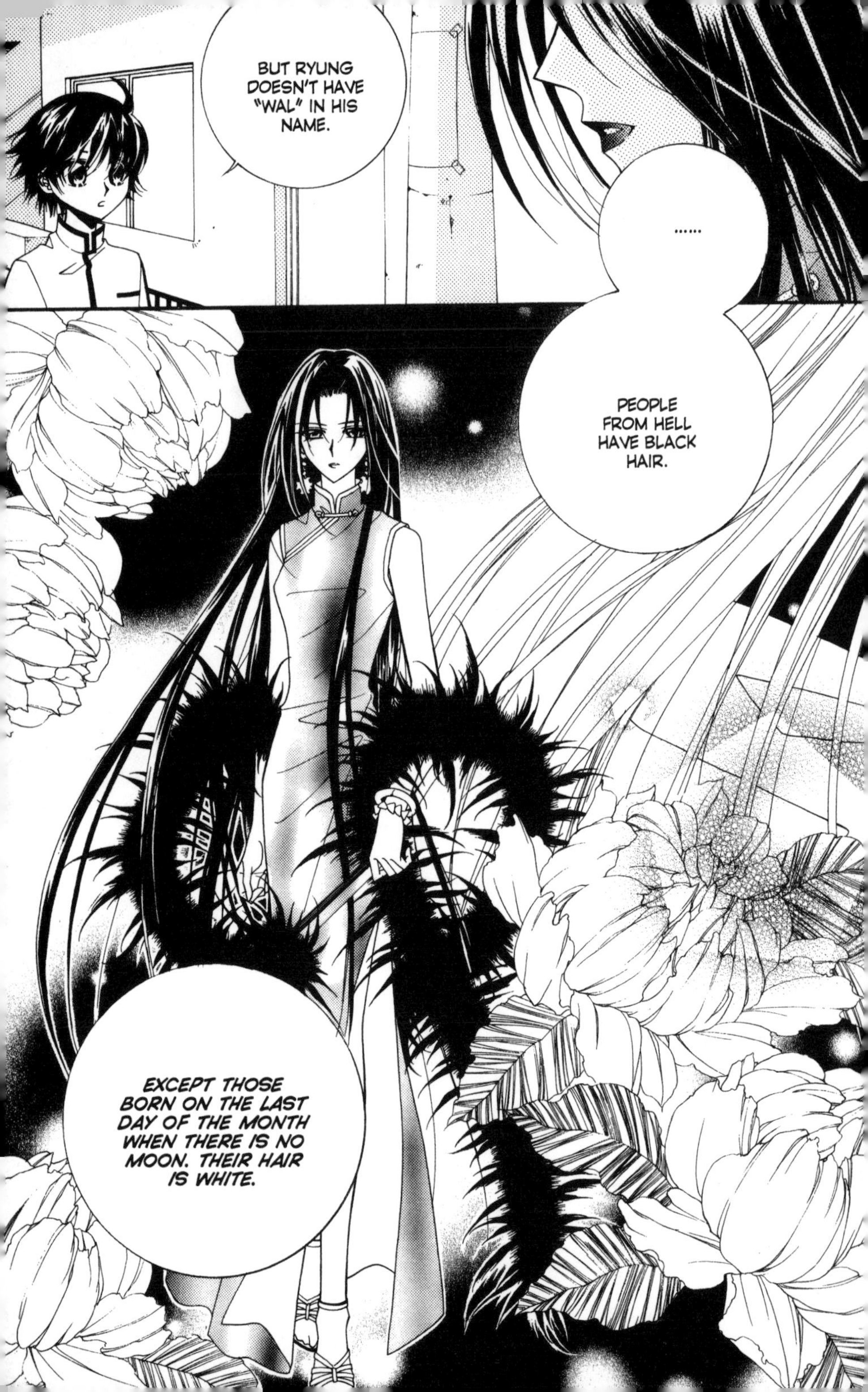

BUT RYUNG DOESN'T HAVE "WAL" IN HIS NAME.
......
PEOPLE FROM HELL HAVE BLACK HAIR.
EXCEPT THOSE BORN ON THE LAST DAY OF THE MONTH WHEN THERE IS NO MOON. THEIR HAIR IS WHITE.

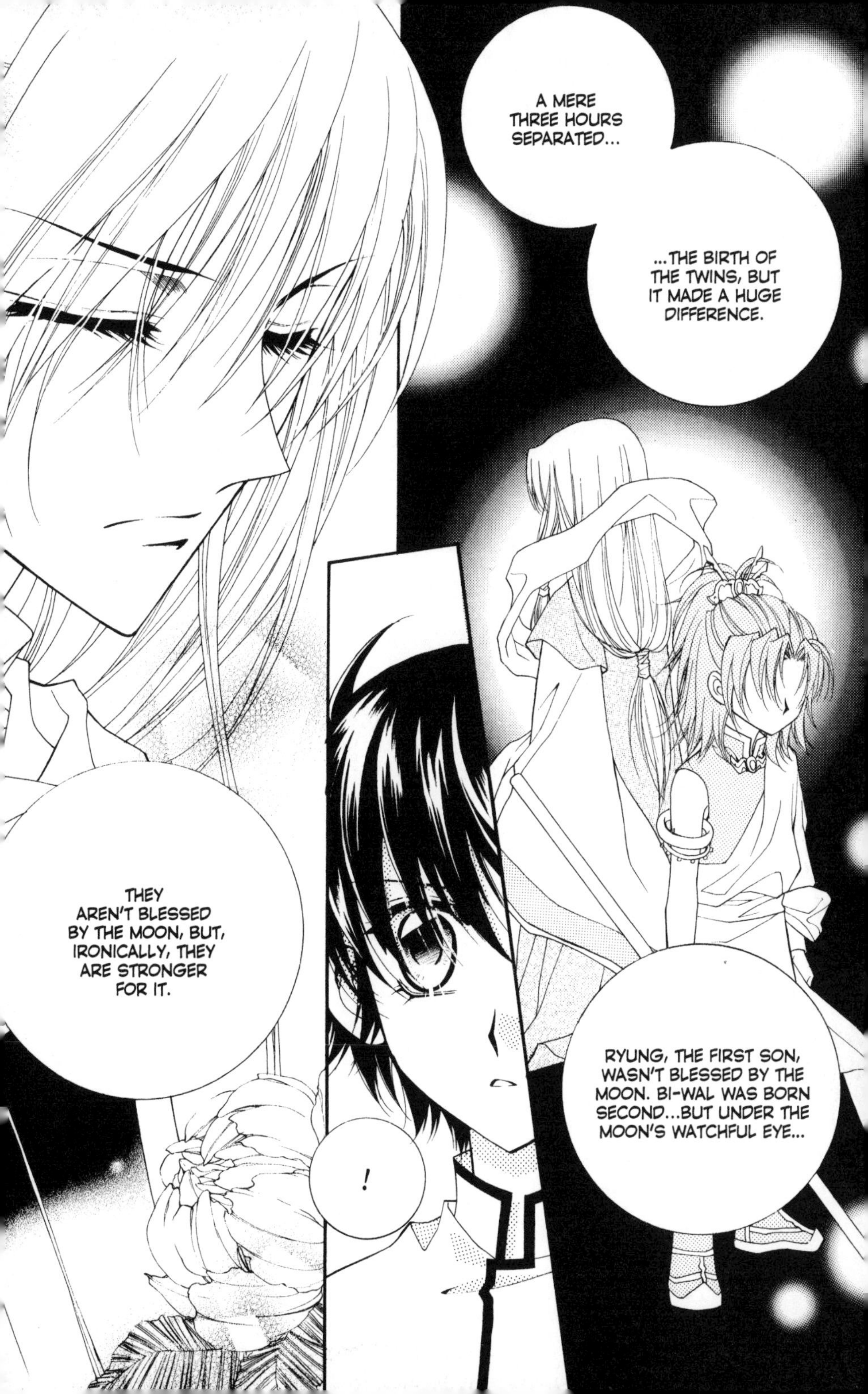
THEY AREN'T BLESSED BY THE MOON, BUT, IRONICALLY, THEY ARE STRONGER FOR IT.
A MERE THREE HOURS SEPARATED...
...THE BIRTH OF THE TWINS, BUT IT MADE A HUGE DIFFERENCE.
RYUNG, THE FIRST SON, WASN'T BLESSED BY THE MOON. BI-WAL WAS BORN SECOND...BUT UNDER THE MOON'S WATCHFUL EYE...
!

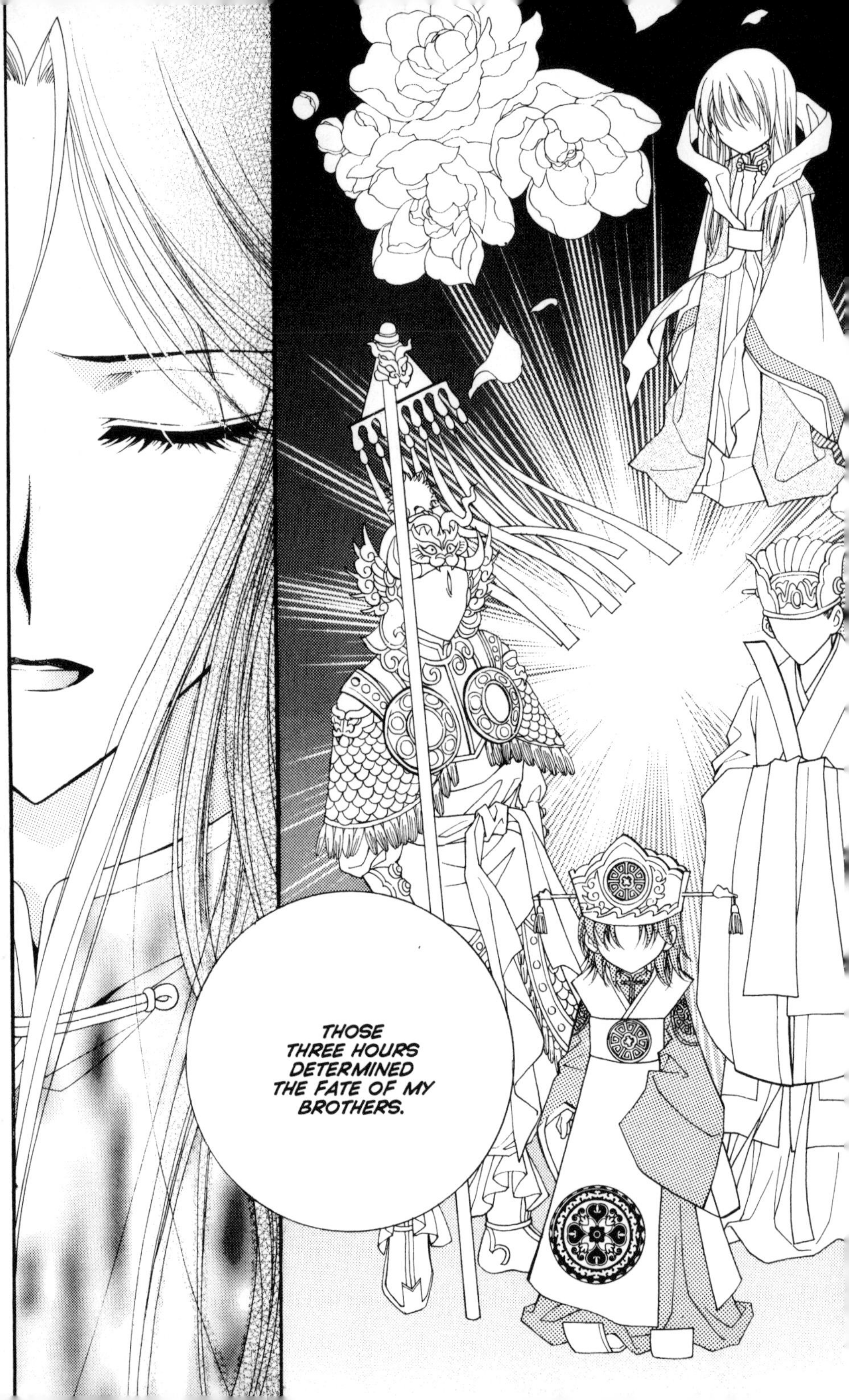
THOSE THREE HOURS DETERMINED THE FATE OF MY BROTHERS.

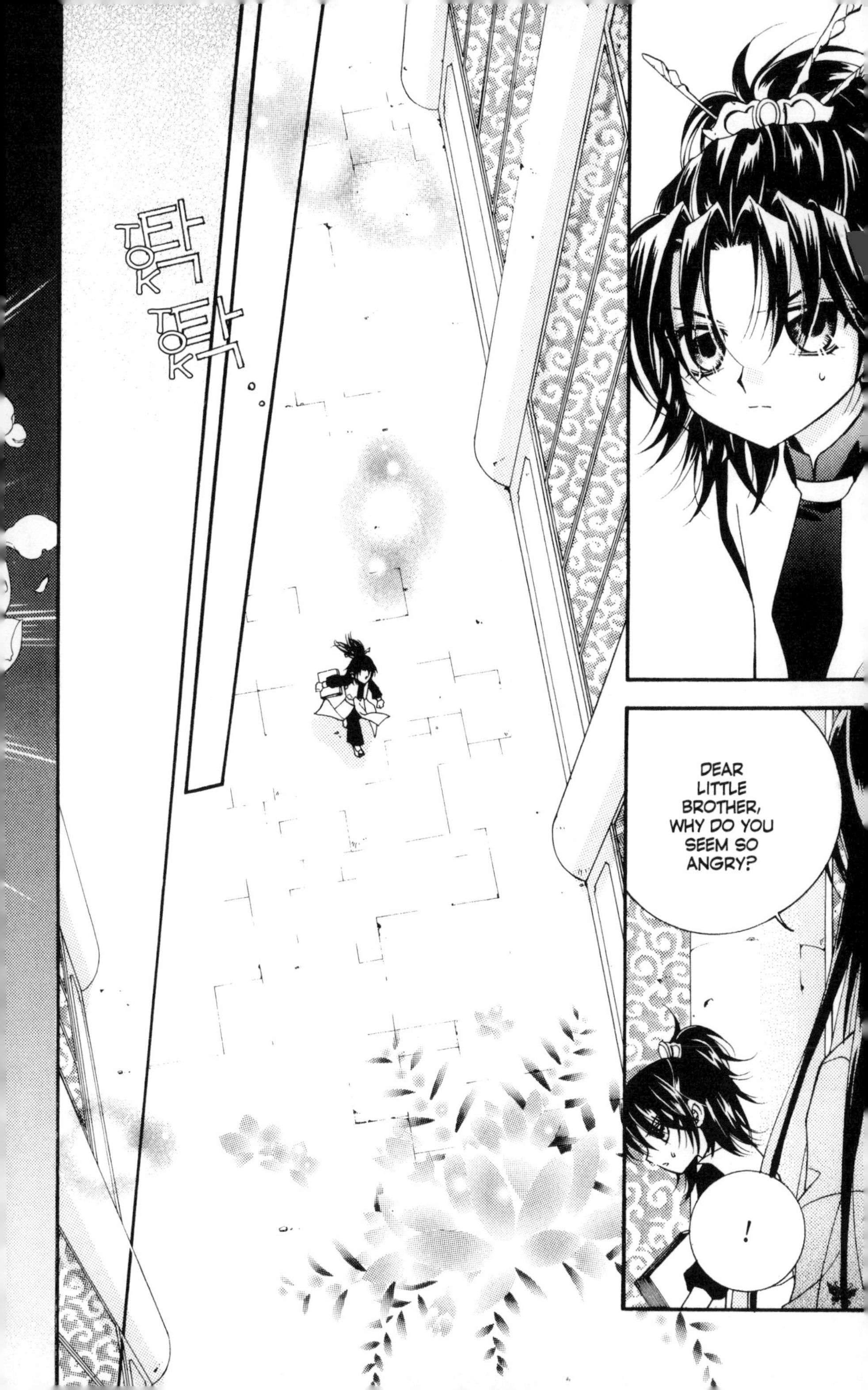
탁 TOK
탁 TOK
DEAR LITTLE BROTHER, WHY DO YOU SEEM SO ANGRY?
!

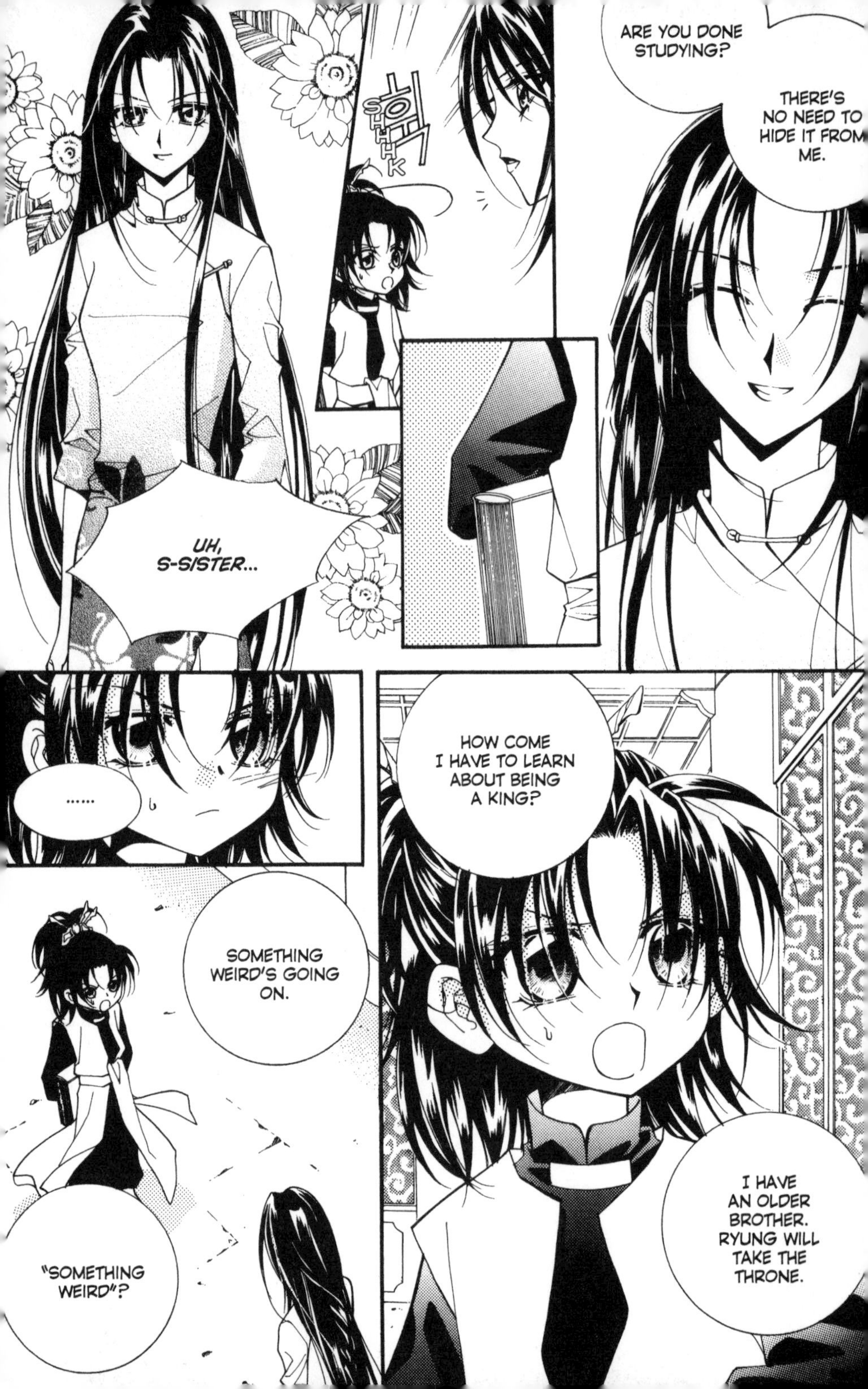
UH, S-SISTER...
SHHHHK
ARE YOU DONE STUDYING?
THERE'S NO NEED TO HIDE IT FROM ME.
......
SOMETHING WEIRD'S GOING ON.
"SOMETHING WEIRD"?
HOW COME I HAVE TO LEARN ABOUT BEING A KING?
I HAVE AN OLDER BROTHER. RYUNG WILL TAKE THE THRONE.

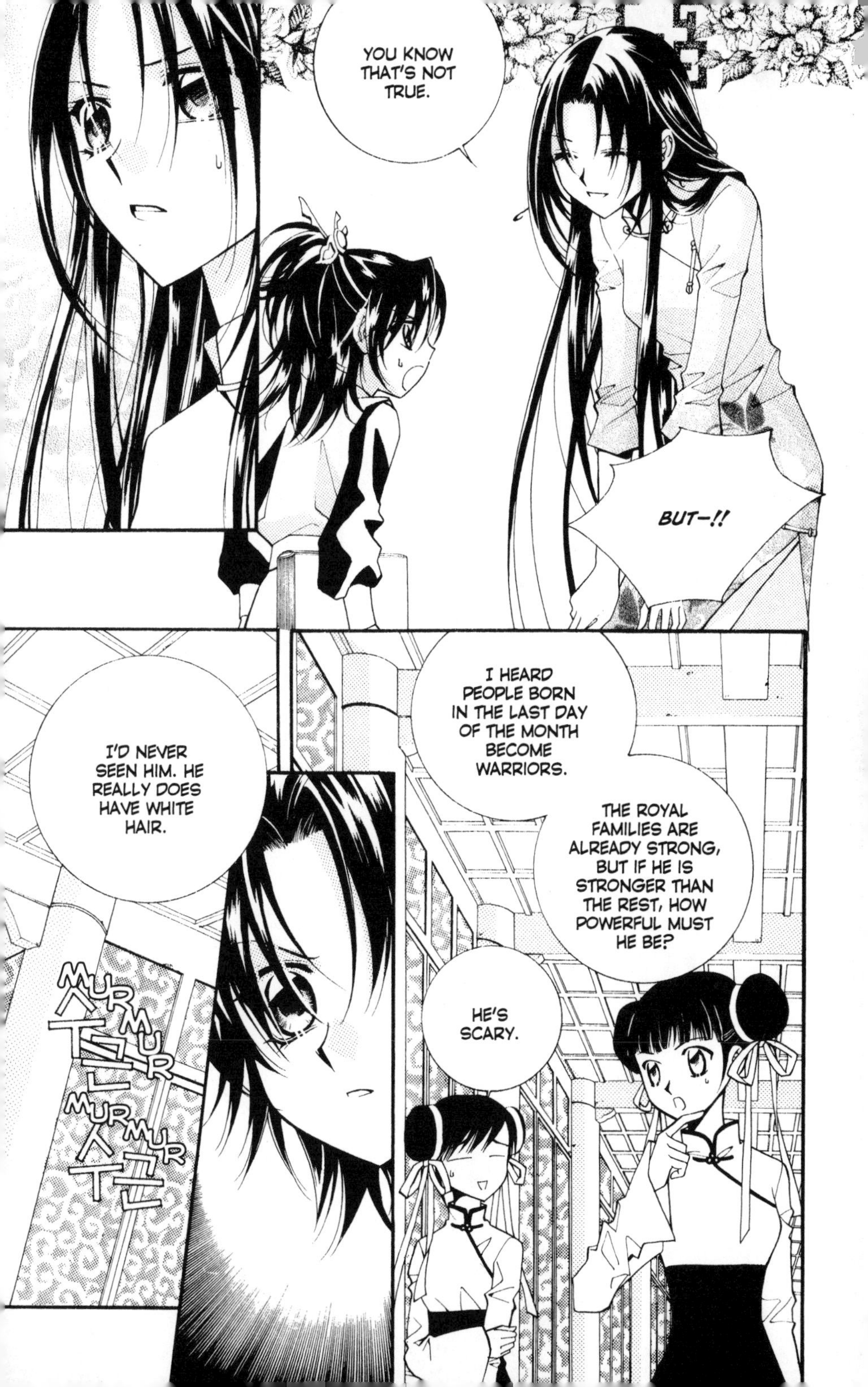
YOU KNOW THAT'S NOT TRUE.
BUT—!!
I'D NEVER SEEN HIM. HE REALLY DOES HAVE WHITE HAIR.
MURMUR
MURMUR
I HEARD PEOPLE BORN IN THE LAST DAY OF THE MONTH BECOME WARRIORS.
THE ROYAL FAMILIES ARE ALREADY STRONG, BUT IF HE IS STRONGER THAN THE REST, HOW POWERFUL MUST HE BE?
HE'S SCARY.

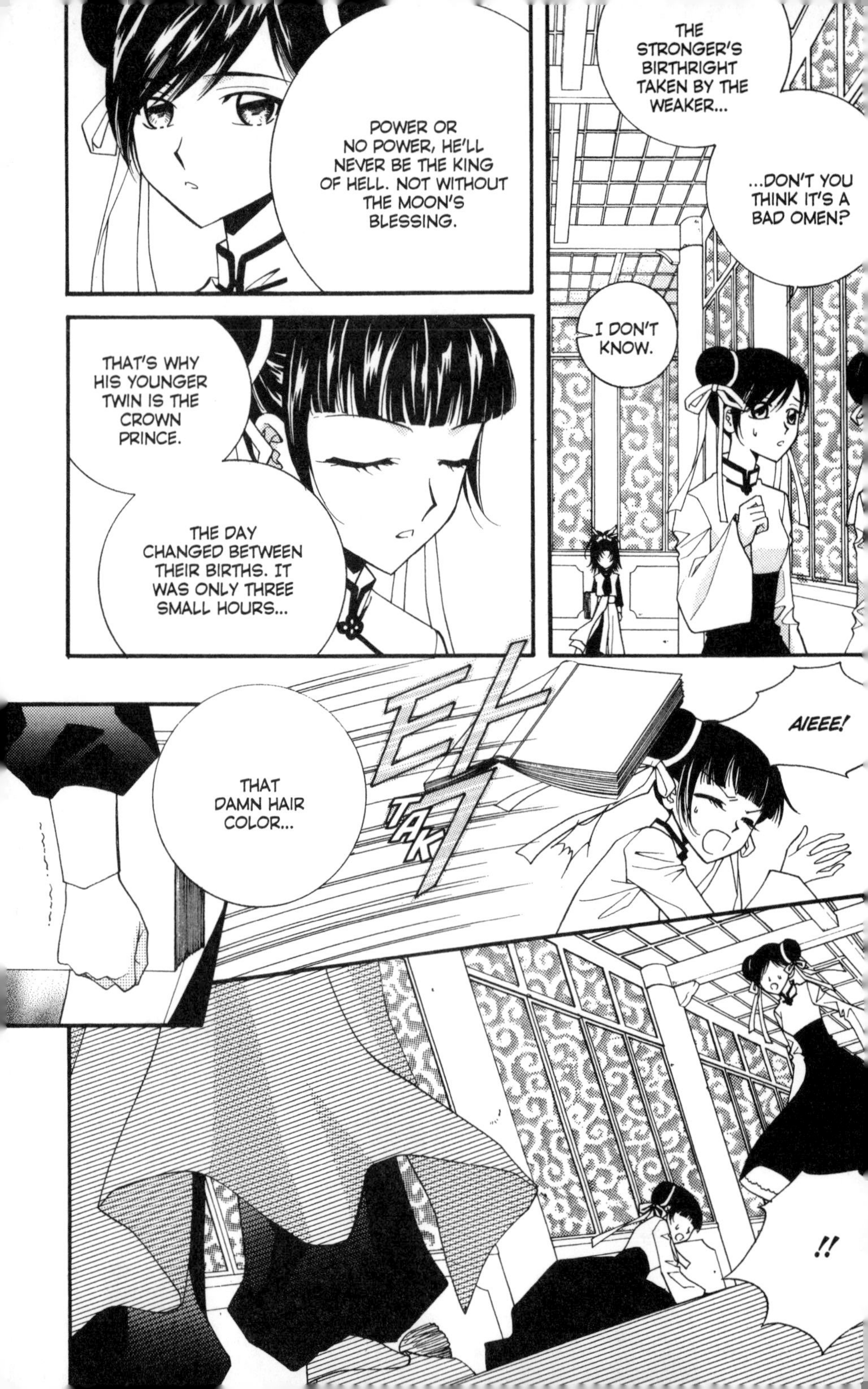
POWER OR NO POWER, HE'LL NEVER BE THE KING OF HELL. NOT WITHOUT THE MOON'S BLESSING.
THAT'S WHY HIS YOUNGER TWIN IS THE CROWN PRINCE.
THE DAY CHANGED BETWEEN THEIR BIRTHS. IT WAS ONLY THREE SMALL HOURS...
THE STRONGER'S BIRTHRIGHT TAKEN BY THE WEAKER...
...DON'T YOU THINK IT'S A BAD OMEN?
I DON'T KNOW.
THAT DAMN HAIR COLOR...
TAK
AIEEE!
!!

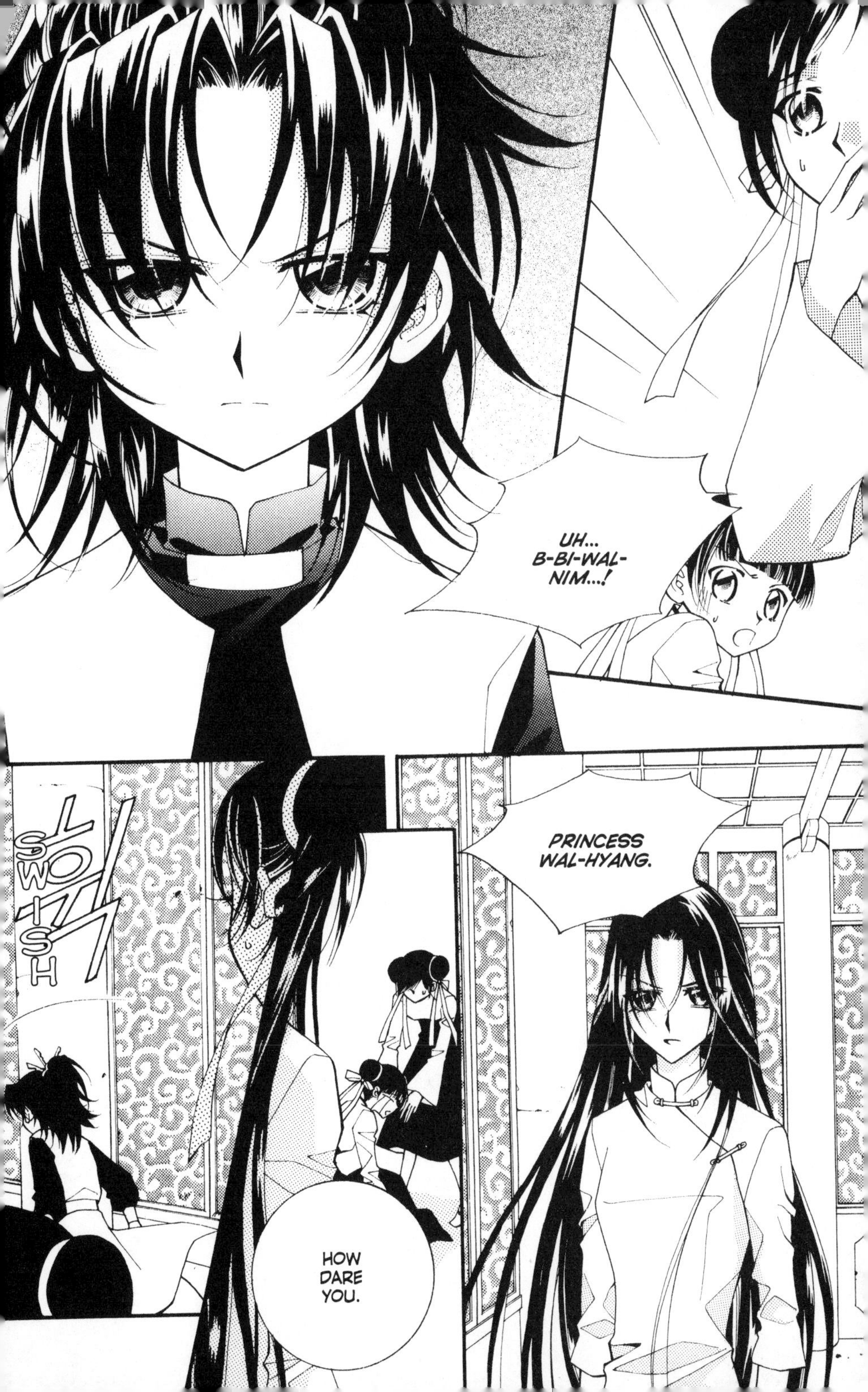
UH... B-BI-WAL-NIM...!
SWISH
PRINCESS WAL-HYANG.
HOW DARE YOU.

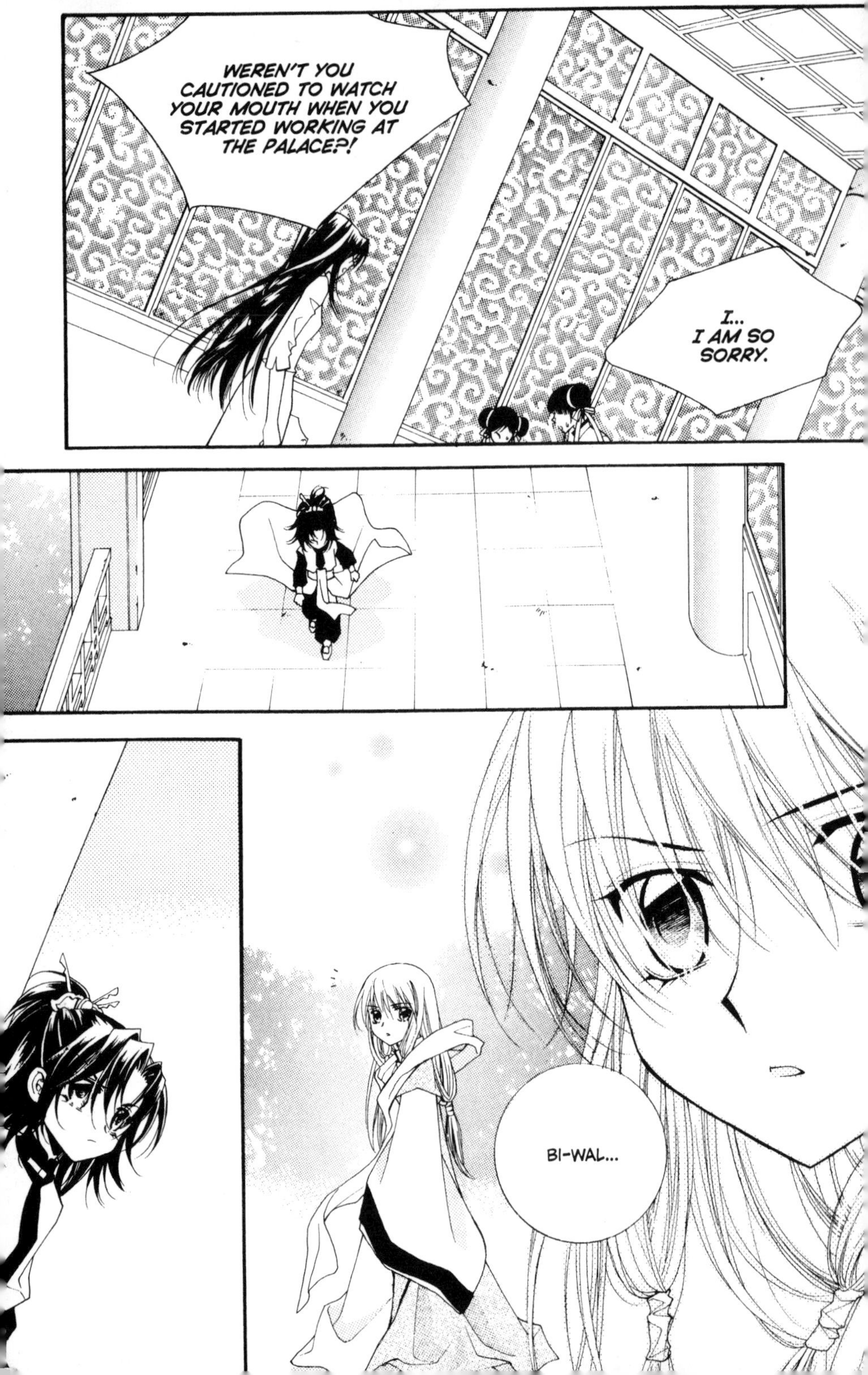
WEREN'T YOU CAUTIONED TO WATCH YOUR MOUTH WHEN YOU STARTED WORKING AT THE PALACE?!
I... I AM SO SORRY.
BI-WAL...

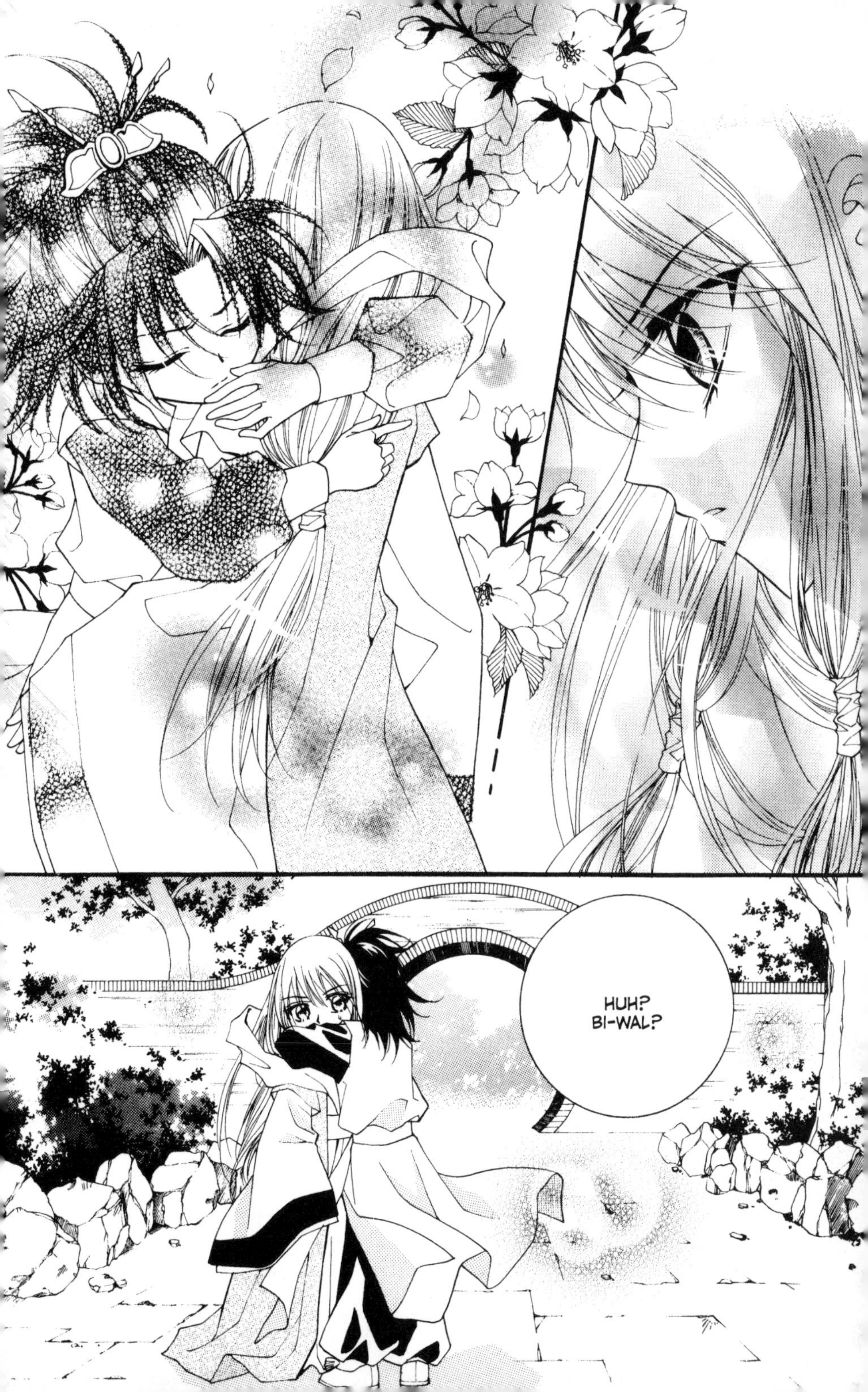
HUH?
BI-WAL?

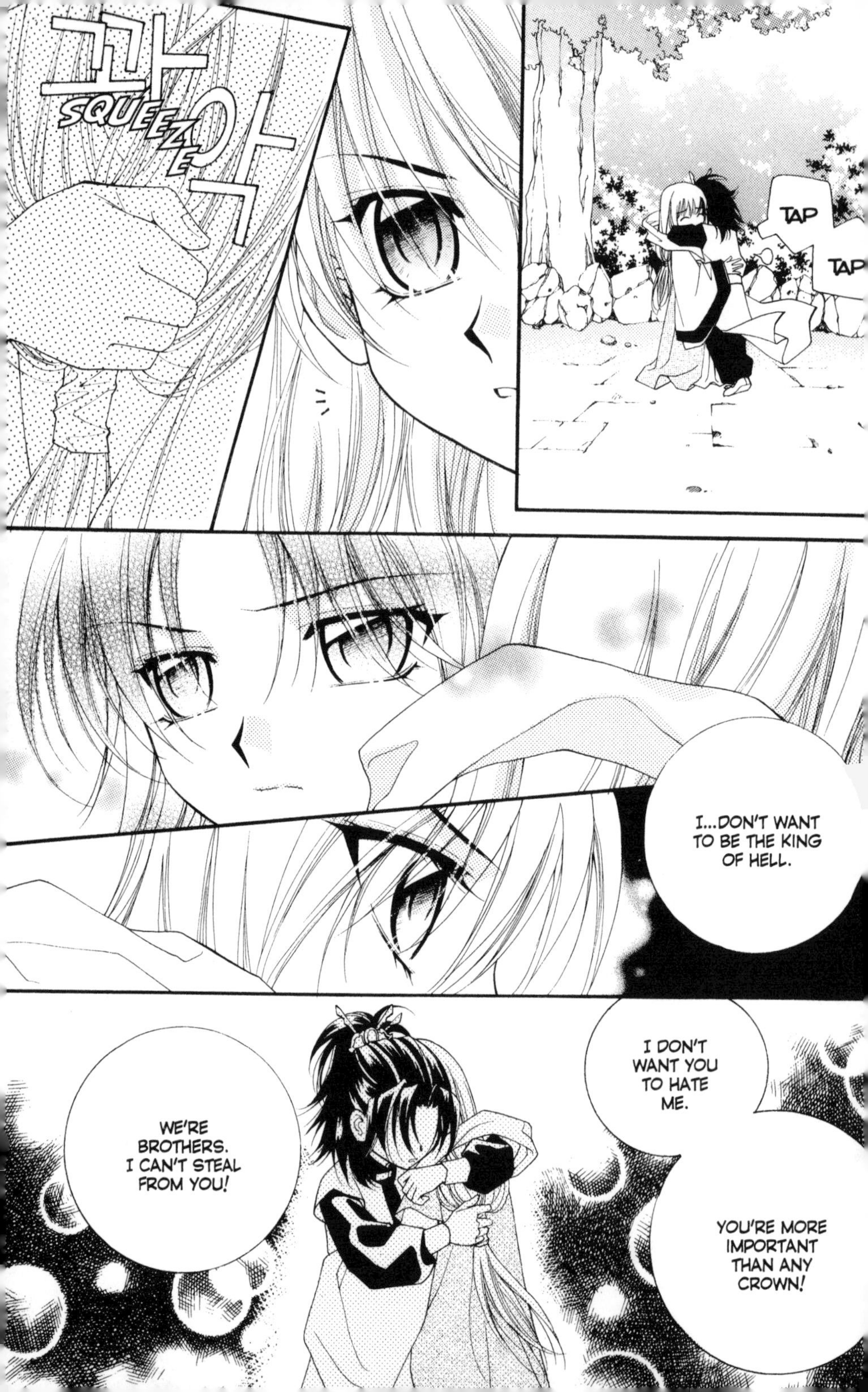
꼬아악
SQUEEZE
TAP
TAP
I...DON'T WANT TO BE THE KING OF HELL.
WE'RE BROTHERS. I CAN'T STEAL FROM YOU!
I DON'T WANT YOU TO HATE ME.
YOU'RE MORE IMPORTANT THAN ANY CROWN!

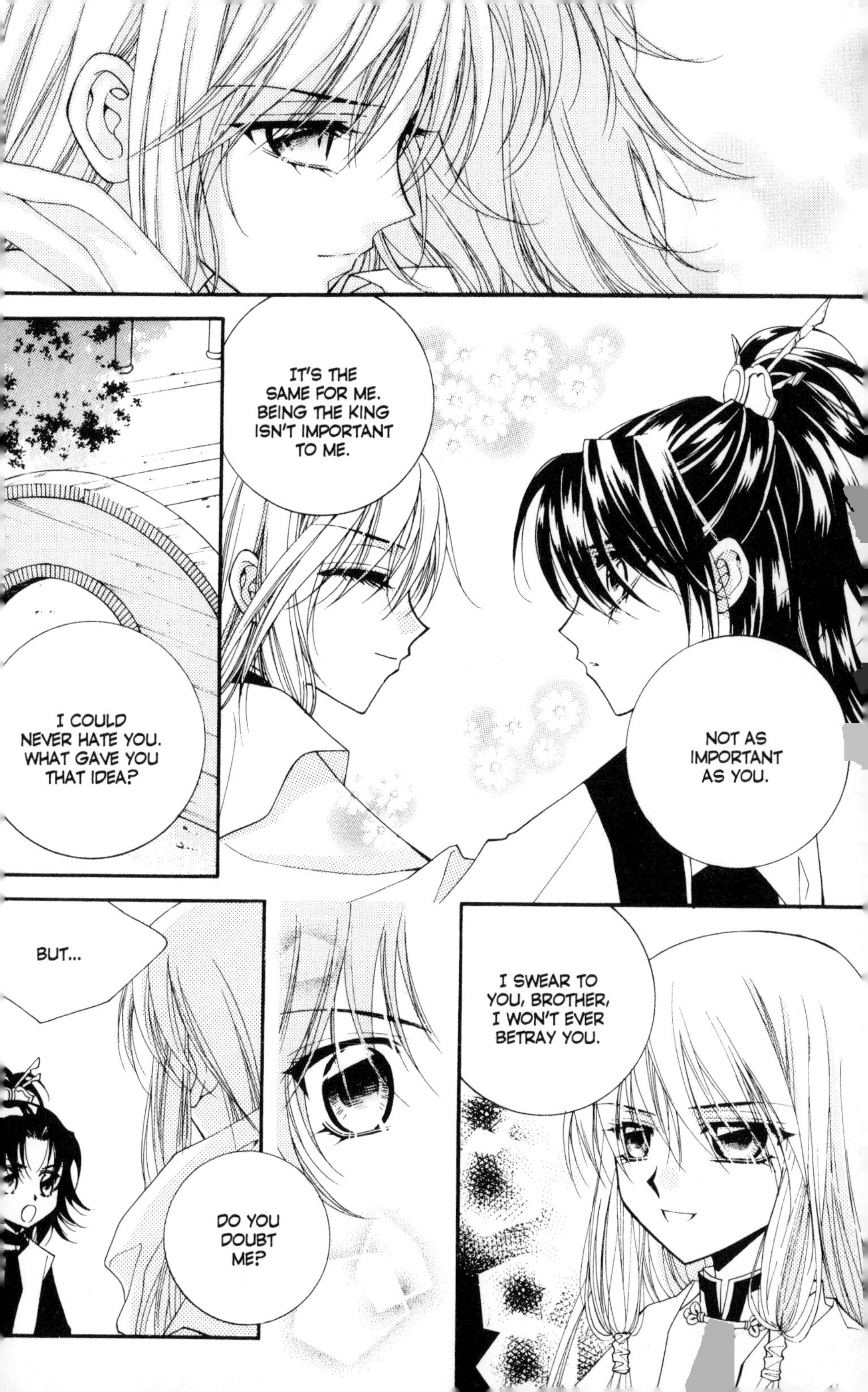
I COULD NEVER HATE YOU. WHAT GAVE YOU THAT IDEA?
IT'S THE SAME FOR ME. BEING THE KING ISN'T IMPORTANT TO ME.
NOT AS IMPORTANT AS YOU.
BUT...
DO YOU DOUBT ME?
I SWEAR TO YOU, BROTHER, I WON'T EVER BETRAY YOU.

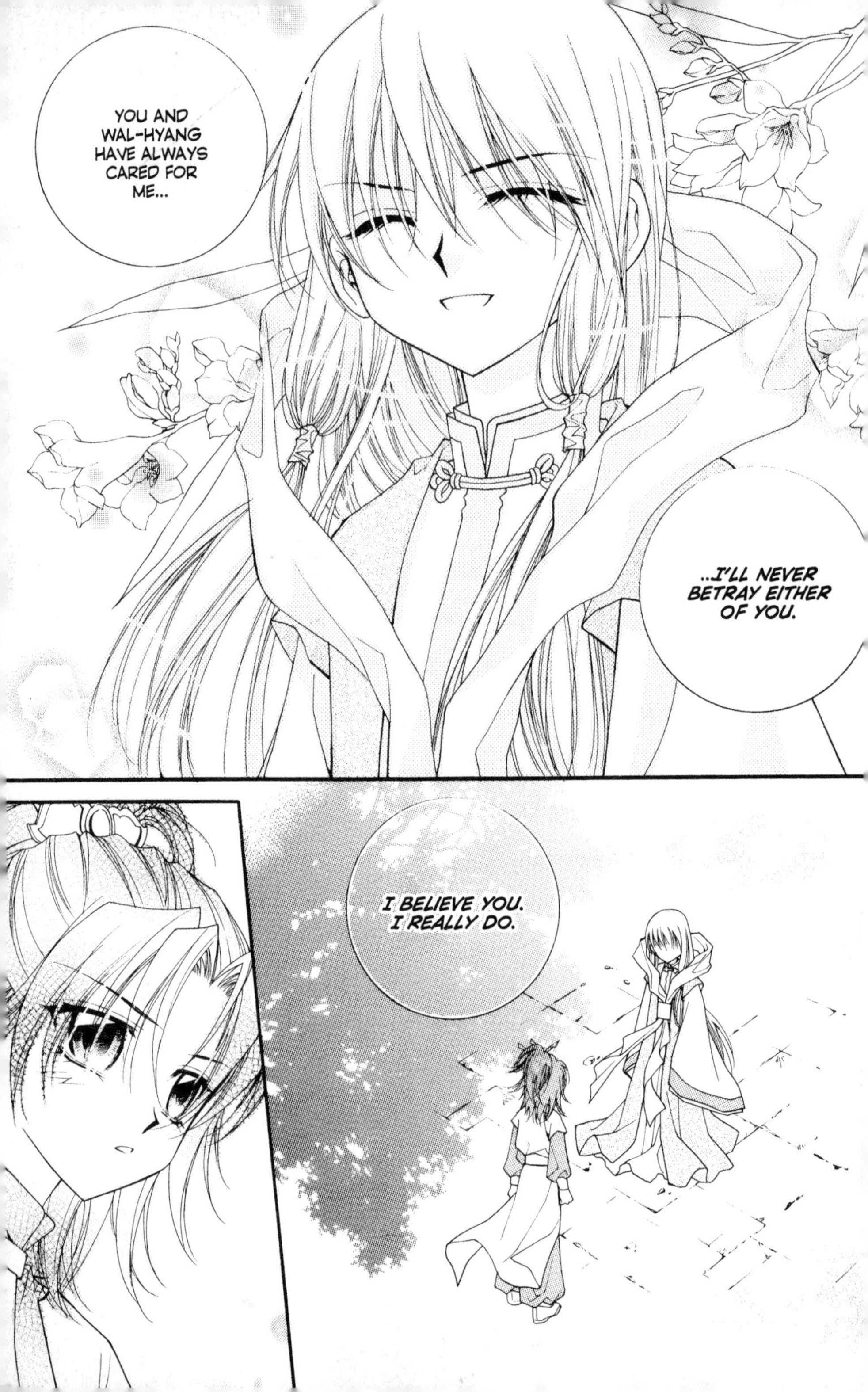
YOU AND WAL-HYANG HAVE ALWAYS CARED FOR ME...
...I'LL NEVER BETRAY EITHER OF YOU.
I BELIEVE YOU. I REALLY DO.

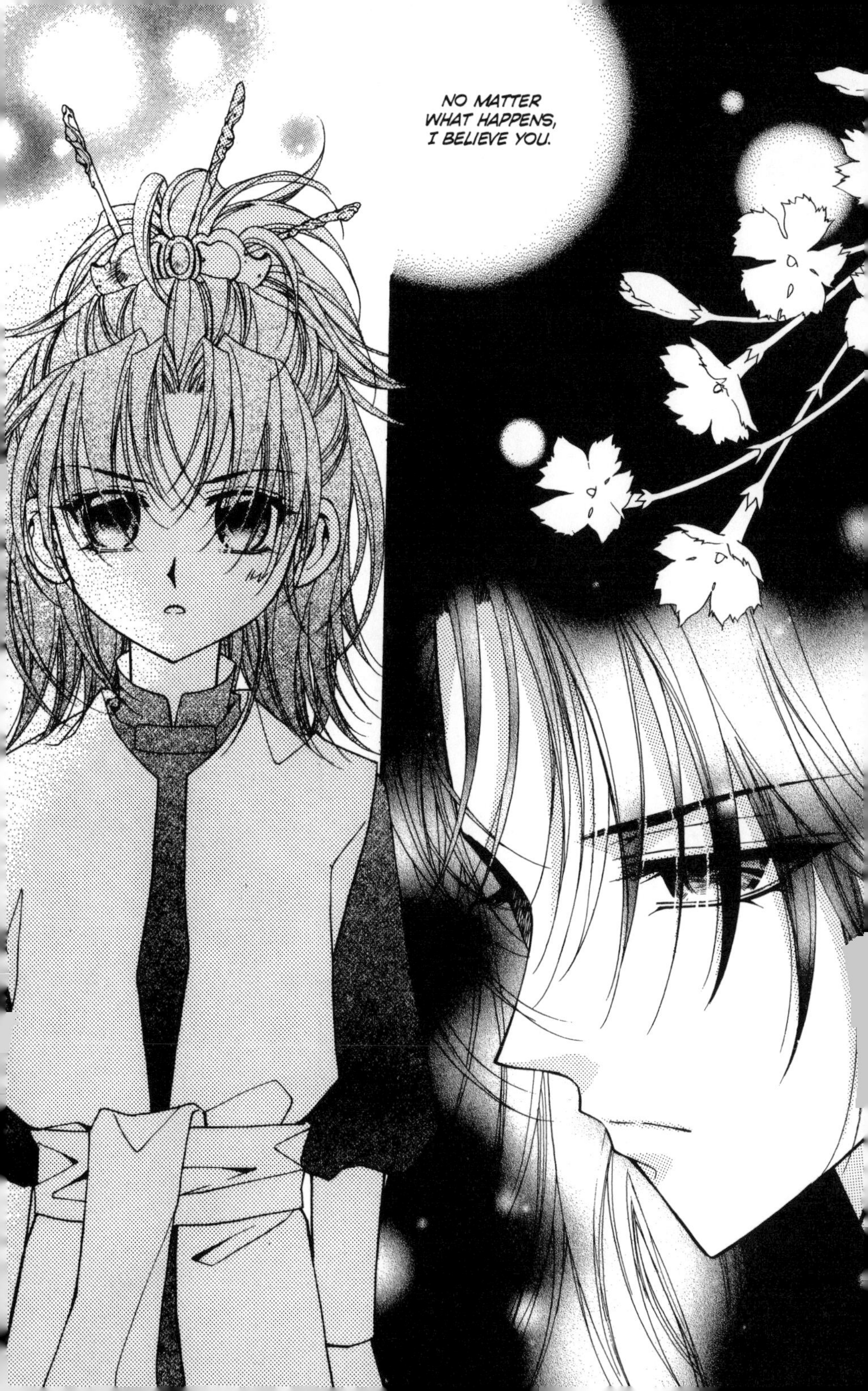
NO MATTER WHAT HAPPENS, I BELIEVE YOU.

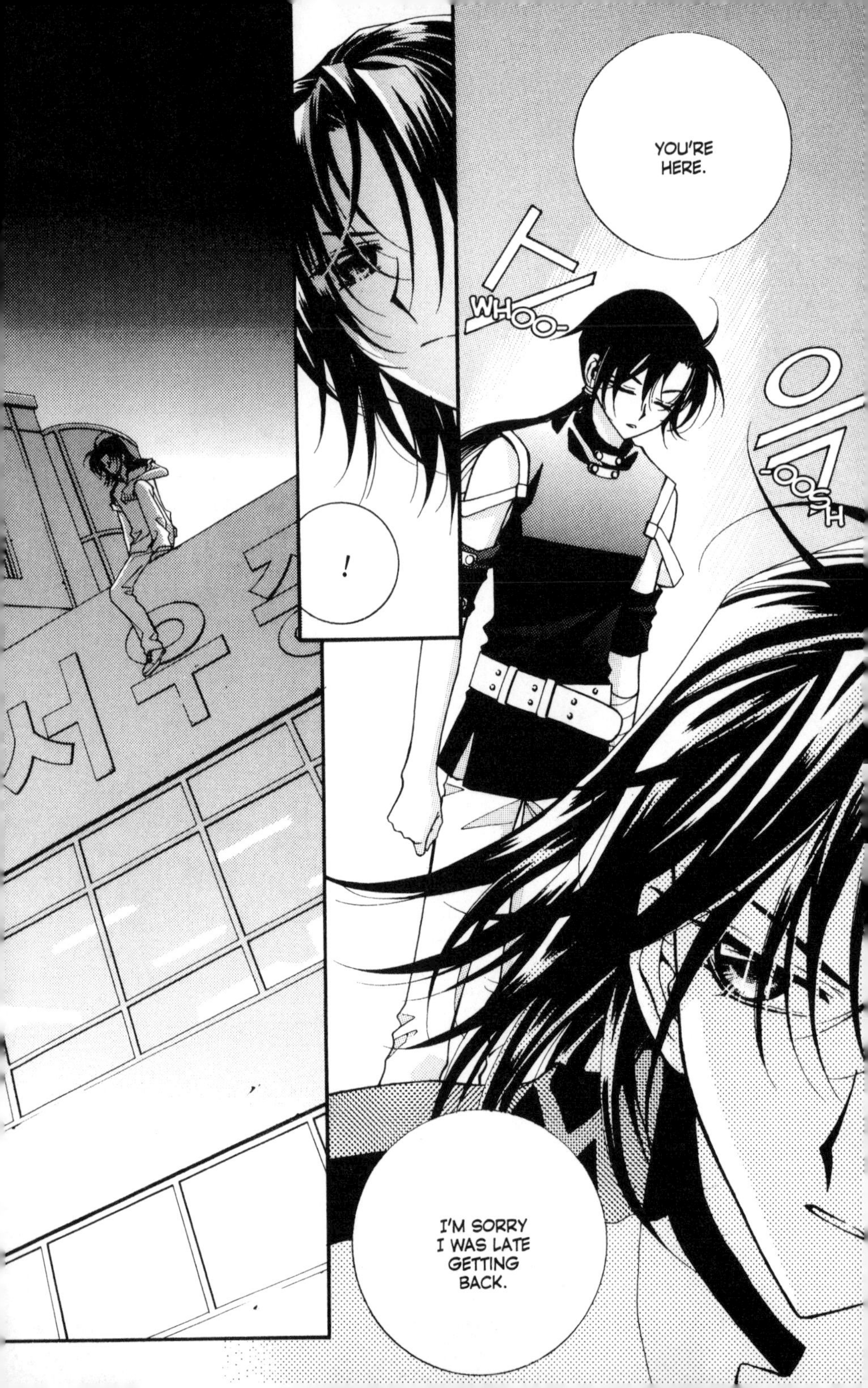
!
YOU'RE HERE.
WHOO-
-OOSH
I'M SORRY I WAS LATE GETTING BACK.

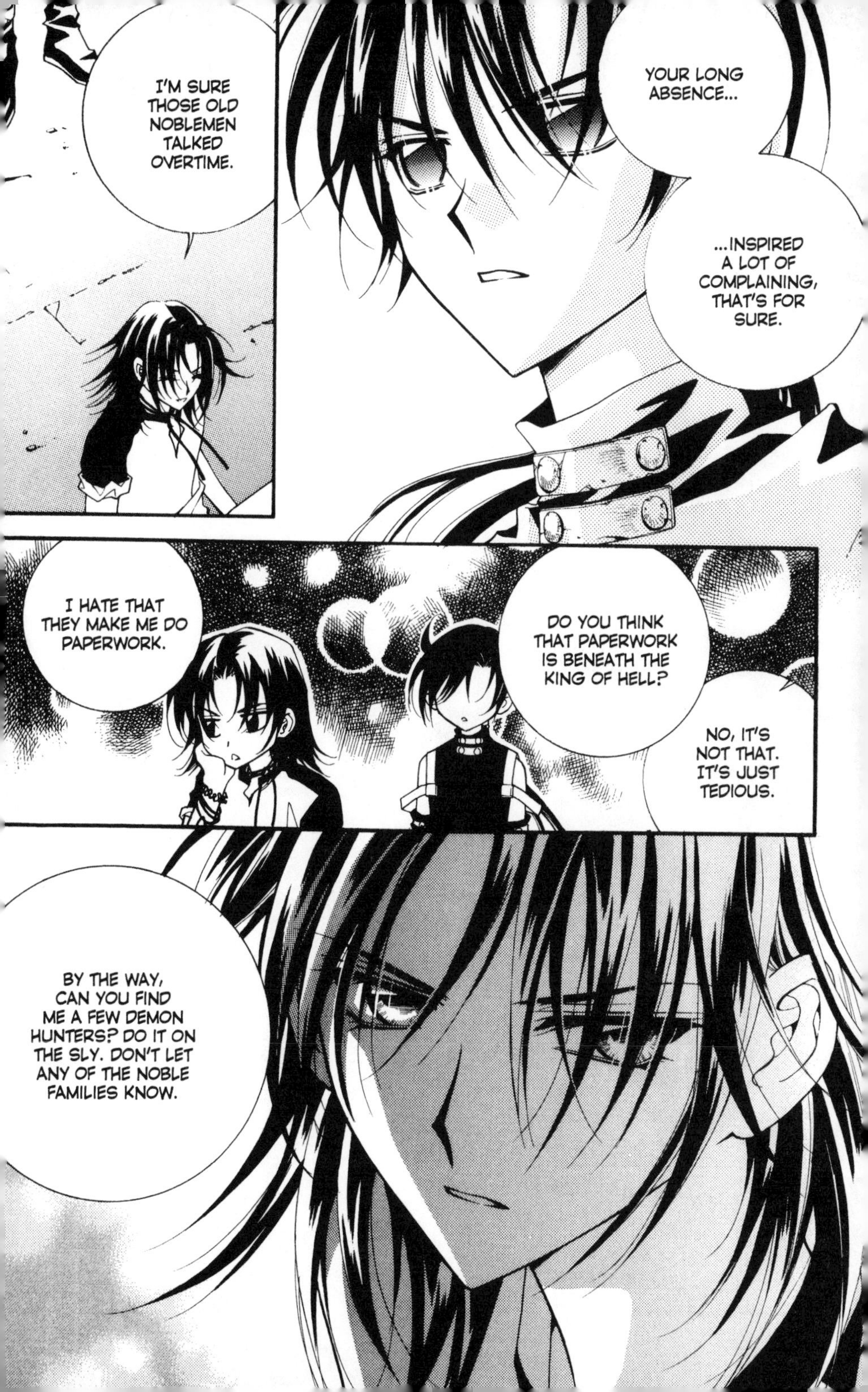
I'M SURE THOSE OLD NOBLEMEN TALKED OVERTIME.
YOUR LONG ABSENCE...
...INSPIRED A LOT OF COMPLAINING, THAT'S FOR SURE.
I HATE THAT THEY MAKE ME DO PAPERWORK.
DO YOU THINK THAT PAPERWORK IS BENEATH THE KING OF HELL?
NO, IT'S NOT THAT. IT'S JUST TEDIOUS.
BY THE WAY, CAN YOU FIND ME A FEW DEMON HUNTERS? DO IT ON THE SLY. DON'T LET ANY OF THE NOBLE FAMILIES KNOW.

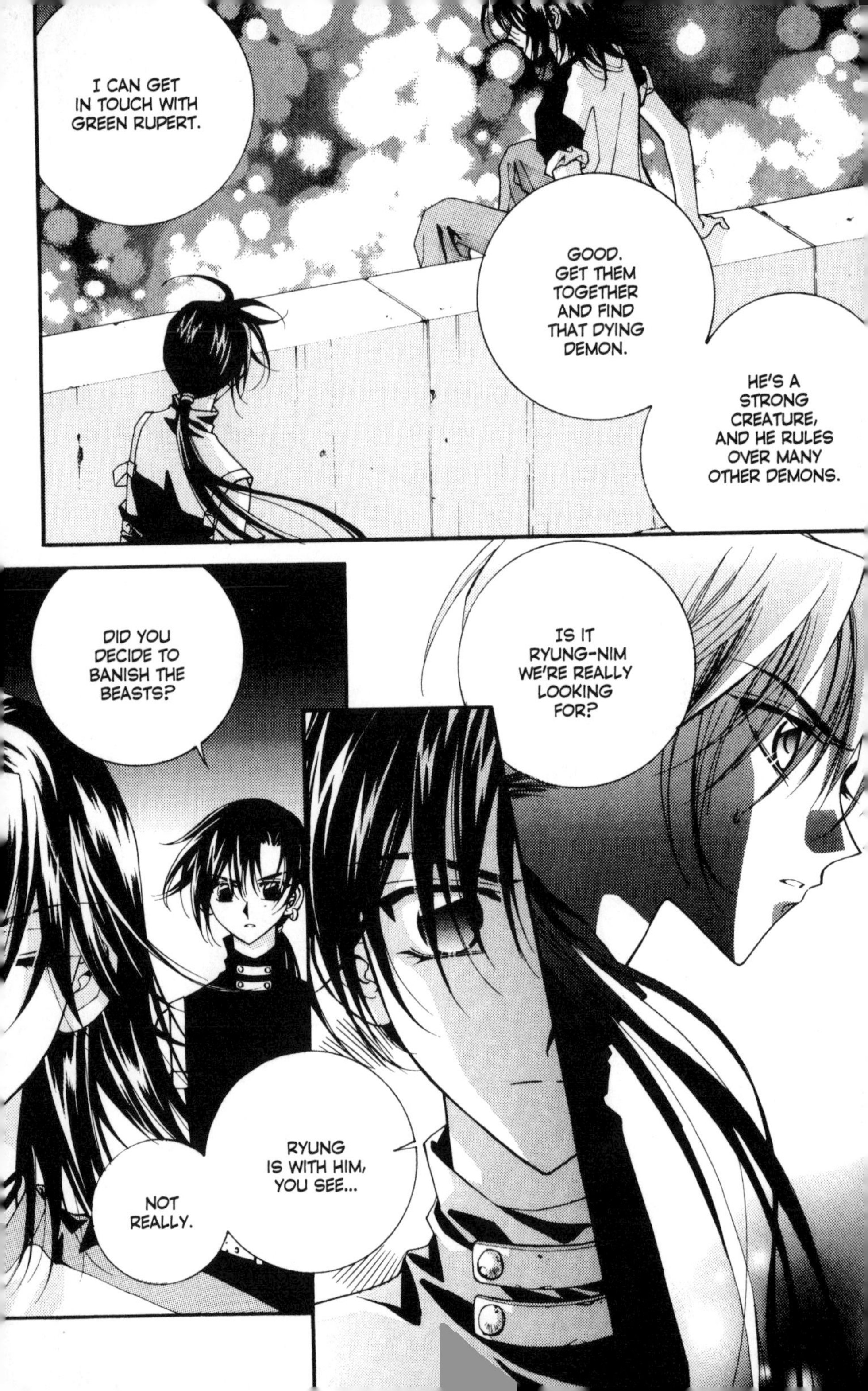
I CAN GET IN TOUCH WITH GREEN RUPERT.
GOOD. GET THEM TOGETHER AND FIND THAT DYING DEMON.
HE'S A STRONG CREATURE, AND HE RULES OVER MANY OTHER DEMONS.
DID YOU DECIDE TO BANISH THE BEASTS?
IS IT RYUNG-NIM WE'RE REALLY LOOKING FOR?
NOT REALLY.
RYUNG IS WITH HIM, YOU SEE...

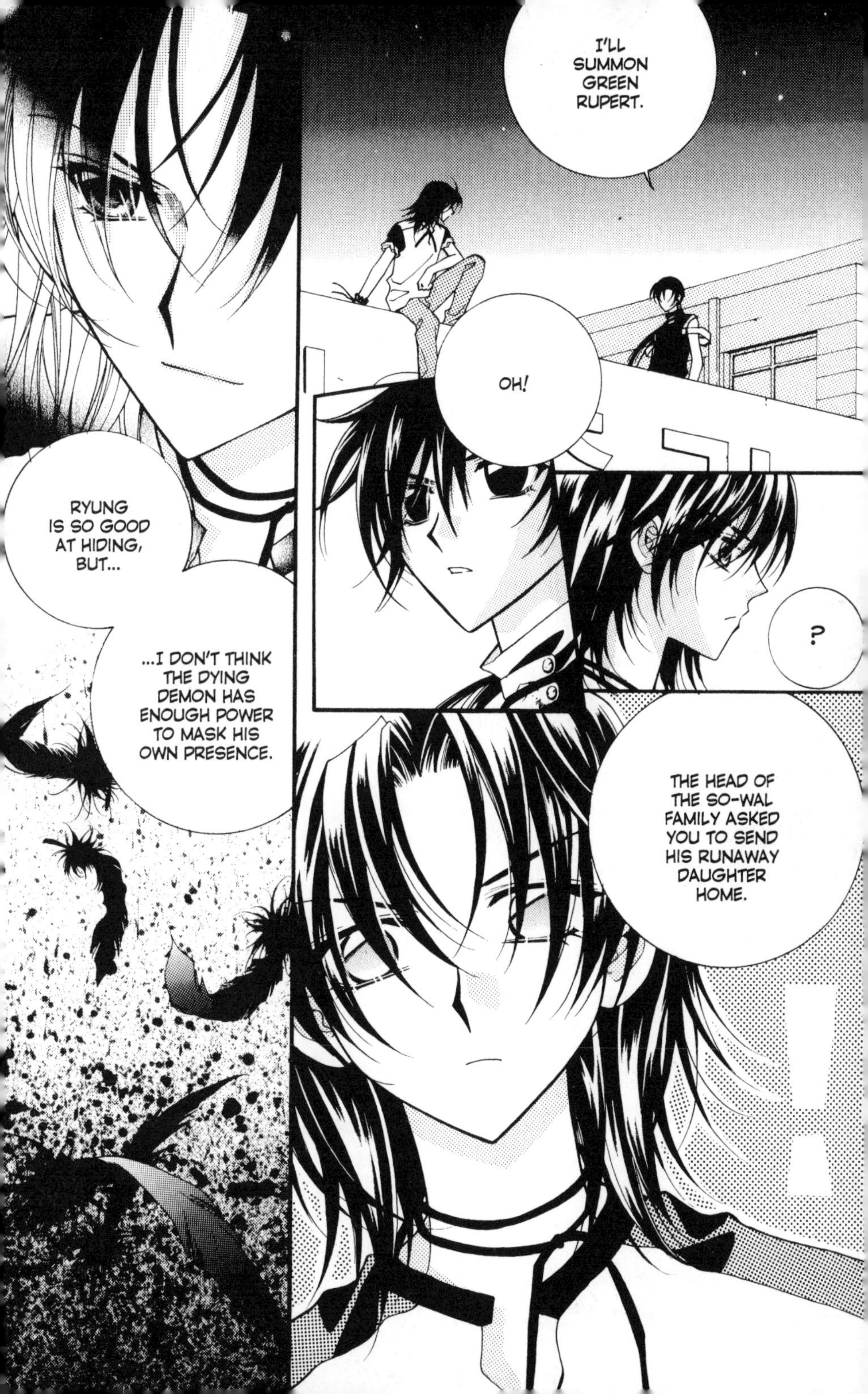
RYUNG IS SO GOOD AT HIDING, BUT...
...I DON'T THINK THE DYING DEMON HAS ENOUGH POWER TO MASK HIS OWN PRESENCE.
I'LL SUMMON GREEN RUPERT.
OH!
?
THE HEAD OF THE SO-WAL FAMILY ASKED YOU TO SEND HIS RUNAWAY DAUGHTER HOME.
!

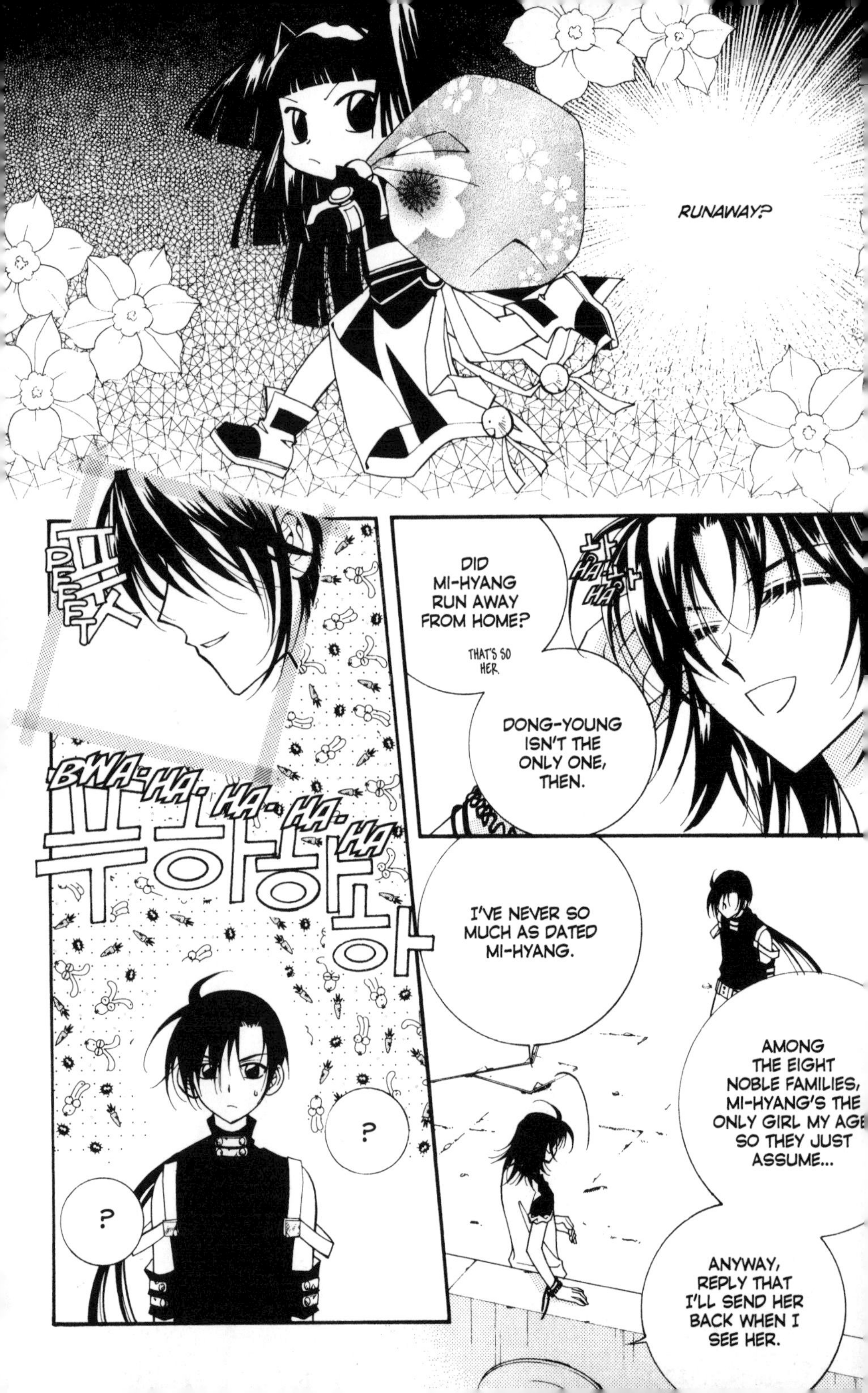

RUNAWAY?
PFFT
DID MI-HYANG RUN AWAY FROM HOME?
HA HA
THAT'S SO HER.
DONG-YOUNG ISN'T THE ONLY ONE, THEN.
BWA-HA-HA-HA-HA
?
?
I'VE NEVER SO MUCH AS DATED MI-HYANG.
AMONG THE EIGHT NOBLE FAMILIES, MI-HYANG'S THE ONLY GIRL MY AGE SO THEY JUST ASSUME...
ANYWAY, REPLY THAT I'LL SEND HER BACK WHEN I SEE HER.

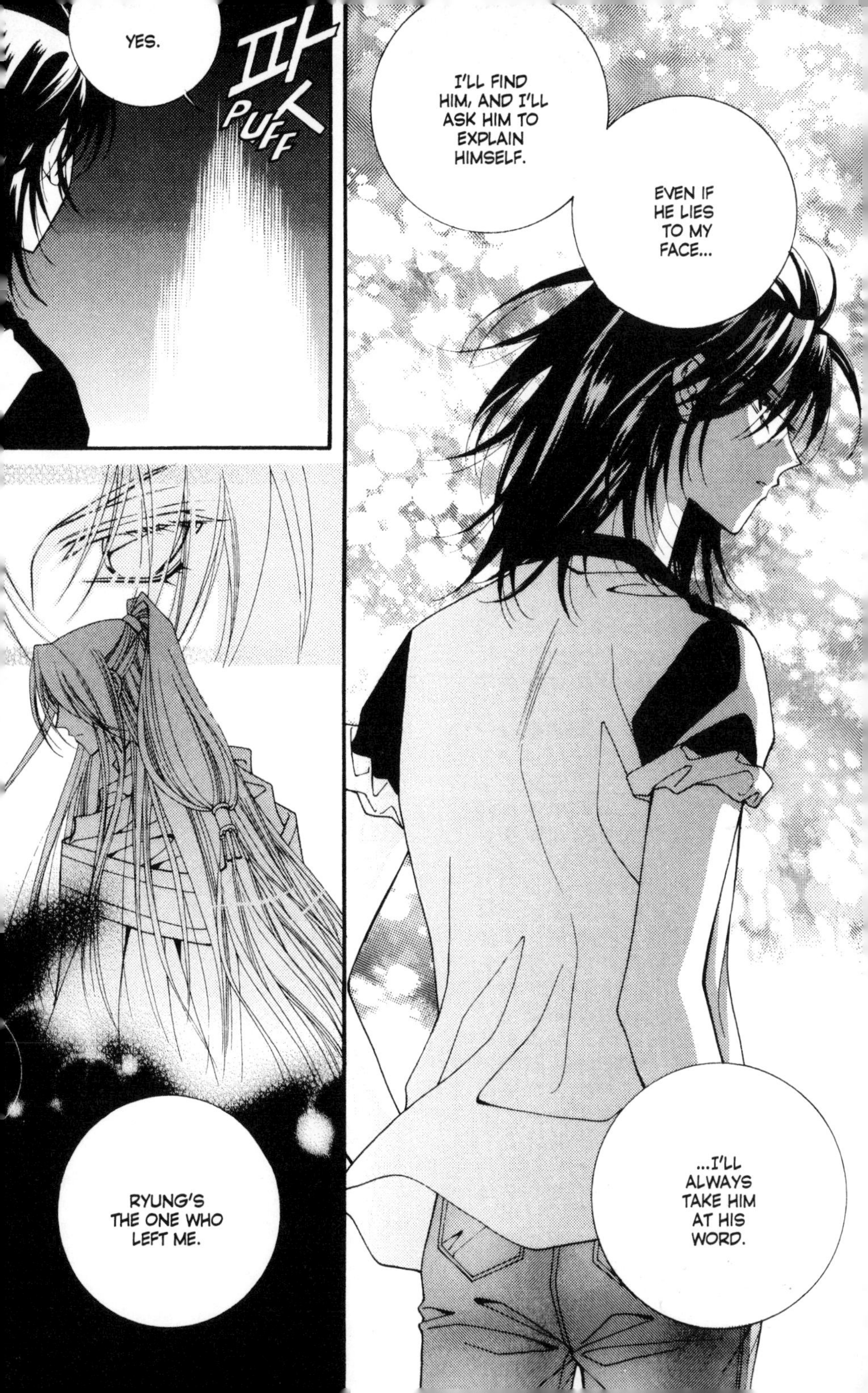
YES.
PUFF
RYUNG'S THE ONE WHO LEFT ME.
I'LL FIND HIM, AND I'LL ASK HIM TO EXPLAIN HIMSELF.
EVEN IF HE LIES TO MY FACE...
...I'LL ALWAYS TAKE HIM AT HIS WORD.

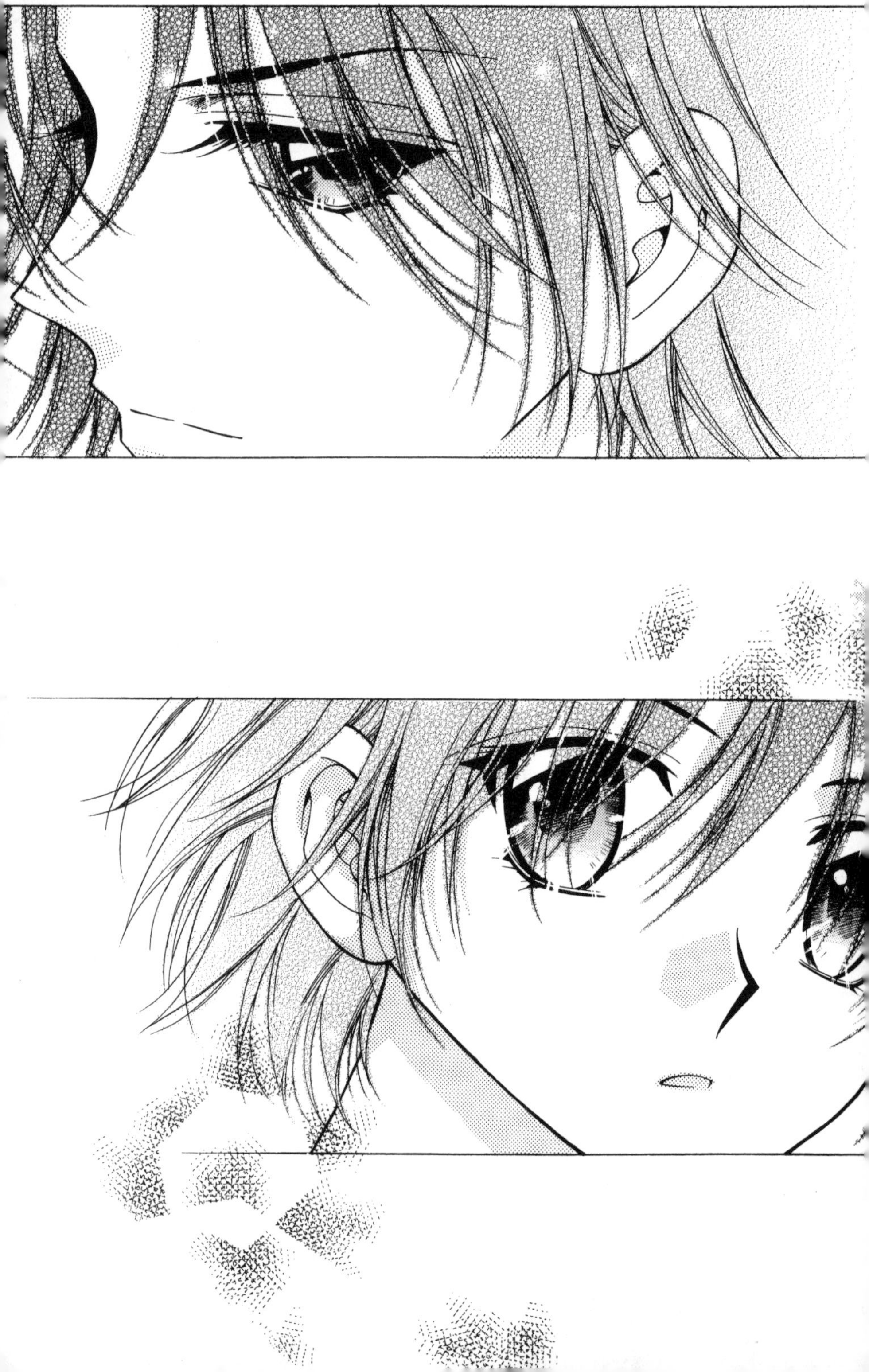

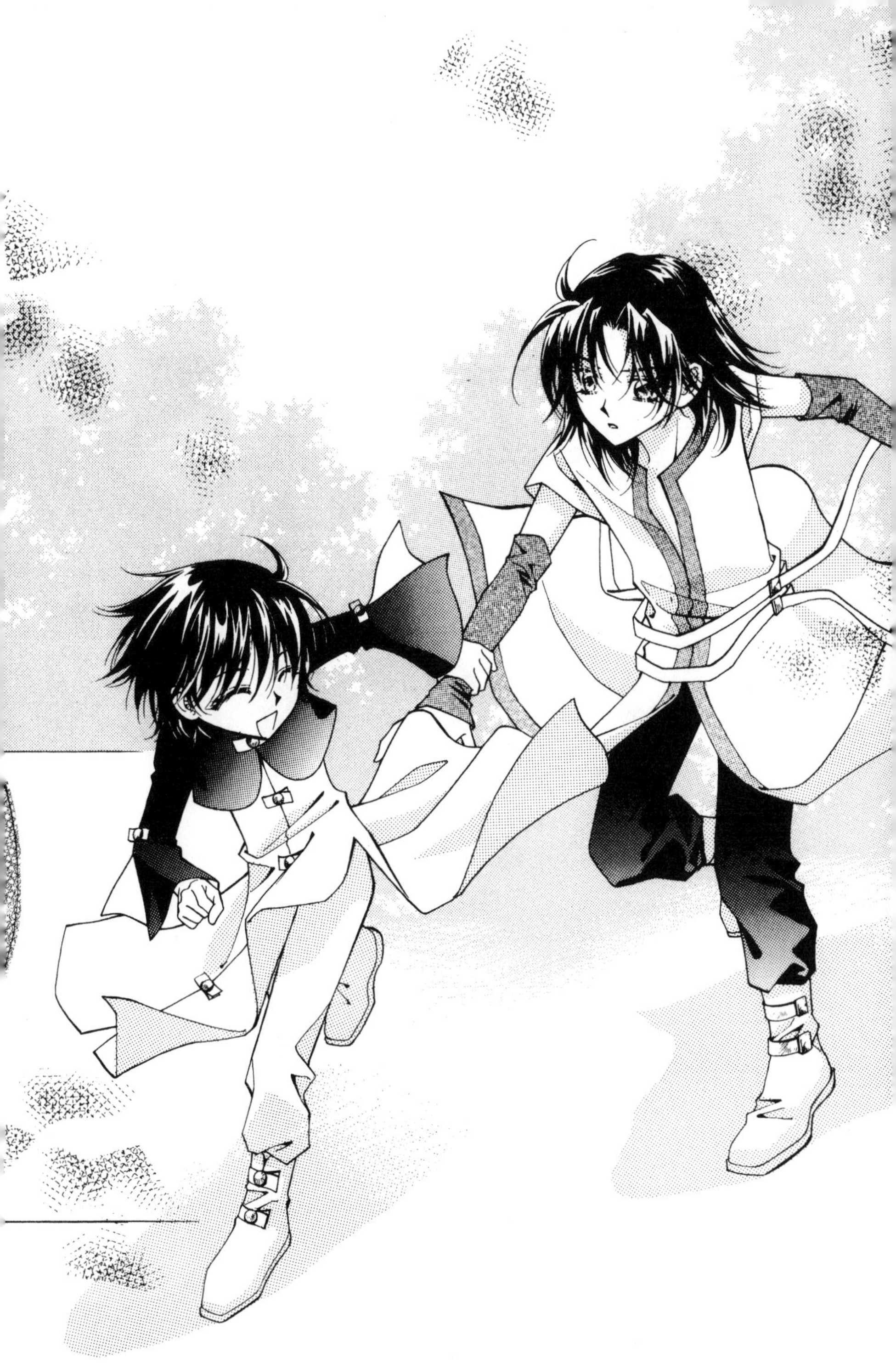

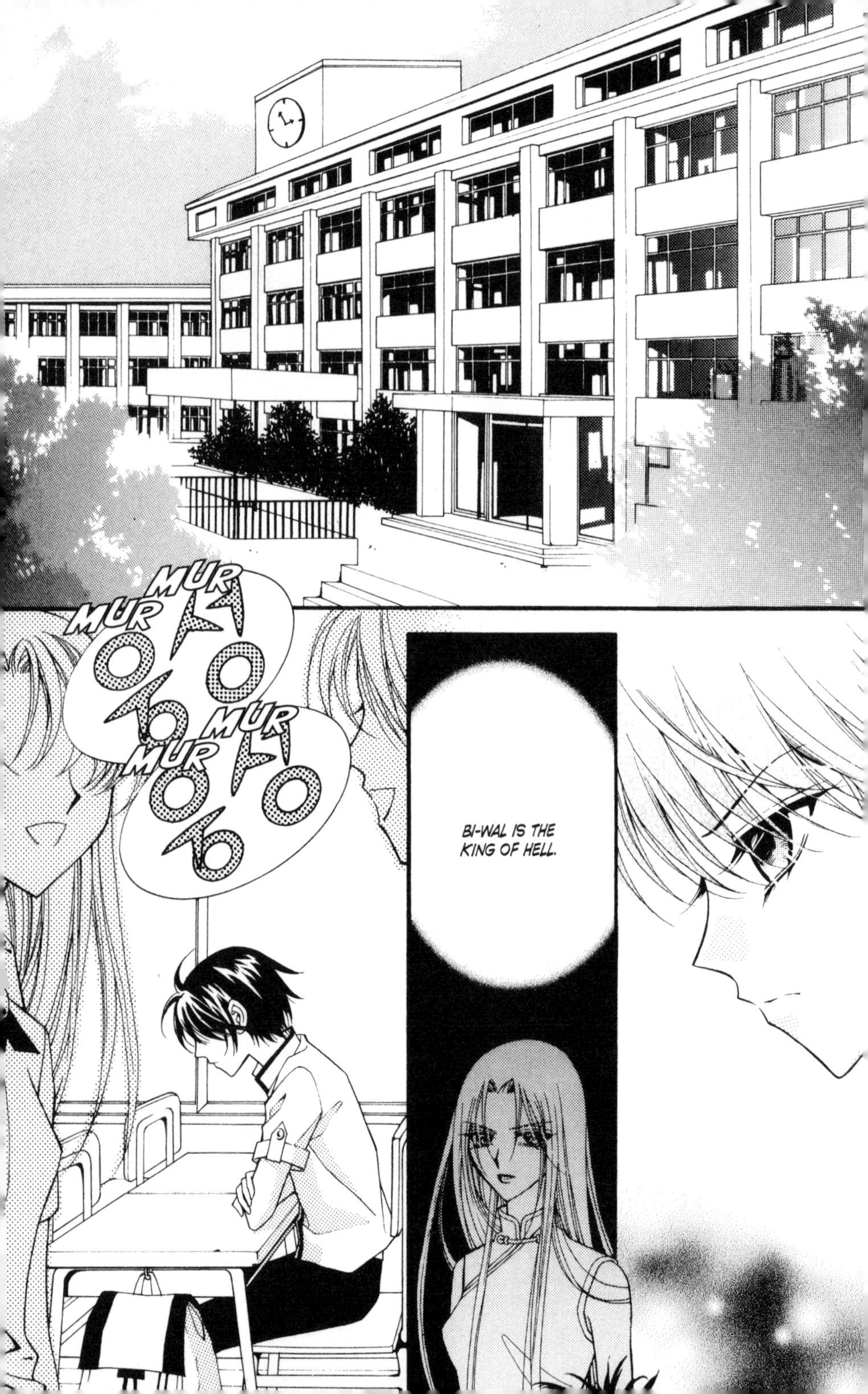
MUR MUR
MUR MUR
BI-WAL IS THE KING OF HELL.

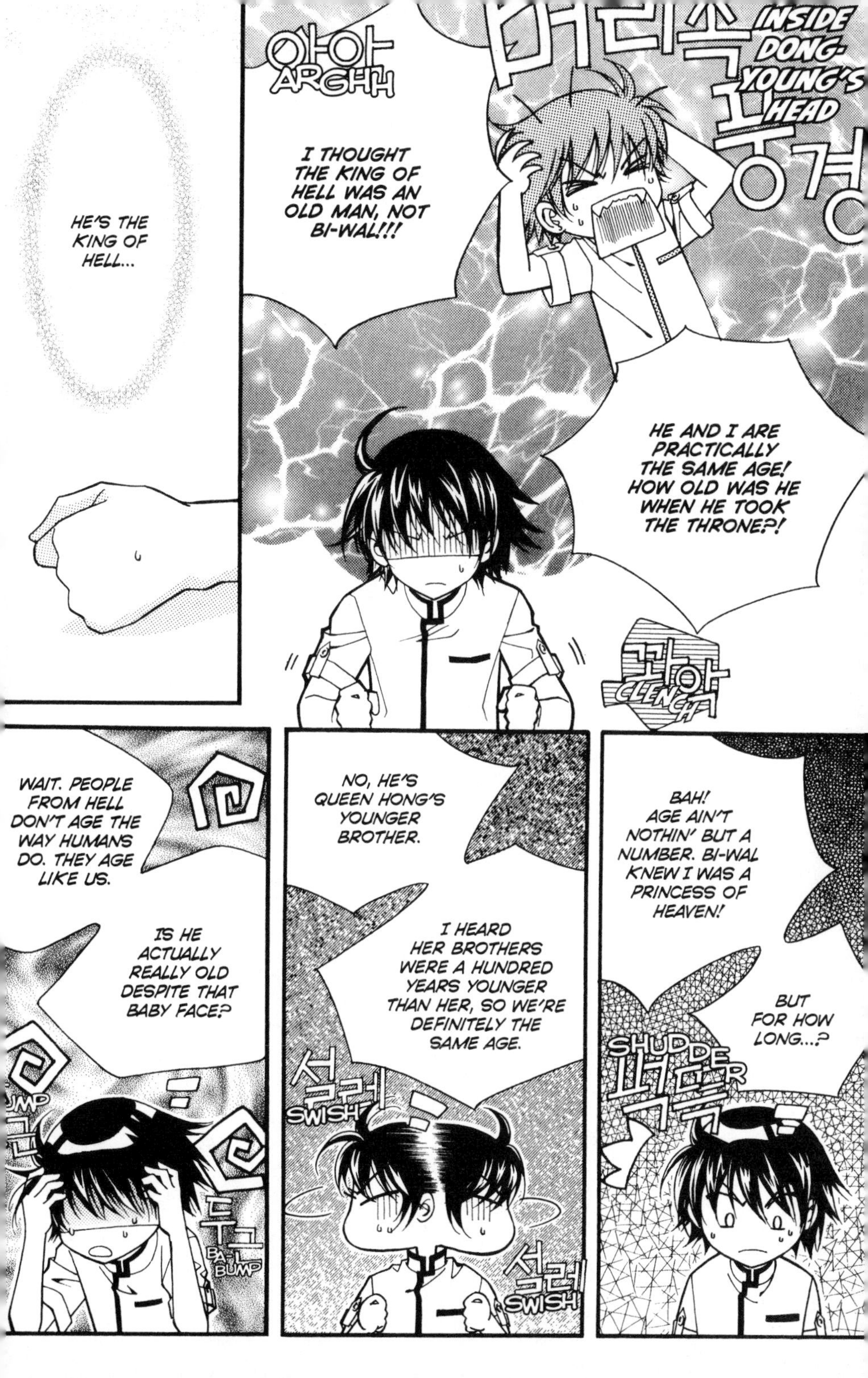
HE'S THE KING OF HELL...
아아
ARGHH
INSIDE DONG-YOUNG'S HEAD
I THOUGHT THE KING OF HELL WAS AN OLD MAN, NOT BI-WAL!!!
HE AND I ARE PRACTICALLY THE SAME AGE! HOW OLD WAS HE WHEN HE TOOK THE THRONE?!
CLENCH
WAIT. PEOPLE FROM HELL DON'T AGE THE WAY HUMANS DO. THEY AGE LIKE US.
IS HE ACTUALLY REALLY OLD DESPITE THAT BABY FACE?
BA-BUMP
NO, HE'S QUEEN HONG'S YOUNGER BROTHER.
I HEARD HER BROTHERS WERE A HUNDRED YEARS YOUNGER THAN HER, SO WE'RE DEFINITELY THE SAME AGE.
SWISH
SWISH
BAH! AGE AIN'T NOTHIN' BUT A NUMBER. BI-WAL KNEW I WAS A PRINCESS OF HEAVEN!
BUT FOR HOW LONG...?
SHUDDER

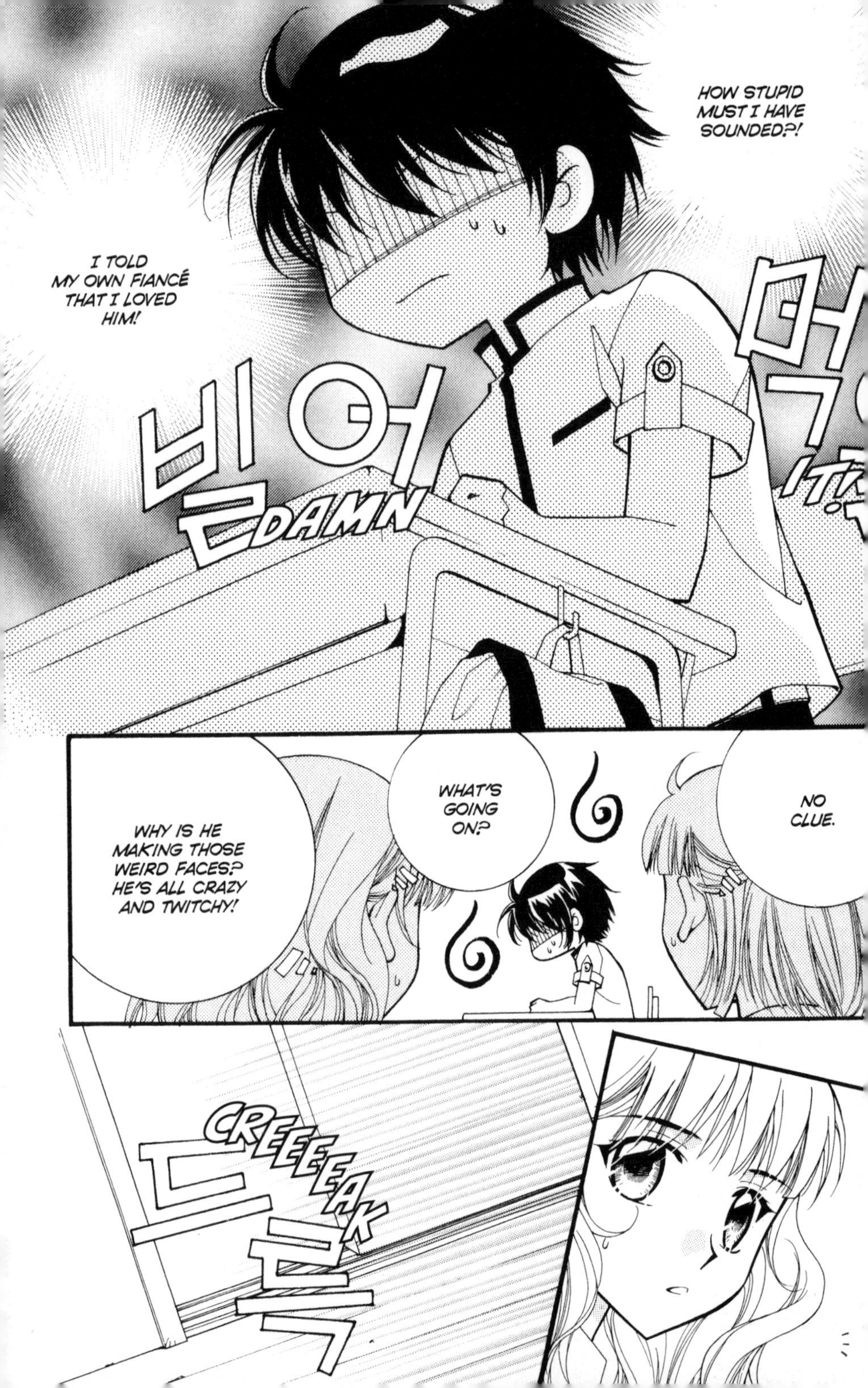
I TOLD MY OWN FIANCÉ THAT I LOVED HIM!
HOW STUPID MUST I HAVE SOUNDED?!
벌어
DAMN
벌떡
IT!
WHY IS HE MAKING THOSE WEIRD FACES? HE'S ALL CRAZY AND TWITCHY!
WHAT'S GOING ON?
NO CLUE.
CREEEEAK
드르륵

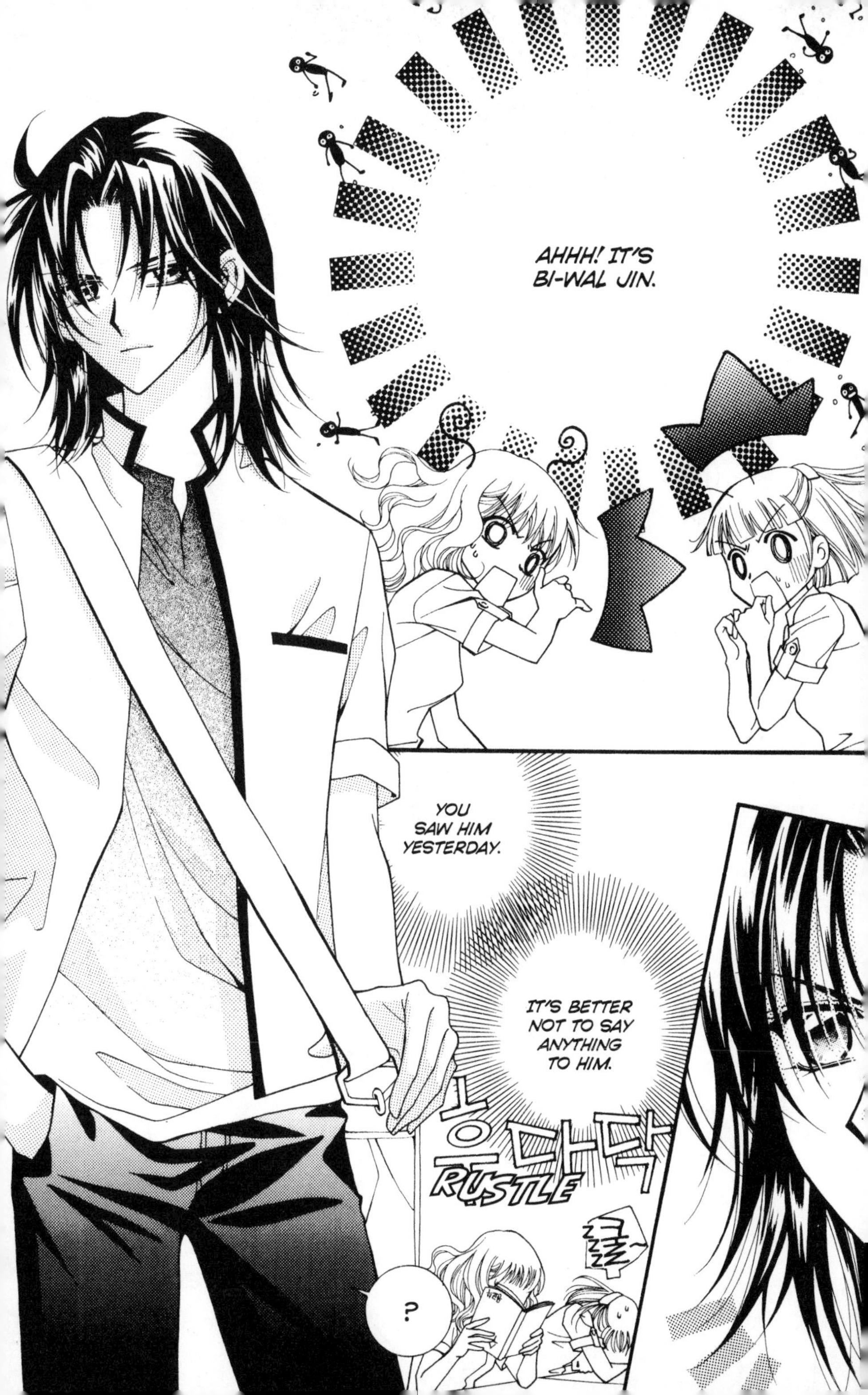
AHHH! IT'S BI-WAL JIN.
YOU SAW HIM YESTERDAY.
IT'S BETTER NOT TO SAY ANYTHING TO HIM.
부스럭
RUSTLE
ZZZZ
?

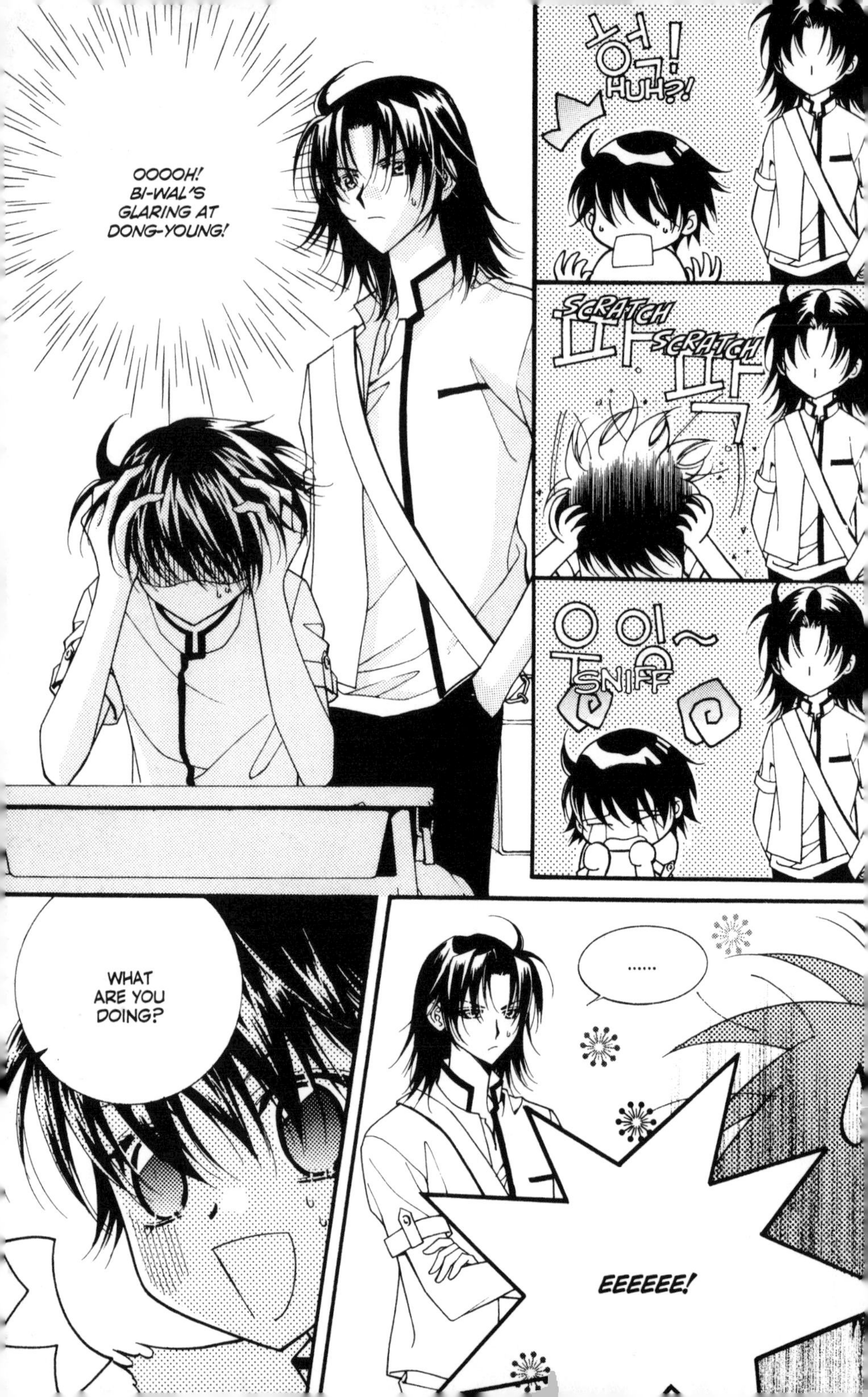

OOOOH! BI-WAL'S GLARING AT DONG-YOUNG!
헉!
HUH?!
SCRATCH
파팍
SCRATCH
우이~
SNIFF
WHAT ARE YOU DOING?
......
EEEEEE!

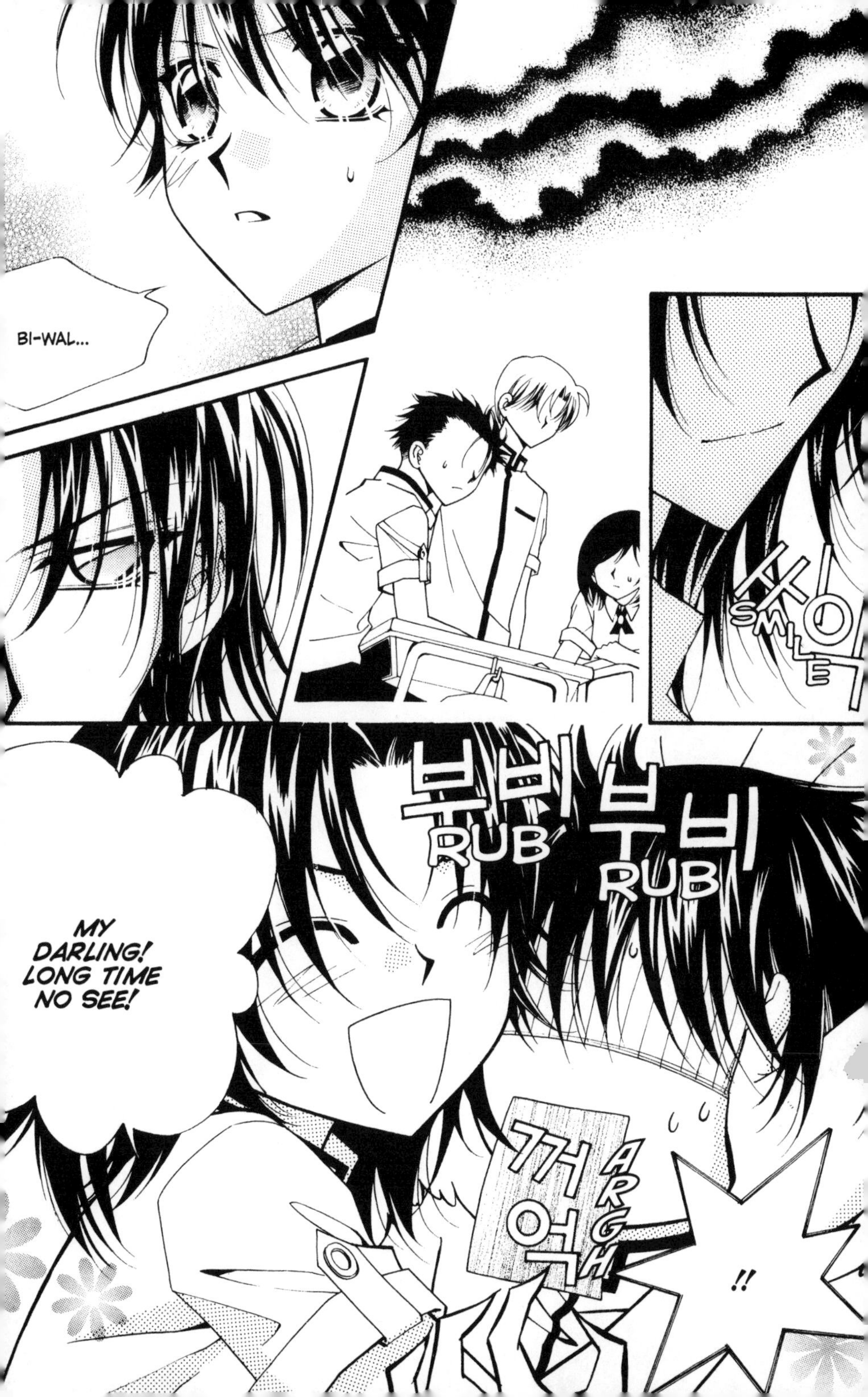
BI-WAL...
SMILE
부비
RUB
부비
RUB
MY DARLING! LONG TIME NO SEE!
ARGH
!!

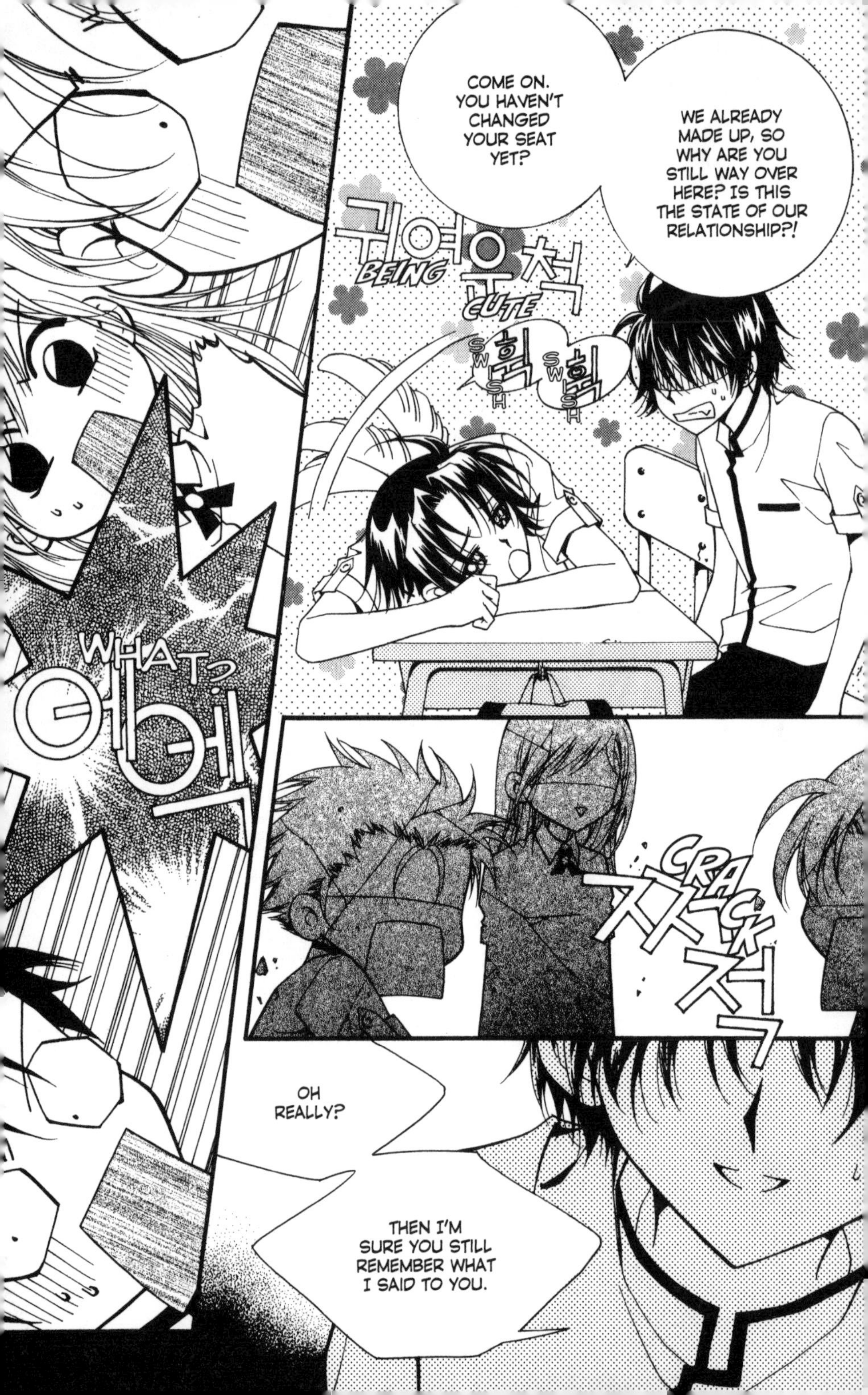
WHAT?
COME ON. YOU HAVEN'T CHANGED YOUR SEAT YET?
WE ALREADY MADE UP, SO WHY ARE YOU STILL WAY OVER HERE? IS THIS THE STATE OF OUR RELATIONSHIP?!
귀여운 척
BEING CUTE
휙
SWISH
휙
SWISH
CRACK
OH REALLY?
THEN I'M SURE YOU STILL REMEMBER WHAT I SAID TO YOU.

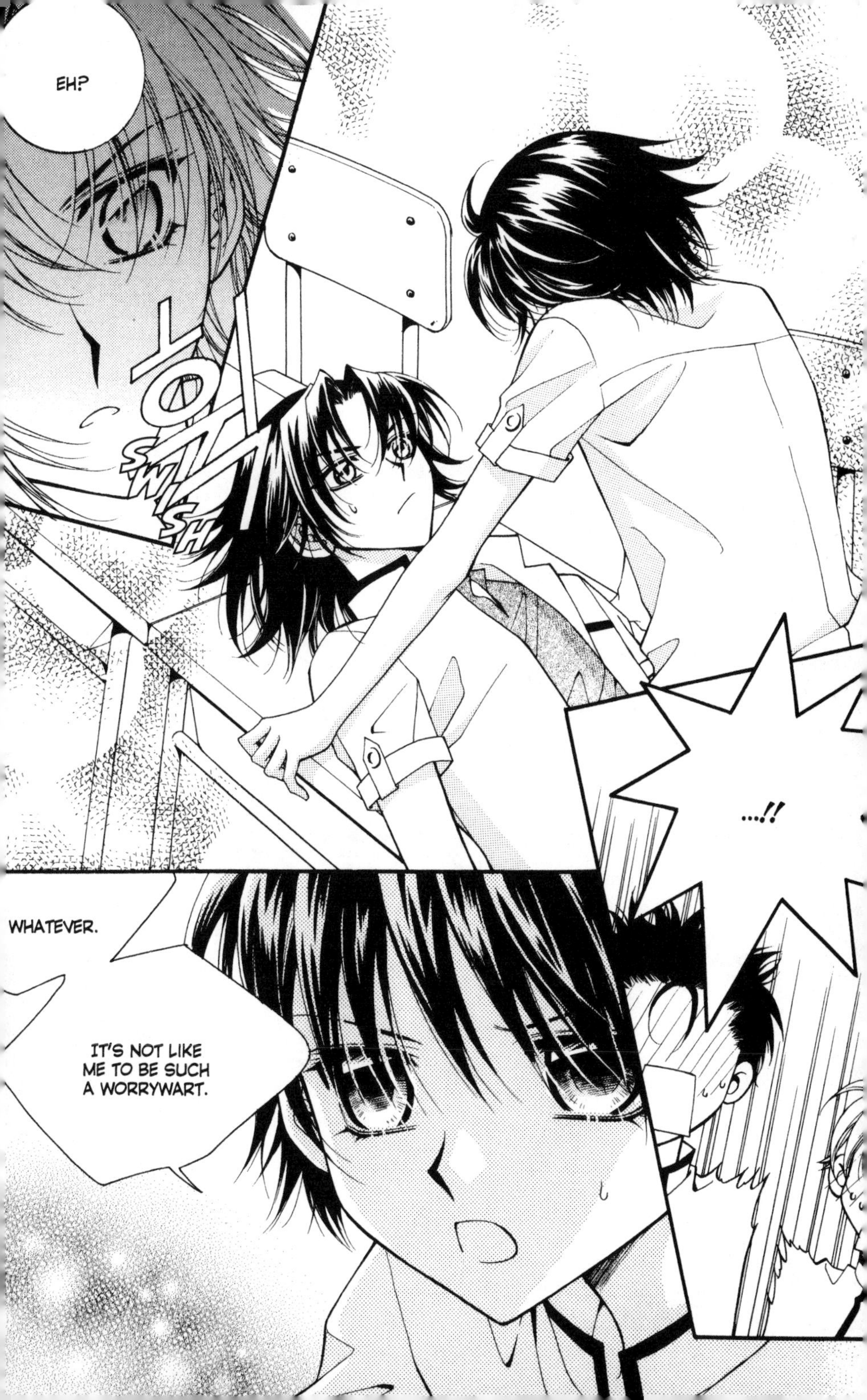
EH?
SWISH
SWISH
...!!
WHATEVER.
IT'S NOT LIKE ME TO BE SUCH A WORRYWART.

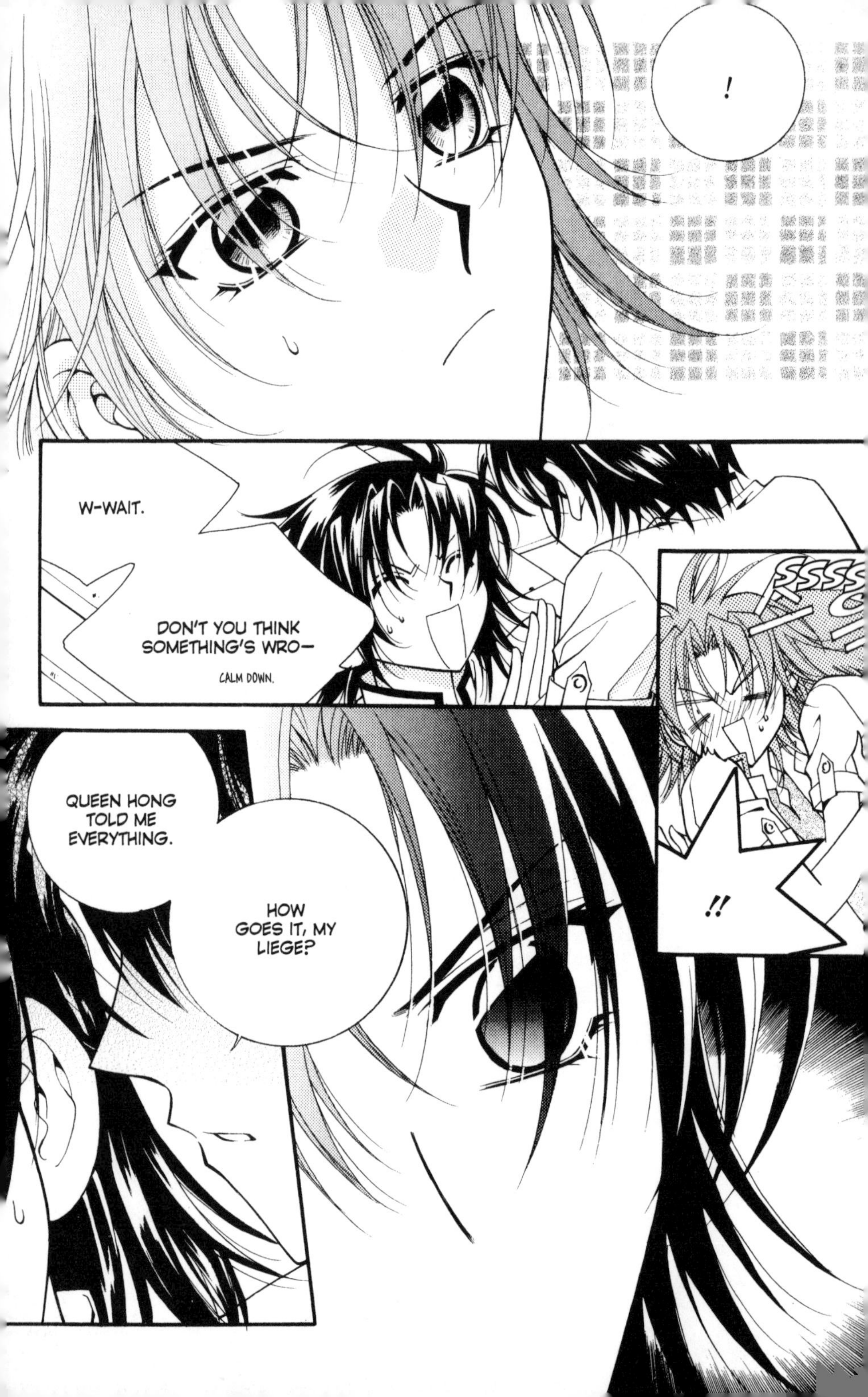
!
W-WAIT.
DON'T YOU THINK SOMETHING'S WRO—
CALM DOWN.
QUEEN HONG TOLD ME EVERYTHING.
HOW GOES IT, MY LIEGE?
!!

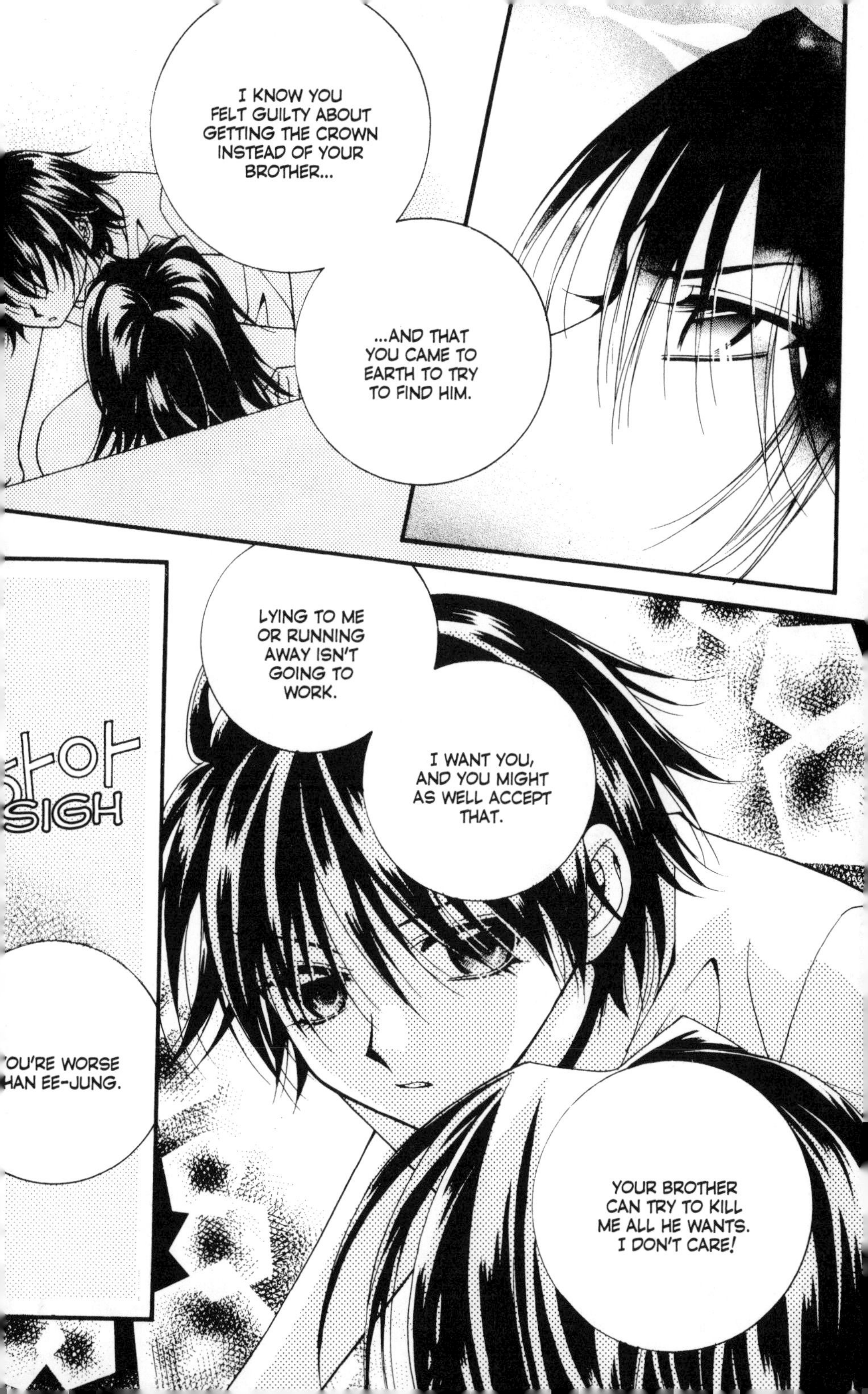
I KNOW YOU FELT GUILTY ABOUT GETTING THE CROWN INSTEAD OF YOUR BROTHER...
...AND THAT YOU CAME TO EARTH TO TRY TO FIND HIM.
LYING TO ME OR RUNNING AWAY ISN'T GOING TO WORK.
I WANT YOU, AND YOU MIGHT AS WELL ACCEPT THAT.
SIGH
OU'RE WORSE HAN EE-JUNG.
YOUR BROTHER CAN TRY TO KILL ME ALL HE WANTS. I DON'T CARE!

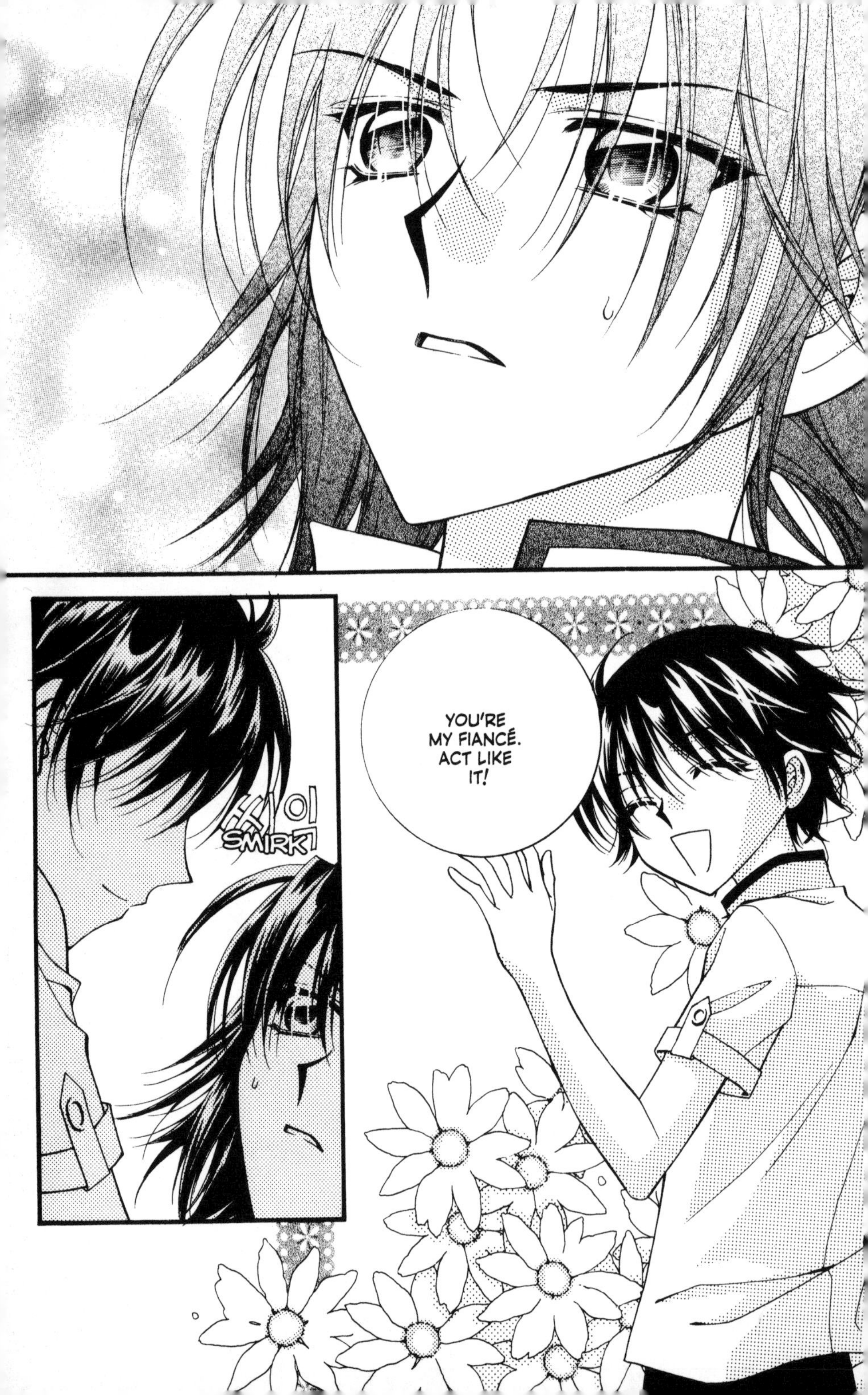
SMIRK!
YOU'RE MY FIANCÉ. ACT LIKE IT!

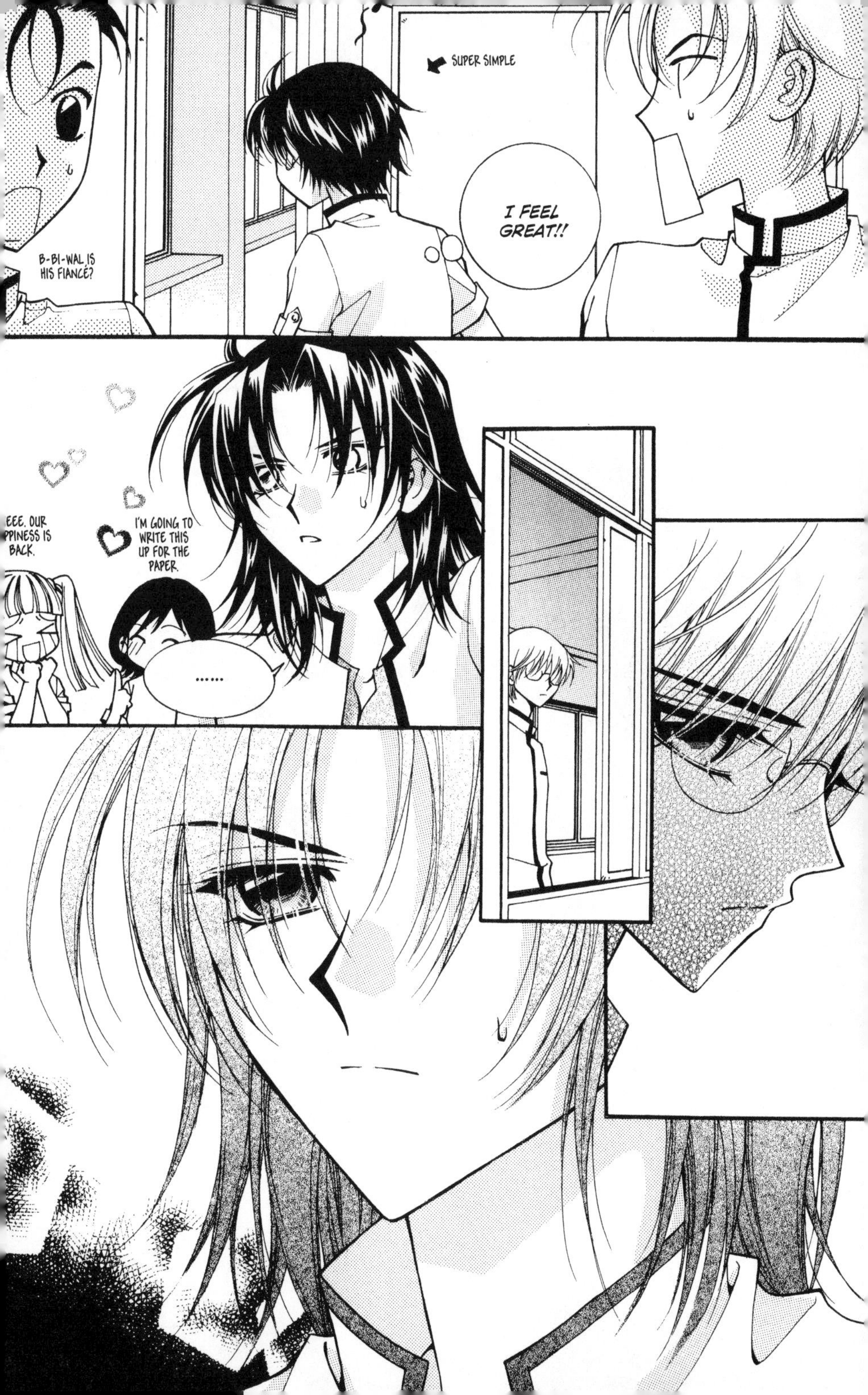
B-BI-WAL IS HIS FIANCÉ?
SUPER SIMPLE
I FEEL GREAT!!
EEE. OUR PPINESS IS BACK.
I'M GOING TO WRITE THIS UP FOR THE PAPER.
......

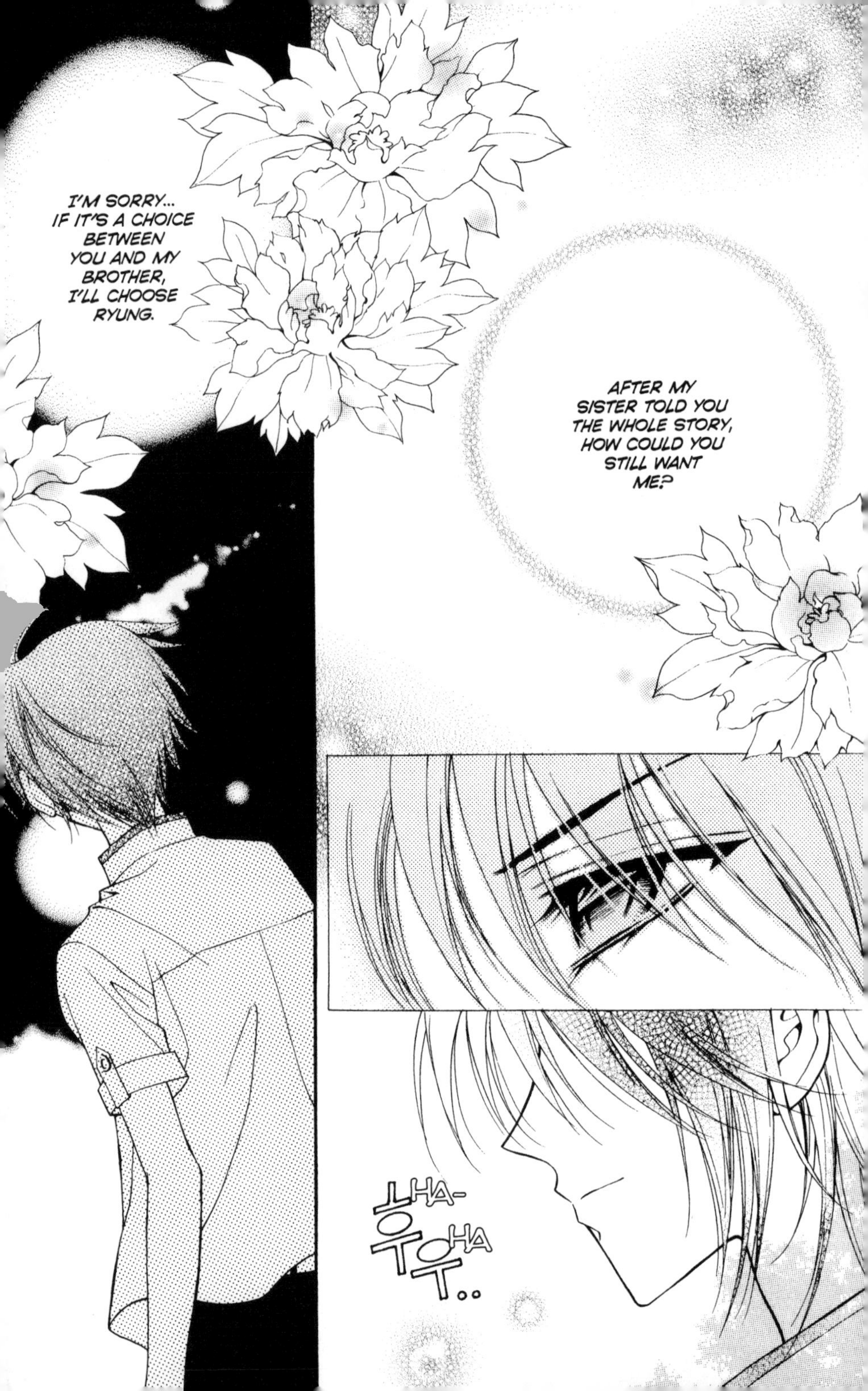
I'M SORRY... IF IT'S A CHOICE BETWEEN YOU AND MY BROTHER, I'LL CHOOSE RYUNG.
AFTER MY SISTER TOLD YOU THE WHOLE STORY, HOW COULD YOU STILL WANT ME?
HA-HA..

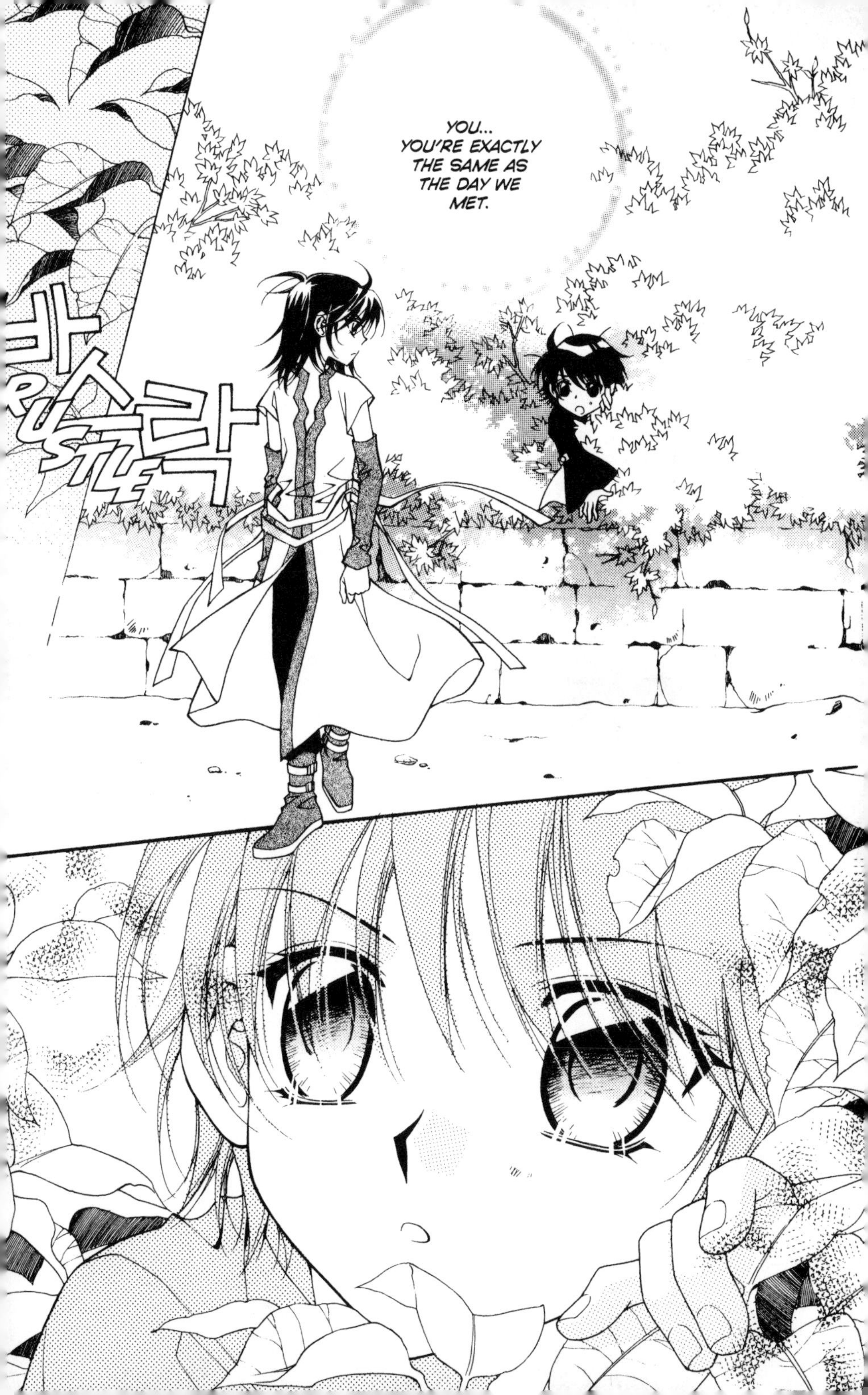
YOU... YOU'RE EXACTLY THE SAME AS THE DAY WE MET.
바스락
RUSTLE

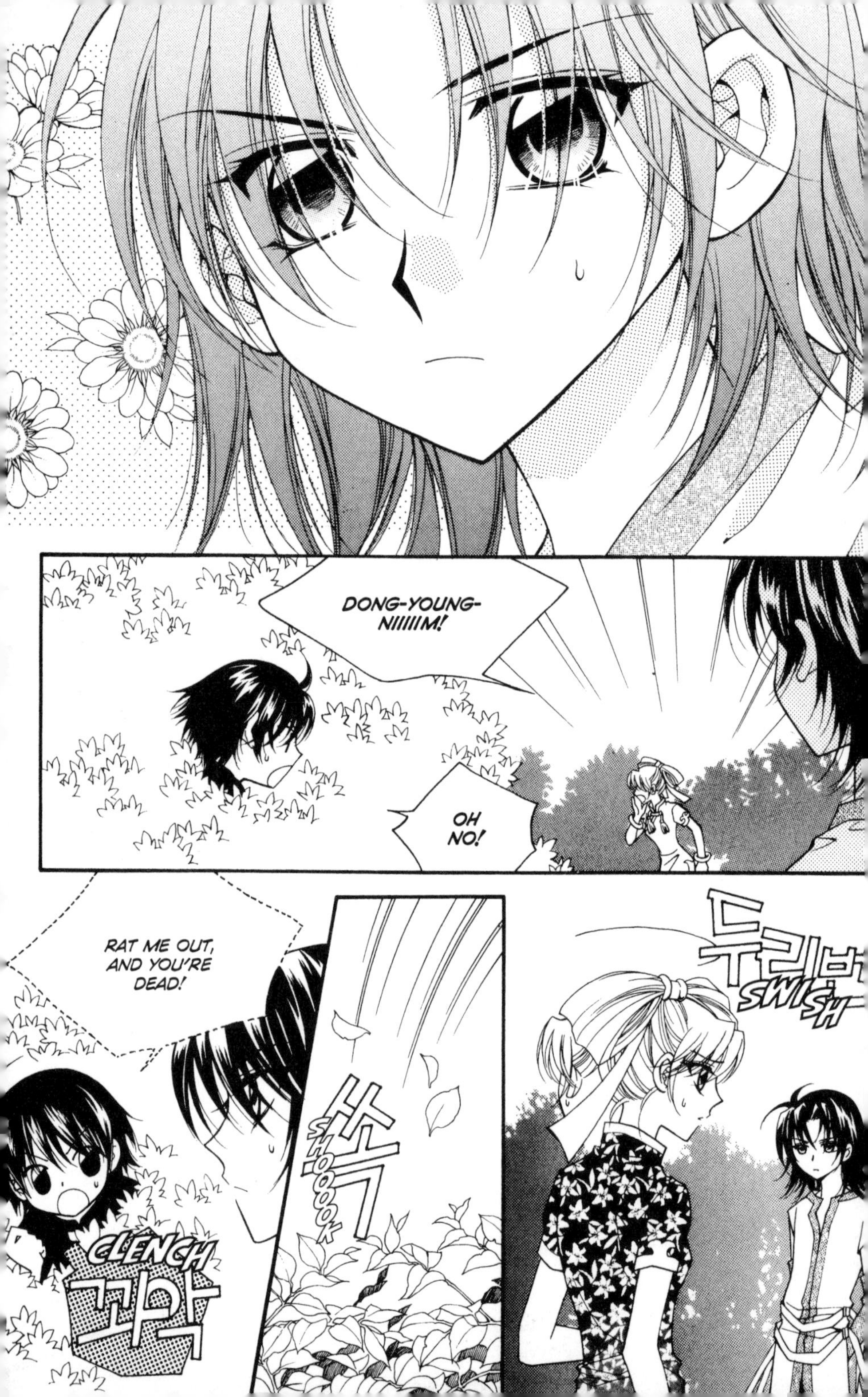
DONG-YOUNG-NIIIIIM!
OH NO!
RAT ME OUT, AND YOU'RE DEAD!
CLENCH
꽈악
쏘옥
SHOOOOOK
두리번
SWISH

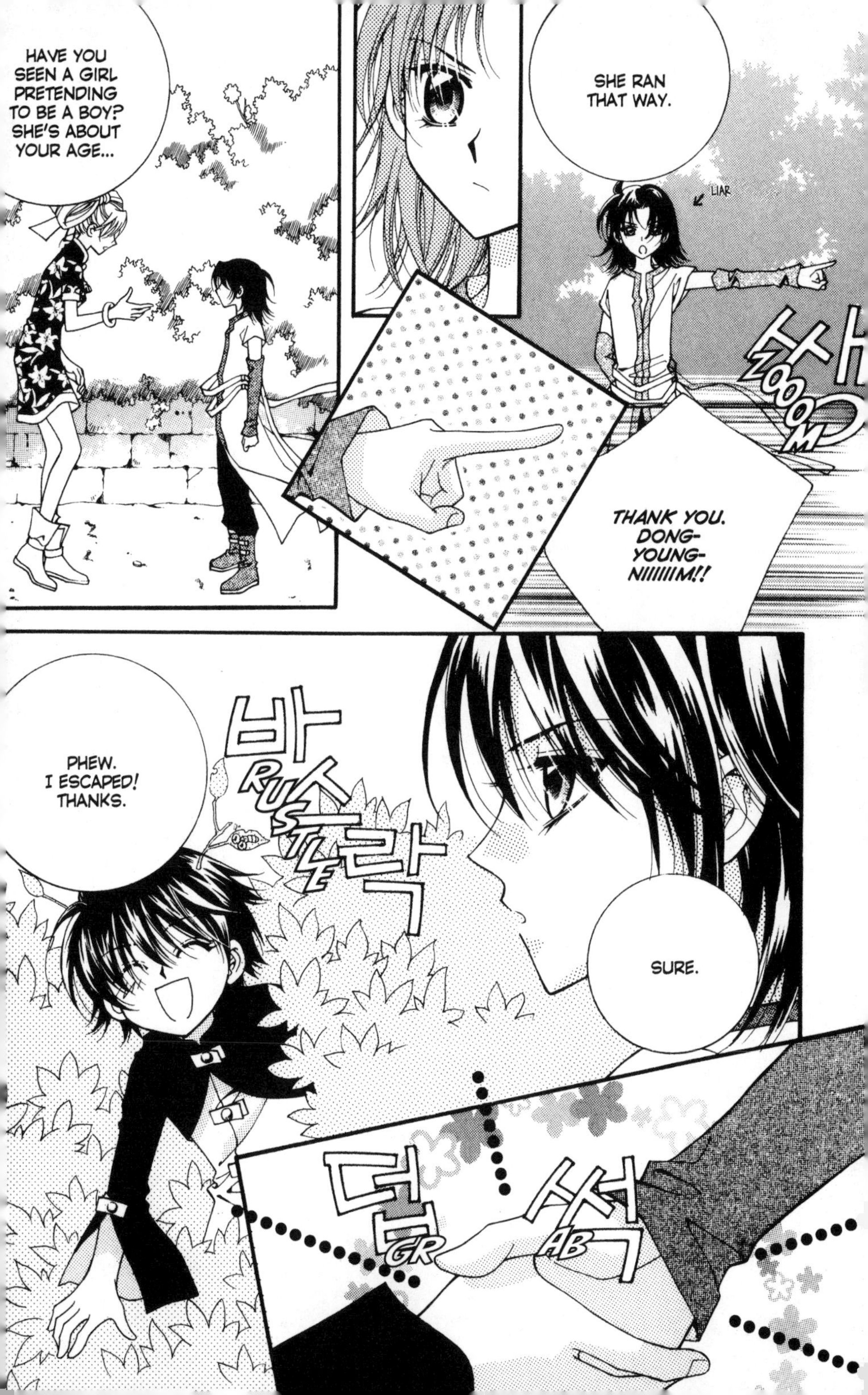
HAVE YOU SEEN A GIRL PRETENDING TO BE A BOY? SHE'S ABOUT YOUR AGE...
SHE RAN THAT WAY.
LIAR
ZOOOM
THANK YOU. DONG-YOUNG-NIIIIIIM!!
바스락
RUSTLE
PHEW. I ESCAPED! THANKS.
SURE.
덥석
GRAB

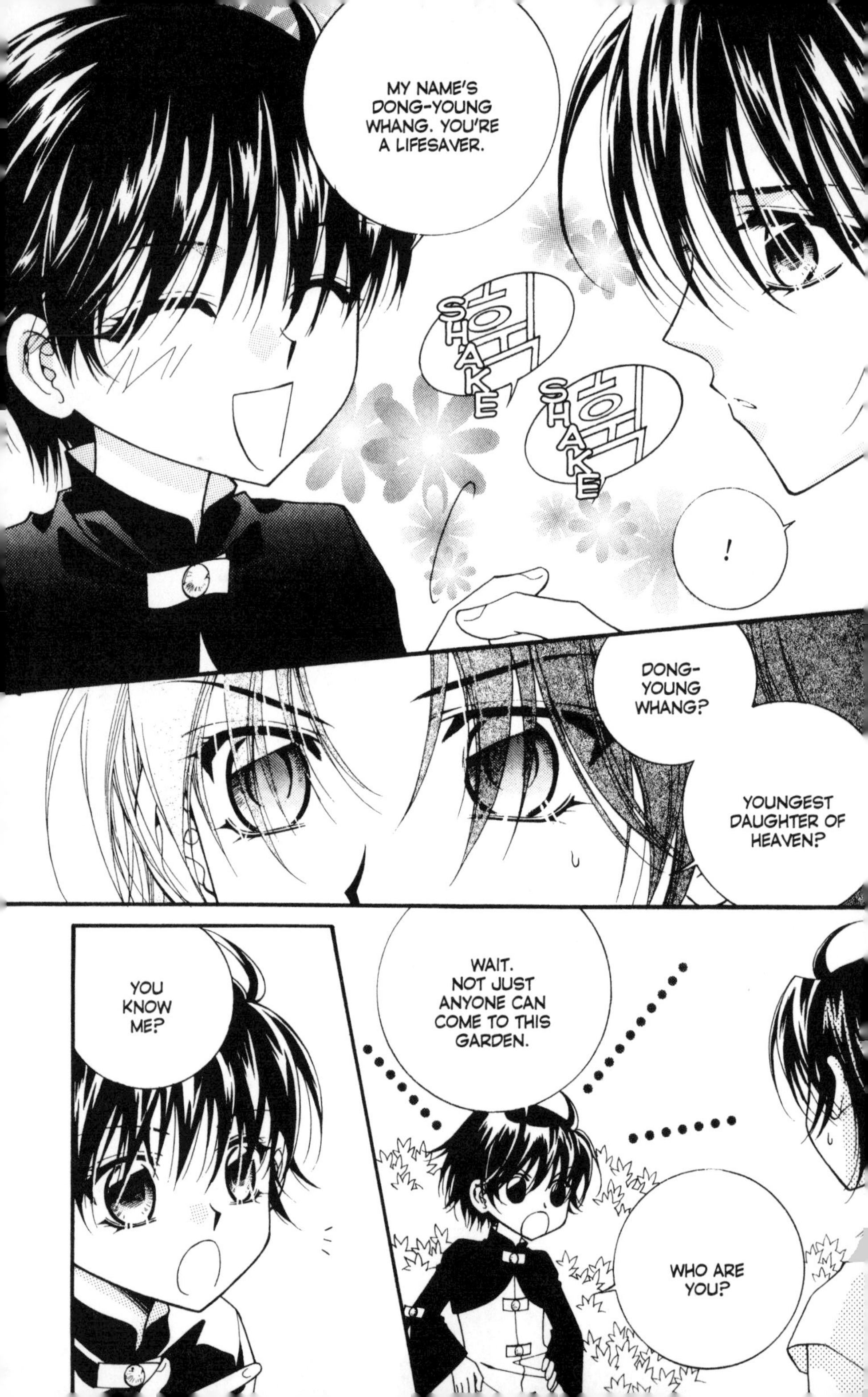
MY NAME'S DONG-YOUNG WHANG. YOU'RE A LIFESAVER.
SHAKE
SHAKE
!
DONG-YOUNG WHANG?
YOUNGEST DAUGHTER OF HEAVEN?
YOU KNOW ME?
WAIT. NOT JUST ANYONE CAN COME TO THIS GARDEN.
WHO ARE YOU?

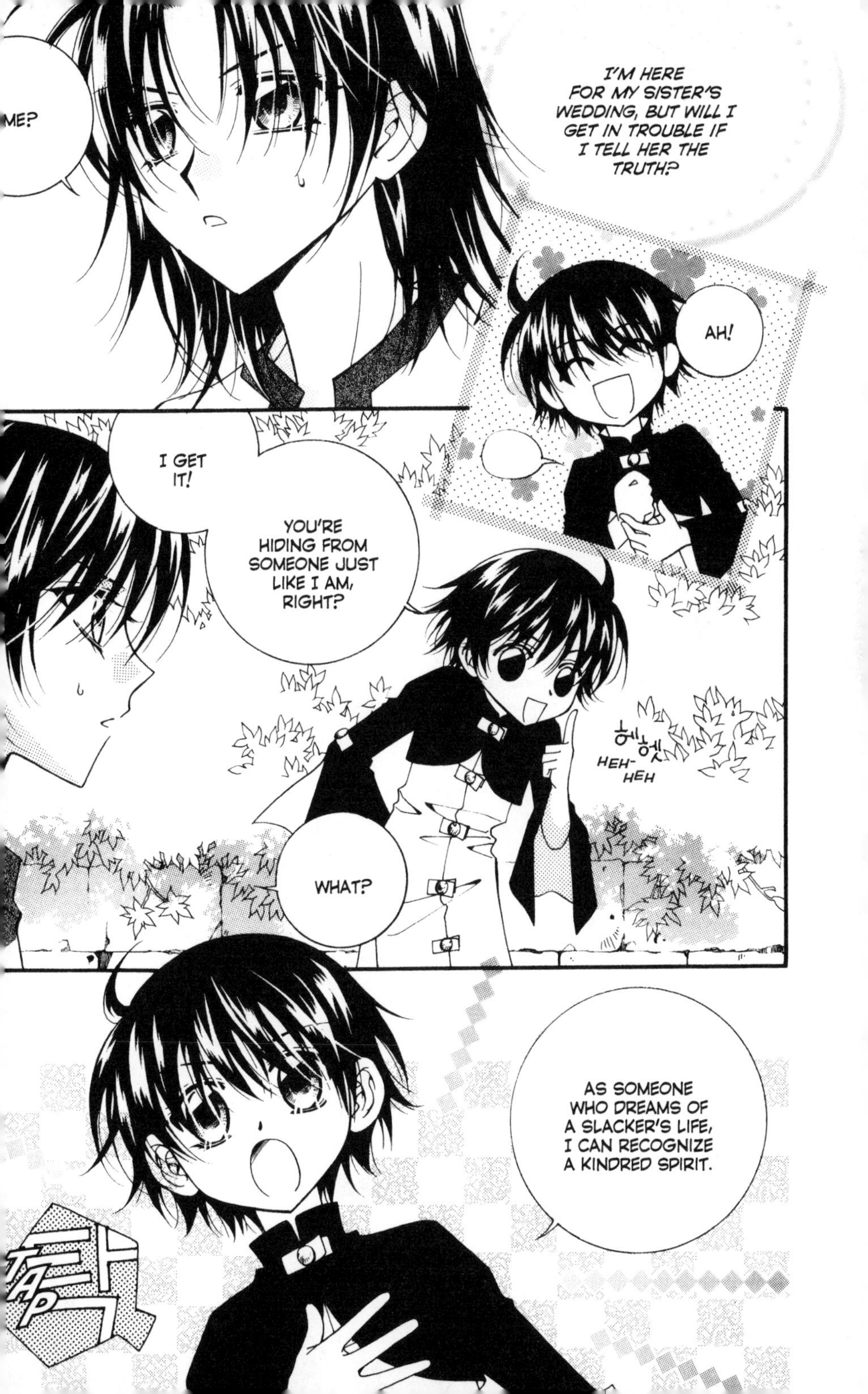

ME?
I'M HERE FOR MY SISTER'S WEDDING, BUT WILL I GET IN TROUBLE IF I TELL HER THE TRUTH?
AH!
I GET IT!
YOU'RE HIDING FROM SOMEONE JUST LIKE I AM, RIGHT?
헤헷
HEH-HEH
WHAT?
AS SOMEONE WHO DREAMS OF A SLACKER'S LIFE, I CAN RECOGNIZE A KINDRED SPIRIT.
TAP

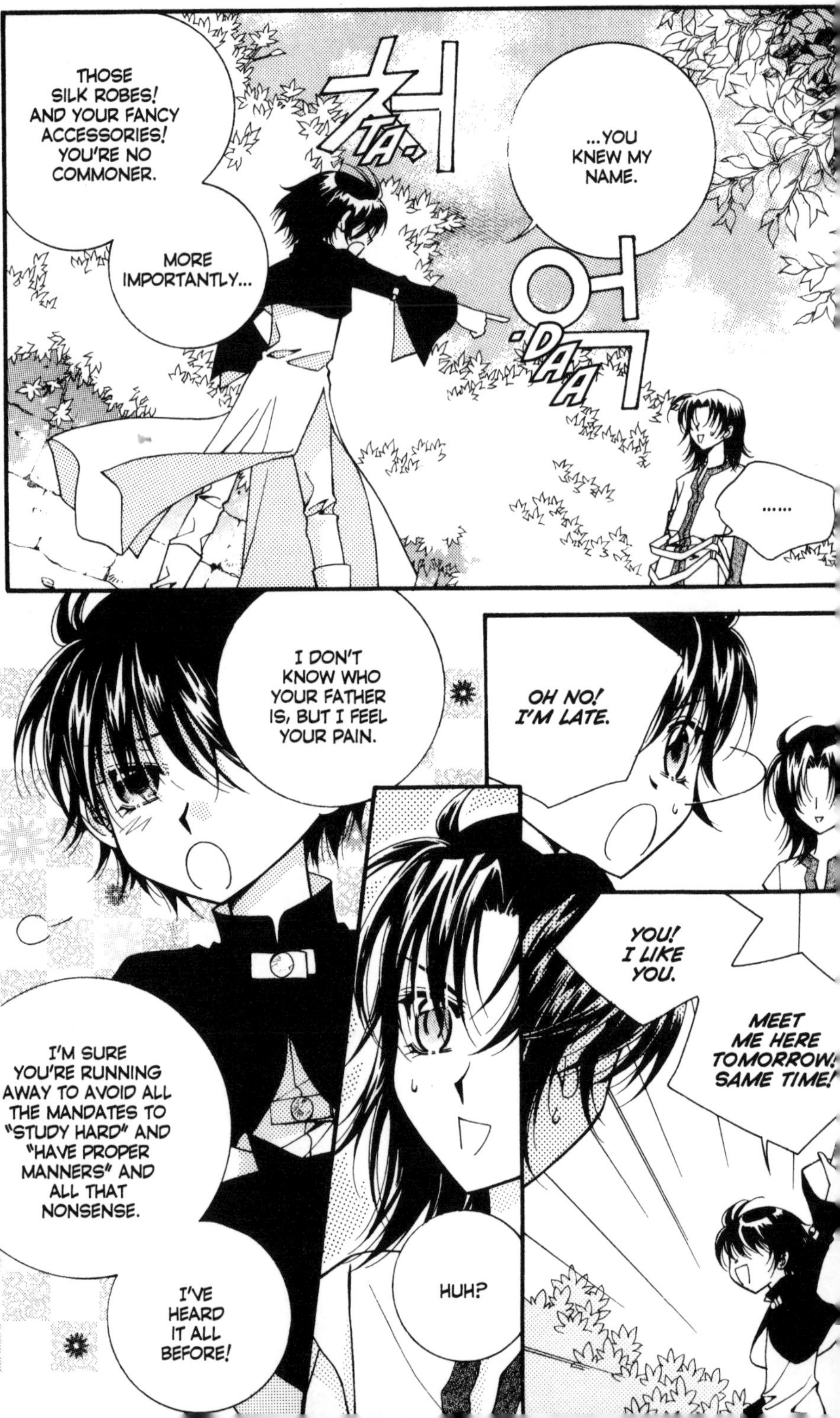
THOSE SILK ROBES! AND YOUR FANCY ACCESSORIES! YOU'RE NO COMMONER.
MORE IMPORTANTLY...
TA-
...YOU KNEW MY NAME.
-DAA
......
I DON'T KNOW WHO YOUR FATHER IS, BUT I FEEL YOUR PAIN.
I'M SURE YOU'RE RUNNING AWAY TO AVOID ALL THE MANDATES TO "STUDY HARD" AND "HAVE PROPER MANNERS" AND ALL THAT NONSENSE.
I'VE HEARD IT ALL BEFORE!
HUH?
OH NO! I'M LATE.
YOU! I LIKE YOU.
MEET ME HERE TOMORROW, SAME TIME!

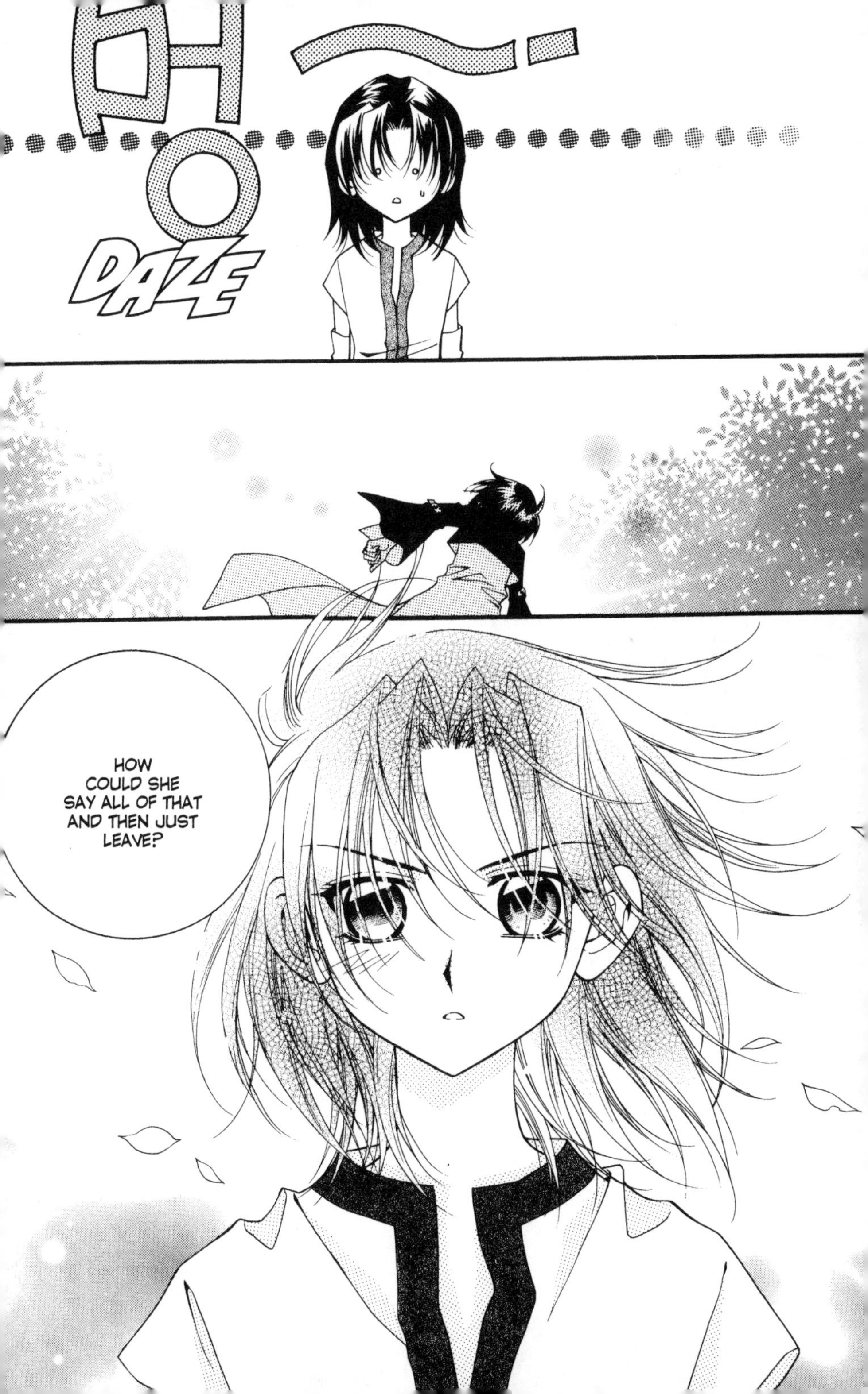
DAZE
HOW COULD SHE SAY ALL OF THAT AND THEN JUST LEAVE?

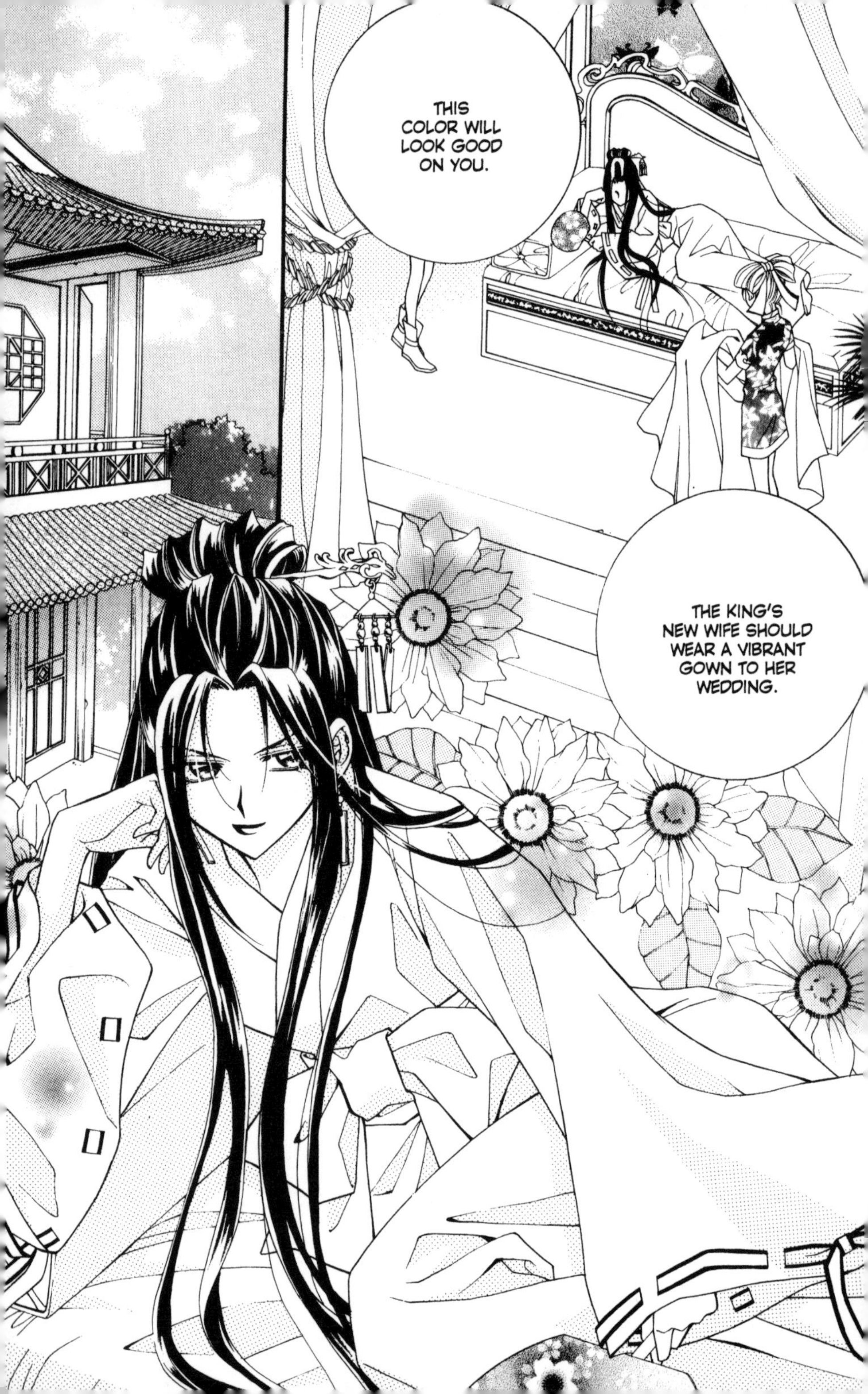
THIS COLOR WILL LOOK GOOD ON YOU.
THE KING'S NEW WIFE SHOULD WEAR A VIBRANT GOWN TO HER WEDDING.

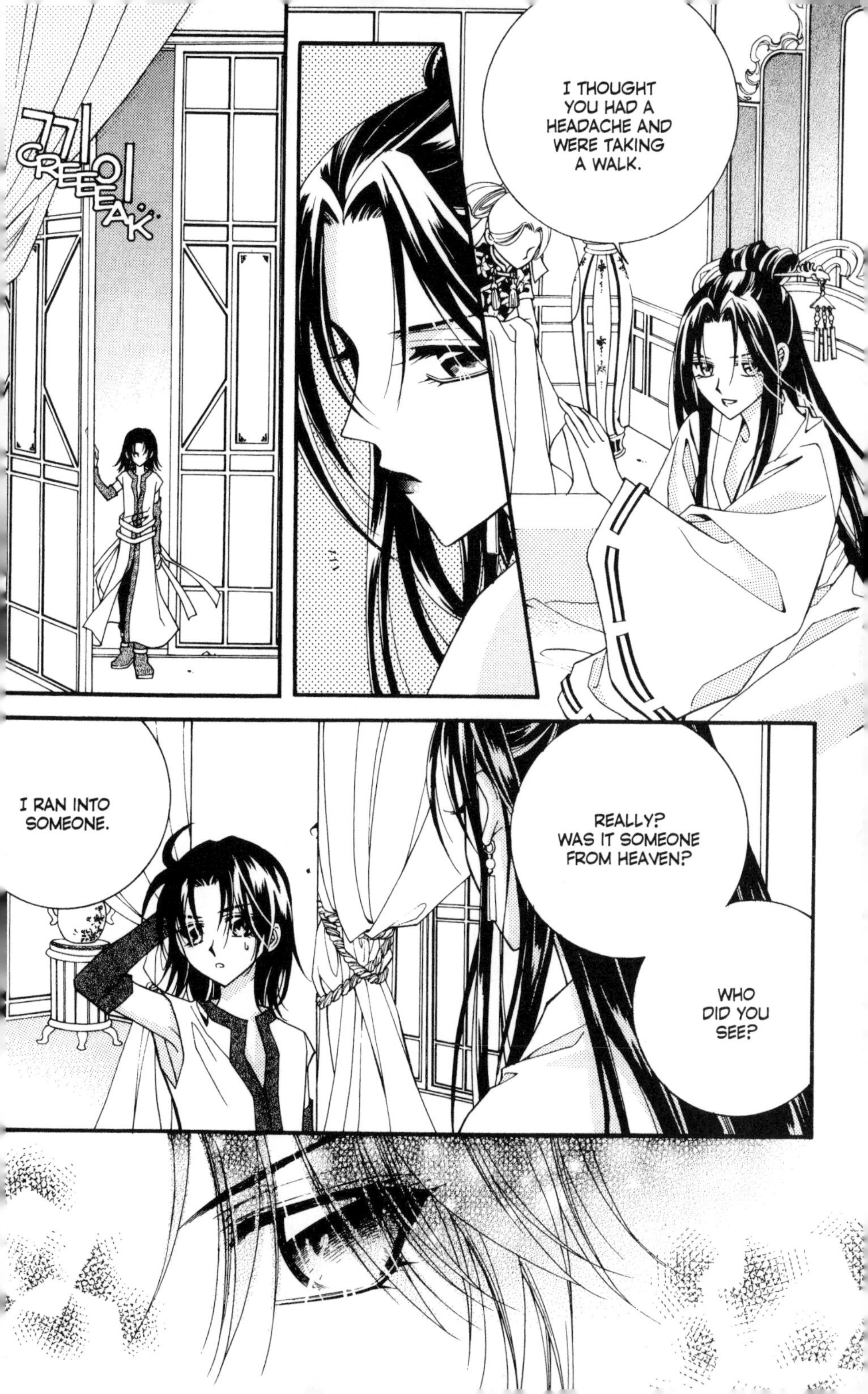

CREEEEAK...
I THOUGHT YOU HAD A HEADACHE AND WERE TAKING A WALK.
I RAN INTO SOMEONE.
REALLY? WAS IT SOMEONE FROM HEAVEN?
WHO DID YOU SEE?

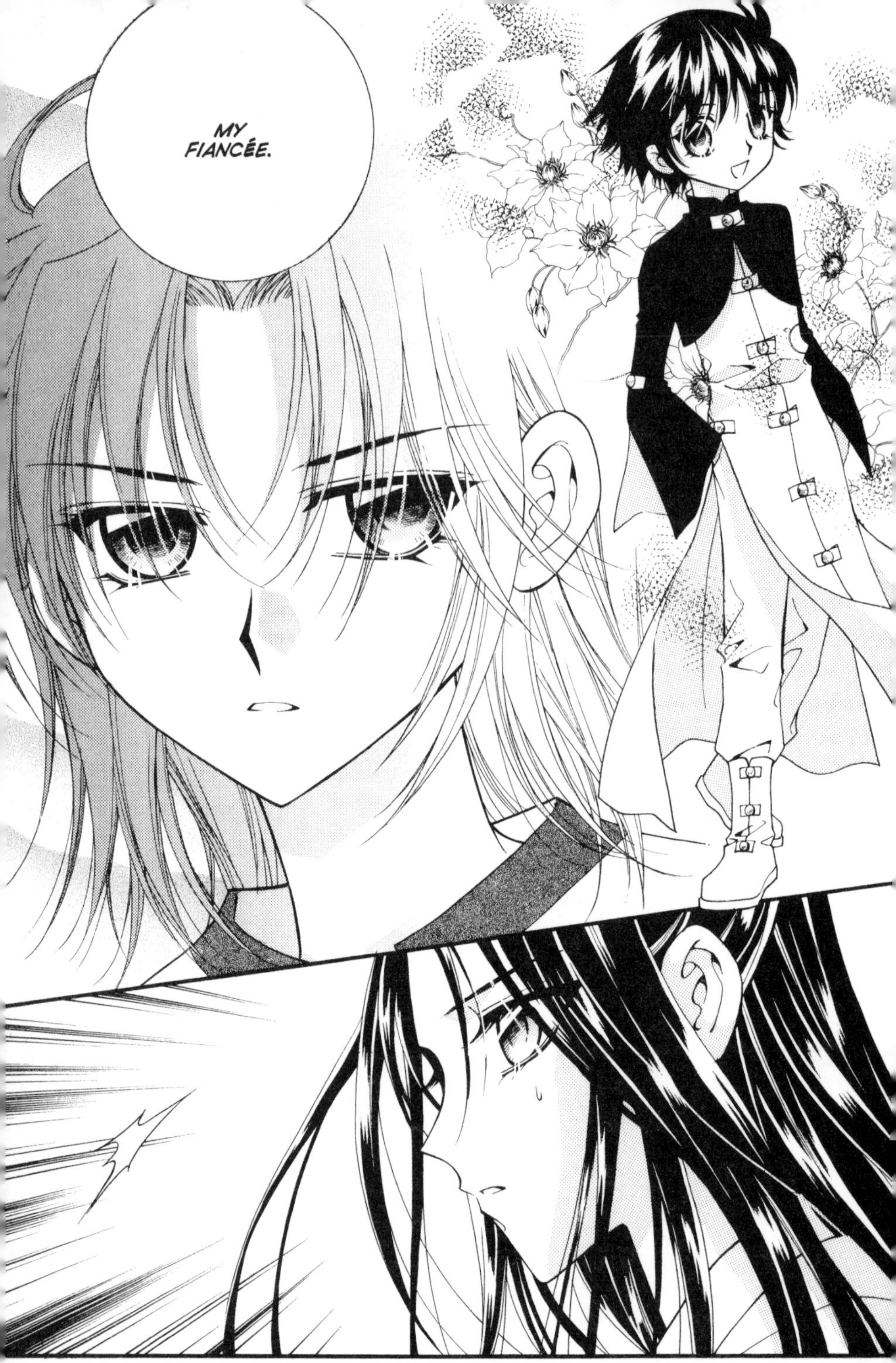
MY FIANCÉE.

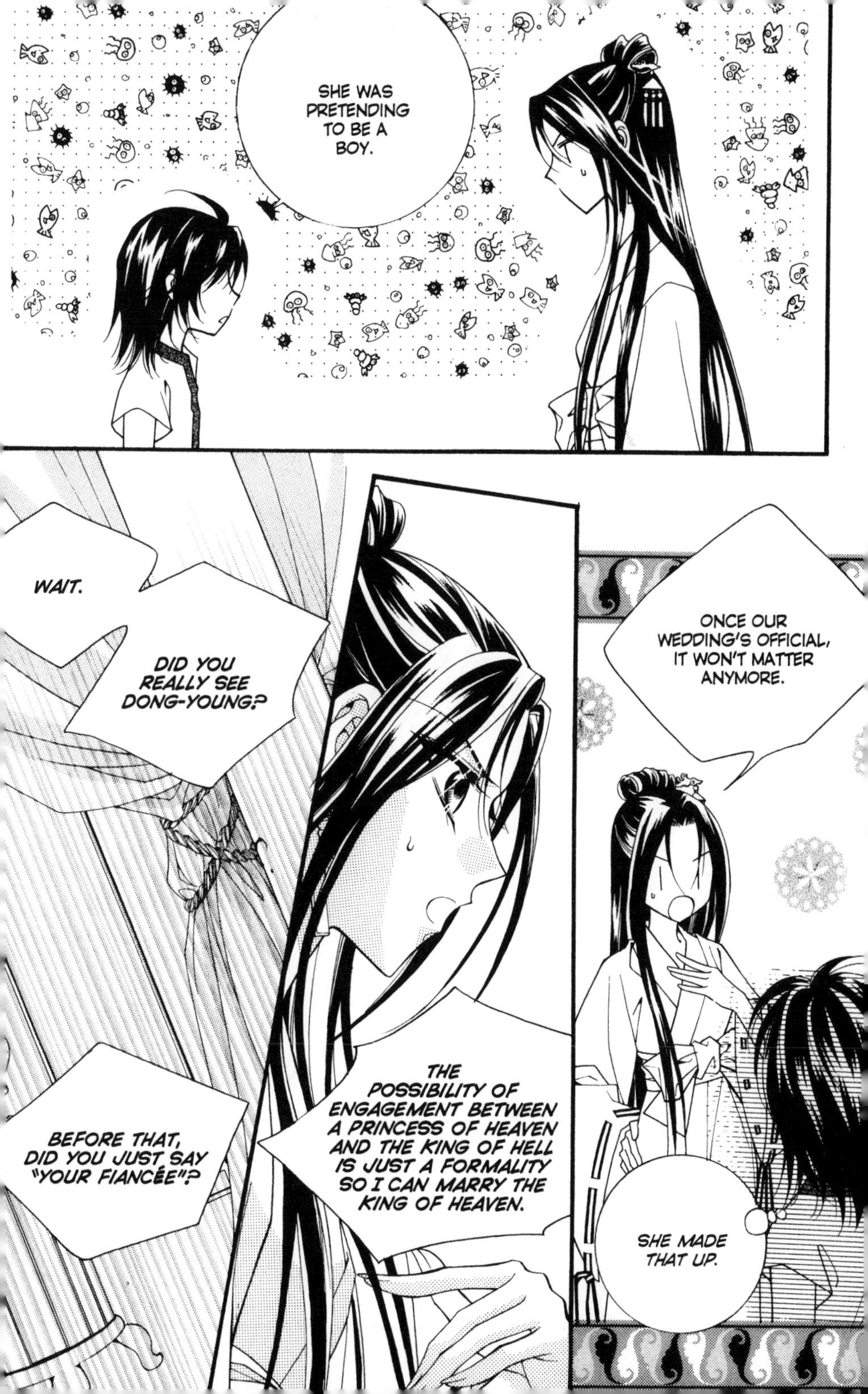
SHE WAS PRETENDING TO BE A BOY.
WAIT.
DID YOU REALLY SEE DONG-YOUNG?
BEFORE THAT, DID YOU JUST SAY "YOUR FIANCÉE"?
THE POSSIBILITY OF ENGAGEMENT BETWEEN A PRINCESS OF HEAVEN AND THE KING OF HELL IS JUST A FORMALITY SO I CAN MARRY THE KING OF HEAVEN.
ONCE OUR WEDDING'S OFFICIAL, IT WON'T MATTER ANYMORE.
SHE MADE THAT UP.

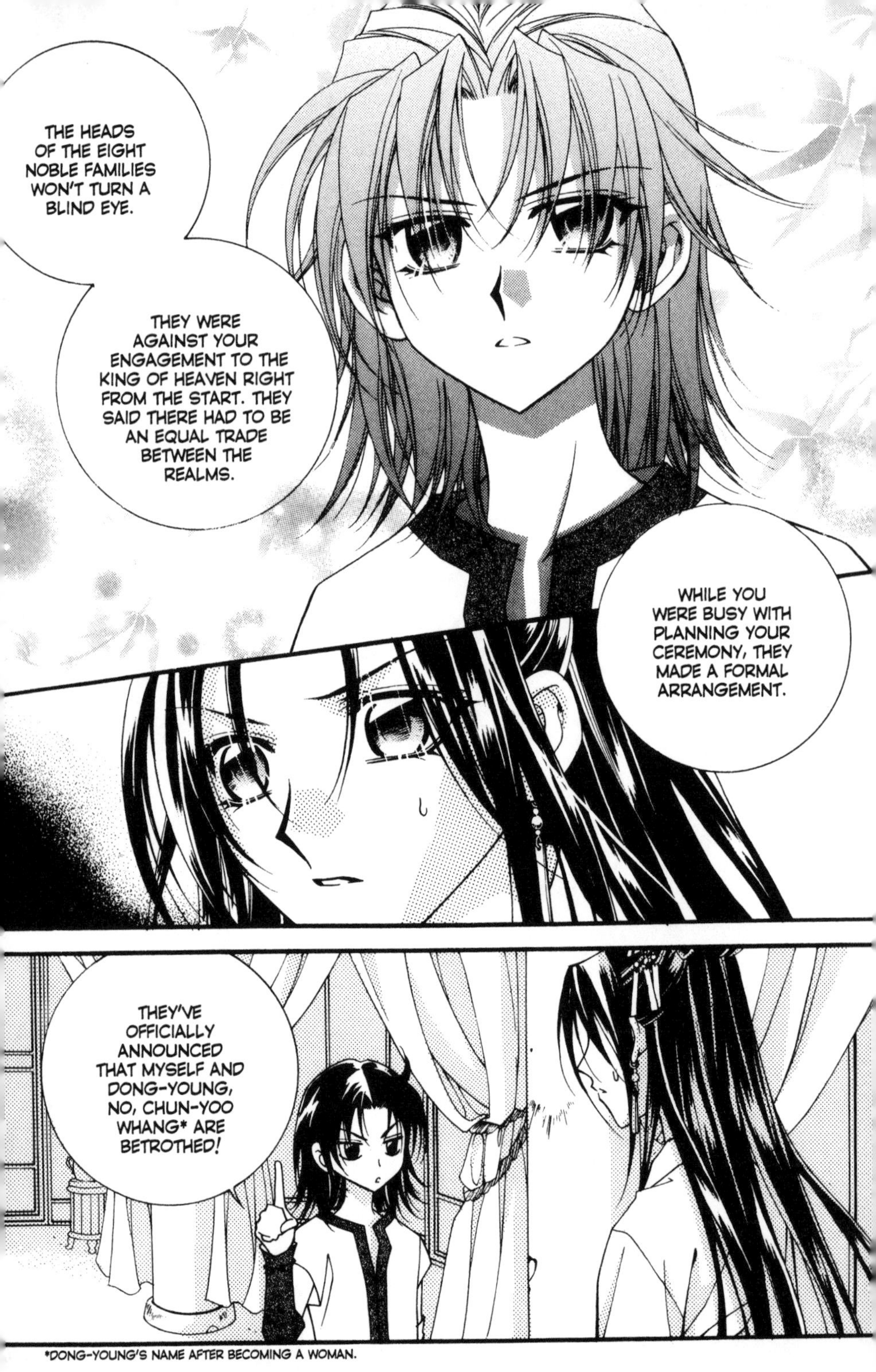
THE HEADS OF THE EIGHT NOBLE FAMILIES WON'T TURN A BLIND EYE.
THEY WERE AGAINST YOUR ENGAGEMENT TO THE KING OF HEAVEN RIGHT FROM THE START. THEY SAID THERE HAD TO BE AN EQUAL TRADE BETWEEN THE REALMS.
WHILE YOU WERE BUSY WITH PLANNING YOUR CEREMONY, THEY MADE A FORMAL ARRANGEMENT.
THEY'VE OFFICIALLY ANNOUNCED THAT MYSELF AND DONG-YOUNG, NO, CHUN-YOO WHANG* ARE BETROTHED!

*DONG-YOUNG'S NAME AFTER BECOMING A WOMAN.

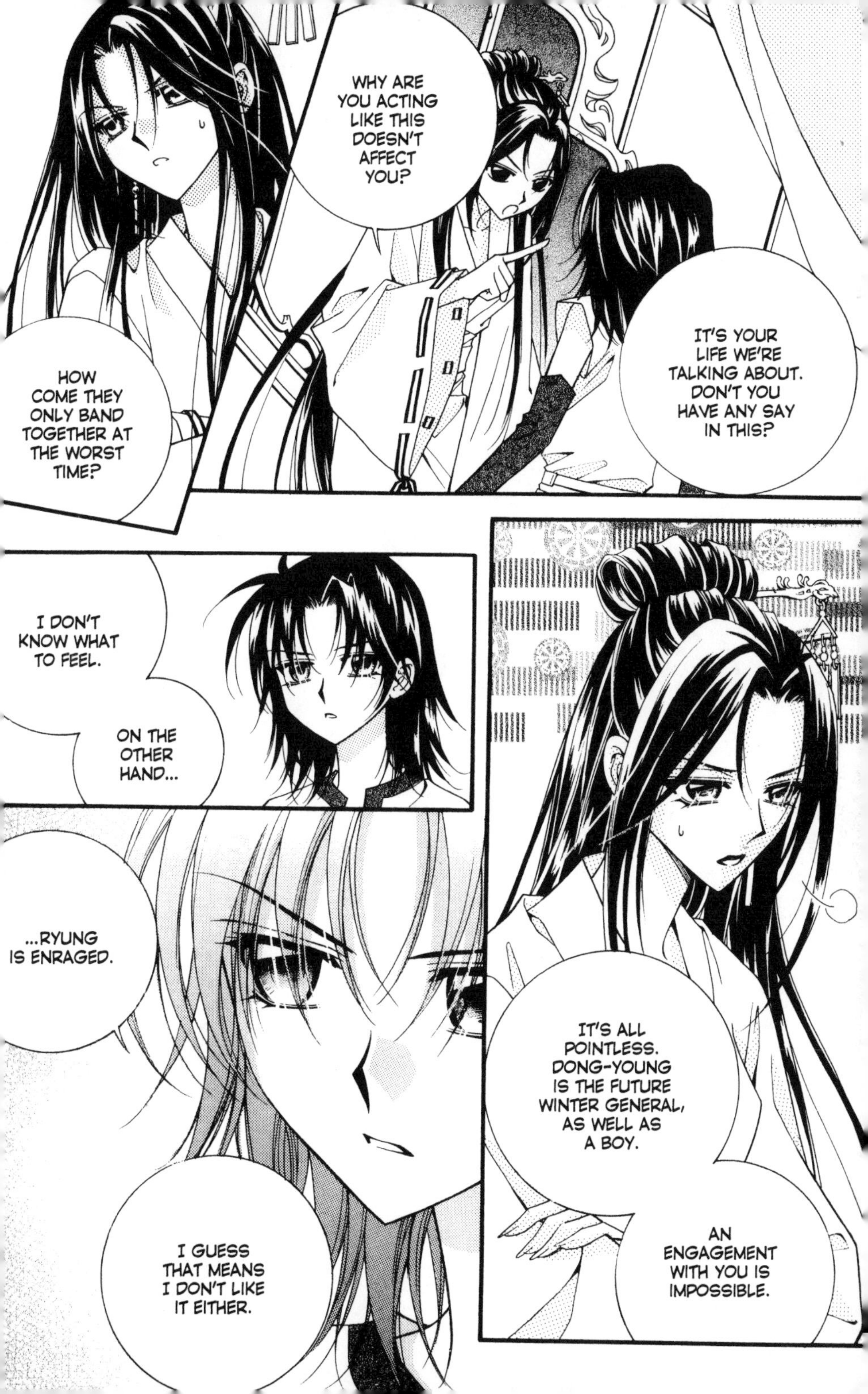
HOW COME THEY ONLY BAND TOGETHER AT THE WORST TIME?
WHY ARE YOU ACTING LIKE THIS DOESN'T AFFECT YOU?
IT'S YOUR LIFE WE'RE TALKING ABOUT. DON'T YOU HAVE ANY SAY IN THIS?
I DON'T KNOW WHAT TO FEEL.
ON THE OTHER HAND...
...RYUNG IS ENRAGED.
I GUESS THAT MEANS I DON'T LIKE IT EITHER.
IT'S ALL POINTLESS. DONG-YOUNG IS THE FUTURE WINTER GENERAL, AS WELL AS A BOY.
AN ENGAGEMENT WITH YOU IS IMPOSSIBLE.

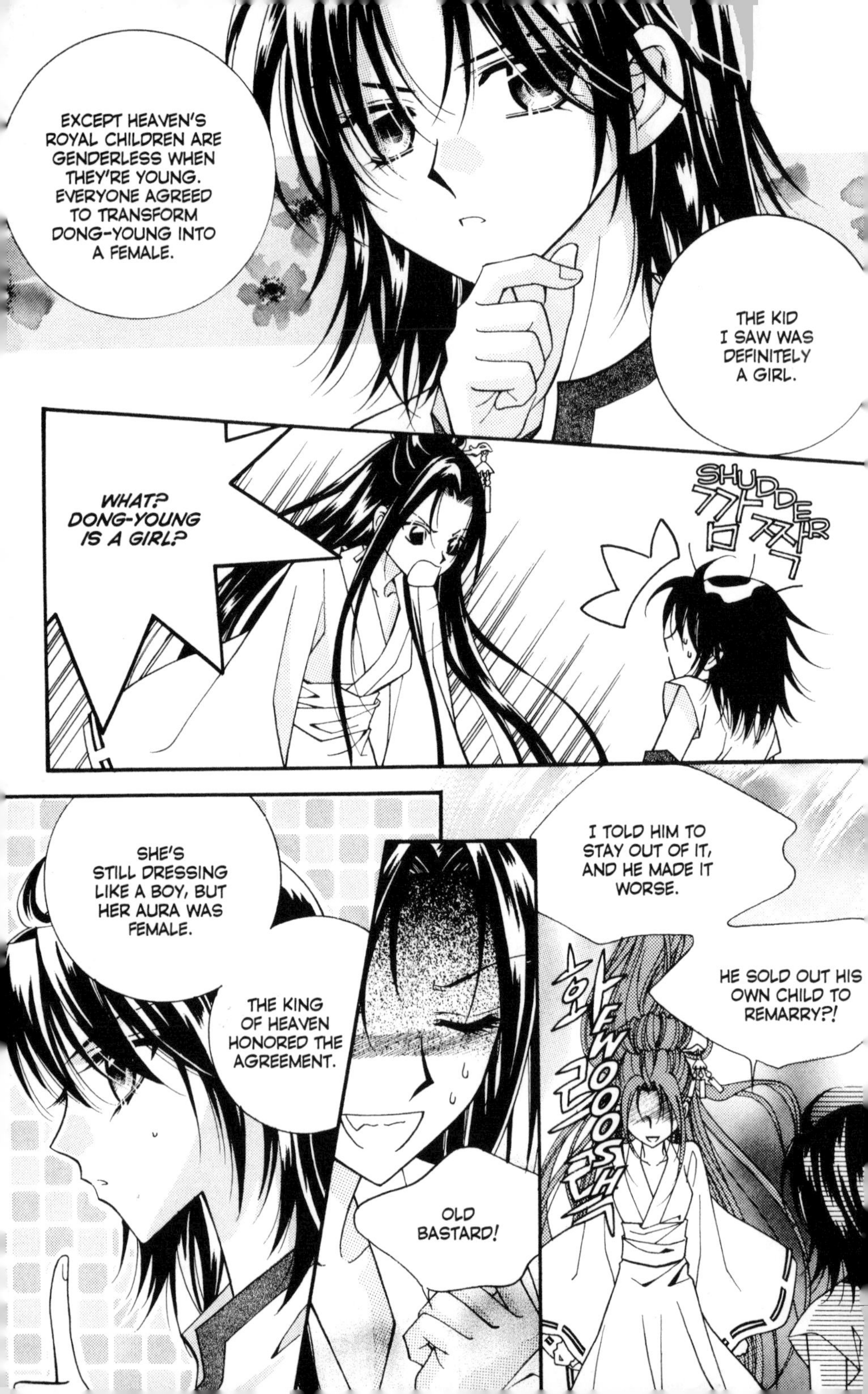
EXCEPT HEAVEN'S ROYAL CHILDREN ARE GENDERLESS WHEN THEY'RE YOUNG. EVERYONE AGREED TO TRANSFORM DONG-YOUNG INTO A FEMALE.
THE KID I SAW WAS DEFINITELY A GIRL.
WHAT? DONG-YOUNG IS A GIRL?
SHUDDER
SHE'S STILL DRESSING LIKE A BOY, BUT HER AURA WAS FEMALE.
THE KING OF HEAVEN HONORED THE AGREEMENT.
OLD BASTARD!
I TOLD HIM TO STAY OUT OF IT, AND HE MADE IT WORSE.
FWOOOOSH
HE SOLD OUT HIS OWN CHILD TO REMARRY?!

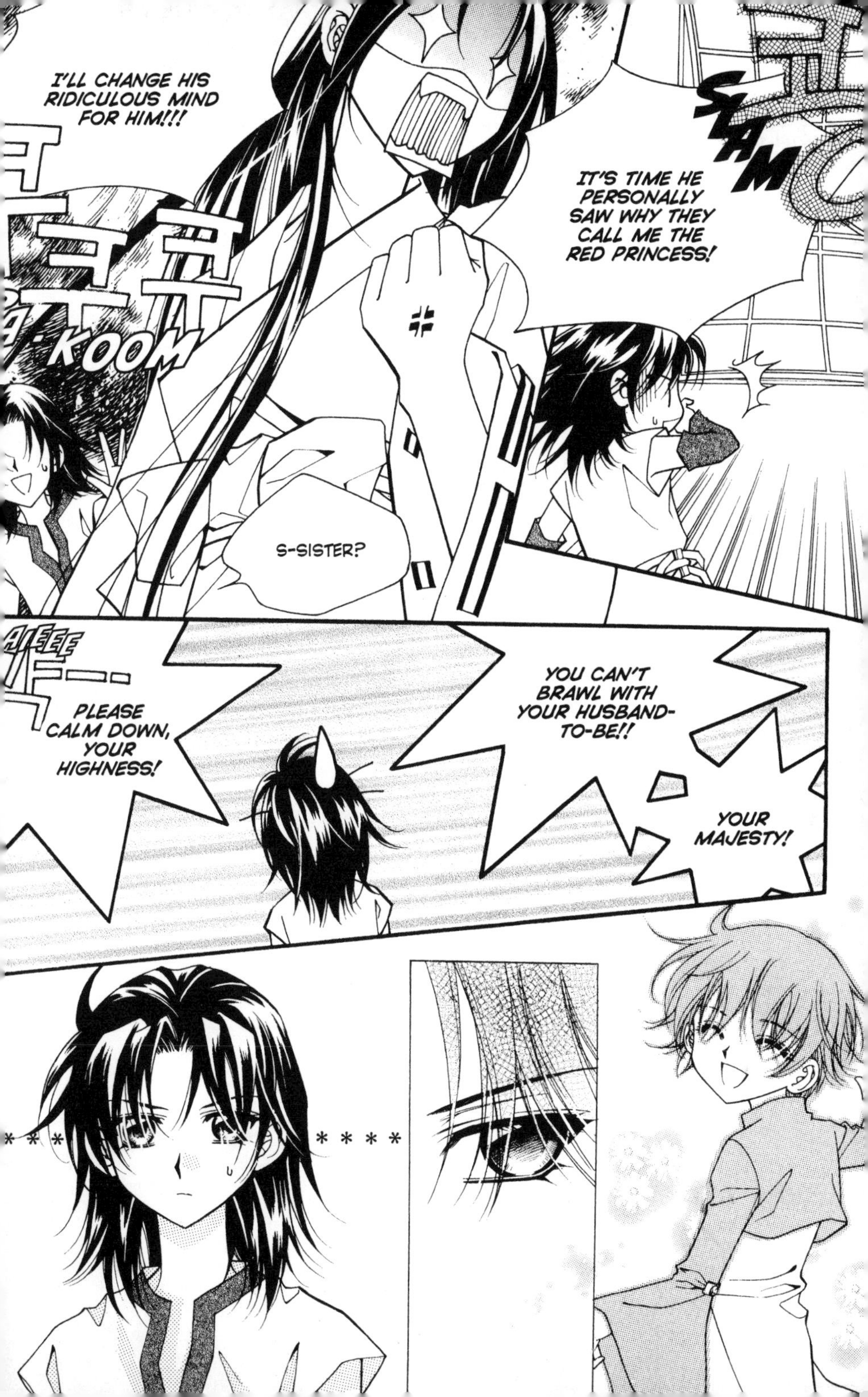
I'LL CHANGE HIS RIDICULOUS MIND FOR HIM!!!
SLAM
IT'S TIME HE PERSONALLY SAW WHY THEY CALL ME THE RED PRINCESS!
KOOM
S-SISTER?
AEEEE
PLEASE CALM DOWN, YOUR HIGHNESS!
YOU CAN'T BRAWL WITH YOUR HUSBAND-TO-BE!!
YOUR MAJESTY!
* * * *
* * * *

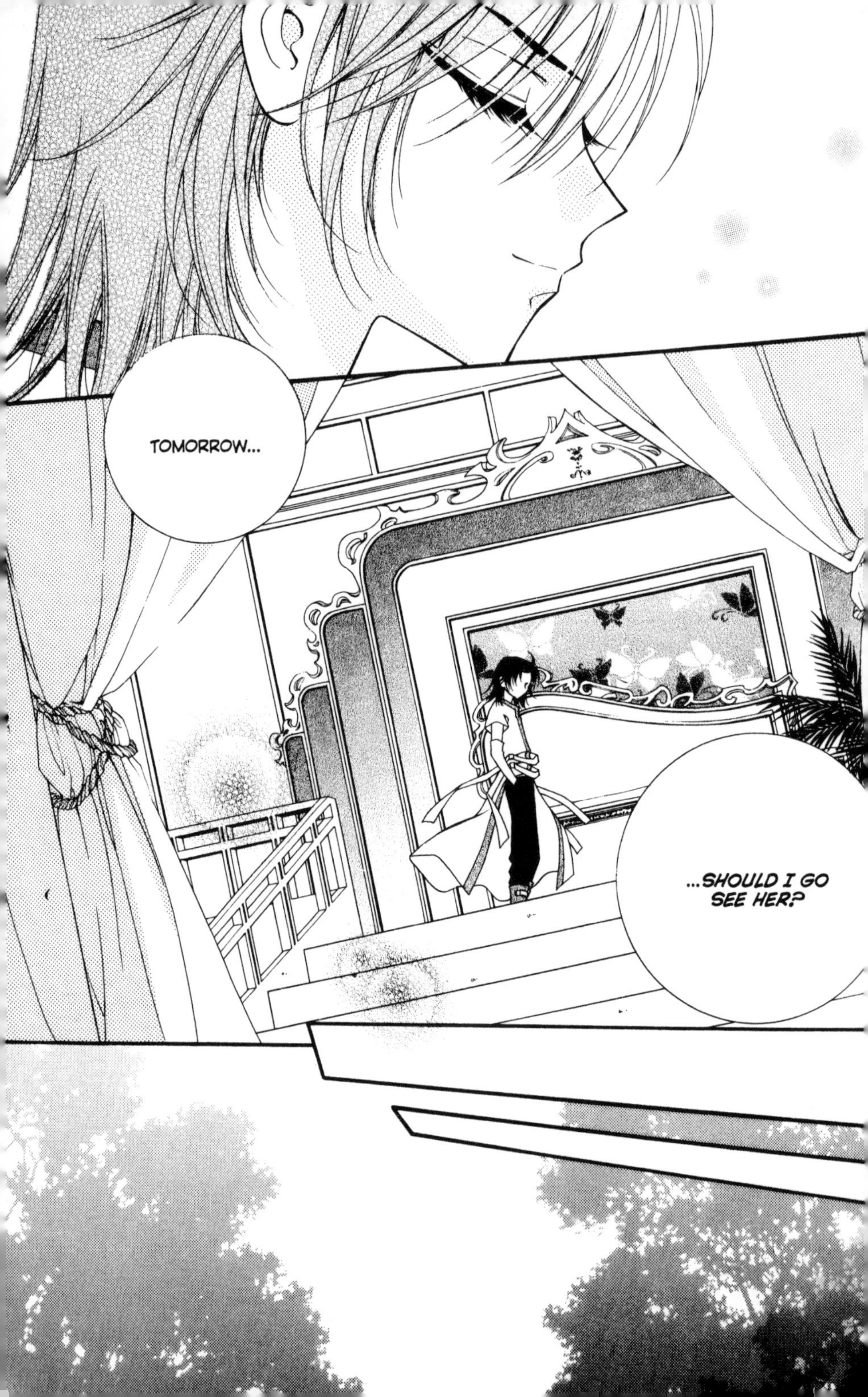
TOMORROW...
...SHOULD I GO SEE HER?

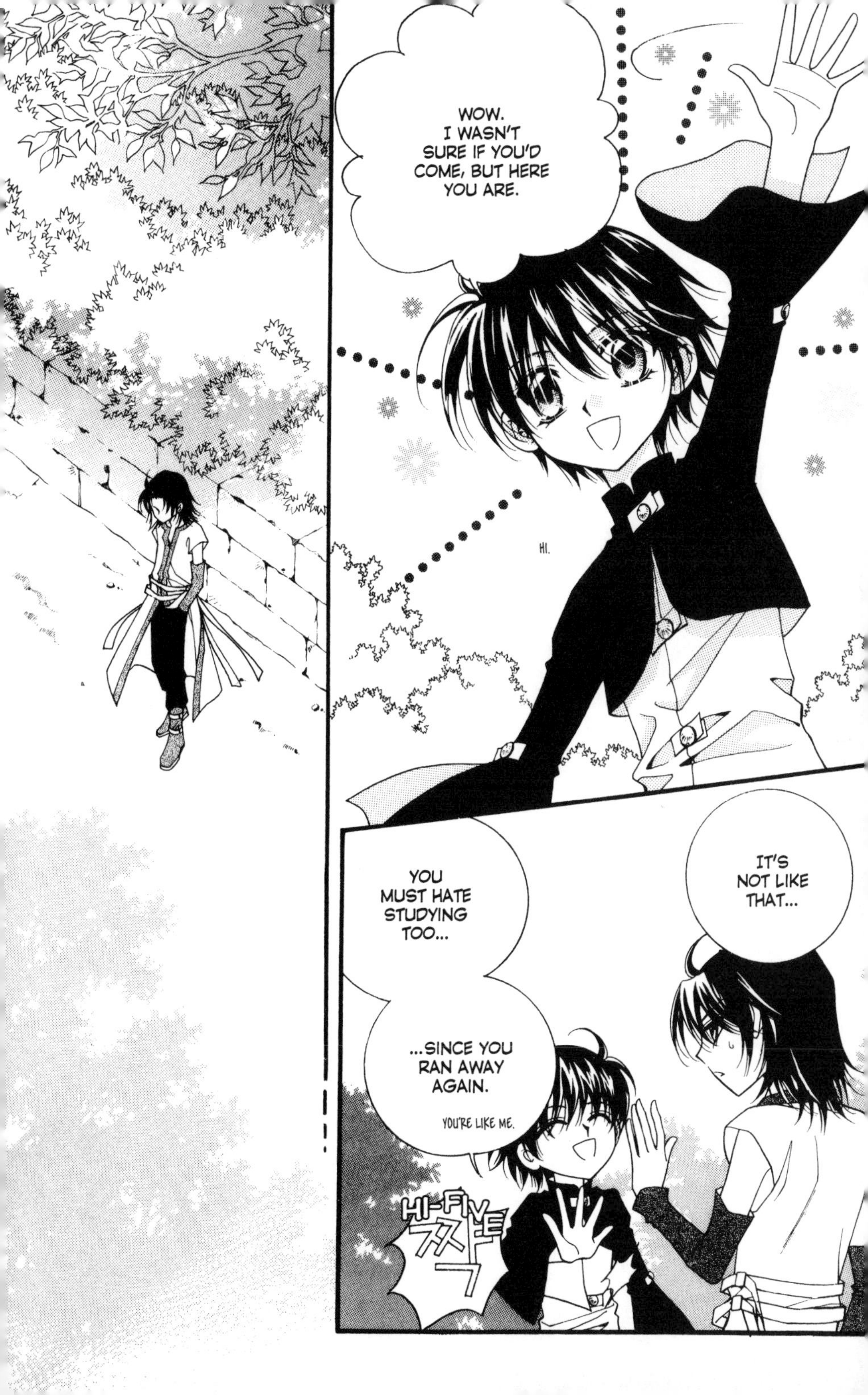
WOW. I WASN'T SURE IF YOU'D COME, BUT HERE YOU ARE.
HI.
YOU MUST HATE STUDYING TOO...
...SINCE YOU RAN AWAY AGAIN.
YOU'RE LIKE ME.
IT'S NOT LIKE THAT...
HI-FIVE

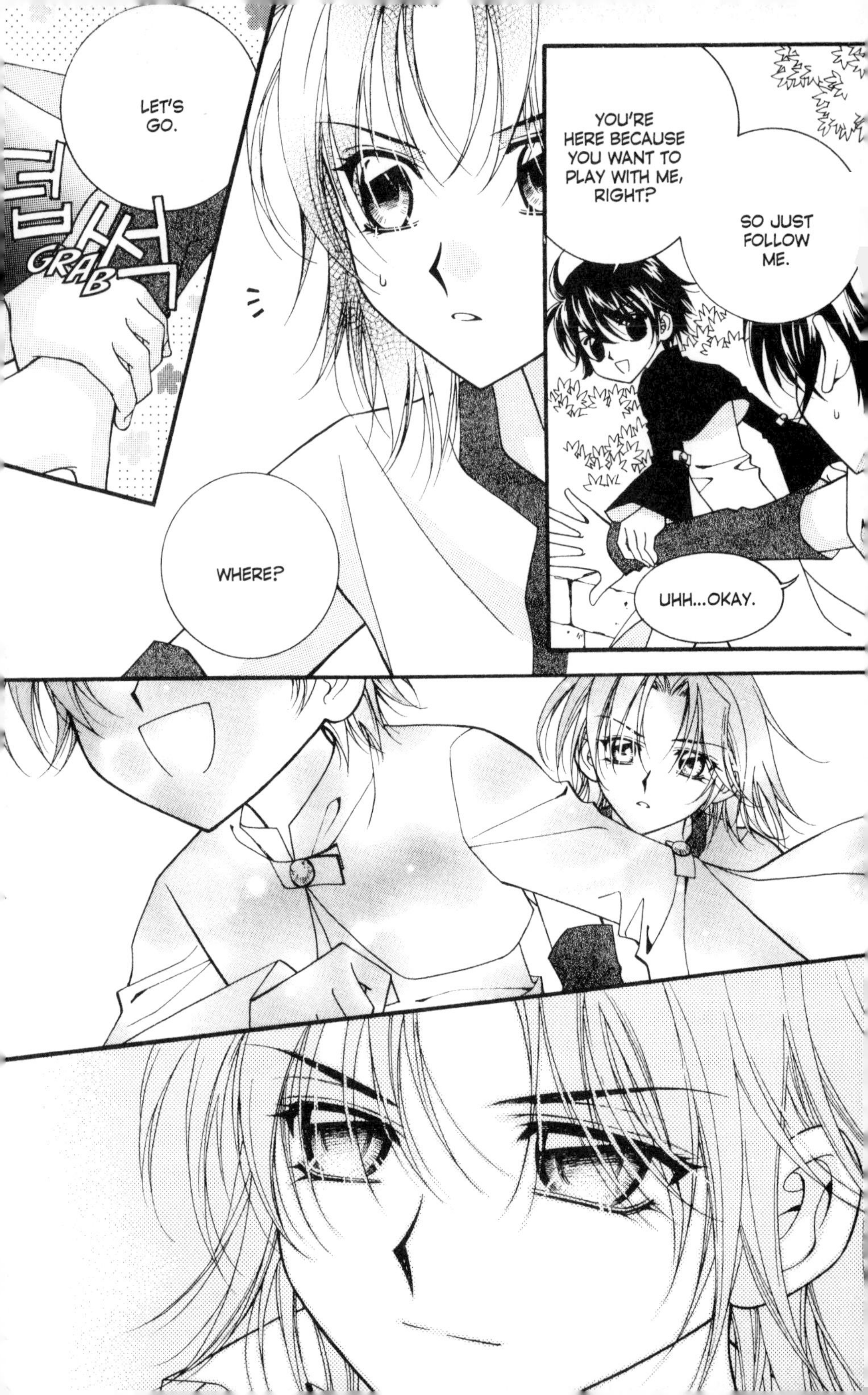
LET'S GO.
GRAB
WHERE?
YOU'RE HERE BECAUSE YOU WANT TO PLAY WITH ME, RIGHT?
SO JUST FOLLOW ME.
UHH...OKAY.

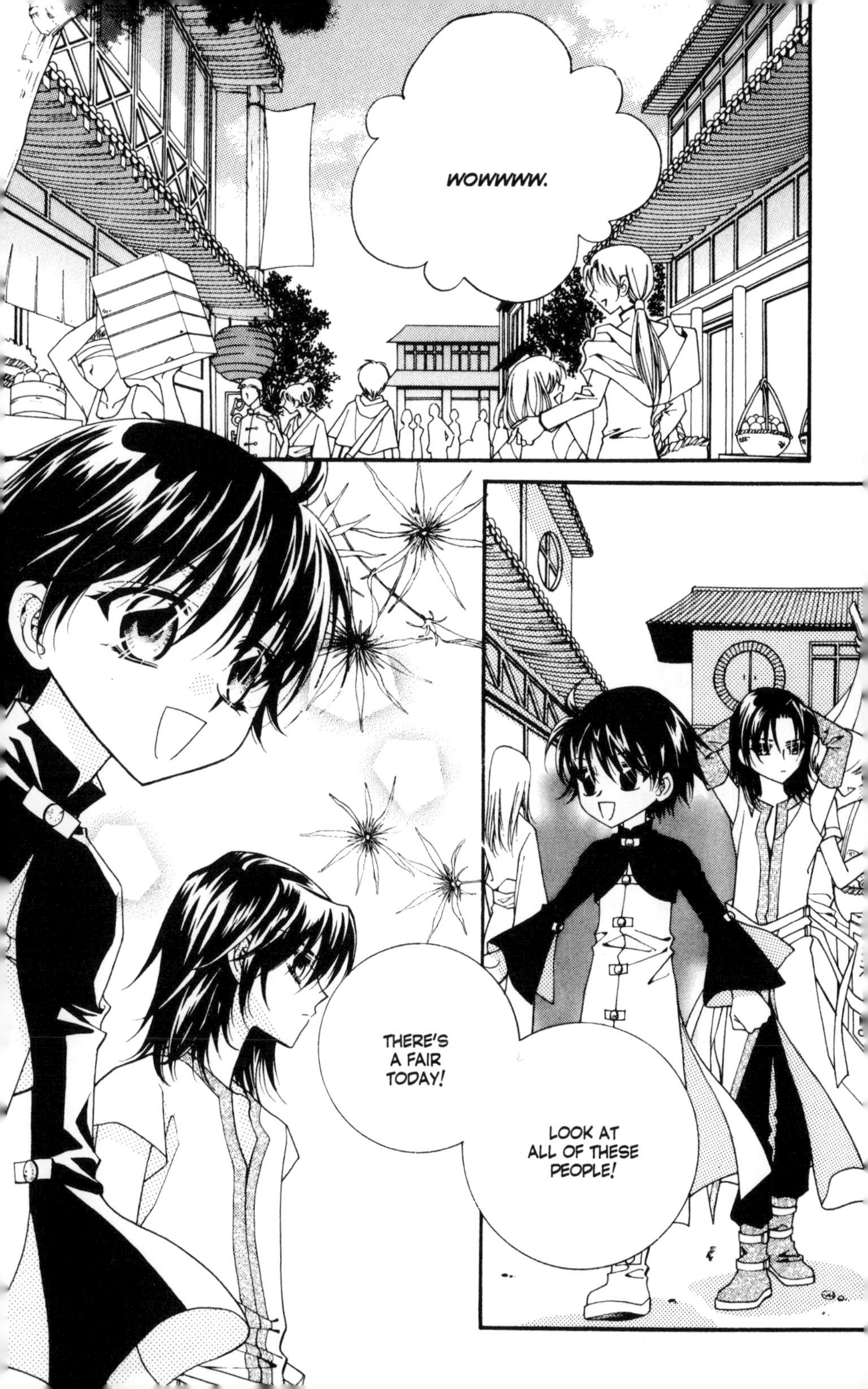
WOWWWW.
THERE'S A FAIR TODAY!
LOOK AT ALL OF THESE PEOPLE!

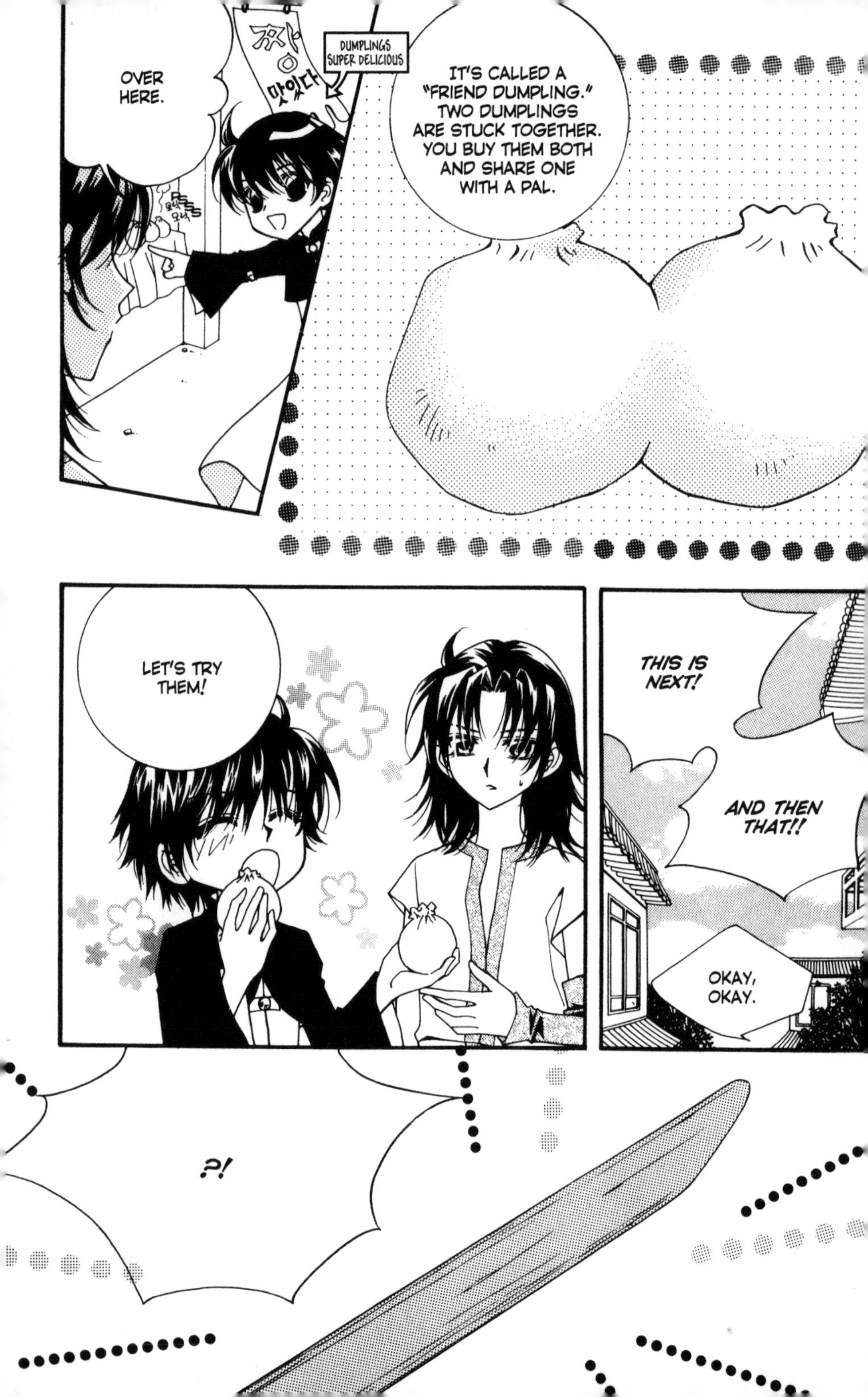
OVER HERE.
꼬치
맛있다
DUMPLINGS SUPER DELICIOUS
IT'S CALLED A "FRIEND DUMPLING." TWO DUMPLINGS ARE STUCK TOGETHER. YOU BUY THEM BOTH AND SHARE ONE WITH A PAL.
LET'S TRY THEM!
THIS IS NEXT!
AND THEN THAT!!
OKAY, OKAY.
?!

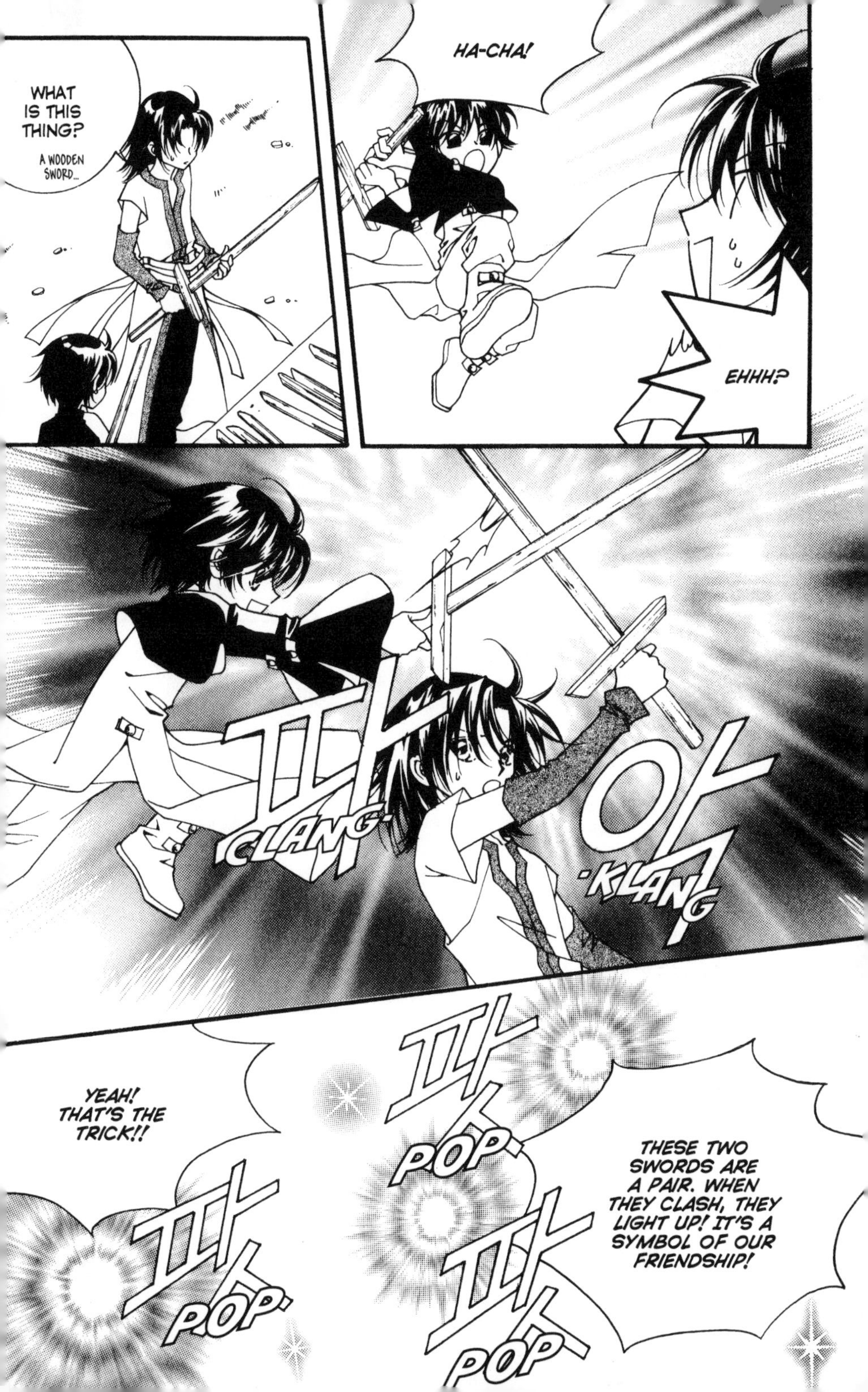
WHAT IS THIS THING?
A WOODEN SWORD...
HA-CHA!
EHHH?
CLANG
KLANG
YEAH! THAT'S THE TRICK!!
POP
POP
THESE TWO SWORDS ARE A PAIR. WHEN THEY CLASH, THEY LIGHT UP! IT'S A SYMBOL OF OUR FRIENDSHIP!
POP
POP

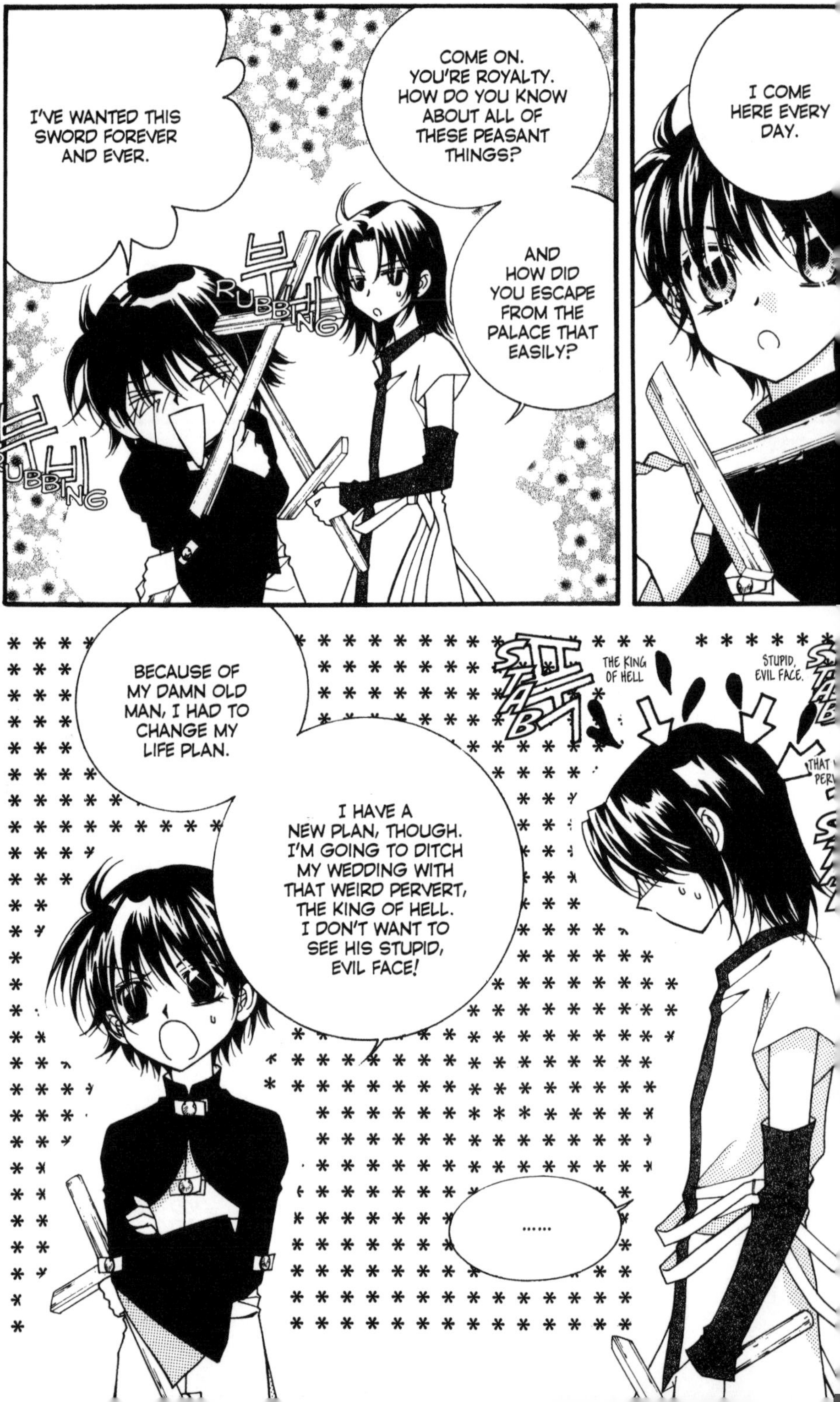
I'VE WANTED THIS SWORD FOREVER AND EVER.
COME ON. YOU'RE ROYALTY. HOW DO YOU KNOW ABOUT ALL OF THESE PEASANT THINGS?
RUBBING
RUBBING
AND HOW DID YOU ESCAPE FROM THE PALACE THAT EASILY?
I COME HERE EVERY DAY.
BECAUSE OF MY DAMN OLD MAN, I HAD TO CHANGE MY LIFE PLAN.
I HAVE A NEW PLAN, THOUGH. I'M GOING TO DITCH MY WEDDING WITH THAT WEIRD PERVERT, THE KING OF HELL. I DON'T WANT TO SEE HIS STUPID, EVIL FACE!
STAB
THE KING OF HELL
STUPID, EVIL FACE.
......

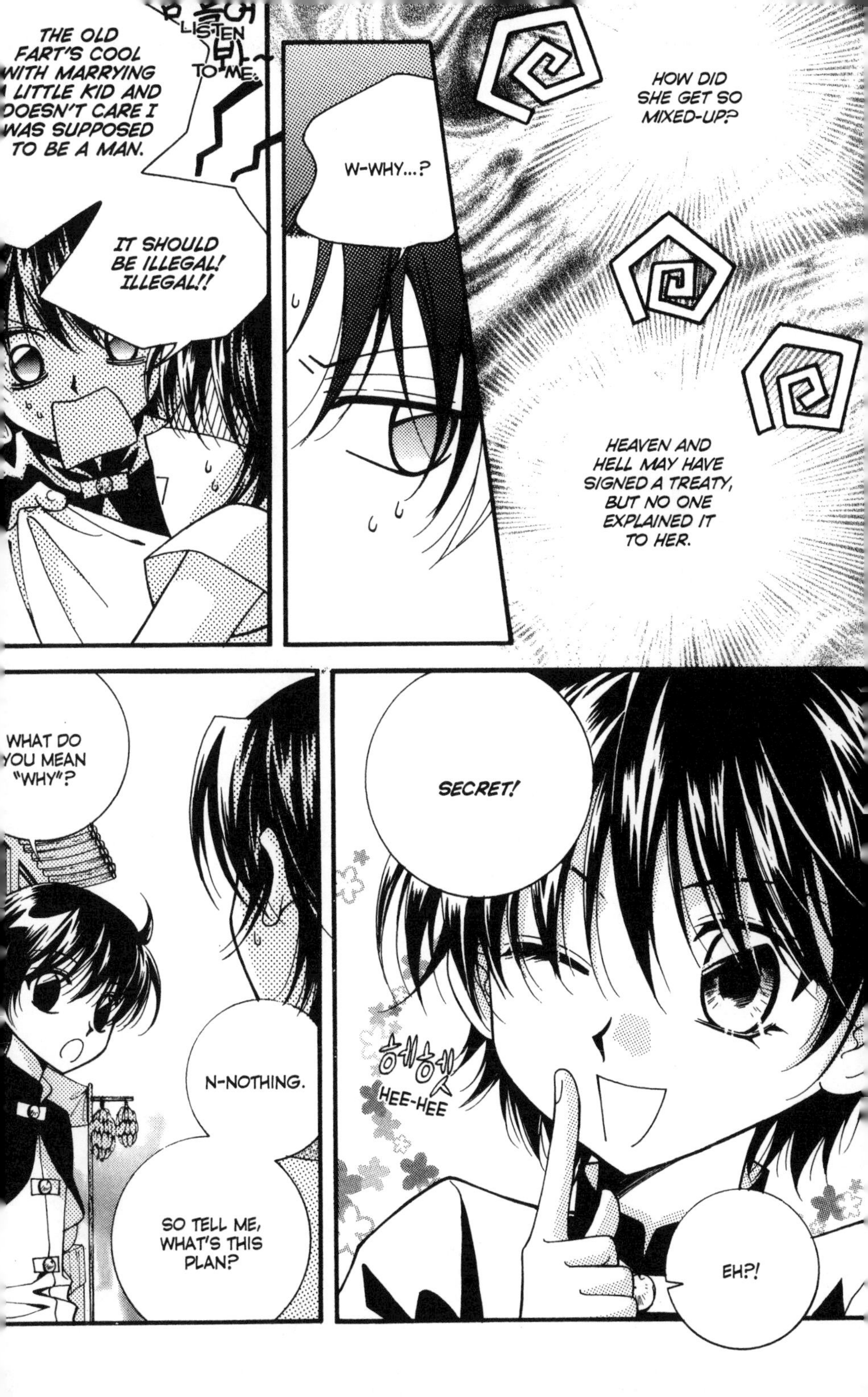
LISTEN TO ME.
THE OLD FART'S COOL WITH MARRYING A LITTLE KID AND DOESN'T CARE I WAS SUPPOSED TO BE A MAN.
IT SHOULD BE ILLEGAL! ILLEGAL!!
W-WHY...?
HOW DID SHE GET SO MIXED-UP?
HEAVEN AND HELL MAY HAVE SIGNED A TREATY, BUT NO ONE EXPLAINED IT TO HER.
WHAT DO YOU MEAN "WHY"?
N-NOTHING.
SO TELL ME, WHAT'S THIS PLAN?
SECRET!
HEE-HEE
EH?!

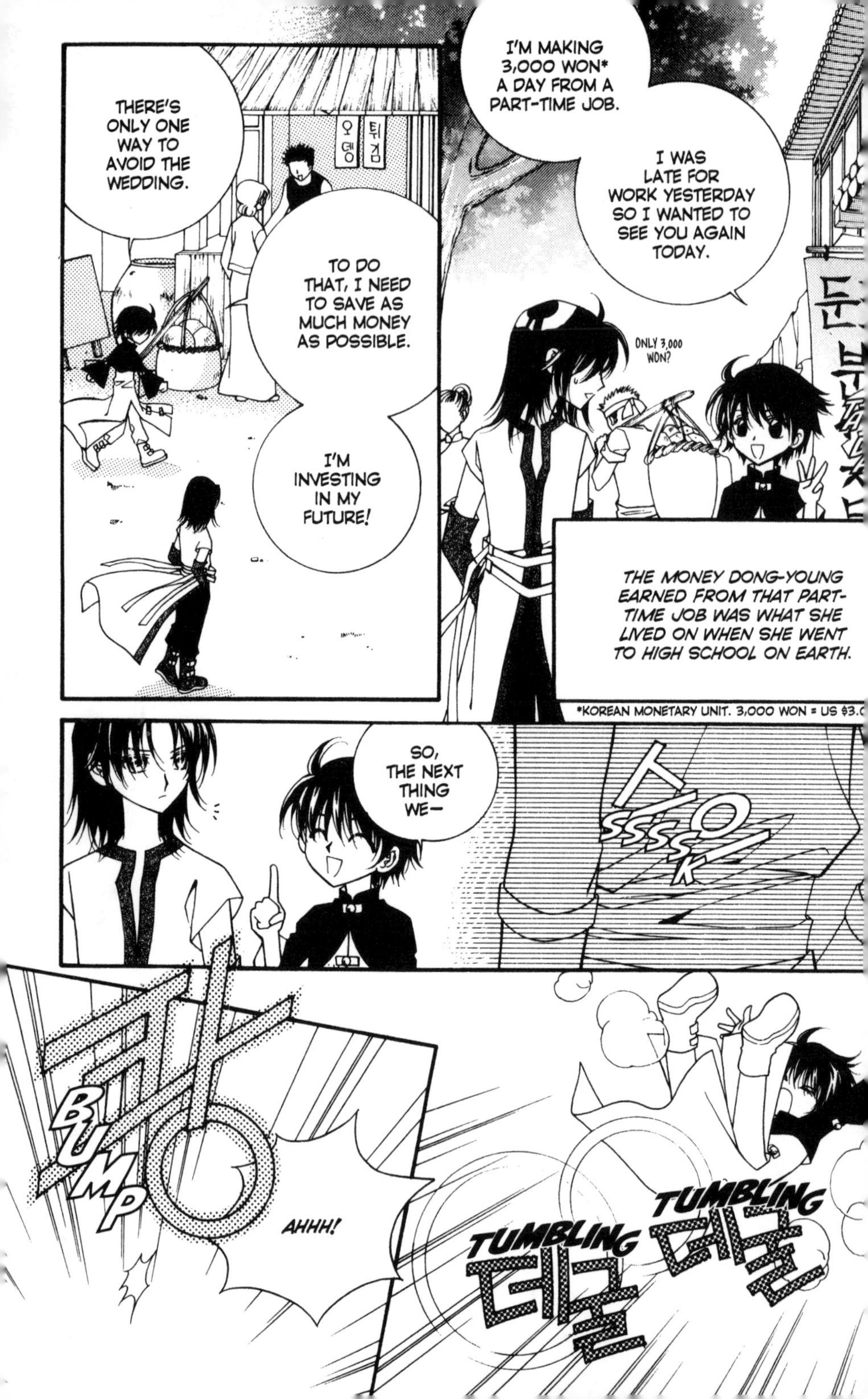
THERE'S ONLY ONE WAY TO AVOID THE WEDDING.
오뎅
튀김
TO DO THAT, I NEED TO SAVE AS MUCH MONEY AS POSSIBLE.
I'M INVESTING IN MY FUTURE!
I'M MAKING 3,000 WON* A DAY FROM A PART-TIME JOB.
I WAS LATE FOR WORK YESTERDAY SO I WANTED TO SEE YOU AGAIN TODAY.
ONLY 3,000 WON?
THE MONEY DONG-YOUNG EARNED FROM THAT PART-TIME JOB WAS WHAT SHE LIVED ON WHEN SHE WENT TO HIGH SCHOOL ON EARTH.
*KOREAN MONETARY UNIT. 3,000 WON = US $3.0
SO, THE NEXT THING WE—
SSSSK
BUMP
AHHH!
TUMBLING
데굴
TUMBLING
데굴

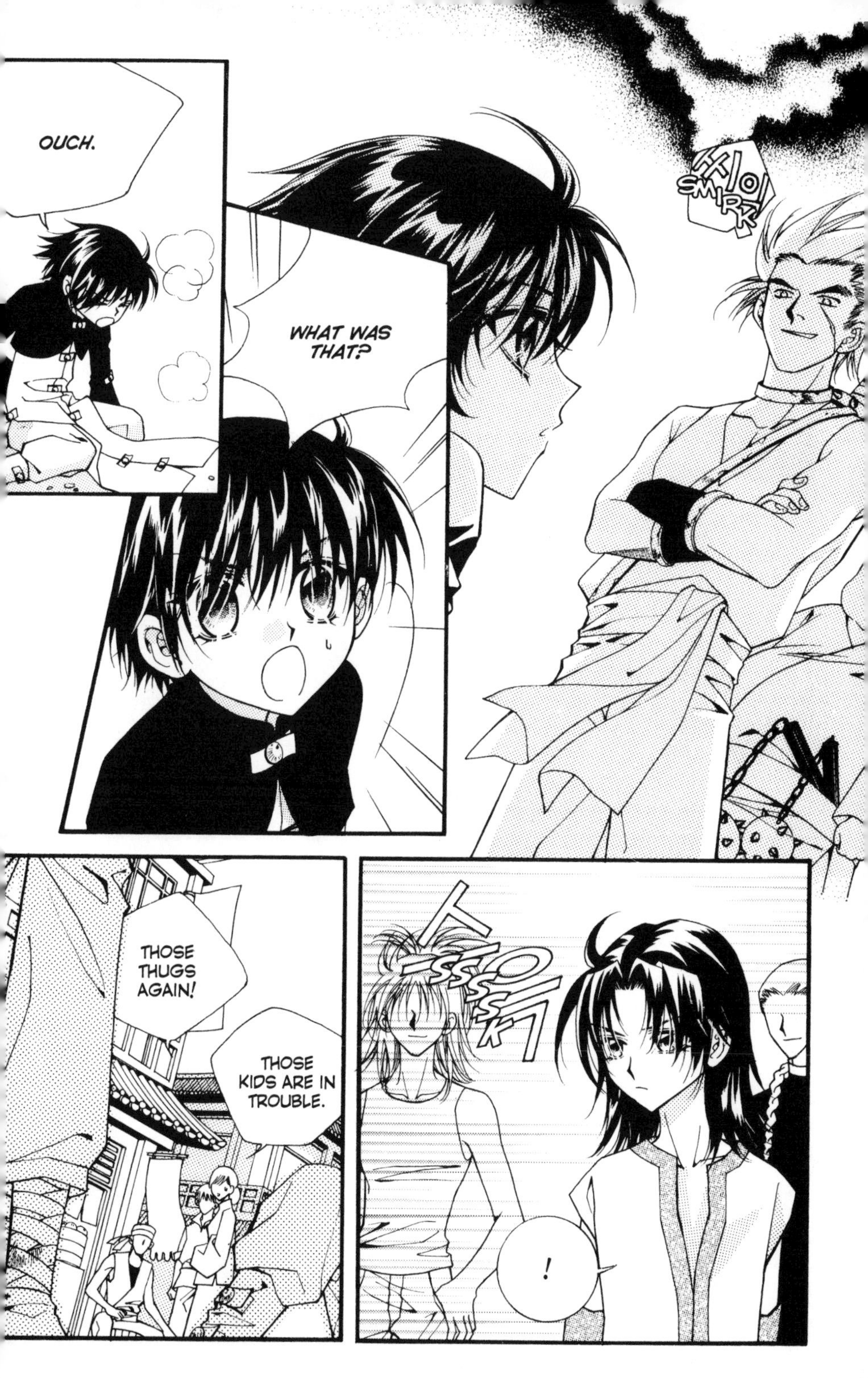
OUCH.
WHAT WAS THAT?
SMIRK
THOSE THUGS AGAIN!
THOSE KIDS ARE IN TROUBLE.
TSSSK
!

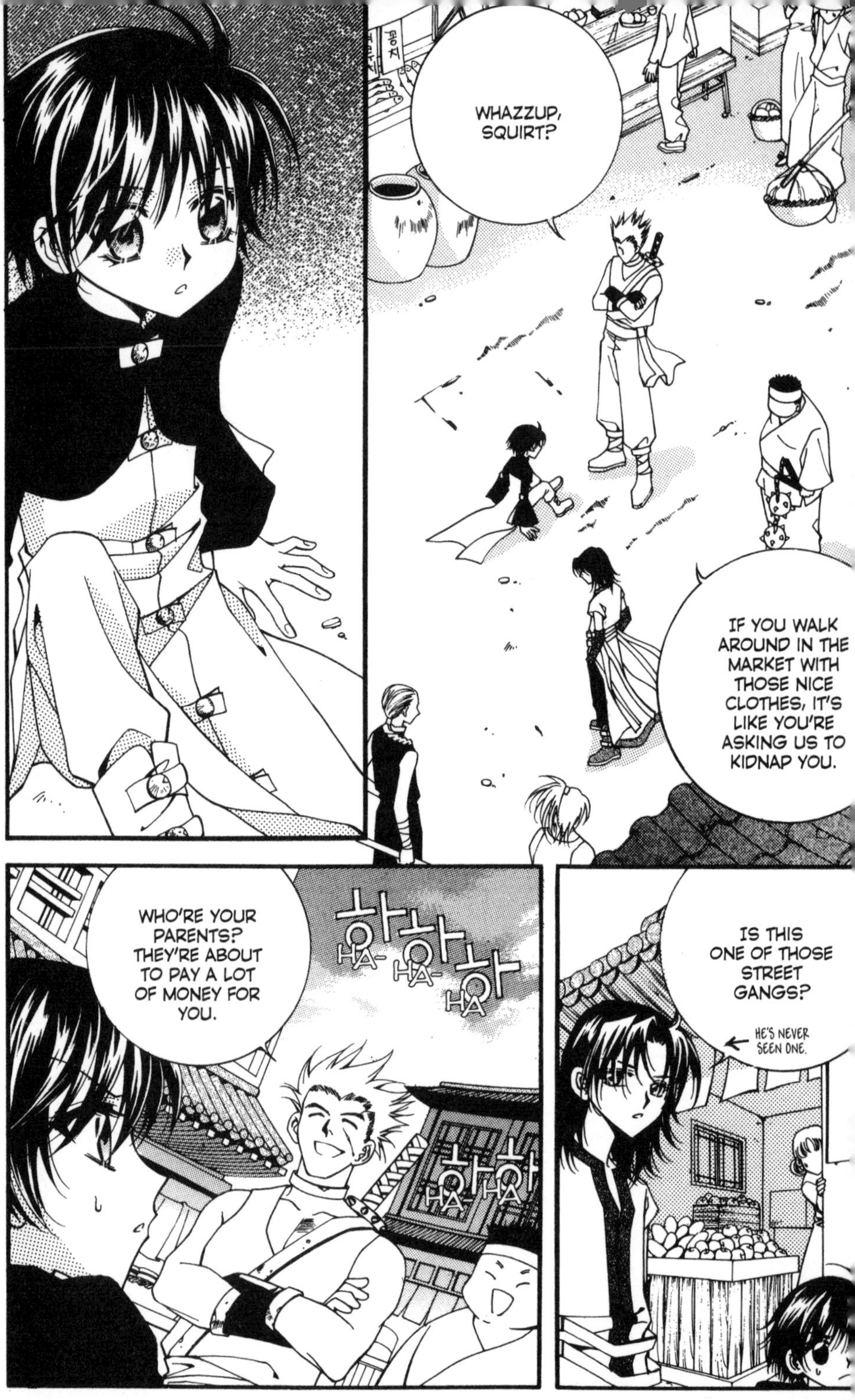
WHAZZUP, SQUIRT?
IF YOU WALK AROUND IN THE MARKET WITH THOSE NICE CLOTHES, IT'S LIKE YOU'RE ASKING US TO KIDNAP YOU.
WHO'RE YOUR PARENTS? THEY'RE ABOUT TO PAY A LOT OF MONEY FOR YOU.
하하하
HA- HA- HA
하하
HA- HA
IS THIS ONE OF THOSE STREET GANGS?
HE'S NEVER SEEN ONE.

WHAT? ISN'T IT OBVIOUS?!

IF THEY GET CAUGHT, THEY'LL BE BANISHED TO EARTH.

CRIMINALS OF HEAVEN ARE REBORN AS ANIMALS DOWN THERE SO THEY CAN'T COMMIT MORE CRIME.

IT TAKES GUTS AND RECKLESSNESS TO BE A BAD GUY UP HERE.

OH-HO.

IN HELL, WE SEND OUR CRIMINALS TO JAIL. IT'S NOT THE SAME.

EITHER THAT, OR THEY'RE REALLY STUPID TO BE DOING THIS IN PUBLIC.

MURMUR

MURMUR

THOSE KIDS AREN'T SCARED OF THE GANGSTERS.

I KNOW.

THEY'RE TALKING LIKE THE BANGERS AREN'T EVEN THERE!

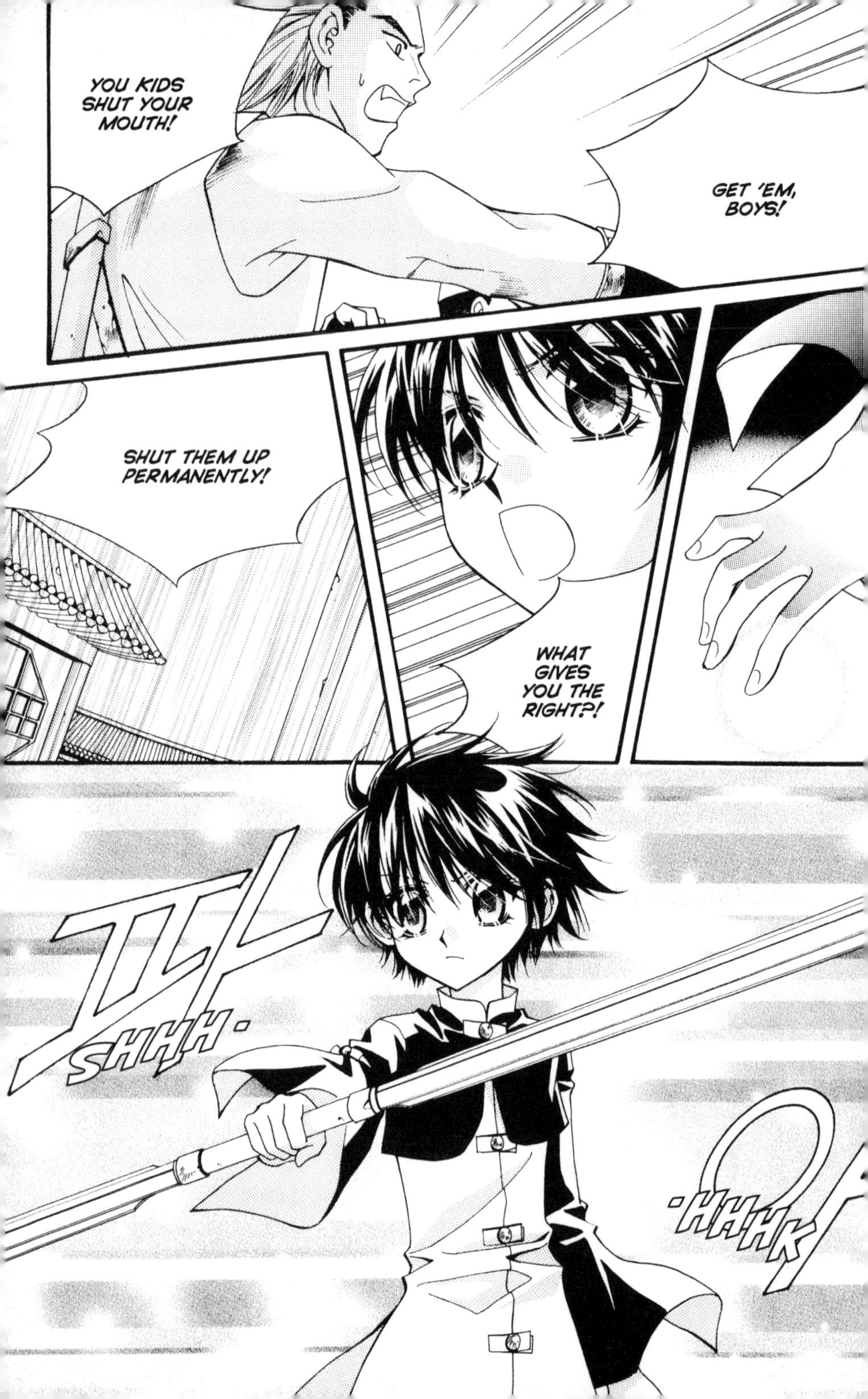
YOU KIDS SHUT YOUR MOUTH!
GET 'EM, BOYS!
SHUT THEM UP PERMANENTLY!
WHAT GIVES YOU THE RIGHT?!
SHHH-
-HHHK

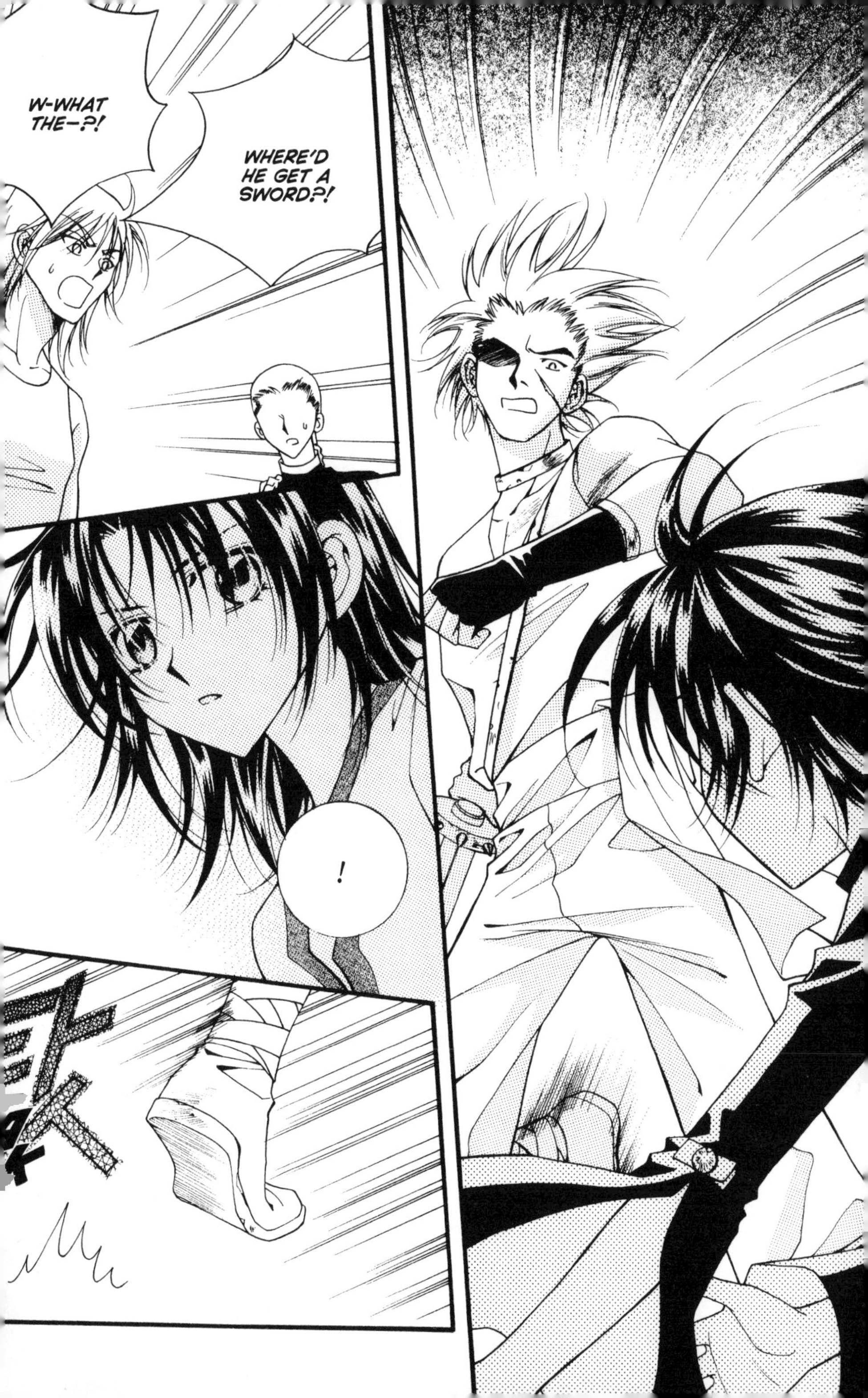
W-WHAT THE–?!
WHERE'D HE GET A SWORD?!
!

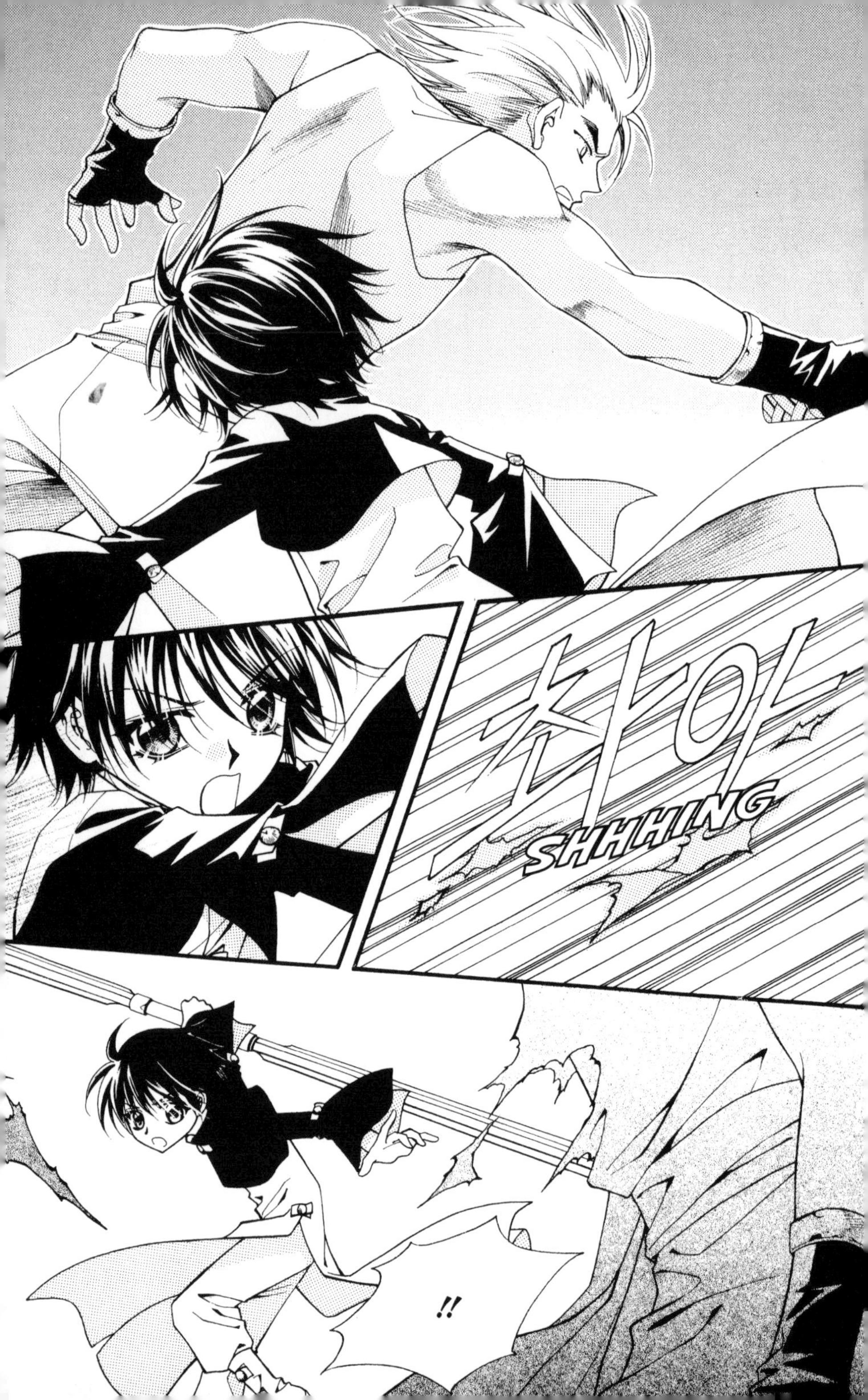

SHHHING
!!

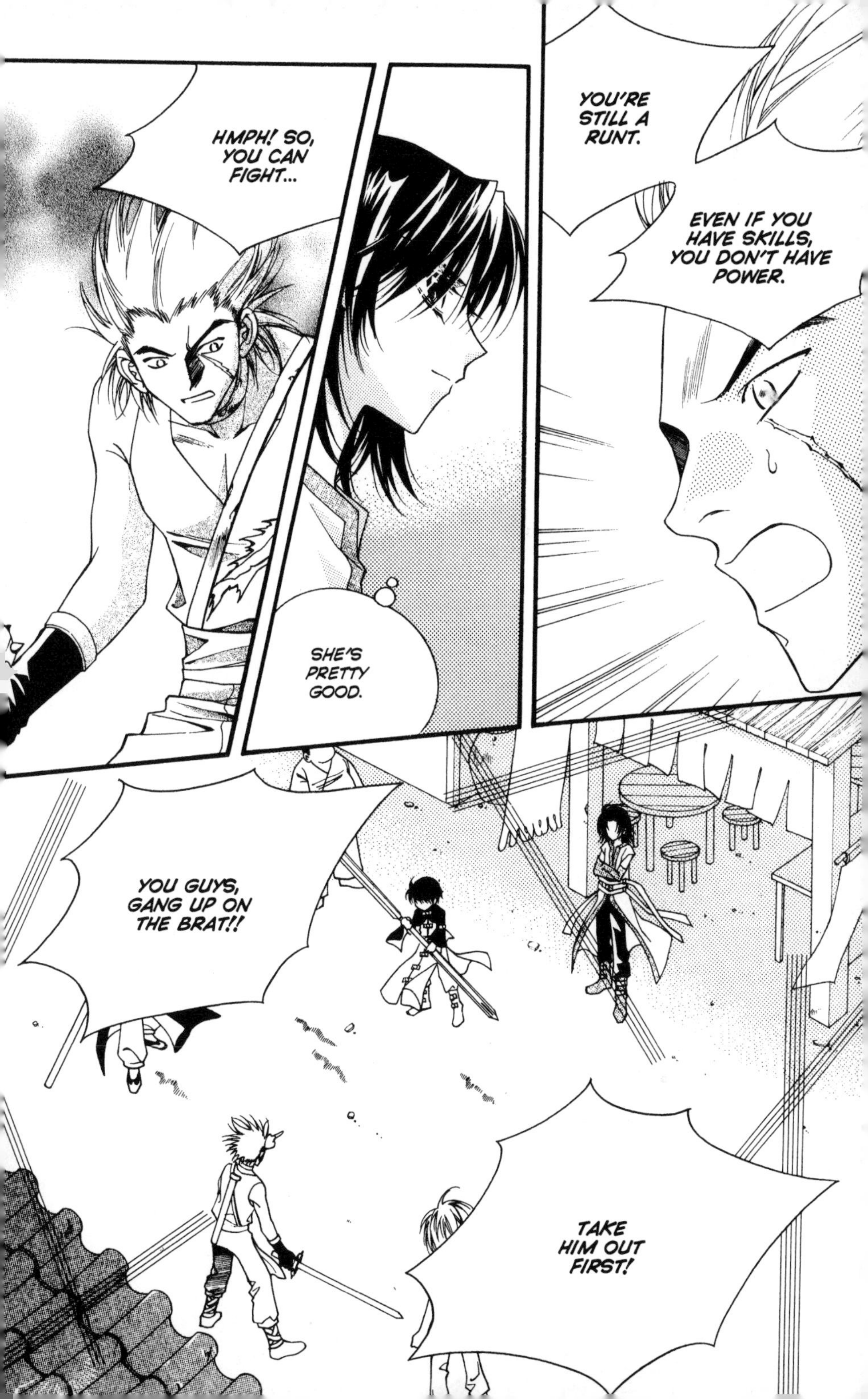
HMPH! SO, YOU CAN FIGHT...
SHE'S PRETTY GOOD.
YOU'RE STILL A RUNT.
EVEN IF YOU HAVE SKILLS, YOU DON'T HAVE POWER.
YOU GUYS, GANG UP ON THE BRAT!!
TAKE HIM OUT FIRST!

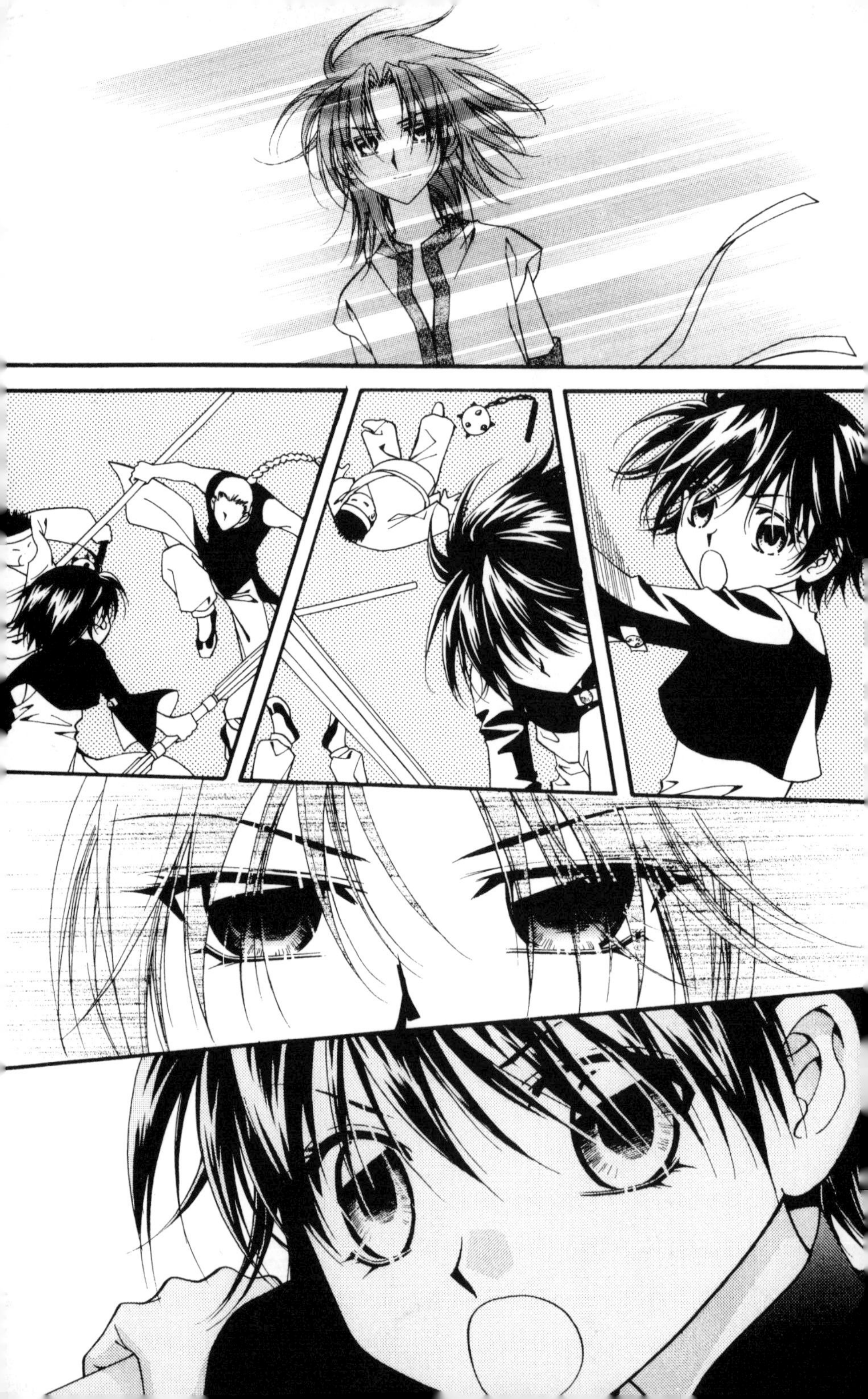

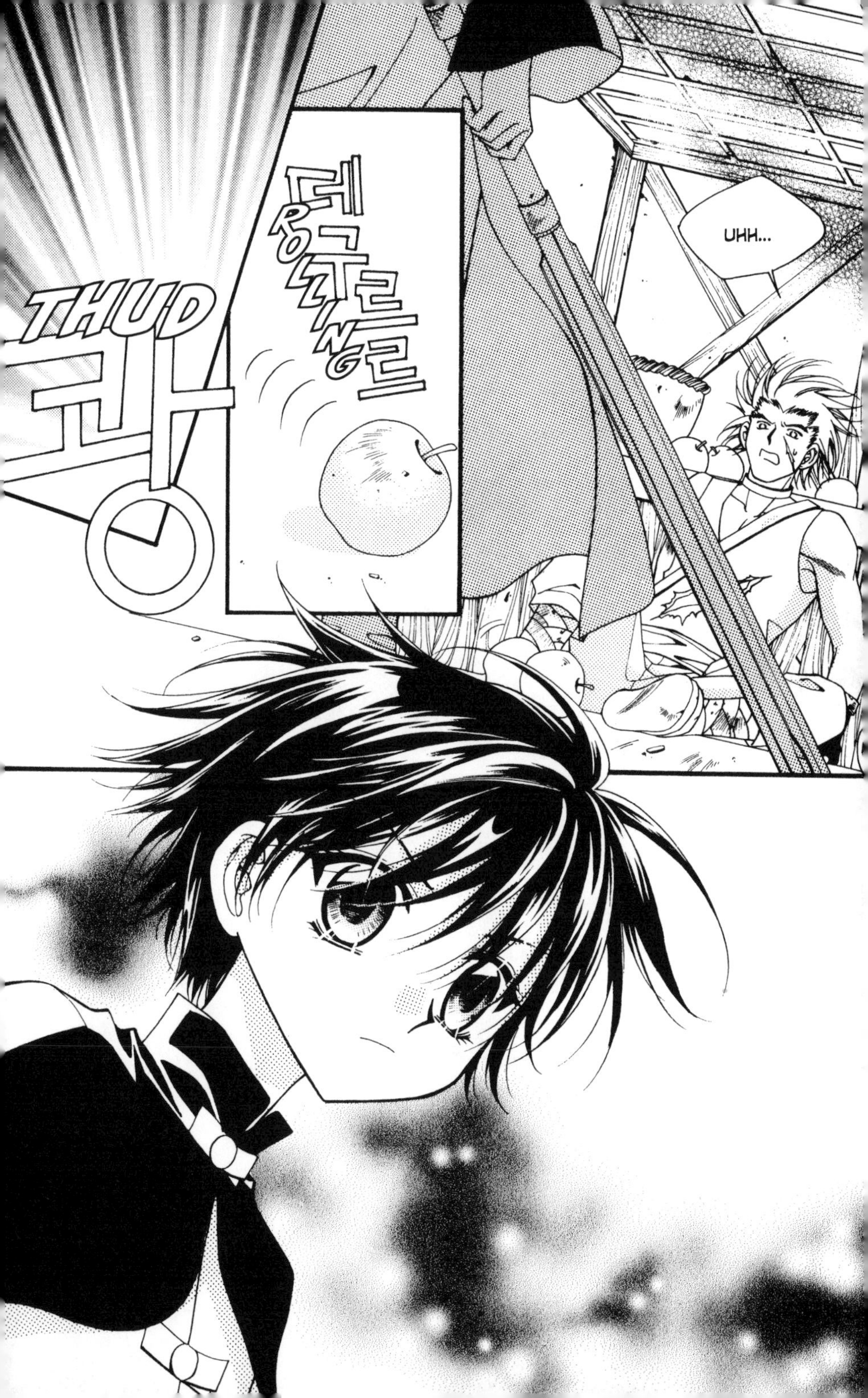
THUD
콰앙
ROLLING
데구르르
UHH...

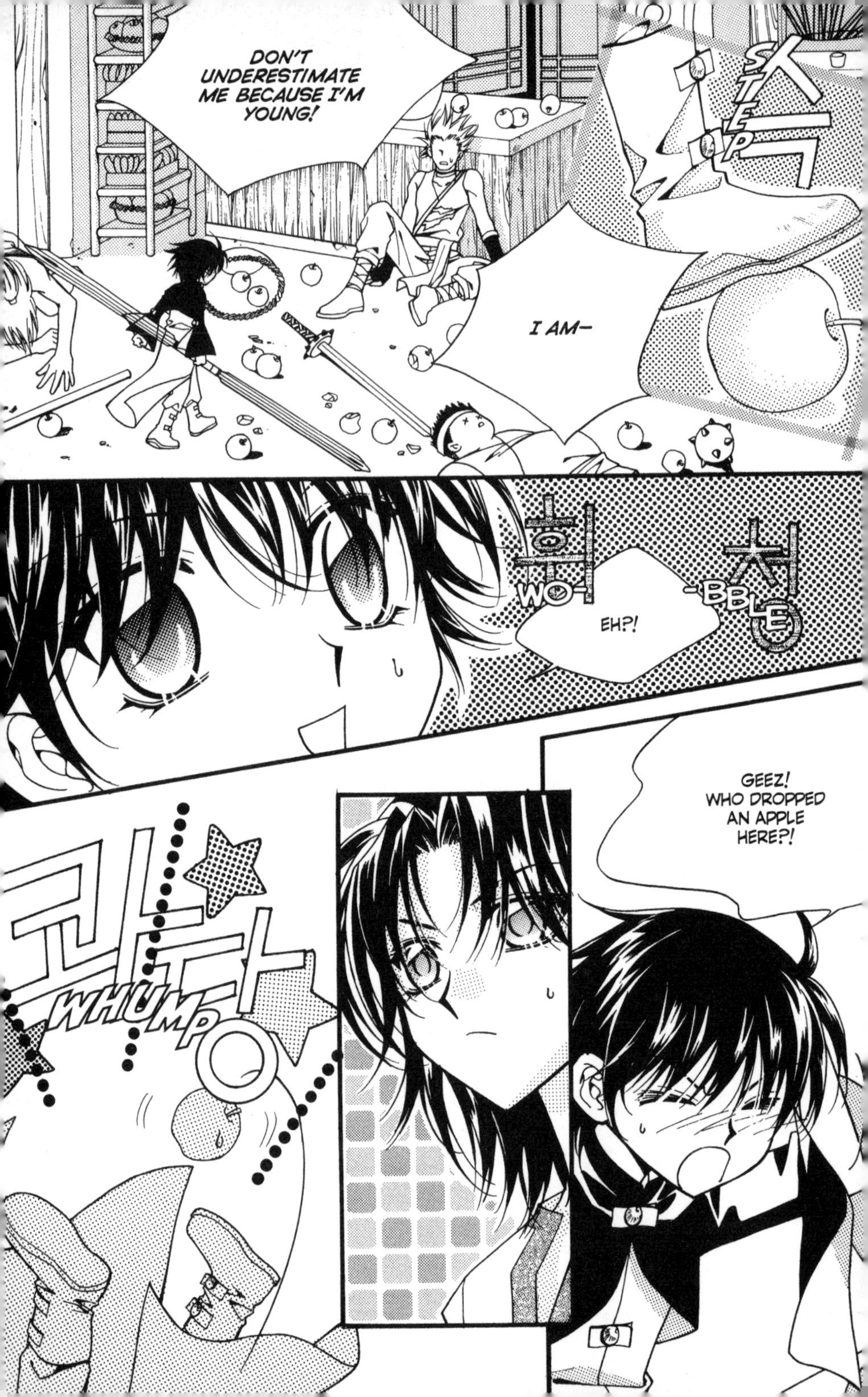
DON'T UNDERESTIMATE ME BECAUSE I'M YOUNG!
STEP
I AM—
WO-
EH?!
-BBLE
WHUMP
GEEZ! WHO DROPPED AN APPLE HERE?!

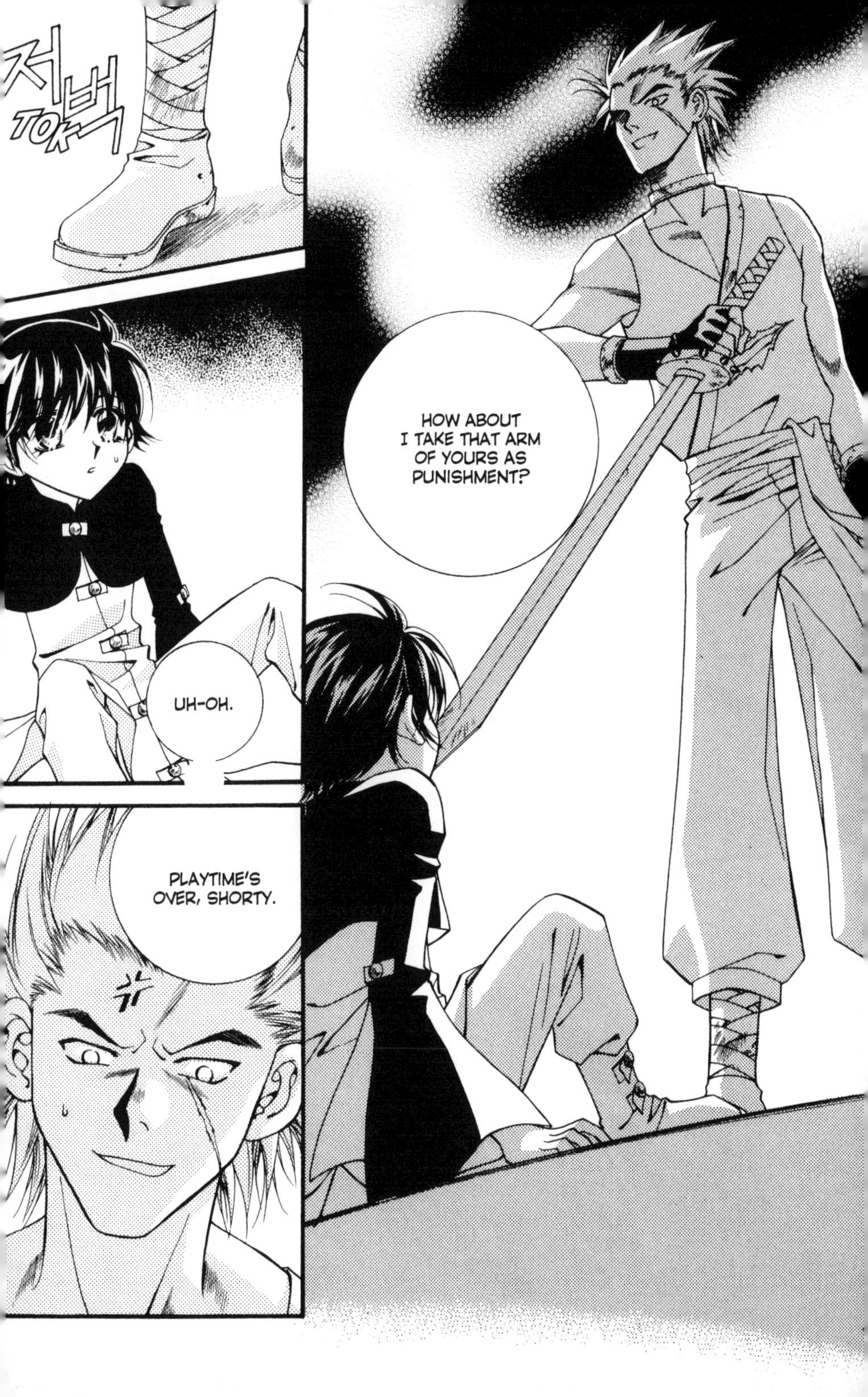
저벅
TOK
UH-OH.
PLAYTIME'S OVER, SHORTY.
HOW ABOUT I TAKE THAT ARM OF YOURS AS PUNISHMENT?

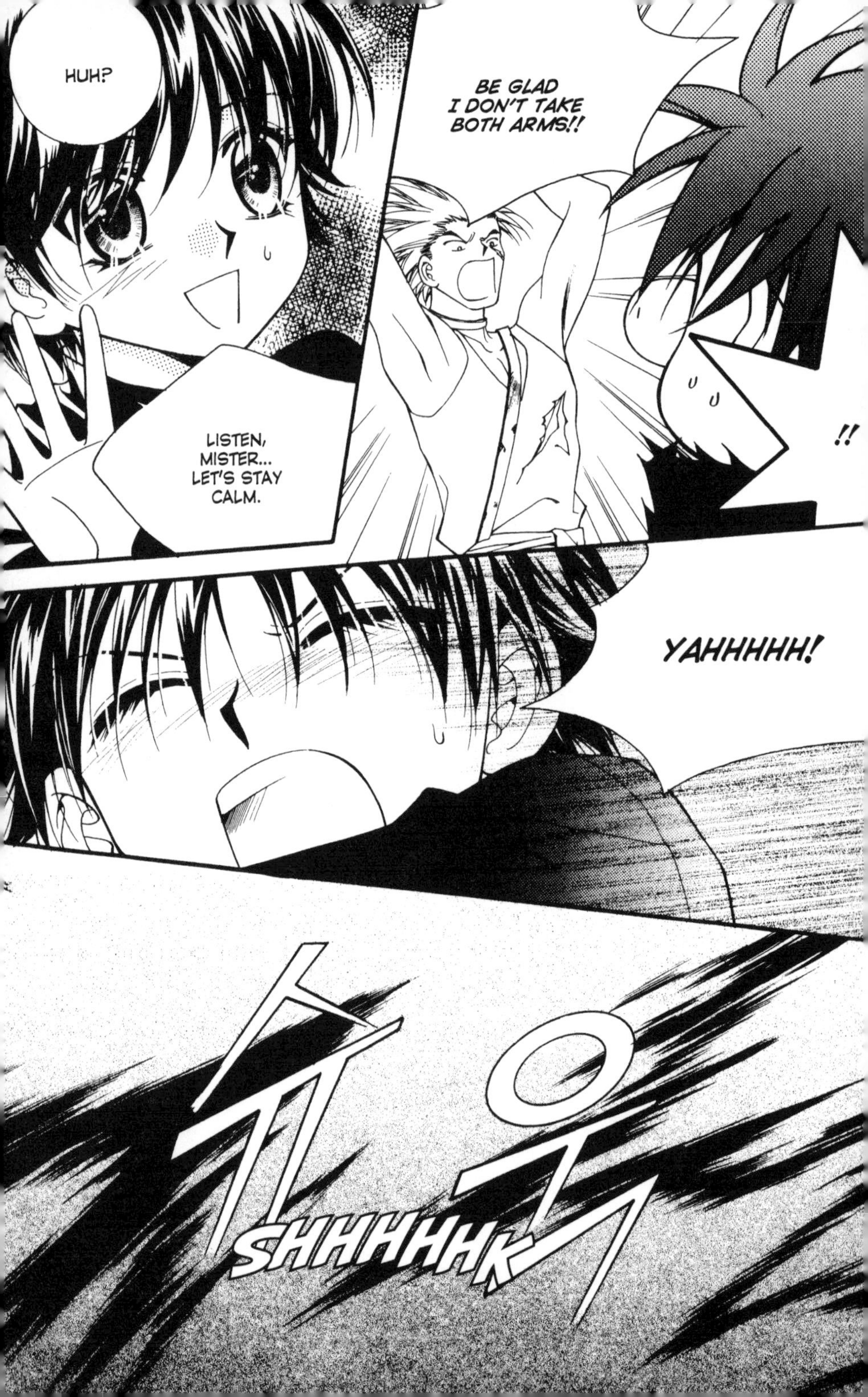
HUH?
LISTEN, MISTER... LET'S STAY CALM.
BE GLAD I DON'T TAKE BOTH ARMS!!
!!
YAHHHHH!
SHHHHHK

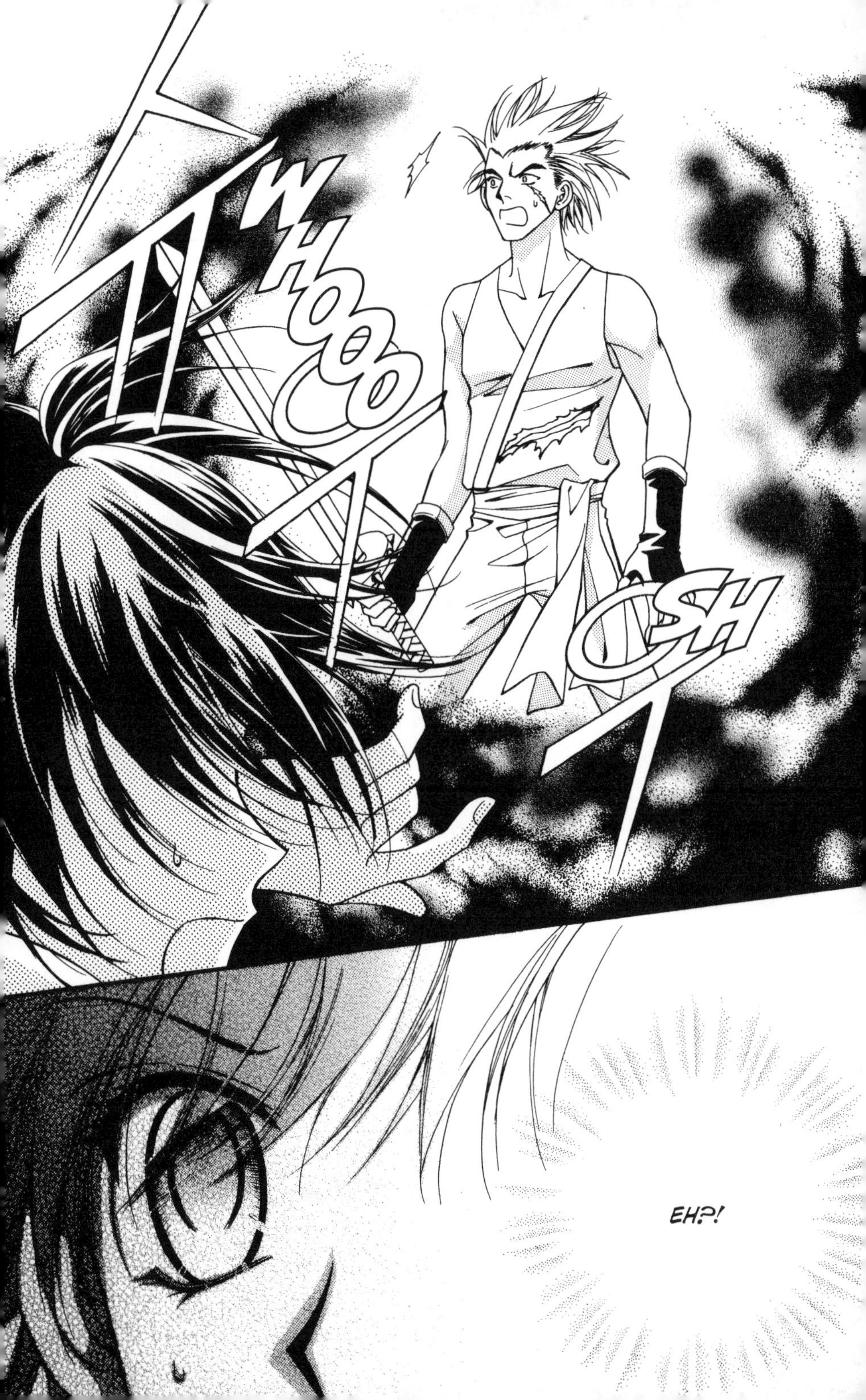
WHOOO
CSH
EH?!

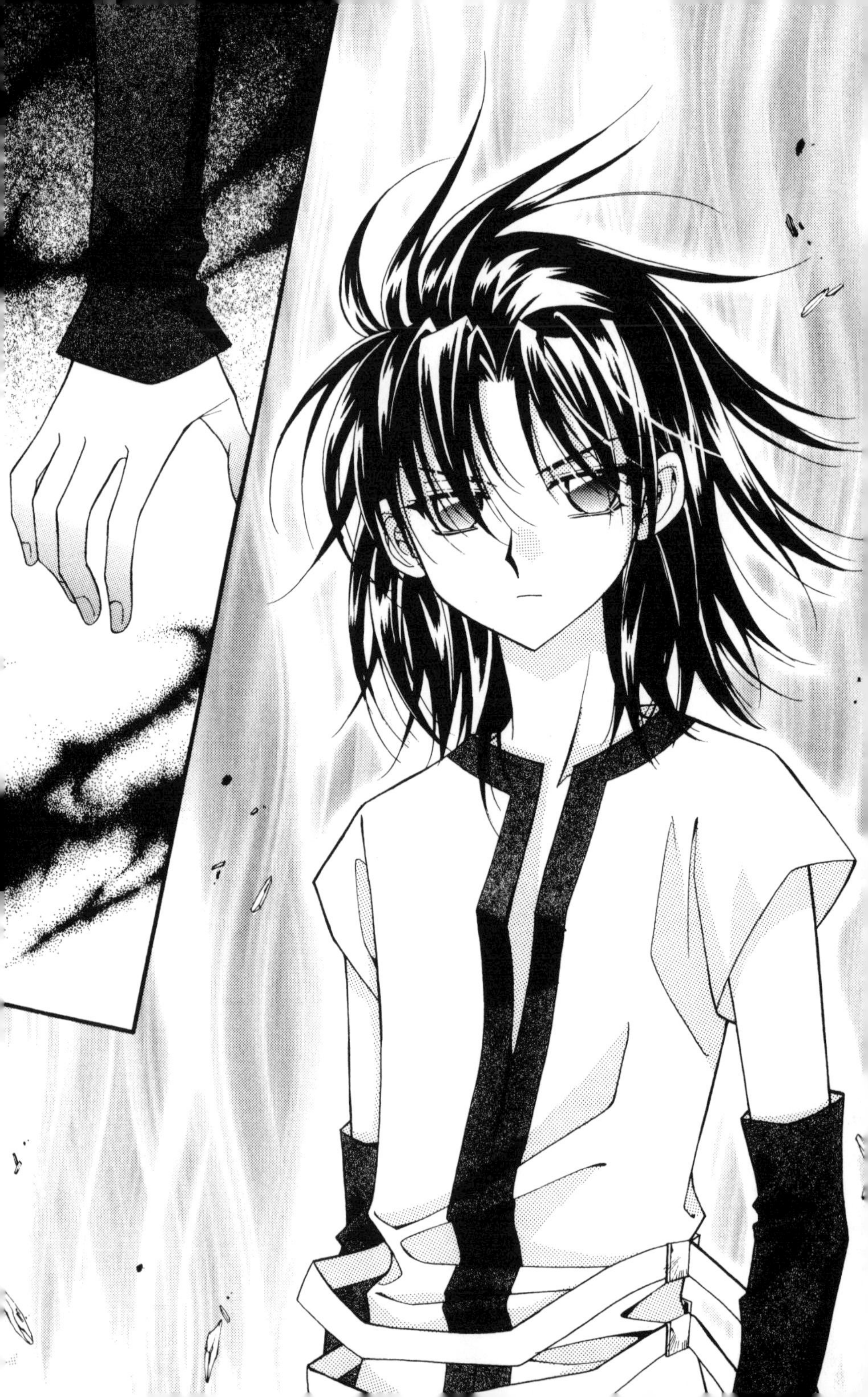

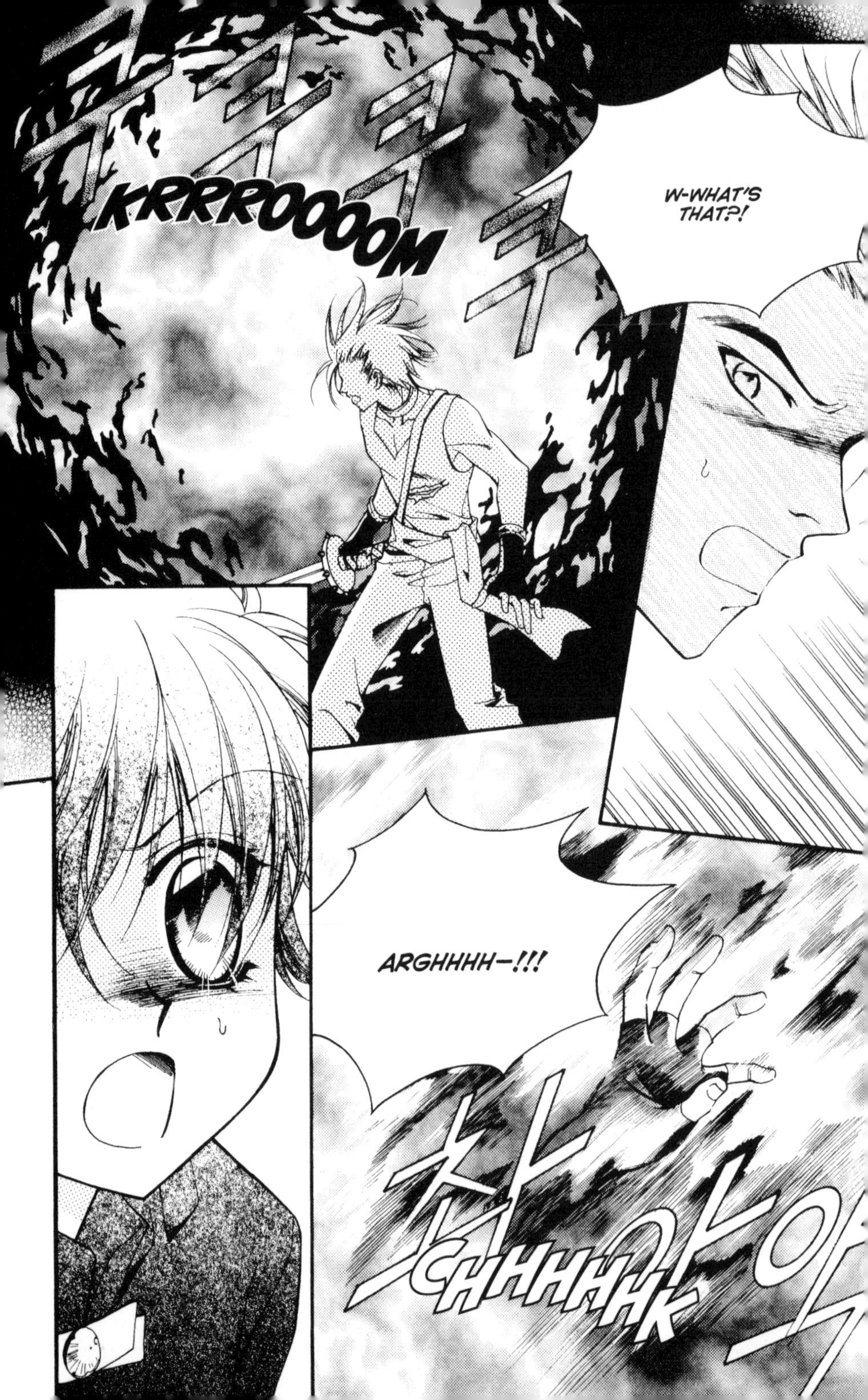
KRRROOOOM
W-WHAT'S THAT?!
ARGHHHH-!!!
CHHHHHHK

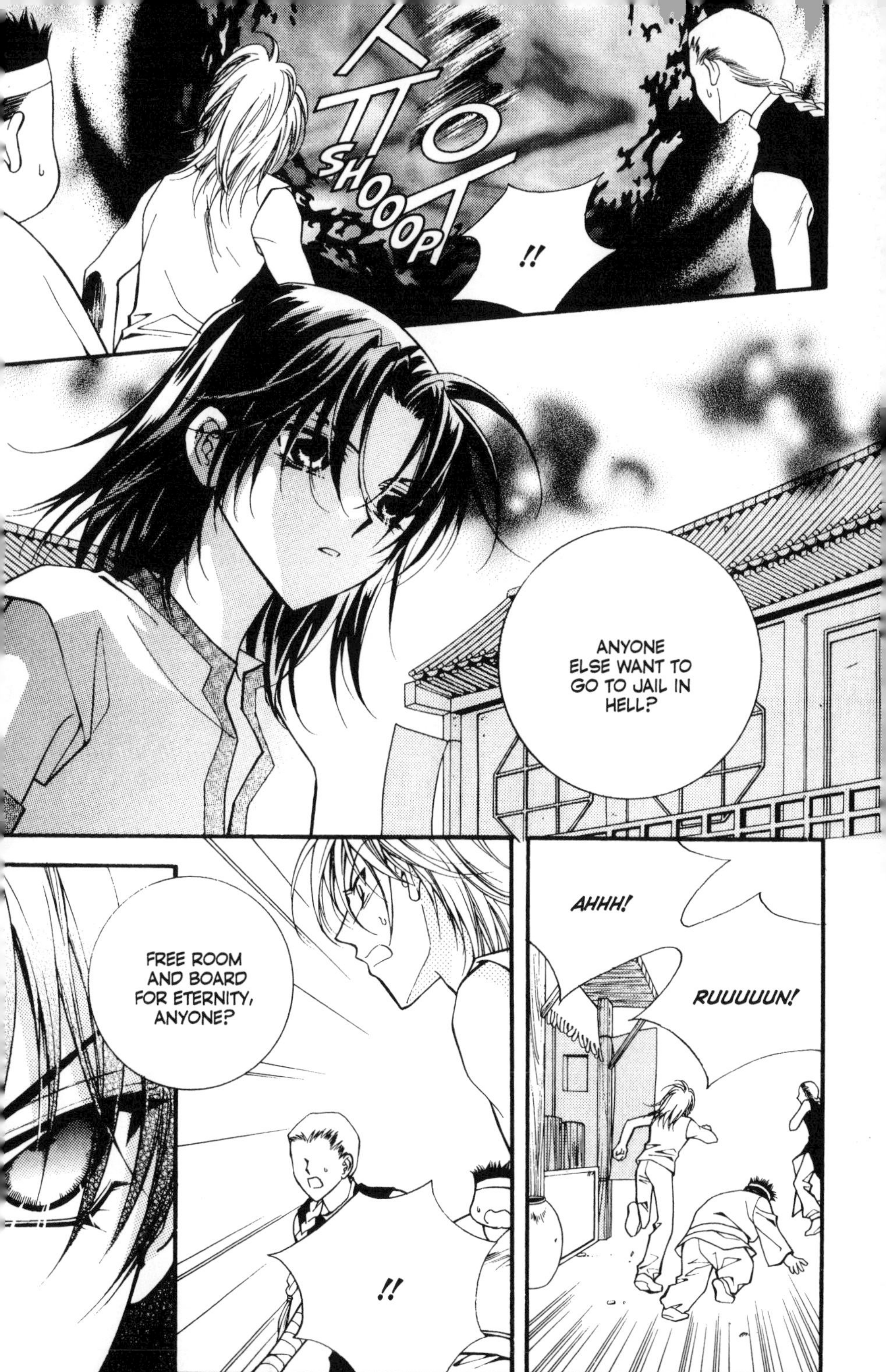
SHOOOP
!!
ANYONE ELSE WANT TO GO TO JAIL IN HELL?
FREE ROOM AND BOARD FOR ETERNITY, ANYONE?
!!
AHHH!
RUUUUUN!

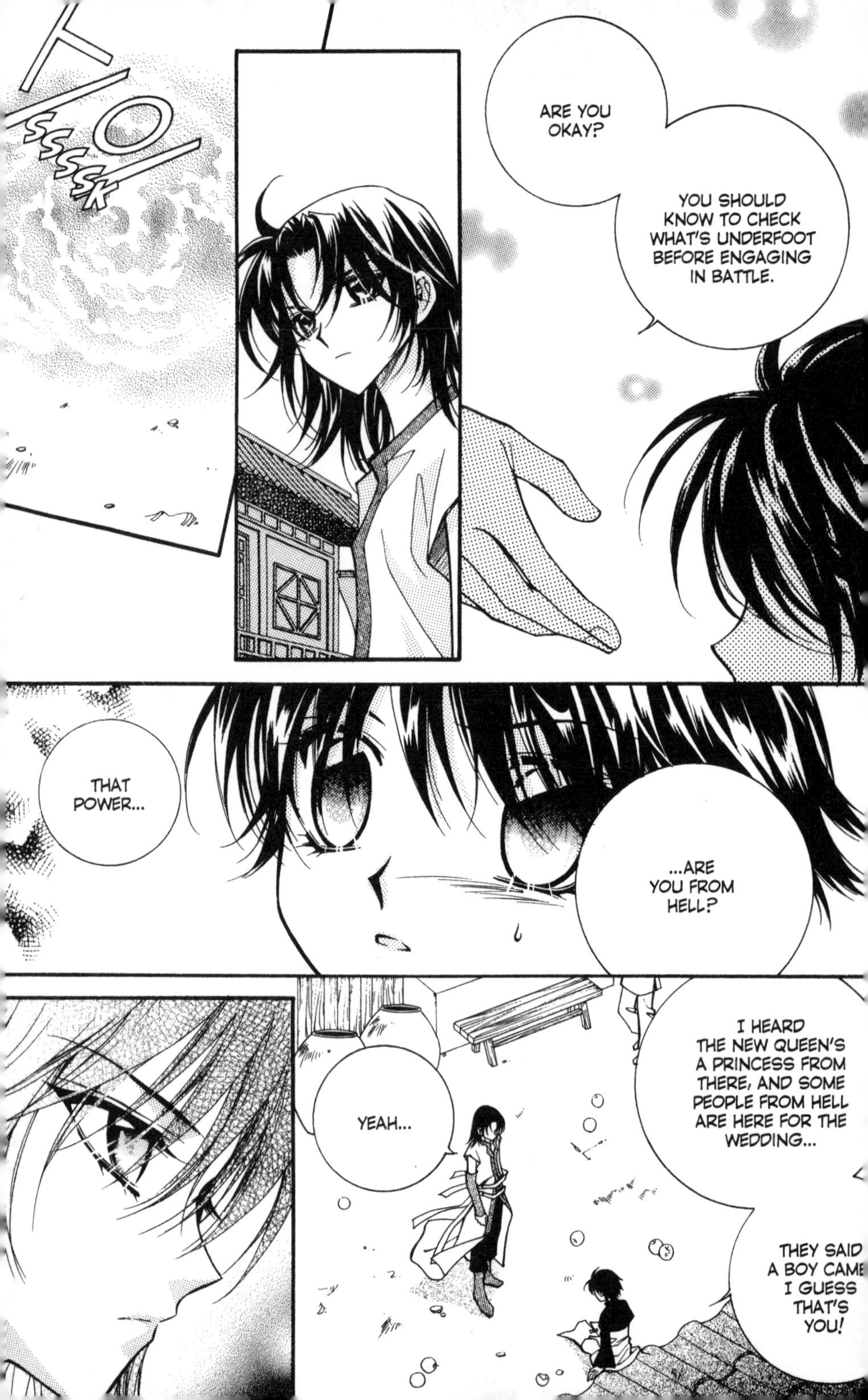
SSSSK
ARE YOU OKAY?
YOU SHOULD KNOW TO CHECK WHAT'S UNDERFOOT BEFORE ENGAGING IN BATTLE.
THAT POWER...
...ARE YOU FROM HELL?
YEAH...
I HEARD THE NEW QUEEN'S A PRINCESS FROM THERE, AND SOME PEOPLE FROM HELL ARE HERE FOR THE WEDDING...
THEY SAID A BOY CAME I GUESS THAT'S YOU!

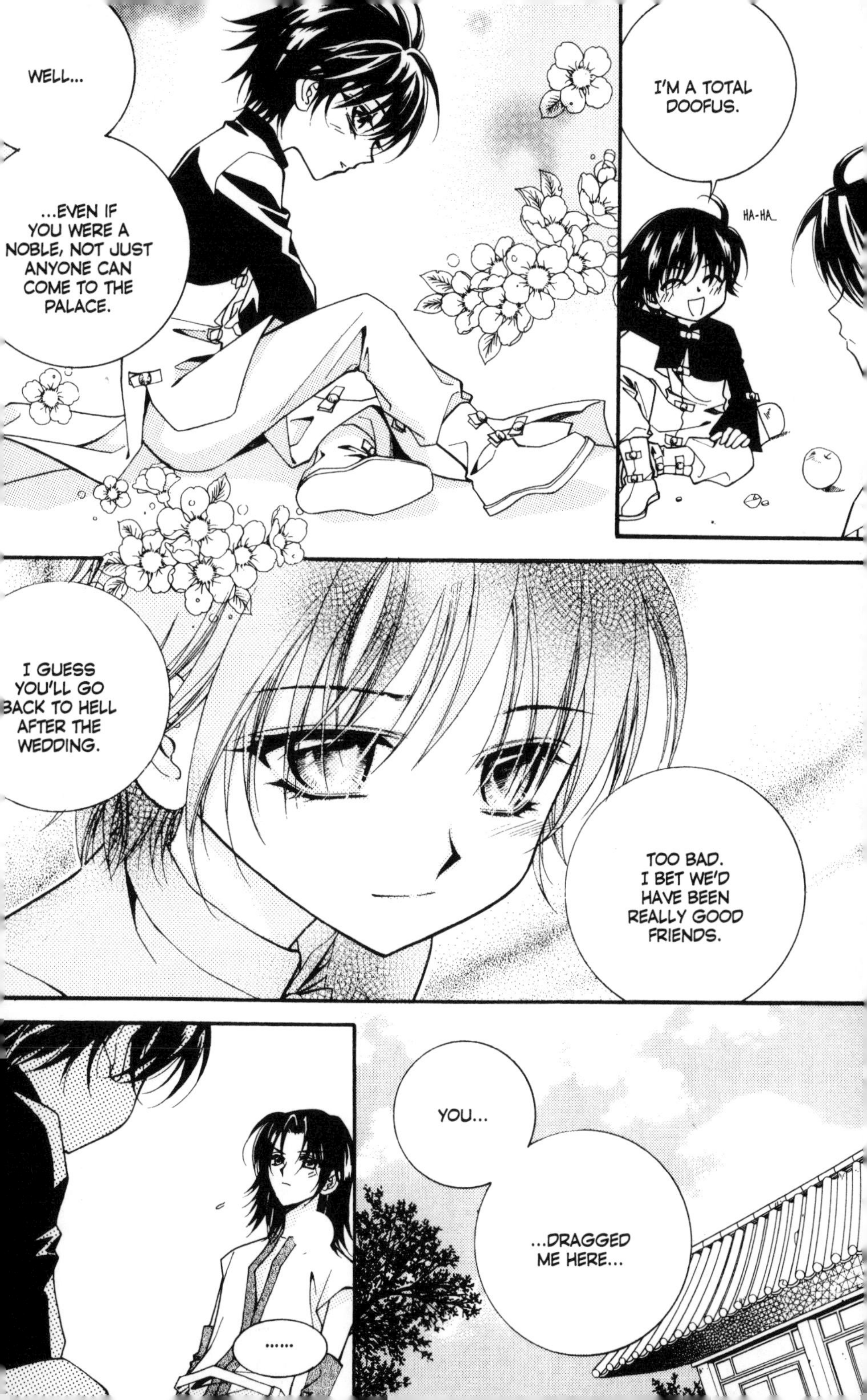
WELL...
...EVEN IF YOU WERE A NOBLE, NOT JUST ANYONE CAN COME TO THE PALACE.
I'M A TOTAL DOOFUS.
HA-HA...
I GUESS YOU'LL GO BACK TO HELL AFTER THE WEDDING.
TOO BAD. I BET WE'D HAVE BEEN REALLY GOOD FRIENDS.
......
YOU...
...DRAGGED ME HERE...

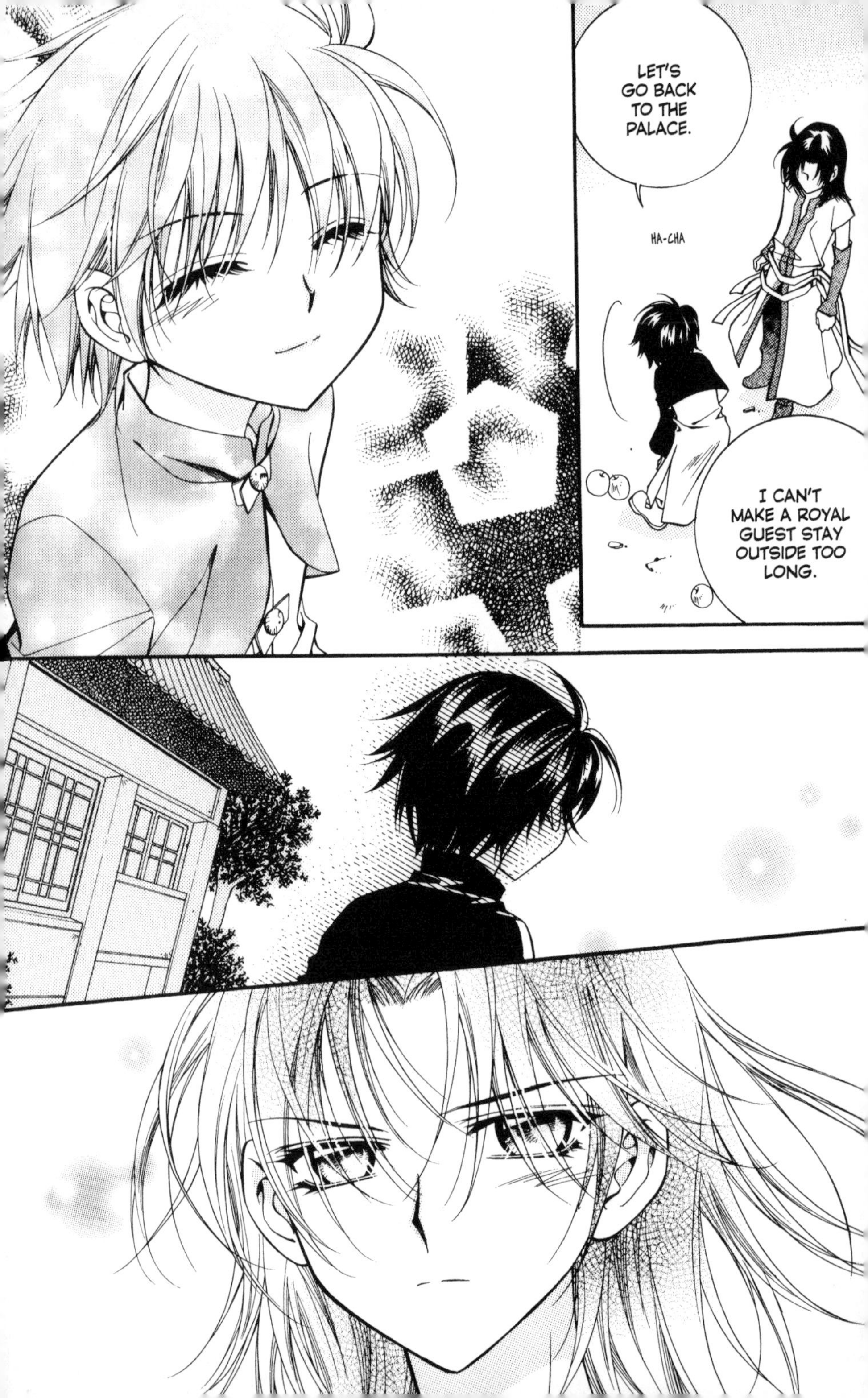
LET'S GO BACK TO THE PALACE.
HA-CHA
I CAN'T MAKE A ROYAL GUEST STAY OUTSIDE TOO LONG.

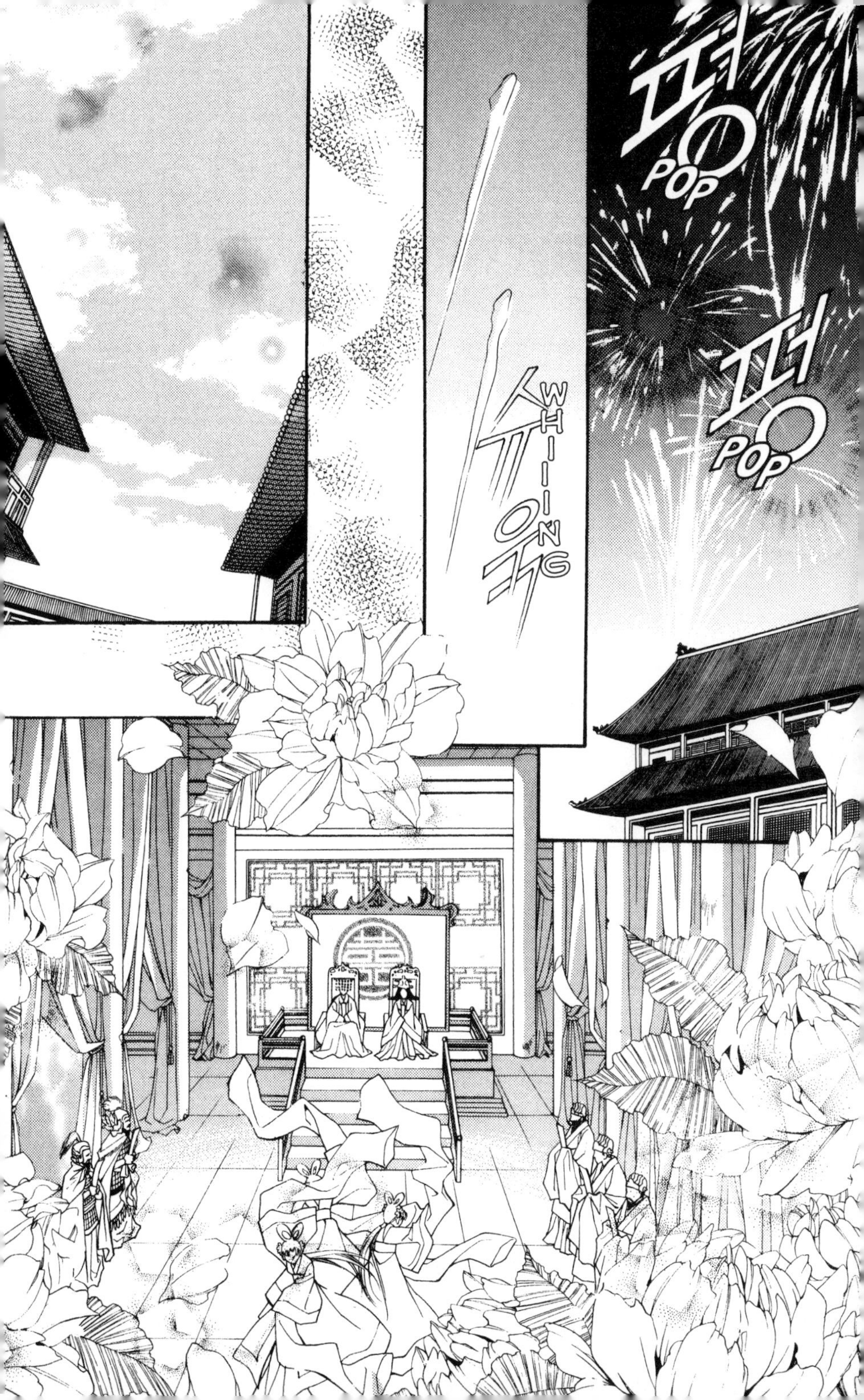
WHIIIING
POP
POP

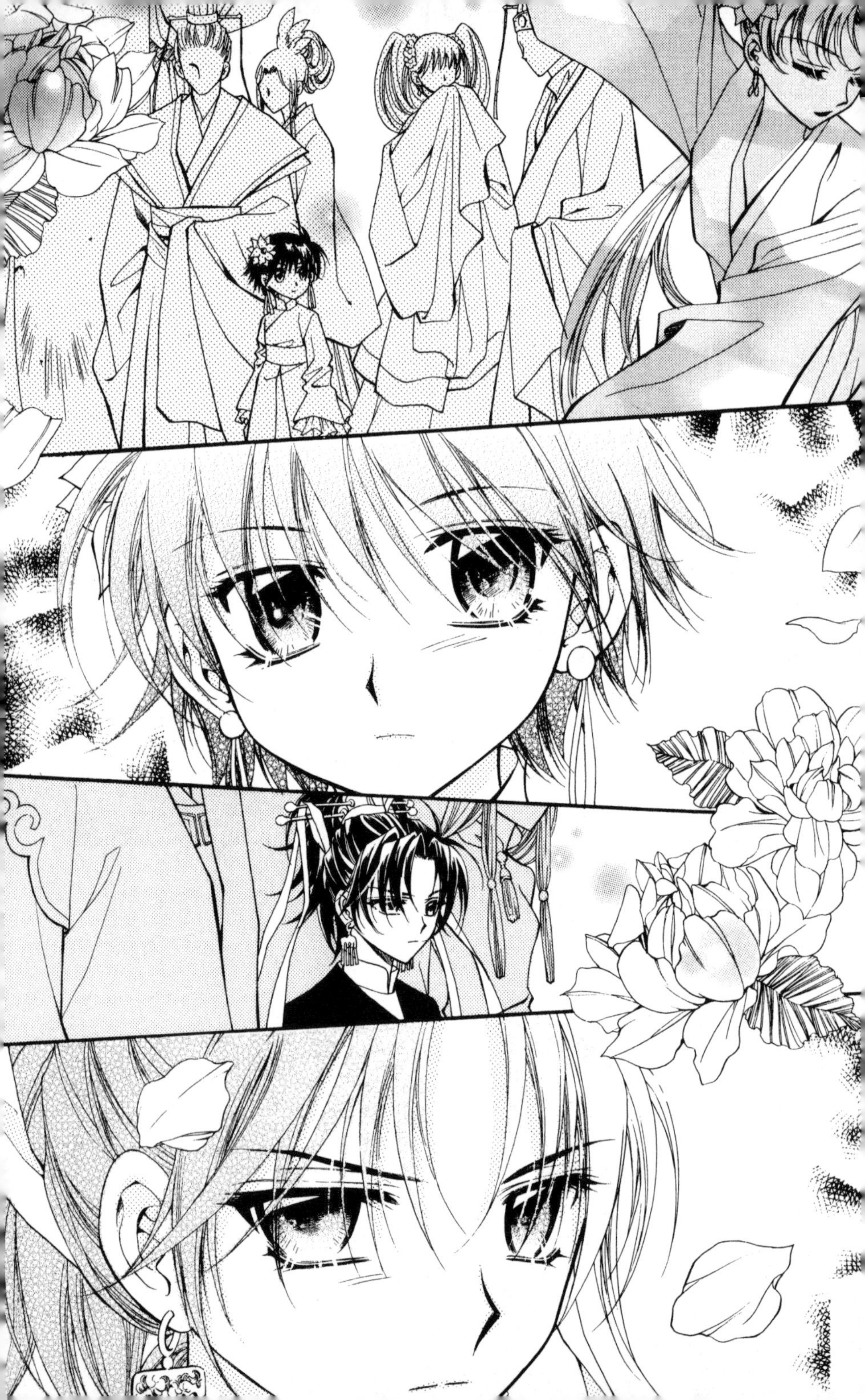

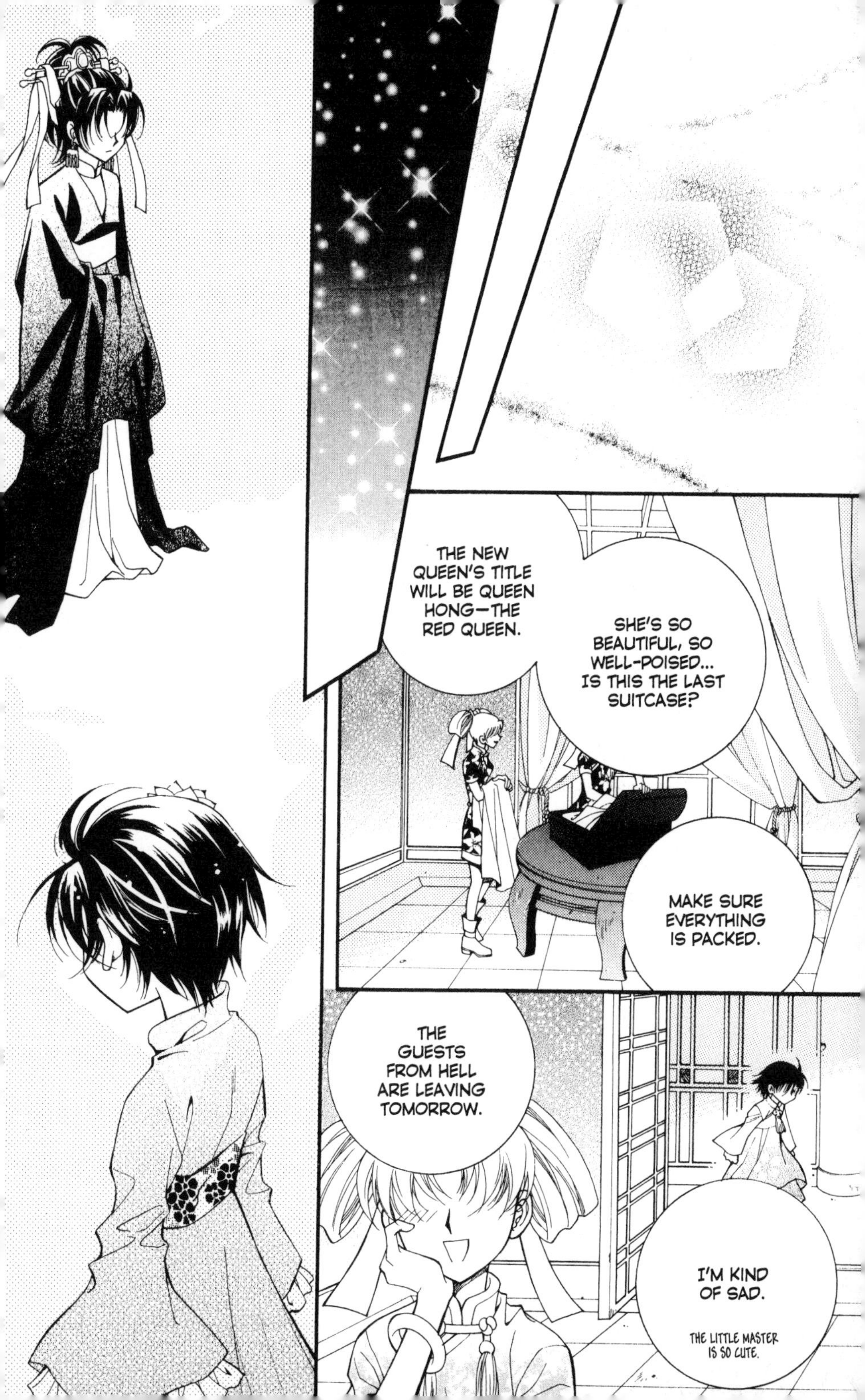
THE NEW QUEEN'S TITLE WILL BE QUEEN HONG—THE RED QUEEN.
SHE'S SO BEAUTIFUL, SO WELL-POISED... IS THIS THE LAST SUITCASE?
MAKE SURE EVERYTHING IS PACKED.
THE GUESTS FROM HELL ARE LEAVING TOMORROW.
I'M KIND OF SAD.
THE LITTLE MASTER IS SO CUTE.

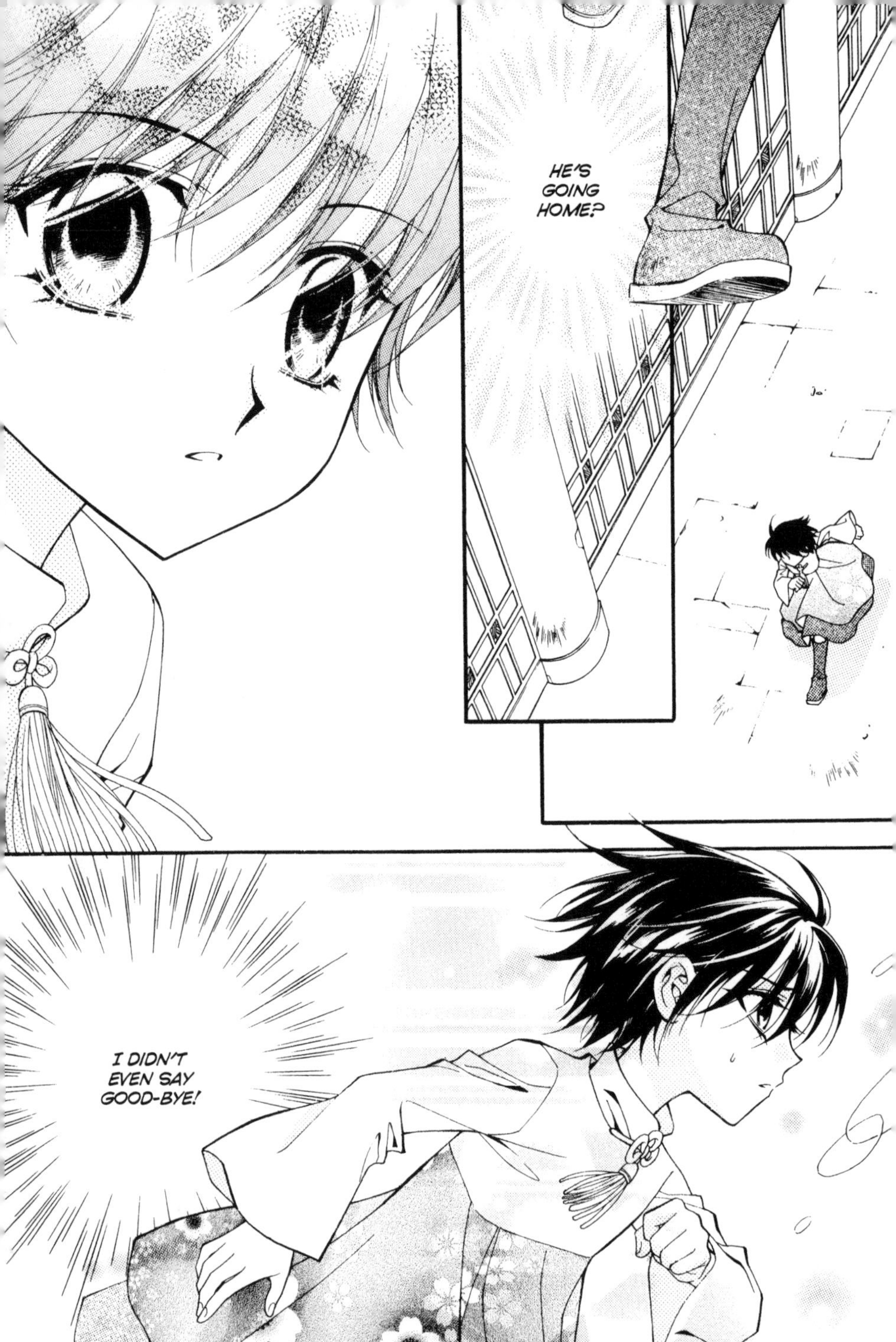
HE'S GOING HOME?
I DIDN'T EVEN SAY GOOD-BYE!

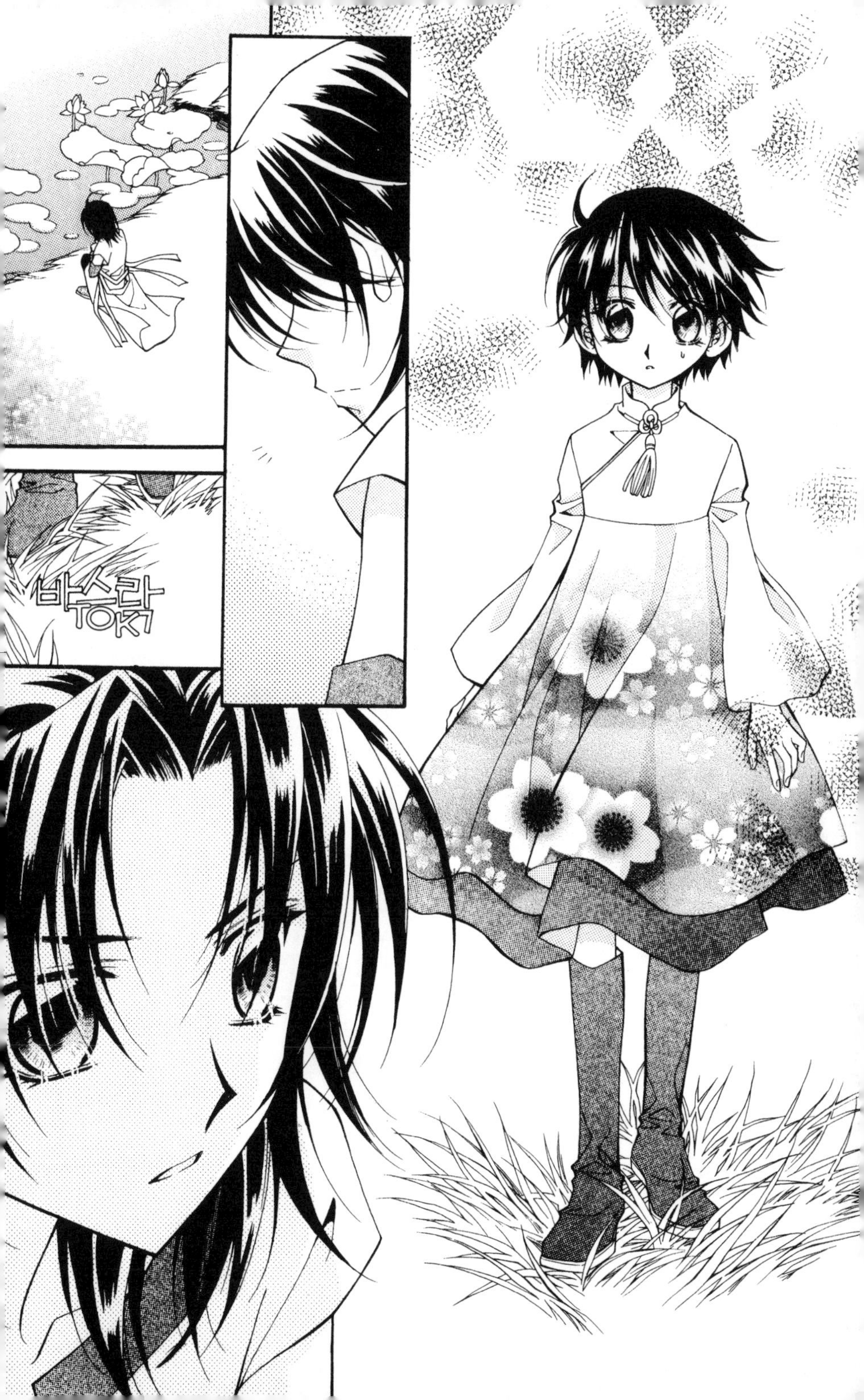
바스락
TOK7

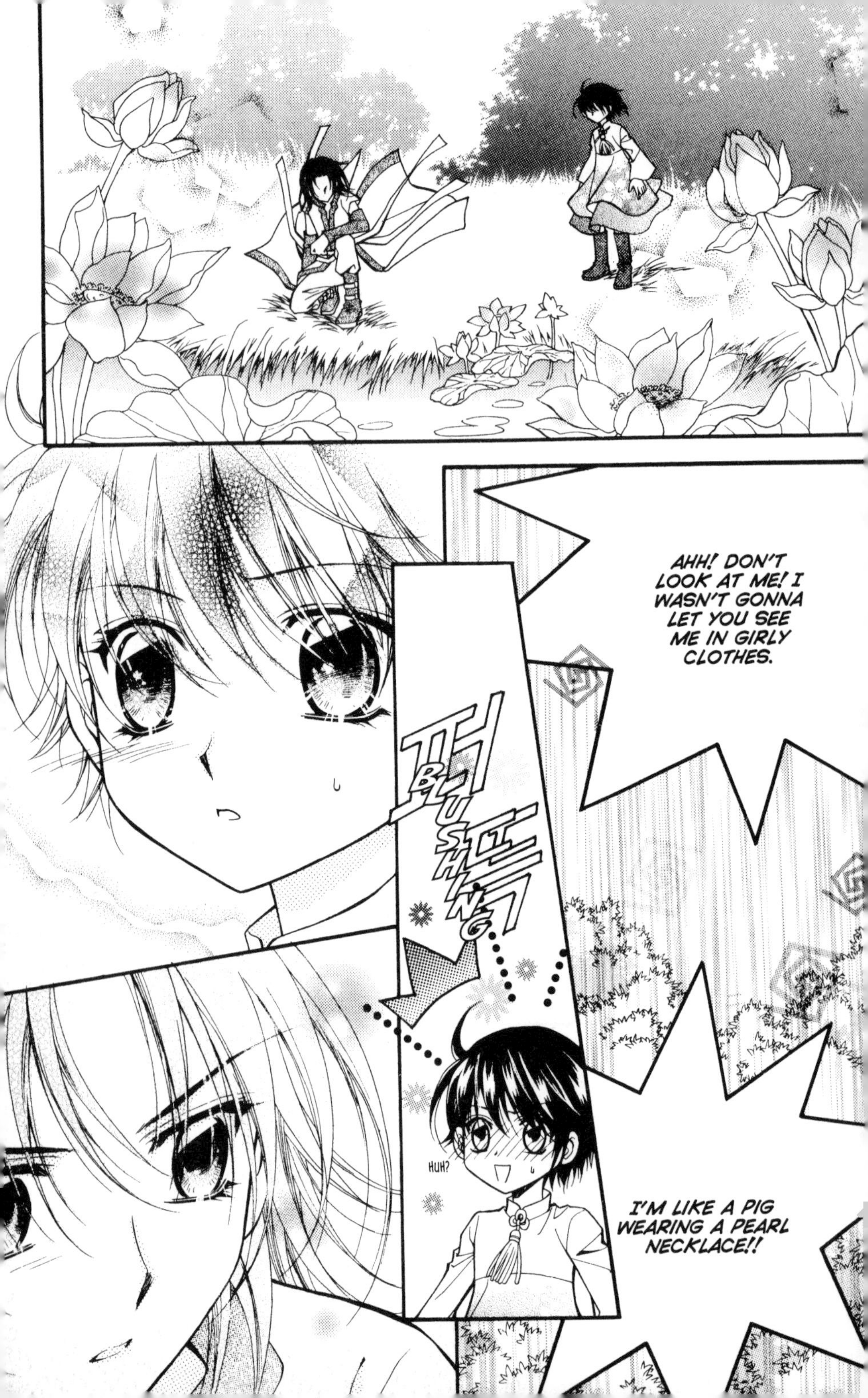
AHH! DON'T LOOK AT ME! I WASN'T GONNA LET YOU SEE ME IN GIRLY CLOTHES.
BLUSHING
HUH?
I'M LIKE A PIG WEARING A PEARL NECKLACE!!

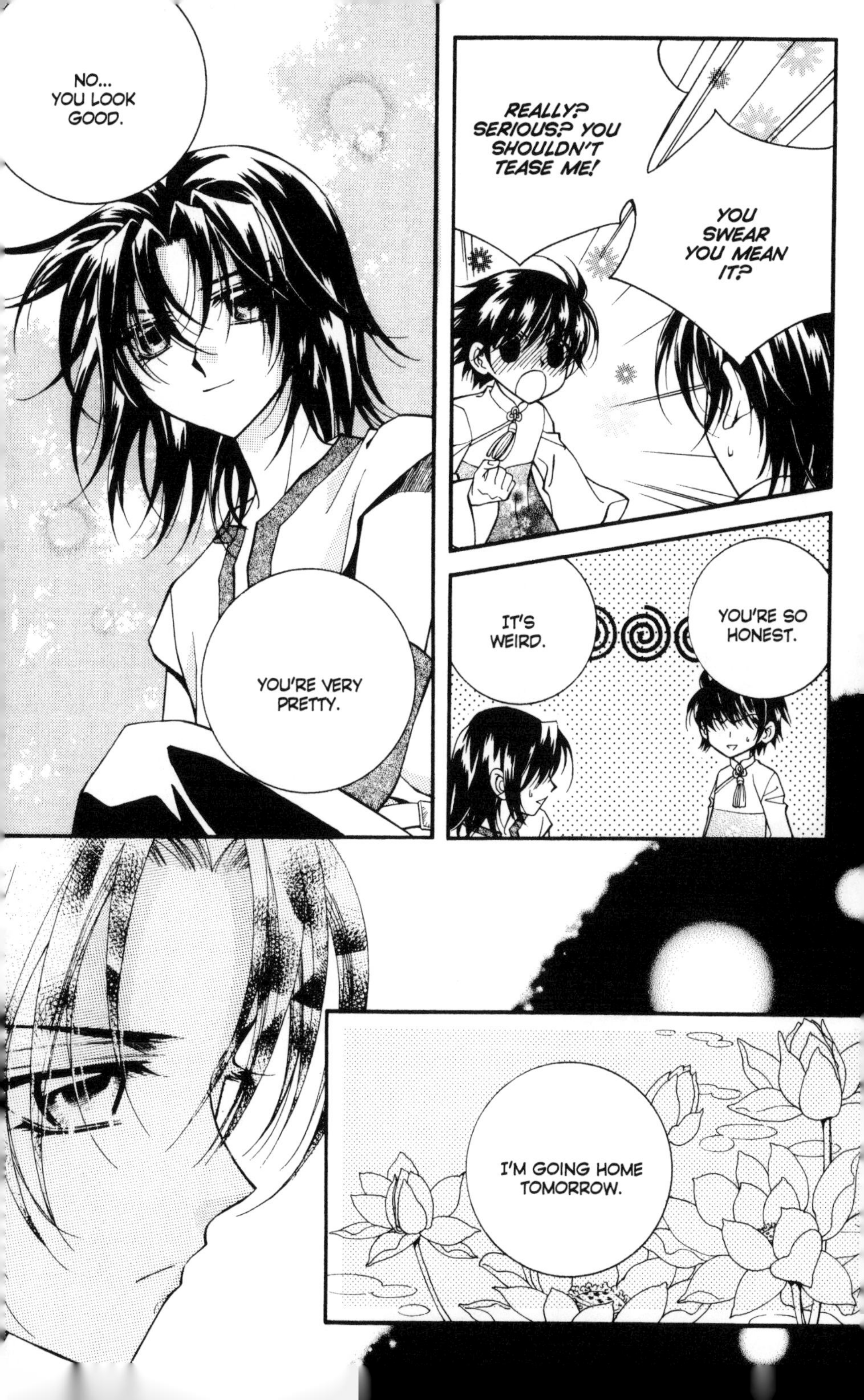
NO... YOU LOOK GOOD.
YOU'RE VERY PRETTY.
REALLY? SERIOUS? YOU SHOULDN'T TEASE ME!
YOU SWEAR YOU MEAN IT?
IT'S WEIRD.
YOU'RE SO HONEST.
I'M GOING HOME TOMORROW.

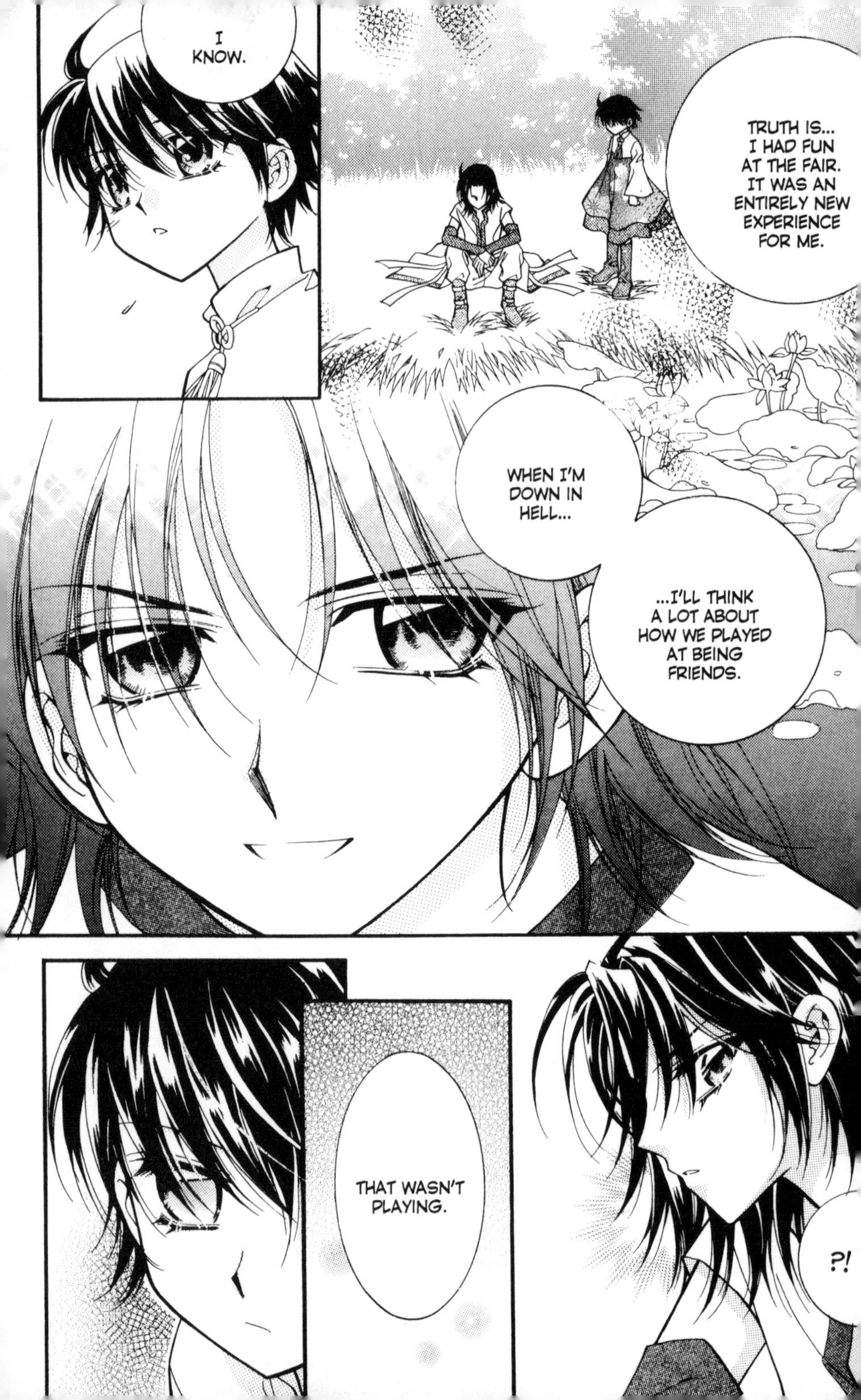
I KNOW.
TRUTH IS... I HAD FUN AT THE FAIR. IT WAS AN ENTIRELY NEW EXPERIENCE FOR ME.
WHEN I'M DOWN IN HELL...
...I'LL THINK A LOT ABOUT HOW WE PLAYED AT BEING FRIENDS.
THAT WASN'T PLAYING.
?!

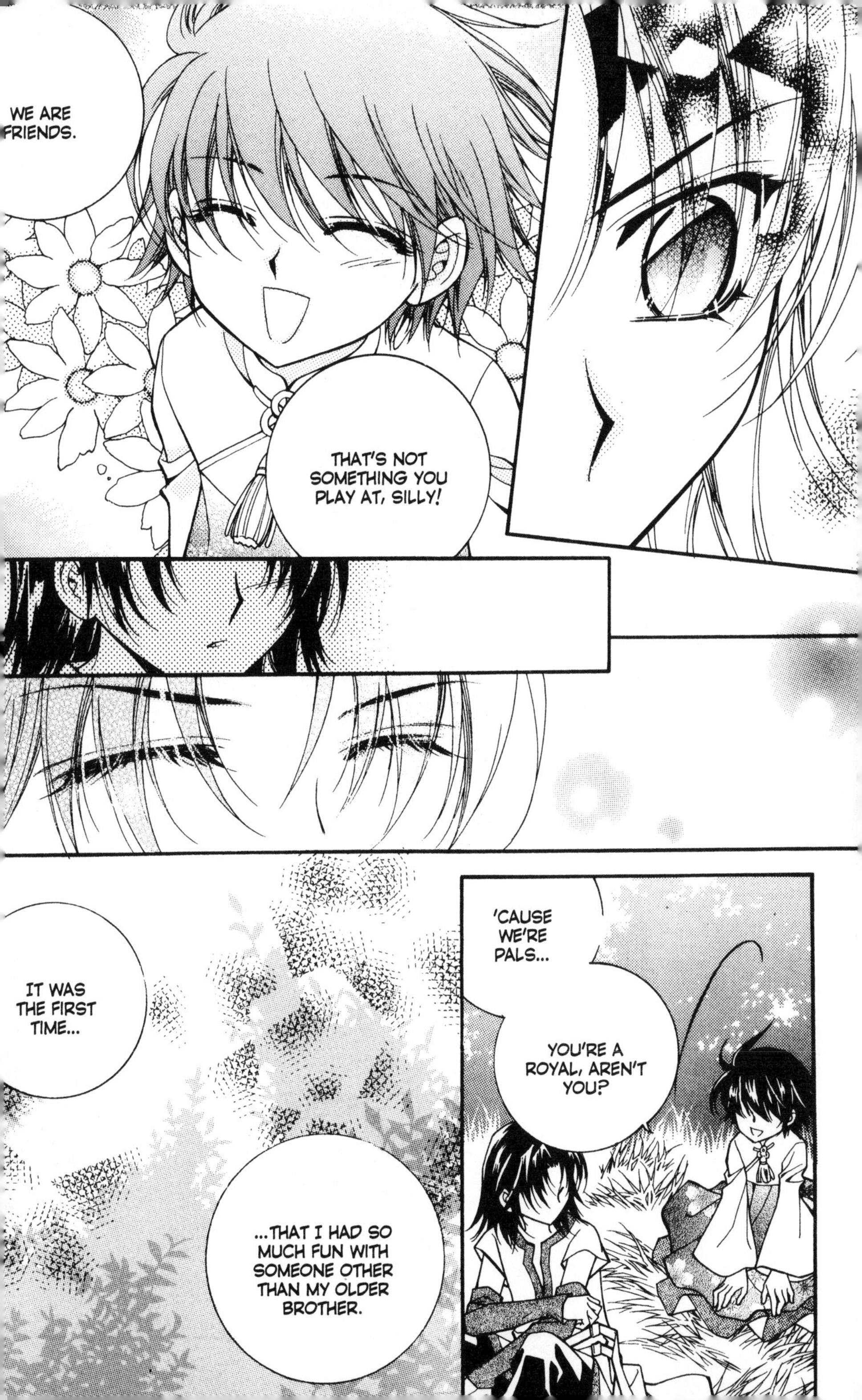
WE ARE FRIENDS.
THAT'S NOT SOMETHING YOU PLAY AT, SILLY!
IT WAS THE FIRST TIME...
...THAT I HAD SO MUCH FUN WITH SOMEONE OTHER THAN MY OLDER BROTHER.
'CAUSE WE'RE PALS...
YOU'RE A ROYAL, AREN'T YOU?

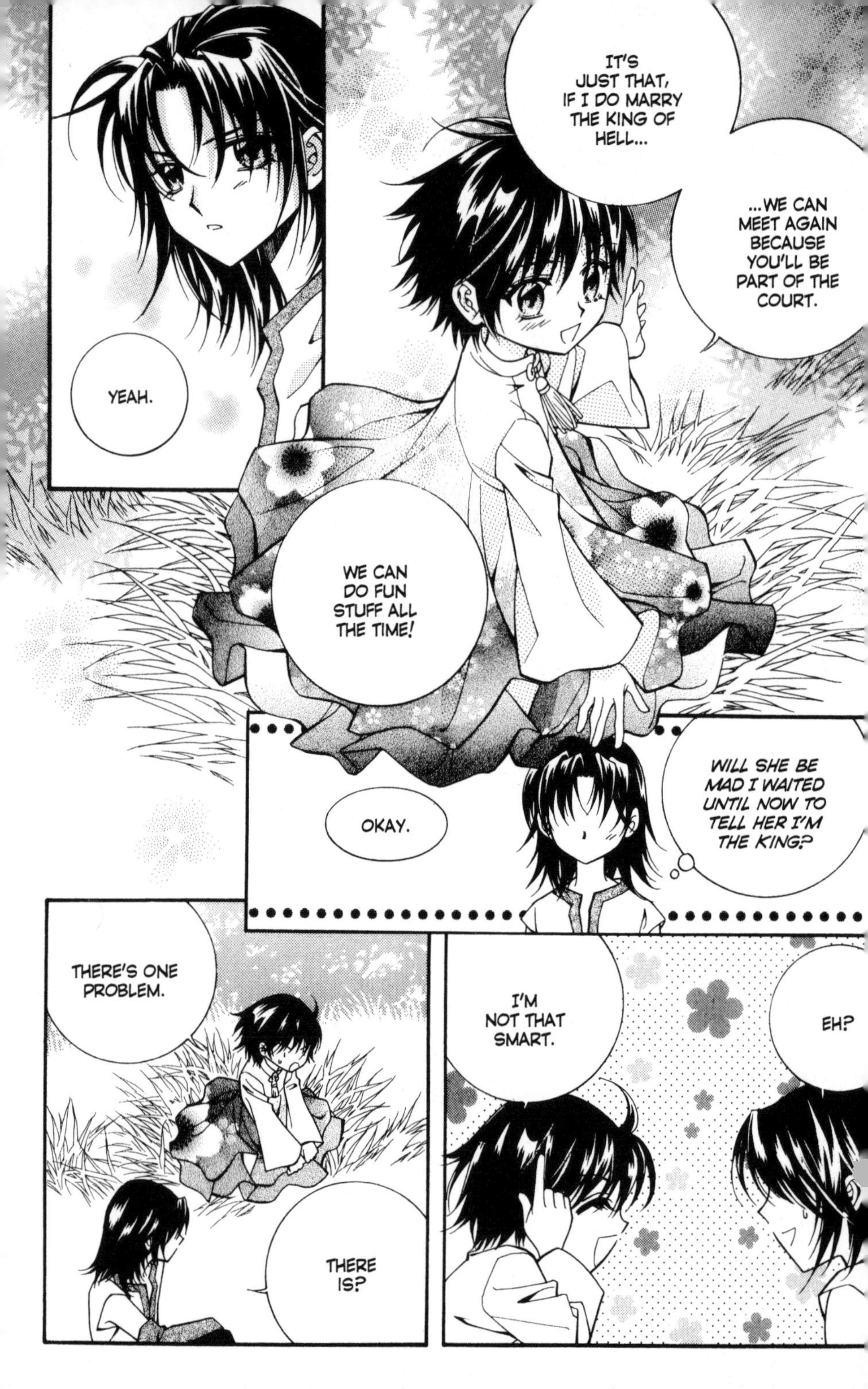
YEAH.
IT'S JUST THAT, IF I DO MARRY THE KING OF HELL...
...WE CAN MEET AGAIN BECAUSE YOU'LL BE PART OF THE COURT.
WE CAN DO FUN STUFF ALL THE TIME!
OKAY.
WILL SHE BE MAD I WAITED UNTIL NOW TO TELL HER I'M THE KING?
THERE'S ONE PROBLEM.
THERE IS?
I'M NOT THAT SMART.
EH?

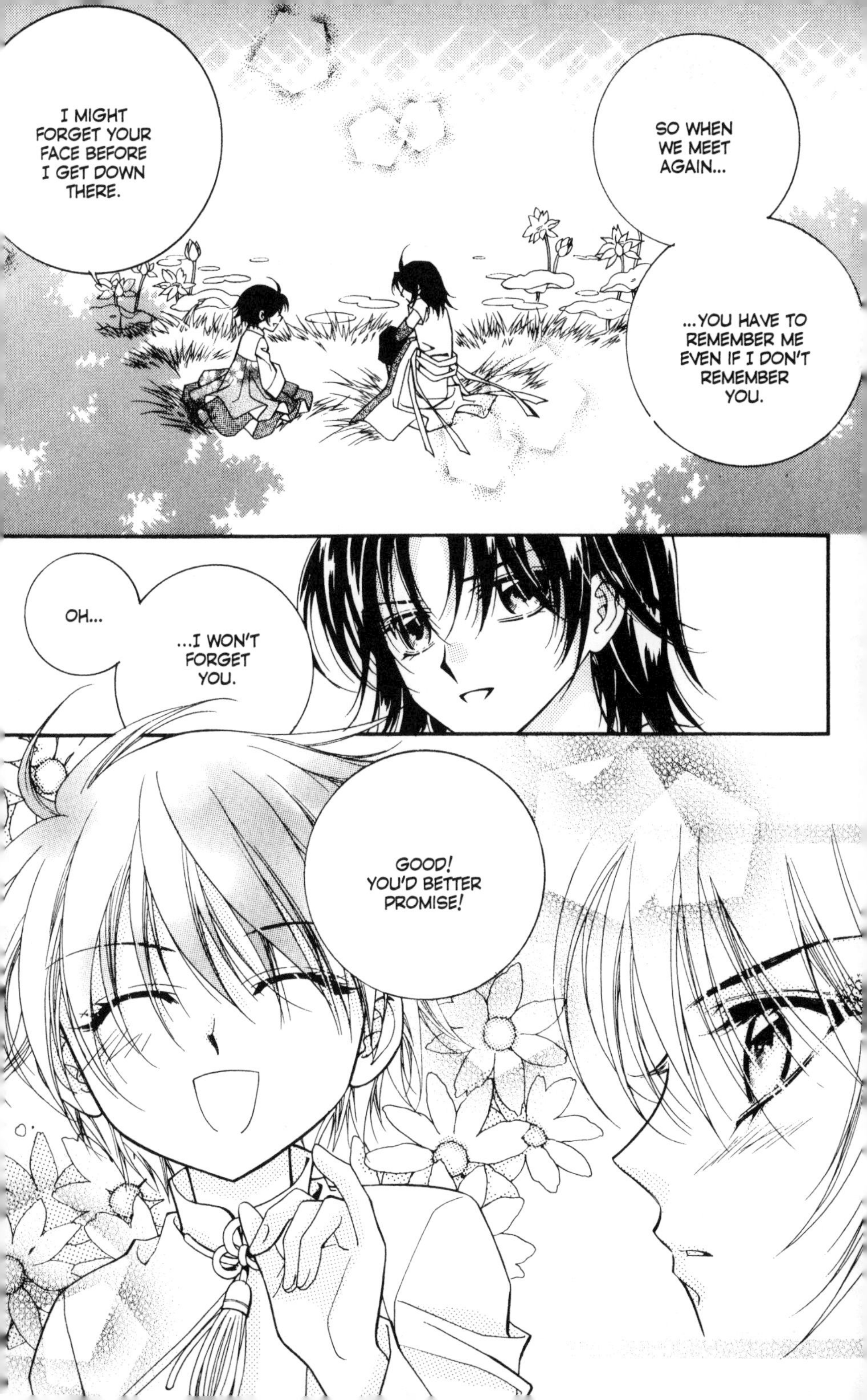

I MIGHT FORGET YOUR FACE BEFORE I GET DOWN THERE.
SO WHEN WE MEET AGAIN...
...YOU HAVE TO REMEMBER ME EVEN IF I DON'T REMEMBER YOU.
OH...
...I WON'T FORGET YOU.
GOOD! YOU'D BETTER PROMISE!

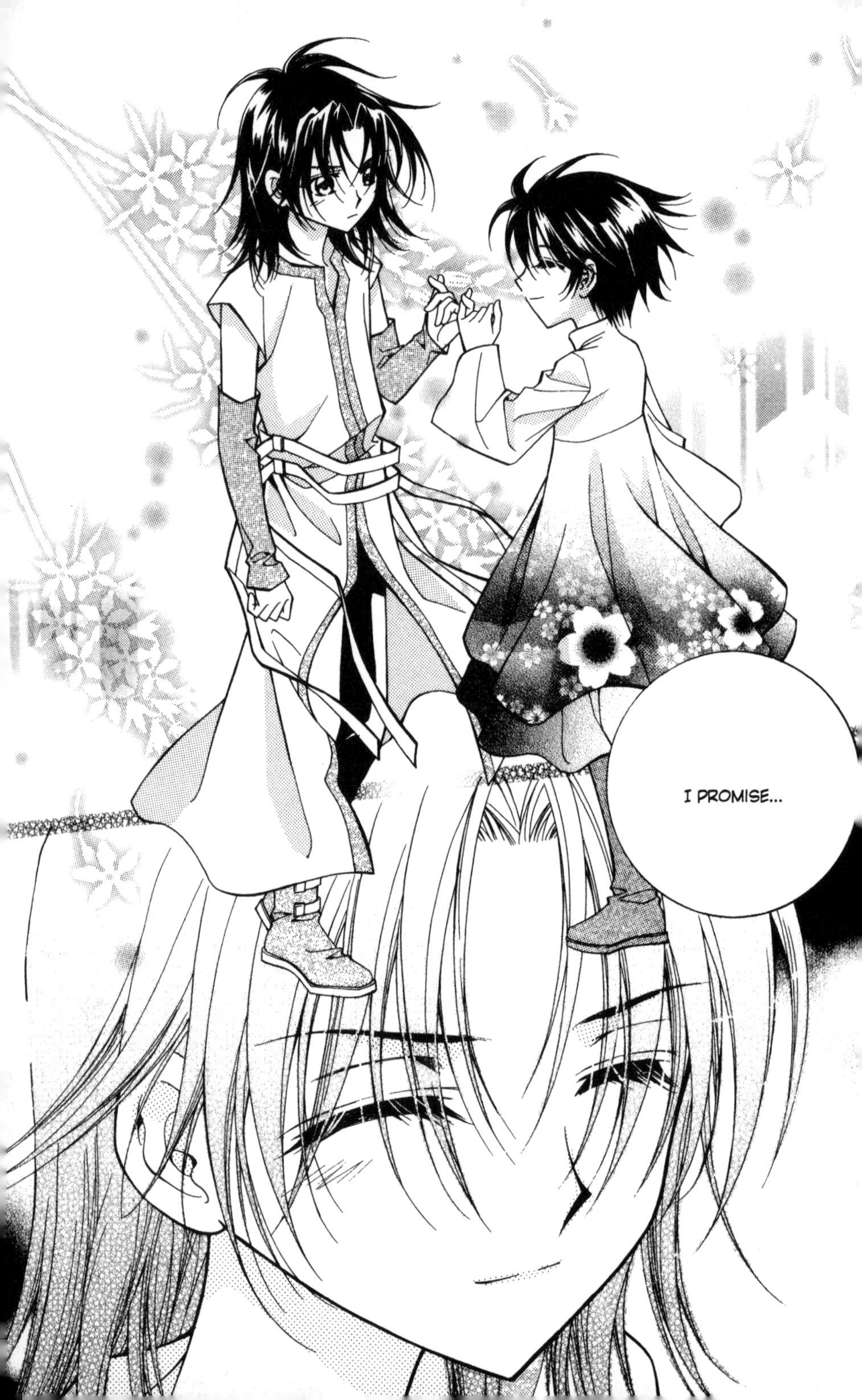
I PROMISE...

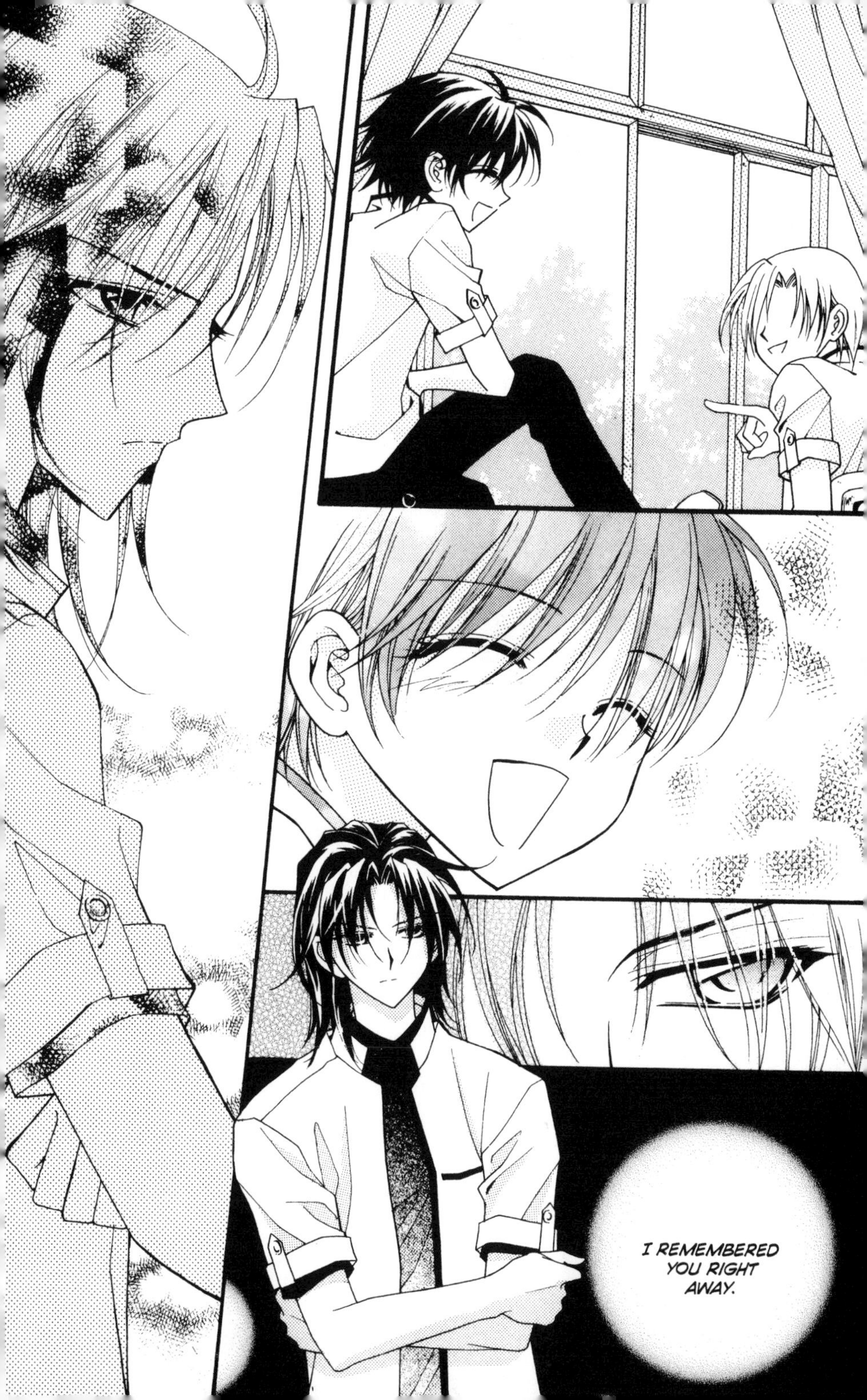
I REMEMBERED YOU RIGHT AWAY.

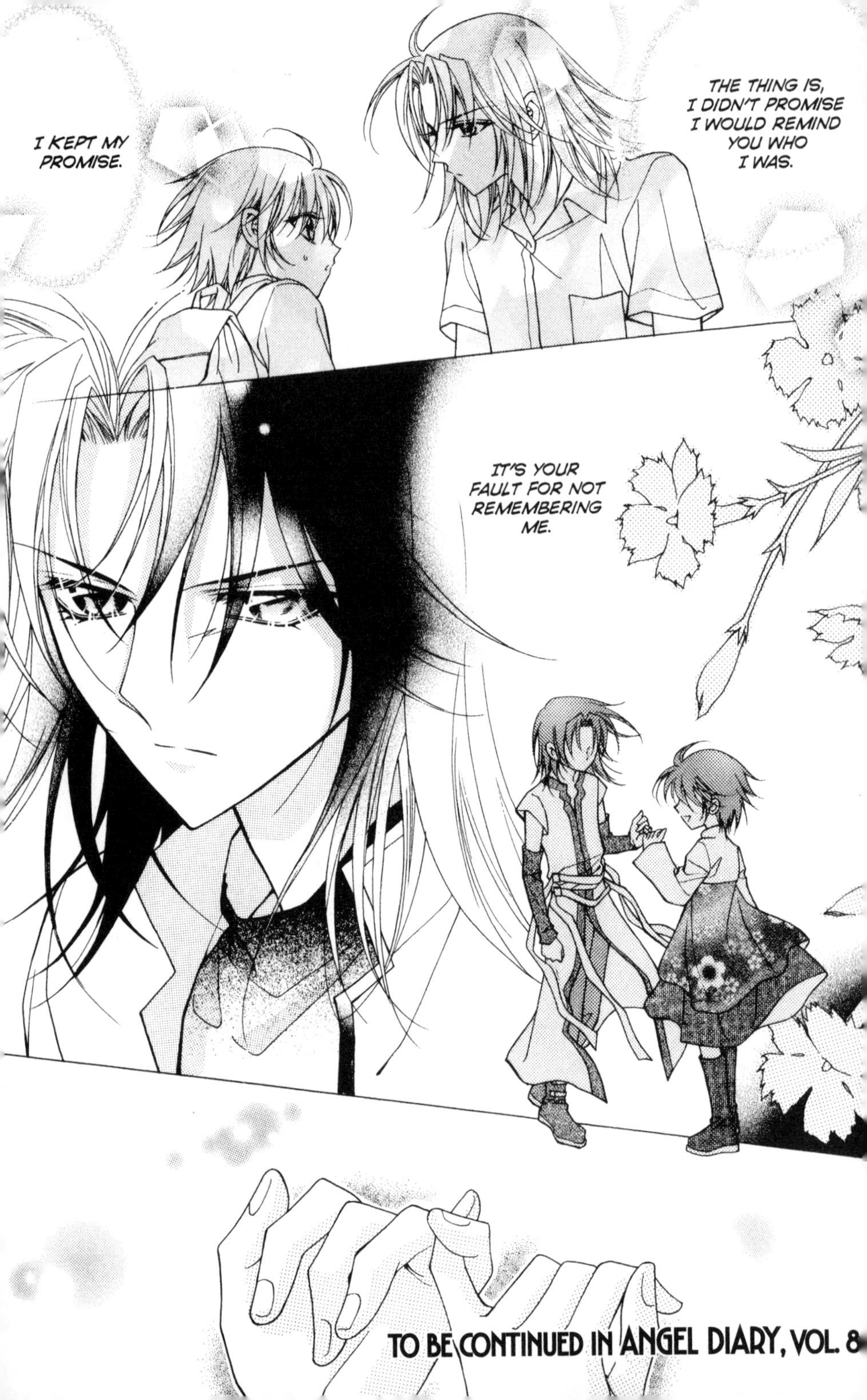
I KEPT MY PROMISE.
THE THING IS, I DIDN'T PROMISE I WOULD REMIND YOU WHO I WAS.
IT'S YOUR FAULT FOR NOT REMEMBERING ME.
TO BE CONTINUED IN ANGEL DIARY, VOL. 8

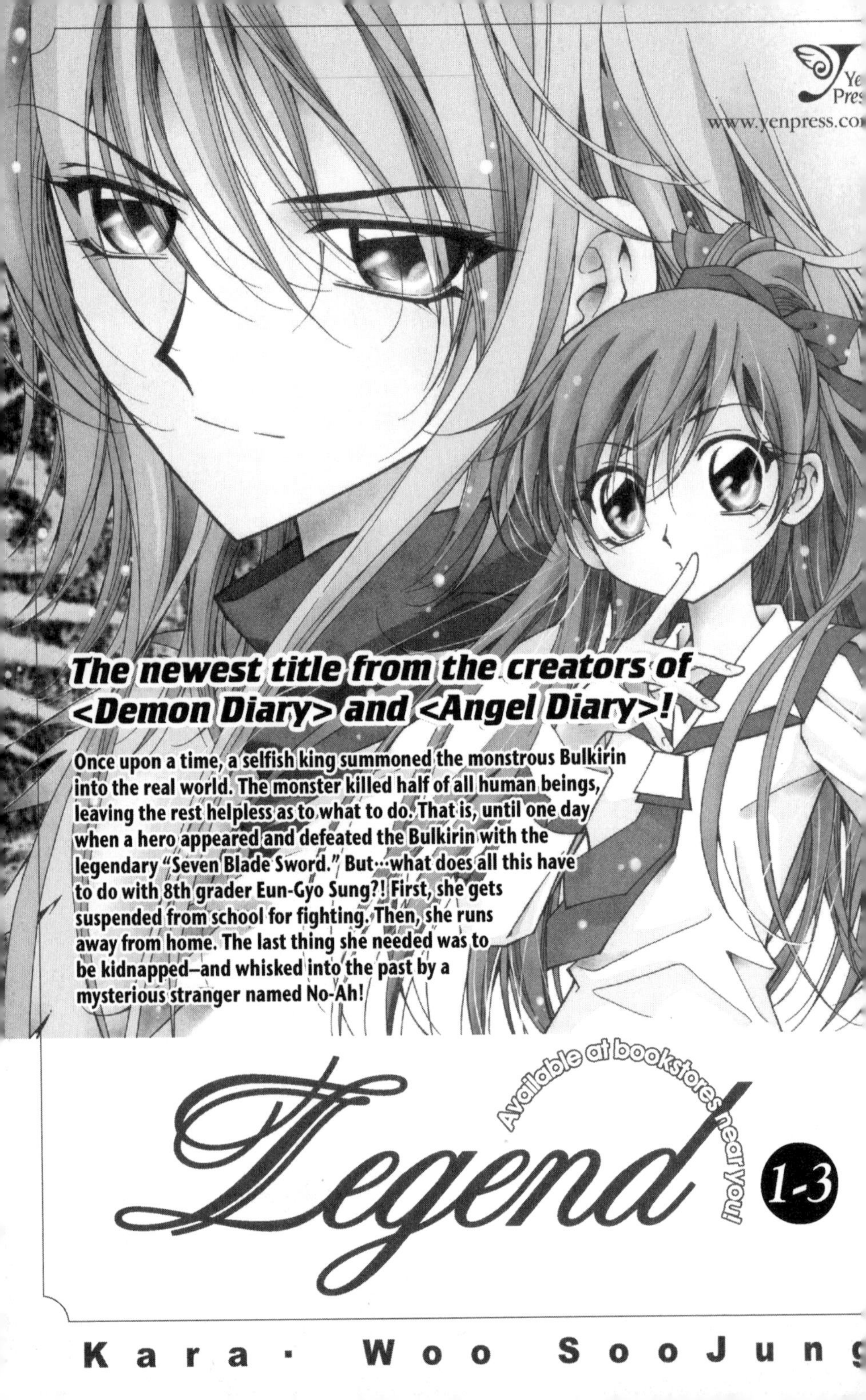
www.yenpress.co
The newest title from the creators of <Demon Diary> and <Angel Diary>!
Once upon a time, a selfish king summoned the monstrous Bulkirin into the real world. The monster killed half of all human beings, leaving the rest helpless as to what to do. That is, until one day when a hero appeared and defeated the Bulkirin with the legendary "Seven Blade Sword." But···what does all this have to do with 8th grader Eun-Gyo Sung?! First, she gets suspended from school for fighting. Then, she runs away from home. The last thing she needed was to be kidnapped–and whisked into the past by a mysterious stranger named No-Ah!
Available at bookstores near you!
Legend
1-3
Kara · Woo SooJung

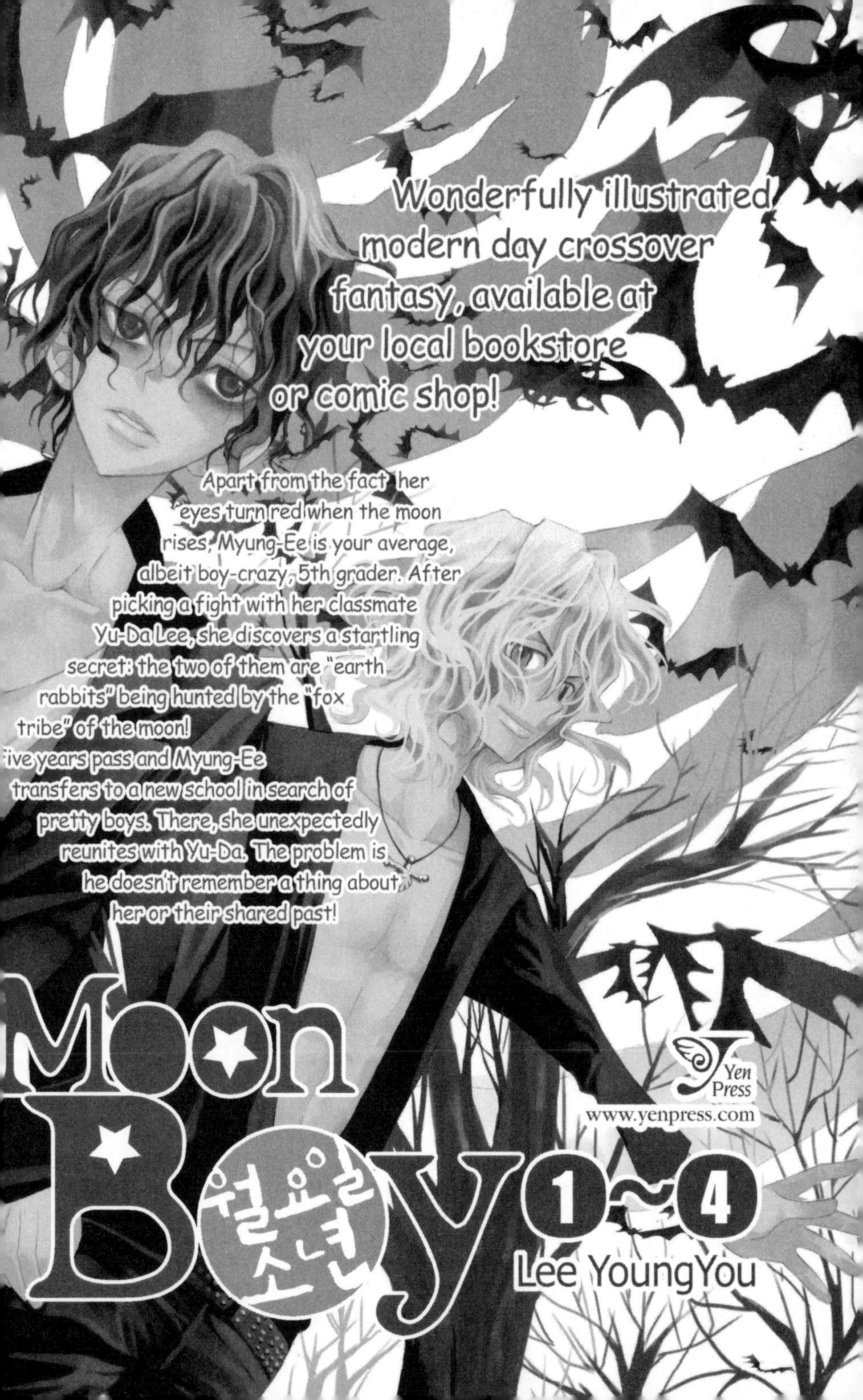
Wonderfully illustrated modern day crossover fantasy, available at your local bookstore or comic shop!
Apart from the fact her eyes turn red when the moon rises, Myung-Ee is your average, albeit boy-crazy, 5th grader. After picking a fight with her classmate Yu-Da Lee, she discovers a startling secret: the two of them are "earth rabbits" being hunted by the "fox tribe" of the moon!
Five years pass and Myung-Ee transfers to a new school in search of pretty boys. There, she unexpectedly reunites with Yu-Da. The problem is he doesn't remember a thing about her or their shared past!
Moon Boy
월요일 소년
1~4
Lee YoungYou
Yen Press
www.yenpress.com

Available at bookstores near you!

CHOCOLAT
1~6
Shin JiSang · Geo

Kum-ji was a little late getting under the spell
of the chart-topping band, DDL. Unable to
join the DDL fan club, she almost gives up
on meeting her idols, until she develops a
cunning plan–to become a member of a
rival fan club for the brand-new boy band
Yo-I. This way she can act as Yo-I's fan
club member and also be near Yo-I,

How far would you go to meet your favorite boy band?

who always seem to be in the
same shows as DDL. Perfect
plan...except being a fanatic is a lot
more complicated than she
expects. Especially when you're
actually a fan of someone else. This
full-blown love comedy about a fan
club will make you laugh, cry, and
laugh some more.

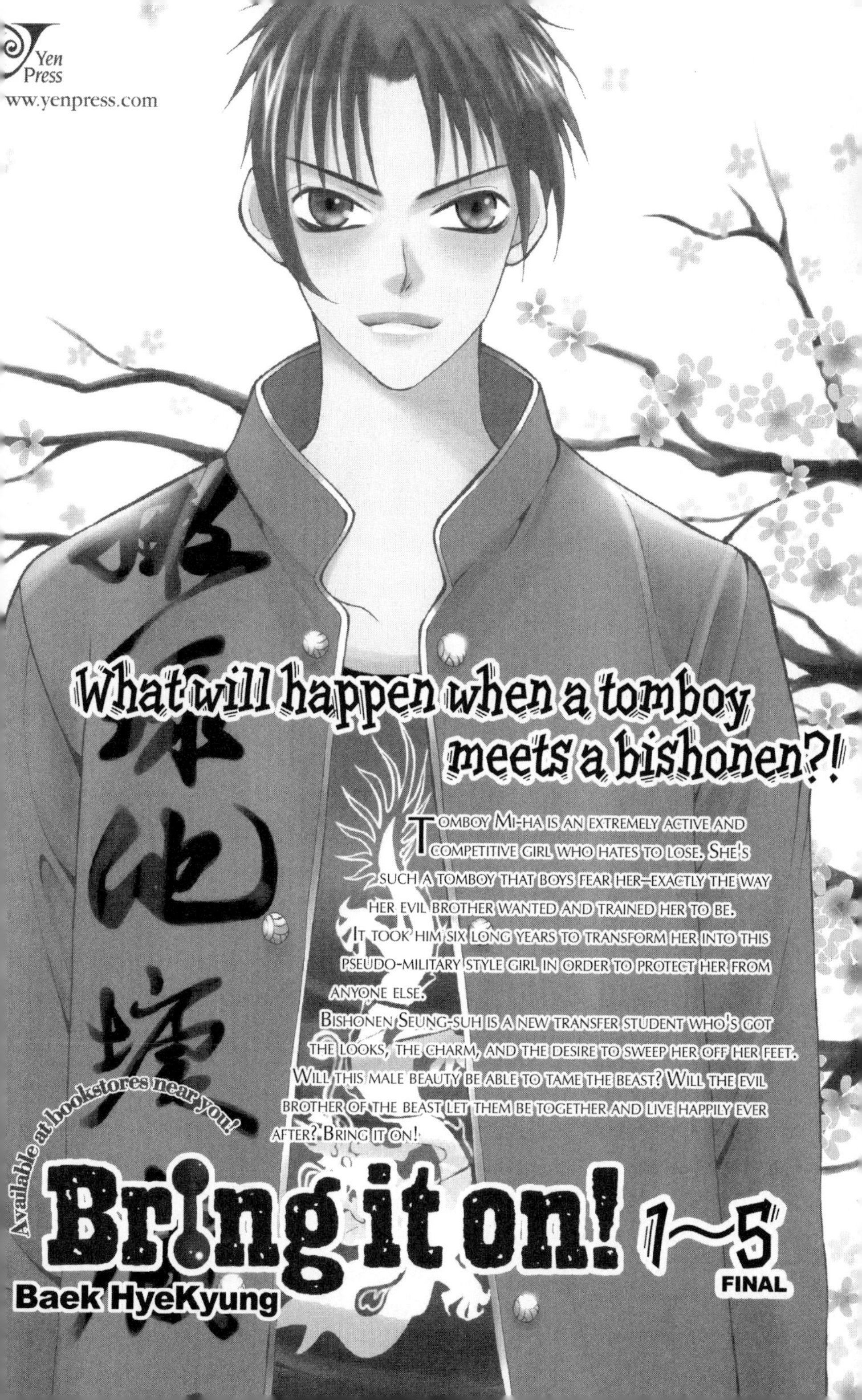

Yen Press
www.yenpress.com
What will happen when a tomboy meets a bishonen?!
Tomboy Mi-ha is an extremely active and competitive girl who hates to lose. She's such a tomboy that boys fear her—exactly the way her evil brother wanted and trained her to be.
It took him six long years to transform her into this pseudo-military style girl in order to protect her from anyone else.
Bishonen Seung-suh is a new transfer student who's got the looks, the charm, and the desire to sweep her off her feet. Will this male beauty be able to tame the beast? Will the evil brother of the beast let them be together and live happily ever after? Bring it on!
Available at bookstores near you!
Bring it on! 1~5
FINAL
Baek HyeKyung

Yen
Press
www.yenpress.com

Becoming the princess... Isn't that every girl's dream?!

Monarchy rule ended long ago in Korea, but there are still other countries with kings, queens, princes and princesses. What if Korea had continued monarchism? What if all the beautiful palaces, which are now only historical relics, were actually filled with people? What if the glamorous royal family still maintained the palace customs? Welcome to a world where Korea still has the royal family living in their everyday lives! Only for this one high school girl, Chae-Kyung, is this a tragedy, since she has to marry the prince — who apparently is a total bastard!

THE ROYAL PALACE

Goong

vol.1~2

Park SoHee

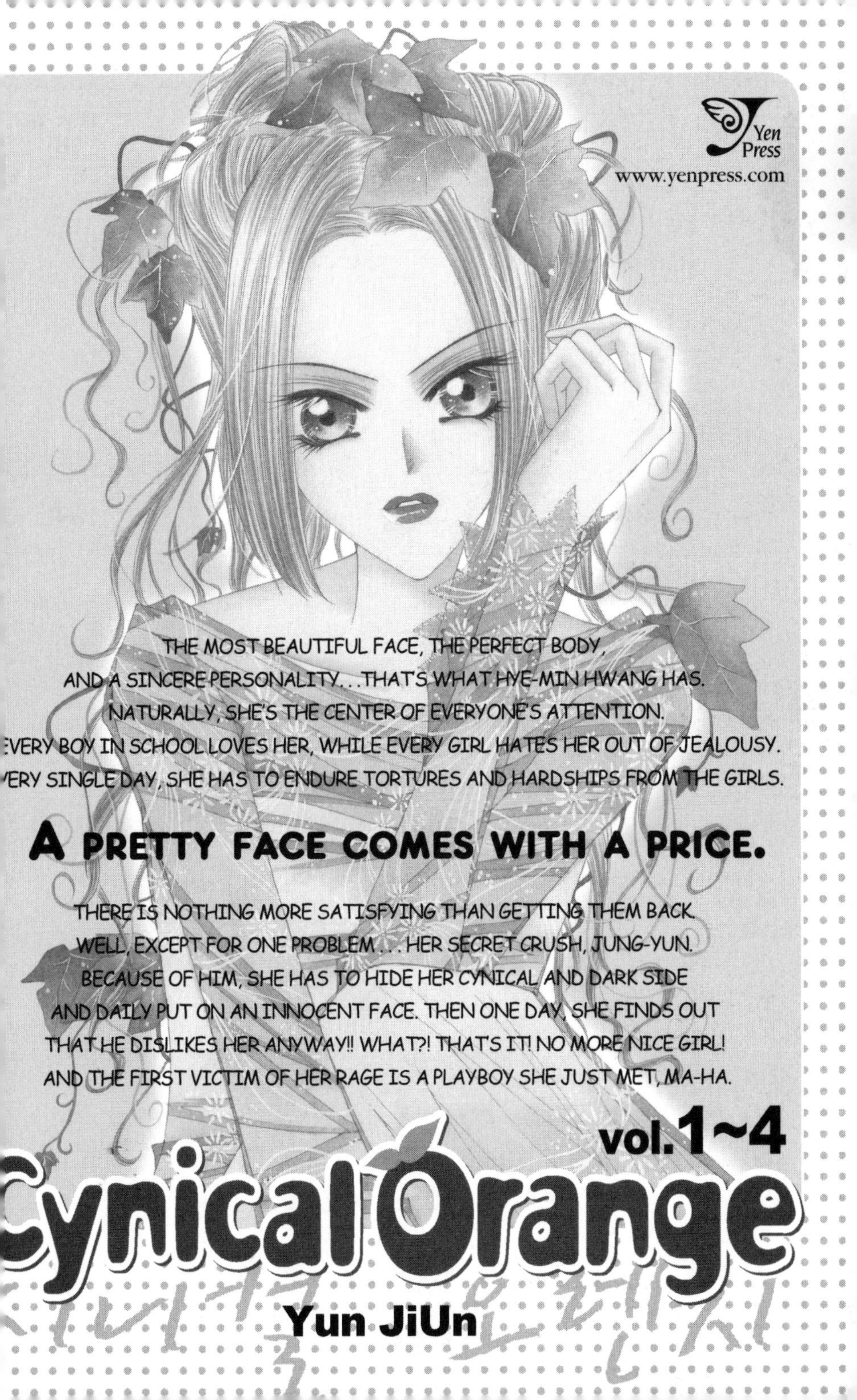
Yen Press
www.yenpress.com
THE MOST BEAUTIFUL FACE, THE PERFECT BODY,
AND A SINCERE PERSONALITY. . . THAT'S WHAT HYE-MIN HWANG HAS.
NATURALLY, SHE'S THE CENTER OF EVERYONE'S ATTENTION.
EVERY BOY IN SCHOOL LOVES HER, WHILE EVERY GIRL HATES HER OUT OF JEALOUSY.
EVERY SINGLE DAY, SHE HAS TO ENDURE TORTURES AND HARDSHIPS FROM THE GIRLS.
A PRETTY FACE COMES WITH A PRICE.
THERE IS NOTHING MORE SATISFYING THAN GETTING THEM BACK.
WELL, EXCEPT FOR ONE PROBLEM . . . HER SECRET CRUSH, JUNG-YUN.
BECAUSE OF HIM, SHE HAS TO HIDE HER CYNICAL AND DARK SIDE
AND DAILY PUT ON AN INNOCENT FACE. THEN ONE DAY, SHE FINDS OUT
THAT HE DISLIKES HER ANYWAY!! WHAT?! THAT'S IT! NO MORE NICE GIRL!
AND THE FIRST VICTIM OF HER RAGE IS A PLAYBOY SHE JUST MET, MA-HA.
vol. 1~4
Cynical Orange
Yun JiUn

Yen
Press
www.yenpress.com

Sometimes, just being a teenager is hard enough.

Da-Eh, an aspiring manhwa artist who lives with her father and her little brother, comes across Sun-Nam, a softie whose ultimate goal is simply to become a "Tough guy." Whenever these two meet, trouble follows. Meanwhile, Ta-Jun, the hottest guy in town, finds himself drawn to the one girl that his killer smile does not work on–Da-Eh. With their complicated family history hanging on their shoulders, watch how these three teenagers find their way out into the world!

Available at bookstores near you!

HISSING 1~4
한숨

Kang EunYoung

Totally new Arabian nights, where Shahrazad is a guy!

Everyone knows the story of Shahrazad and her wonderful tales from the Arabian Nights. For one thousand and one nights, the stories that she created entertained the mad Sultan and eventually saved her life. In this version, Shahrazad is a guy who wanted to save his sister from the mad Sultan by disguising himself as a woman. When he puts his life on the line, what kind of strange and unique stories would he tell? This new twist on one of the greatest classical tales might just keep you awake for another ONE THOUSAND AND ONE NIGHTS.

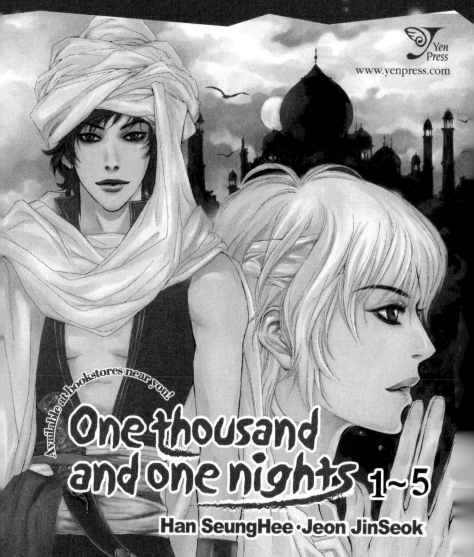

Yen Press

www.yenpress.com

Available at bookstores near you!

One thousand and one nights 1~5

Han SeungHee · Jeon JinSeok

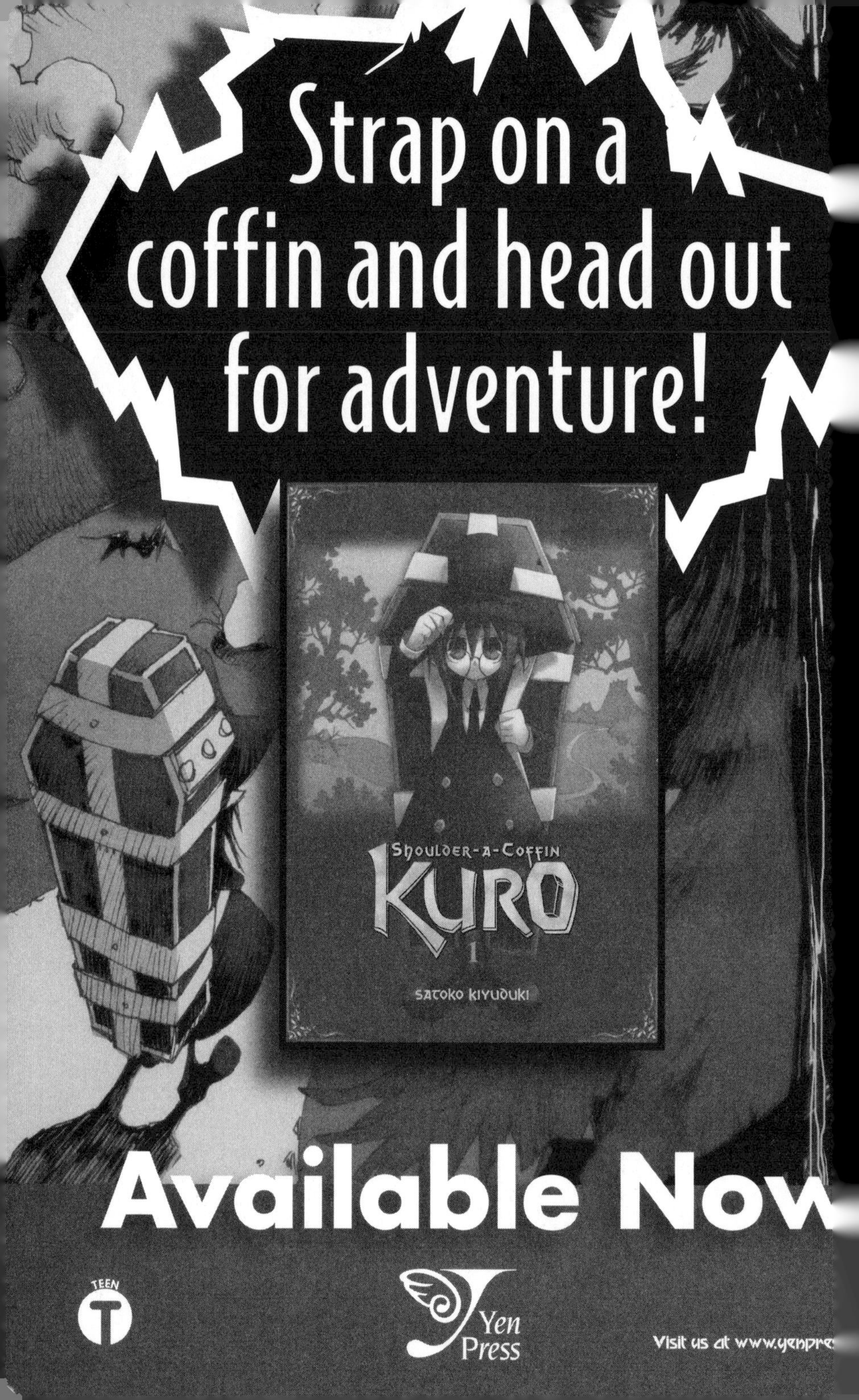

**DEALING WITH THE DEAD IS EVEN
WORSE THAN DEALING WITH THE DEVIL!**

ZOMBIE-LOAN

BY PEACH-PIT

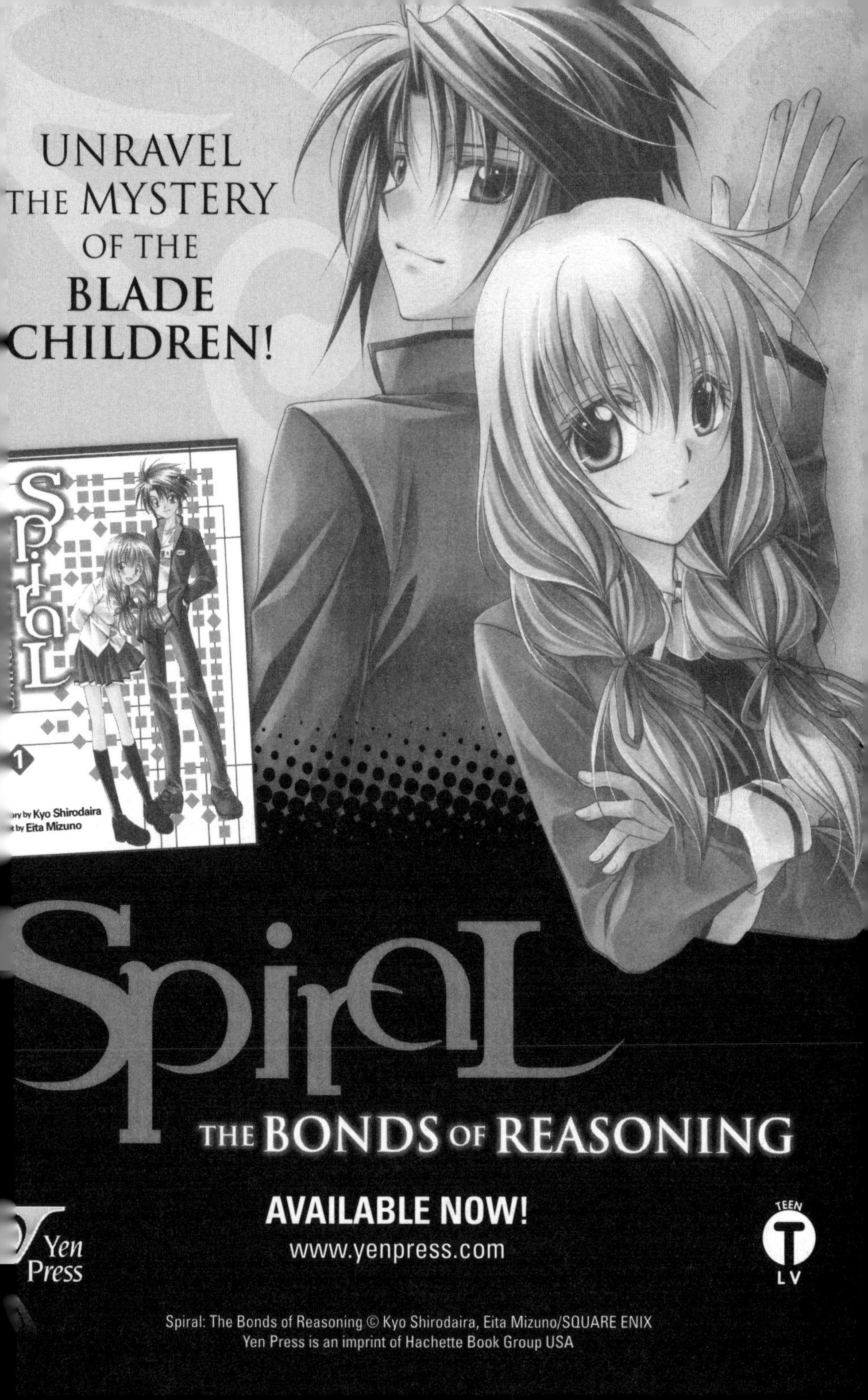
UNRAVEL
THE MYSTERY
OF THE
BLADE
CHILDREN!
Kyo Shirodaira
Eita Mizuno
Spiral
THE BONDS OF REASONING
AVAILABLE NOW!
www.yenpress.com
Yen Press
TEEN
T
LV
Spiral: The Bonds of Reasoning © Kyo Shirodaira, Eita Mizuno/SQUARE ENIX
Yen Press is an imprint of Hachette Book Group USA

Angel Diary vol. 7

Story by YunHee Lee
Art by Kara

Translation: HyeYoung Im
English Adaptation: Jamie S. Rich
Lettering: Terri Delgado

ANGEL DIARY, Vol. 7 © 2004 Kara · YunHee Lee. All rights reserved. First published in Korea in 2004 by Sigongsa Co., Ltd.

English translation © 2008 Hachette Book Group USA, Inc.

Yen Press
Hachette Book Group USA
237 Park Avenue, New York, NY 10017

Visit our Web sites at www.HachetteBookGroupUSA.com and www.YenPress.com.

Yen Press is an imprint of Hachette Book Group USA, Inc. The Yen Press name and logo are trademarks of Hachette Book Group USA, Inc.

First Yen Press Edition: October 2008

ISBN-10: 0-7595-3006-8
ISBN-13: 978-0-7595-3006-5

10 9 8 7 6 5 4 3 2 1

BVG

Printed in the United States of America